BLACK MUSLIM FREEDOM DREAMS

Black Muslim Freedom Dreams

Islamic Education, Pan-Africanism, and Collective Care

Samiha Rahman

New York University Press

New York

NEW YORK UNIVERSITY PRESS
New York
www.nyupress.org

© 2026 by New York University
All rights reserved

Chapter 4, "To Be Young, Gifted, and Black: Qur'anic Education as Collective Care," is a revision of an article previously published in *Curriculum Inquiry* 51, no. 1 (2021). Reprinted with permission from Taylor & Francis Ltd.

Please contact the Library of Congress for Cataloging-in-Publication data.

ISBN: 9781479838202 (hardback)
ISBN: 9781479838219 (paperback)
ISBN: 9781479838233 (library ebook)
ISBN: 9781479838240 (consumer ebook)

This book is printed on acid-free paper, and its binding materials are chosen for strength and durability. We strive to use environmentally responsible suppliers and materials to the greatest extent possible in publishing our books.

The manufacturer's authorized representative in the EU for product safety is Mare Nostrum Group B.V., Mauritskade 21D, 1091 GC Amsterdam, The Netherlands.
Email: gpsr@mare-nostrum.co.uk.

Manufactured in the United States of America

10 9 8 7 6 5 4 3 2 1

Also available as an ebook

In the name of Allah,
To those in the Fayda.

CONTENTS

Introduction: Mapping Paths to Freedom ... 1

1. The Prophetic and the Political: Islam, Sufism, and Revolutionary Pan-Africanism ... 33

2. Launching the Dream: Building Black Muslim Worlds from the U.S. to Senegal ... 53

3. Pedagogy of Place: Everyday Islamic Education in Medina Baye ... 101

4. To Be Young, Gifted, and Black: Qur'anic Education as Collective Care ... 149

5. Time to Work: Living, Dreaming, and Doing Khidma ... 189

6. From American to Cisse: The Tijani Tariqa and the Making of Pan-African Families ... 229

Epilogue: Freedom Dreaming in Frightening Times ... 267

Glossary ... 277

Notes ... 281

Bibliography ... 289

Acknowledgments ... 311

Index ... 313

About the Author ... 328

Introduction

Mapping Paths to Freedom

Early one chilly evening in January 2010, just as the light blues of the sky transformed into orange and pink, I walked down a tree-lined block of the Bedford-Stuyvesant neighborhood of Brooklyn, New York City. I stopped at a three-story brownstone building. I glanced at a text message on my cellphone to confirm that I had arrived at the correct address: the location of the *zawiya*[1] (community center) of the Tijani Sufi *tariqa* (path). I had come for what my friend had promised would be a night of nice *dhikr* (remembrance), good company, and great food. The last two were standard offerings at many Islamic gatherings, but I was especially intrigued by the first—dhikr, a devotional practice that is often associated with Muslims who embrace Sufism, or the inner, mystical dimension of Islam.

I opened the door to the brownstone and passed through an oak wood-paneled hallway adorned with picture frames featuring stoic Black Muslim men and Arabic calligraphy artwork. On the ground were an array of sneakers and winter boots—some thoughtfully placed in a neat line and others scattered haphazardly, likely thrown off in a hurry. I unlaced my shoes and stepped into a large, open room. With the lights turned off and curtains pulled shut, my eyes took a moment to adjust. I faintly made out the geometric patterns on the rug and the outlines of about thirty women and men sitting on the floor, with a few children wiggling around restlessly.

The adults in the room were Muslims whose yearnings to go deeper into their understanding of Islam had propelled them to join the Tijani tariqa, which is one of many systematized Sufi paths that Muslims throughout the world have followed for centuries. As Tijanis, or members of the Tijani tariqa, these women and men embraced a Sufi guide who led them on a journey to spiritual liberation. These spiritual seekers committed to doing a daily routine of dhikr beyond the essential practices that are obligated for all Muslims, with the goal of reaching their highest human potential and arriving at *marifa* (experiential knowledge of Allah)—a powerful and transformative understanding of themselves and their Lord that no system of racism or social hierarchy could deprive them of.

I was swept away by an ocean of voices making *dhikrul jummah* (the Friday dhikr), one of the consistent, extra practices of remembrance that Tijanis commit to doing once they join the tariqa. Tijanis make dhikrul jummah once a week, on Friday evenings before *maghrib* (sunset prayer), preferably aloud with fellow Tijanis. The women and men gathered in the room proclaimed *"la illaha illallah"* (there is no God but Allah) over and over again, their chests heaving, their voices rising, and their speed hastening, until they reached one thousand utterances. These believers lived and worked in a society where the norm was to chase money, status, power, and pleasure, but they carved out some time on a Friday night to remind themselves that there was truly nothing worthy of worship except Allah.

When the dhikr ended, a young brother[2] made the *adhan* (call to prayer) for maghrib. As everyone did their best to arrange themselves, shoulder to shoulder, foot to foot, mustering up the focus to pray as if it would be their last prayer, the scene at the Tijani zawiya quickly returned to what might be observed at any mosque in any part of the U.S. or corner of the globe—a gathering of Muslims who had come together for one of their five daily prayers. Imam[3] Sayed Abdus-Salaam[4] (1942–2017) led us in *salat* (prayer). Imam Sayed was an elderly Black American[5] man from Harlem, New York. Back in his youth, when he was around 18 years old, he joined the Nation of Islam (NOI). From the late 1960s into the 1970s, Imam Sayed served as the assistant imam of the Mosque of Islamic Brotherhood, an orthodox mosque in Harlem that emerged out of the Muslim Mosque Inc., the religious organization that Malcolm X started after he left the NOI. In the late 1970s, Imam Sayed became the first-known Black American man to join the Tijani tariqa. For more than three decades, Imam Sayed served as a pillar in the Tijani community in the U.S., and since the early 2000s, led the Tijani zawiya in Brooklyn.

After maghrib, it was time for *wazifa*, another daily dhikr that Tijanis do, preferably aloud in congregation. With their voices swelling and softening in harmony, the believers earnestly called on their Lord in Arabic. They sought forgiveness from Allah (*istighfar*), recited *salawat* (prayers of praise) upon Prophet Muhammad—their guide along the straight path to Allah—and proclaimed la illaha illallah 100 times.

When wazifa was finished, another young brother flicked on the lights. The sea of strangers transformed into friendly faces with wide, inviting smiles. Many sisters were dressed in shiny garments sewn of *bizaan* (Senegalese fabric) that they had gotten tailor-made during their last trip to the African continent. Other sisters wore outfits made of bright African wax print, some sewn into *dashikis* (loose shirts inspired by African styles and remixed and popularized in the diaspora) and others sewn as long dresses. One elderly woman had on a *melfa*, a flowing garment made of six meters of fabric that is commonly worn by women in parts of Mauritania and Senegal. Many of the brothers were dressed in starched, glossy West African-style *grand boubous* (three-piece outfits that consist of a knee-length shirt, pants, and a top layer that expands widthwise the distance between one's outstretched arms and extends lengthwise from one's shoulders down to one's ankles). Around these brothers' wrists were hundred-count dhikr beads wrapped in multiple loops, purchased during their visits to Senegal or Morocco. Several men were adorned with tall *kufis* (hats) associated with the Hausa, an ethnic group from Nigeria, Ghana, and other parts of West Africa. Others wore Moroccan-style *jalabiyas* (hooded gowns) over their t-shirts and jeans. Their clothes reflected an African-diasporic Muslim aesthetic that blended fashions from West Africa, North Africa, and the U.S.

As people greeted one another, a few brothers and sisters slipped out of the room. They returned with several platters—each filled with stewed chicken and an onion sauce over a bed of saffron rice. Between mouthfuls, attendees expressed enormous appreciation for Nadirah[6], a Black American woman in her early twenties who had learned (and, most would argue, now had mastered) how to make the dish during her adolescent years attending an international Islamic boarding school in Senegal. When we finished eating, a few other brothers and sisters cleared our plates, wiped up the grains of rice and bits of sauce that had scattered from the mats onto the carpet, and scrubbed the dishes clean. These hospitable gestures were acts of *khidma*, an Arabic word that describes a religiously blessed act of service. According to those at the zawiya, khidma was a big part of what it meant to live and be in community as a Tijani. With so many people doing khidma, the task of cleaning up after a large gathering was finished in less than ten minutes. When the attendees trickled out, the Tijani zawiya transformed back into its daily character: the modest home of Imam Sayed and his Afro-Puerto Rican wife, Hajjah[7] Najah Abdus-Salaam, who portioned off the ground floor of their home for their Sufi community.

The Tijani zawiya in Brooklyn was a space of communal fellowship where an intergenerational community of believers shared spiritual experiences, religious knowledge, home-cooked meals, and stories with one another at the end of a long week. They often talked about Shaykh[8] Hassan Aliou Cisse (pronounced "see-say") (1945–2008), a Senegalese Islamic scholar who first visited the U.S. in 1976. Most people at the zawiya had known Shaykh Hassan personally. Shaykh Hassan brought word of the Tijani tariqa—which originated in North Africa during the eighteenth century—to Black American Muslims and sparked what ultimately became the largest Black Sufi community in the U.S. Shaykh Hassan was the spiritual heir of a Tijani community led by his grandfather, Shaykh Ibrahim Niasse (pronounced "nee-yass") (1900–1975), a Senegalese Islamic scholar, Sufi shaykh, and pan-Africanist who oversaw the largest religious movement in Africa during the twentieth century. Several elders recalled that Shaykh Hassan was the first Islamic scholar and Sufi shaykh from overseas they encountered who treated Black Americans with respect. They recalled the lessons they had learned from Shaykh Hassan, who always reminded them of the importance of knowing Allah, loving Prophet Muhammad, and caring for Allah's creation.

The zawiya was one node within a pan-African Sufi network that centered the perspectives, experiences, needs, and dreams of Black Muslim Tijanis[9] across generations. Another node was Medina Baye (pronounced "by"), a sacred city in rural Senegal that Shaykh Ibrahim had founded and where Shaykh Hassan was born and raised. Many elders recalled how, starting in the late 1970s, Shaykh Hassan personally invited them to visit Medina Baye. Shaykh Hassan took care of the daunting logistics associated with what was for most of the Black Americans their first trip to Africa, a continent they had long dreamed of visiting and were finally able to go to—not just as tourists but also as spiritual seekers. Some of these elders saw Medina Baye as a place of possibility for themselves and their children. Starting in the 1980s, these parents enrolled their daughters and sons at an international Islamic boarding school there. These mothers and fathers hoped and prayed that their children would thrive in Medina Baye, living and learning under Shaykh Hassan's care in a nurturing society-wide environment that parents believed was unlike anything that was accessible to Black Muslim youth in the U.S. At the zawiya in Brooklyn, there were also several adults in their thirties and forties who recounted their experiences as young people studying in Medina Baye, a place where they felt that being Black and Muslim was not just normal but celebrated. They described how the lessons they learned in Medina Baye stayed with them after they returned to the U.S. and moved into adulthood. By the 2010s, some of these women and men had become parents of school-aged children, and they, like their parents before them, withdrew their children from schools in the U.S. and sent them to Medina Baye.

This book explores the dreams, sacrifices, struggles, and joys of this multi-generational community of Black Muslims in the Tijani tariqa who live and learn between the U.S. and Senegal. It argues that their experiences of Islamic education and pan-African exchange in Medina Baye are oriented towards collective care—an Islamic and Black radical way of being and belonging that promises spiritual liberation and material relief from racial capitalism and white supremacy. They strive to reach their greatest human potential, achieve new spiritual heights, and cultivate relationships with one another and Allah in ways that reject the political, economic, and social systems designed to exploit and denigrate them.

From Brooklyn to Medina Baye

Shaykh Ibrahim Niasse—Shaykh Hassan's grandfather—established Medina Baye in 1930 as a safe haven and sacred site for members of his Sufi movement at a time when the region was under French colonial domination. Medina Baye is located approximately 200 kilometers (or 125 miles) northeast of Senegal's capital city of Dakar in the rural region of Kaolack. There is no official population count in Medina Baye, but conservative estimates place the stable year-round population as low as 55,000 residents while other estimates suggest that the city hosts more than half a million people during peak times, such as the *gamou* (an event commemorating Prophet Muhammad's birthday) and the 27th night of Ramadan. The Tijani tariqa was present in West Africa prior to Shaykh Ibrahim's time. However, Shaykh Ibrahim was seen to have brought the *fayda* (flood) of divine knowledge, a metaphor that indexed the magnitude of his spiritual insights, which poured out and spread to become the most prominent branch of the Tijani tariqa, with more than one hundred million *murids* (disciples) in Africa and beyond.[10] From its early years, Shaykh Ibrahim's movement, which is often referred to in shorthand as the fayda, was pan-African in makeup. The fayda quickly spread beyond Senegal and attracted Muslims from throughout Africa, including from Nigeria, Ghana, Mauritania, Gambia, Burkina Faso, Côte d'Ivoire, Guinea, Guinea-Bissau, Niger, Benin, Togo, Sierra Leone, Cameroon, the Central African Republic, Chad, and Sudan. Shaykh Ibrahim's father, al-Hajj Abdoulaye Niasse, predicted the wide reach of his son's movement, and advised him at a young age: "If you but sit, people will come to you. It is the duty of a river to be full. If the neighboring cows do not come to drink, those from afar will" (as cited in Cisse 1984, 198).

By the late twentieth century and into the twenty-first century, under the leadership of Shaykh Ibrahim's grandsons Shaykh Hassan, Imam Cheikh[11] Tijani Aliou Cisse, and Shaykh Mouhamadou Mahy Cisse (or as they are usually called, Imam Cheikh and Shaykh Mahy, respectively), the movement spread across the continent—all the way to South Africa and Namibia, among others. It also gained traction among African-diasporic Muslims in the U.S., the United Kingdom, Trinidad, Bermuda, and elsewhere, as well as among Muslims in countries including Mexico, Brazil, and Singapore. Black Americans who came to Medina Baye thus found themselves in community with Tijanis from throughout Africa and the world.

I took my first trip to Medina Baye in 2012. During that trip, I met Ismail, a 14-year-old Black American male from Atlanta, Georgia. Ismail attended the African American Islamic Institute (AAII) School, the international Islamic boarding school started by Shaykh Hassan and Hajjah Kareemah Abdul-Kareem, a Black American Tijani woman

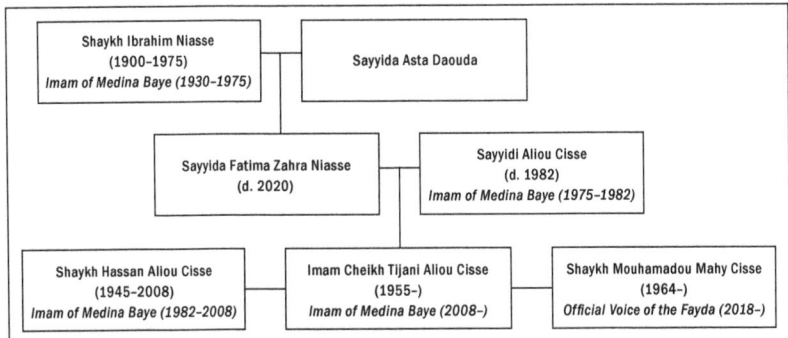

Figure I.1. Partial Niasse-Cisse family tree.

from Harlem, New York who was the first American Tijani *muqaddama* (woman in a position of spiritual leadership). Hajjah Kareemah visited Medina Baye first in 1977 and then again in 1982. She was very impressed by young people's educational experiences in the city. She wanted her daughter and other Black American children and youth to be able to study there and learn about their religion and history as Muslims of African descent. In 1983, Hajjah Kareemah helped Shaykh Hassan bring this dream to life by moving from New York City to Medina Baye to open AAII. Throughout the 1980s, Hajjah Kareemah's children, Shaykh Hassan's children, nieces, and nephews, and Imam Sayed's children were among the first generation of students at AAII. Nadirah, who cooked our delicious dinner at the zawiya in Brooklyn, was among the thousands of Black American and African youth who attended AAII over the next four decades.

Ismail was the ninth Black American student in the history of AAII to become a *hafiz* (one who has memorized the entire Qur'an in Arabic)—an accomplishment that Muslims understand to be incredibly sacred and blessed, yet also quite intellectually, emotionally, and psychologically difficult. Ismail's mother, grandmother, and great-aunt flew in from Atlanta to celebrate his accomplishment. The family vacillated between nervous anticipation, heart-swelling pride, and deep gratitude, watching with bated breath as Ismail recited a quarter of the Qur'an each evening in front of the people of Medina Baye, until four days had passed and he had recalled the entire holy book from memory, without even a single glance at the physical text.

Figure I.2. The final recitation and graduation ceremony for another Black American hafiz from AAII. The student holds the microphone and recites the Qur'an from memory as a group of people sit and listen to him, November 2017. Photo courtesy of the author.

As I talked to Ismail's family, I learned that he belonged to a multigenerational legacy. He was the third person in his extended family to have memorized the entire Qur'an in Medina Baye. Starting in the late 1970s, Ismail's grandmother was among those adults who, like Imam Sayed and Hajjah Kareemah, met Shaykh Hassan in the U.S. and joined the Tijani tariqa. During the 1980s and 1990s, Ismail's grandmother was one of dozens of parents who enrolled their children at AAII. Most of these parents could not relocate to Medina Baye, so they entrusted their daughters and sons to the care of Shaykh Hassan, Hajjah Kareemah, and other adults who vowed to raise these young people as their own. Ismail's mother and her siblings all attended AAII. From the 2000s onwards, Ismail's mother, aunts, and uncles were among the many Black American alumni who sent their own children to Medina Baye. These alumni, like their parents before them, entrusted their children to local caregivers. By then, Shaykh Hassan's younger brother Shaykh Mahy and his wife Sayyida[12] Kubra

Askari-Cisse (a woman from Atlanta who had attended AAII alongside Ismail's mother and who in 2000 became the fifth Black American to finish memorizing Qur'an at the school) continued Shaykh Hassan's precedent of caring for boarding students. Shaykh Mahy and Sayyida Kubra became the adoptive parents for young people like Ismail, who lived at Sayyida Kubra's house with about 15 other students, some of whom were from Atlanta, New York, or Detroit and the rest of whom were from Senegal, Ghana, Nigeria, Gambia, Burkina Faso, or elsewhere in West Africa. Ismail and his peers shared meals, bedrooms, and the ups and downs of being apart from their families as they memorized the Qur'an. Over their years of studying in Medina Baye, they forged new family bonds with one another and learned about the possibilities and responsibilities that came at the intersection of being young, Black, and Muslim.

Black Muslim Freedom Dreams

From the families who gathered at the Tijani zawiya in Brooklyn, to the young people who studied in Medina Baye, this book tells the stories of Black American Muslims' pursuit of Islamic education, spiritual transformation, and pan-African exchange between the U.S. and Senegal. As they lived and learned within a transnational community of Black Muslims in the Tijani tariqa, they strived to actualize what Robin D. G. Kelley terms freedom dreams. In his seminal text by the same title, Kelley recollects the perspective that his mother inculcated within him and his older sister. Kelley (2002) writes,

> She simply wanted us to live through our third eyes, to see life as possibility.... She wanted us to visualize a more expansive, fluid, "cosmopolitan" definition of blackness, to teach us that we are not merely inheritors of a culture but its makers.... She dreamed of land, a spacious house, fresh air, organic food, and endless meadows without boundaries, free of evil and violence, free of toxins and environmental hazards, free of poverty, racism, and sexism ... just free. (2)

Kelley's mother was part of a broader tradition of Black radical activists who dreamed of better futures and led grassroots social movements to turn those dreams into realities.

Throughout the twentieth century, many Black Americans who embraced Islam saw the religion as a freedom dream. Islam offered them more empowering understandings of themselves, their history, and their place within the world. Islam provided them with a radical alternative to the dehumanizing narratives imposed upon Black people. For Black American Muslim adults who met Shaykh Hassan and his brothers, joined the Tijani tariqa, visited Medina Baye, and relocated their children there, their decisions built upon freedom dreams anchored in the liberatory potential of Islam. This book maps the freedom dreams of this multi-generational community who saw life through a boundless lens of possibility and sought refuge in a new world that promised them spiritual liberation alongside material relief. This was a world where they were empowered to know Allah and achieve their highest human potential, and where they could live freely and fully away from the anti-Black violence, anti-Muslim racism, and economic marginalization that characterized urban life in the twentieth and twenty-first century U.S.

As Muslims, these Black Americans considered themselves to be part of the *ummah*, an Islamic concept that describes the global community of Muslims. Yet as members of Shaykh Ibrahim's branch of the Tijani tariqa, they became directly connected, through intimate spiritual relationships, to a contemporary Muslim community that included tens of millions of members in Africa alone. Black Americans plugged into a Sufi movement anchored in West Africa, the region that their ancestors had likely been kidnapped from and where Islam had been practiced since the eleventh century. In Medina Baye, they gained unprecedented access to a radically different world where they strove to deepen their understanding of Islam, emulate the model of Prophet Muhammad, and come to know Allah by studying with prolific scholars whom they saw themselves in.

This book argues that Black Muslims' experiences of Islamic education and pan-African exchange between Medina Baye and the U.S. are oriented towards collective care. The concept of collective care is essential to the argument of this book. I define collective care as a way of being and belonging that offers Black Muslims in the Tijani tariqa spiritual liberation alongside material relief. Collective care is a form of Islamic piety that guides Muslims to know Allah and become those who are most beloved to Him. Collective care is also a Black radical praxis that calls on people to leverage their knowledge, skills, labor, and time to support one another in the face of racial capitalism and white supremacy—two interlocking, oppressive systems that have produced, maintained, and normalized the inequitable world we live in.

Racial capitalism refers to the intertwined processes of economic exploitation and racist oppression that first emerged when Africans were kidnapped and brought to the Americas during the transatlantic slave trade in order to produce the system of capitalism and enable European domination (Robinson 1983). Racial capitalism is closely linked to white supremacy, which is a global system of political, economic, and social domination of nonwhites by whites that naturalizes the exploitation and denigration of nonwhite peoples' lands, resources, labor, cultures, and worldviews (Mills 1997). Racial capitalism and white supremacy work in tandem with one another to divide and dehumanize people on the basis of race in order to justify exploitation and extraction. These systems also influence how people think and act. Racial capitalism and white supremacy celebrate the values of individualism, greed, competition, and inequity, which in turn contribute to the myth that societal oppression is normal, natural, and therefore not worth fighting against. Collective care is a way of being and belonging that fundamentally opposes the systems and values of racial capitalism and white supremacy. Collective care instead emphasizes collectivism, collaboration, and equity in order to create communities where all of Allah's creations are cared for. Collective care is an Islamic and Black radical way of living in community that is just and pleasing to Allah.

From the U.S. to Senegal, I observed how Black Muslims in the Tijani tariqa collectively cared for one another. In Brooklyn, they strove to implement Shaykh Hassan's teachings about emulating prophetic characteristics through an everyday concern for one's community, and they served each other through acts of khidma. In Medina Baye, Senegalese shuyukh and Black American murids hosted adults who came for spiritual pilgrimage, and became the adoptive parents for unaccompanied young people who sought an Islamic education. These students lived and learned with teachers and residents who were part of a pan-African Sufi movement where people collectively cared for one another and strove to become beloved to Allah. Through their everyday experiences in formal and informal settings of Islamic education, young people learned about and searched for their own ways to contribute to a robust system of collective care that defined the Black Muslim Tijani community which spanned the U.S. and Senegal. In so doing, these youth undertook the work of "extending, elaborating, and refining their vision," becoming the latest generation of Black Muslims who freedom dreamed as they engaged in the enduring struggle to actualize a more liberatory world (Kelley 2002, 6).

Collective Care

The concept of collective care offers new insights into scholarship on religion, race, and education. Within the context of religion, collective care shifts away from an individualistic paradigm where a person's religiosity is demonstrated primarily through acts of personal piety and in private spaces. Instead, collective care signals towards twin processes of ethical self-cultivation and intersubjectivity through which believers help one another as a way of obtaining Allah's favor. Within the context of racial formation, collective care resists the impulse to differentiate and hierarchize the interconnected hardships facing various marginalized communities and instead calls on people to cultivate solidarities to actualize self-determination beyond the nation state. Finally, within the context of education, collective care rejects capitalist paradigms of schooling as primarily a path to individual upward socioeconomic mobility and instead calls upon learners to utilize the knowledge they gain as a resource that they are responsible for sharing with their community. Overall, for those who have been marginalized, neglected, and treated as disposable by the state, collective care becomes a strategy for building nurturing spaces of liberation.

For the Black Muslim Tijanis whose stories I share in this book, collective care describes a radical way of being and belonging that resists racial capitalist and white supremacist impulses towards individuality, human hierarchy, and exploitation. Instead, the idea of collective care reminds us that relationships of reciprocity, mutual aid, and shared responsibility offer freedom dreams, or visions and paths towards more liberatory possibilities beyond the present. At the same time, collective care is not just a reaction to or coping mechanism against racist oppression and economic exploitation. While it outlines a route to freedom from material injustices, at the foundation of the concept of collective care are Islamic knowledge, ethics, and practices that predate the oppressive modern systems of racial capitalism and white supremacy. These alternative ways of knowing, being, and belonging have guided Muslims' efforts from the seventh century onwards to live lives that are pleasing to Allah.

For murids in Shaykh Ibrahim's pan-African Sufi movement, collective care is an ethos and everyday practice anchored in the *sunnah* (habits or practices) of Prophet Muhammad, whose exemplary model is one that they strive to emulate in the contemporary era with the guidance of their shuyukh. Collective care describes Tijanis' ways of being and belonging as they journey on the paths towards prophetic excellence and experiential knowledge of Allah by showing concern for others and seeking to improve the material conditions that constrain their communities. These Tijanis' perspectives challenge the false notion that Islam is peripheral to African-diasporic communities and educational movements for Black liberation, as well as the myth that Black people are at the margins of global Muslim networks. Instead, by collectively caring for each other, Black Muslim Tijanis draw upon transnational religious, spiritual, and racial networks to seek Allah's pleasure and build liberatory forms of community beyond racial capitalism and white supremacy.

Theories of Care

Care describes both an emotional attachment ("I care *about* her") and a concrete action ("I care *for* her"). Often, an emotional attachment fuels concrete action; I show that I care about her by caring for her. By showing care *about* and *for* one another, we cultivate bonds of interdependence and interconnectedness. In developing the concept of collective care, I bridge anthropological, educational, and Black radical theories of care.

Anthropological scholarship has shown that care is an often scarce but critical resource that sustains everyday life for oppressed peoples (Han 2012; McKay 2018). Anthropological theories of care build upon the work of scholars in feminist science studies who emphasize the intersubjectivity and reciprocity that is fostered through caring relations. Annemarie Mol (2008) describes care as "a matter of various hands working together (over time) towards a result. Care is not a transaction in which something is exchanged (a product against a price); but an interaction in which the action goes back and forth (in an ongoing process)" (18). Framed in this way, care is "closer to gift exchange between individuals whose relationship to each other really matters. There is an exchange of stories and meanings but also of the raw experience of responsibility and emotional sensibility as in gift giving and receiving among intimate others" (Kleinman 2013, 5).[13] Feminist anthropological theories of care thus point to ways of being that cultivate reciprocity and collaboration.

However, the lived experiences of oppressed people throughout the world remind us that caring relations are embedded within power dynamics. Care can be an exclusionary practice that reifies race, class, and gender inequalities to deem certain people unworthy of care (Black 2018). In the U.S., Black people have long been refused care within a racial capitalist, white supremacist society, as manifested in their treatment in the media (Dixon 2019; Neely 2015), health care settings (Roberts 1997), schools (Dumas 2014; Morris 2016; Noguera 2008; Shange 2019), and beyond.

Yet despite this, Black people have engaged in radical care practices to sustain their communities. Education is a central site in which Black people have shown care about and for one another from slavery to the contemporary era (Anderson 1989; Ginwright 2010; Ladson-Billings 1994; McKinney de Royston et al. 2021; Walker 1996). Black educators have embodied care in their relationship with students, families, and their community (Bass 2012; Beauboeuf-Lafontant 2002; De Royston 2017 et al.; Price 2009; Roberts 2010; Thompson 1998, 2004). These Black educational modes of care, often reflecting Black feminist ethics, represent moral values, political analyses, and visions of change that differ from those promoted in earlier educational research on care, which was anchored in white liberal perspectives (Gilligan 1982; Noddings 1984; Martin 1992). Audrey Thompson (2004) summarizes the contrast between white and Black feminist educational theories of care: "The idealism, individualism, and colorblindness of White ethical and educational traditions contrasts markedly with the political and communal pragmatism of Black traditions of justice and caring" (35). Confronted with slavery and racism, Black peoples' emphasis on interdependence and relational ethics represented "not simply a preferred existential state but a critical component of survival" (Beauboeuf-Lafontant 2002, 82). In this sense, Black feminist theories demonstrate how care is a culturally specific mode of sociality and embodied practice of resistance to racism. Informed by Black feminist perspectives, "caring need not be regarded simply as an interpersonal, dyadic, and apolitical interaction," as is suggested in white liberal frameworks, but rather can be understood as something that holds "potential for communal engagement and political activism" to create liberatory possibilities for all (ibid., 83).

Black feminist educational theories of care build upon Black radical praxes of care. From the maroon societies that self-emancipated Black people created when they fled plantations during the sixteenth through nineteenth centuries (Diouf 2014; Winston 2023), to the farms, mutual aid networks, and cooperatives that Black people sustained during the twentieth century (Nembhard 2014; White 2018), to the social movements for police abolition and Black liberation in the twenty-first century (Harris 2023; Kaba and Ritchie 2022), Black people in the U.S. have long worked to create life-affirming communities.

This book shifts attention from how Black people are denied care to how they care about and for one another. In so doing, it heeds Eve Tuck's call to suspend damaged-centered research and embrace desire-based frameworks. While damage-centered research pathologizes minoritized communities and singularly portrays them in terms of their oppression, desire-based frameworks account "for the loss and despair, but also the hope, the visions, the wisdom of lived lives" (Tuck 2009, 417). Articulated primarily within the context of education research, Tuck's perspective echoes the call among anthropologists to move past studies of the suffering subject towards an anthropology of the good. An anthropology of the good requires scholars to study how "people orientate to and act in a world that outstrips the one most concretely present to them and to avoid dismissing their ideals as unimportant or, worse, as bad-faith alibis for the worlds they actually create" (Robbins 2013, 457).

Research that is anchored in a desire-based framework and attentive to the good honors the legacy of freedom dreaming within the Black radical imagination, where people "envision and make visible a new society, a peaceful, cooperative, loving world without poverty and oppression" (Kelley 2002, 196). Care is a critical site at which to study desire, the good, and freedom dreaming. It is by caring that people articulate hopes and desires as they seek to embody goodness on a personal level and through social relationships in their quest to actualize a liberatory world.

I add the word "collective" to emphasize the scale of care. Collective care signals the ways in which individuals care about and for their community, and the ways in which the community cares about and for each of its members. As we will see, caring is not an uneven burden placed on the most disenfranchised, nor is it *solely* an expectation placed upon those who have greater resources. Instead, collective care refers to a shared ethical obligation in which everyone in the community cares about and for everyone else. The young care for the old, and the old care for the young. Students care for their teachers, and teachers care for their students. Murids care for their shuyukh, and shuyukh care for their murids. All members become incorporated into the affective concerns, ethics, and social and spiritual practices of reciprocity, mutual aid, and interdependence that sustain the collective.

Collective Care Among Muslims in Africa and the Diaspora

The term "collective care" may seem redundant in the context of African and African-diasporic communities, where collectivism and communalism are often seen as core cultural values (Asante 1980; Collins 1990; Ikuenobe 2006), and where peoples' religious identities are often understood to be formed in relation to others (Beliso-De Jesús 2015; Covington-Ward 2016; Covington-Ward and Jouili 2021). However, the scholarship on African peoples' collectivist approaches tends to focus on African traditional religions—a category that seldom includes Islam, even though its presence on the continent dates back to the seventh century and it had a significant presence in West Africa long before the onset of European colonization (Kane 2016; Ogunnaike 2020).[14] However, in observing how Black Muslim Tijanis cared about and for one another, I found that Islam (itself an African religion) played a central role in shaping their ways of being and belonging in the world.

My formulation of collective care thus challenges false narratives of Islam as peripheral to African and African-diasporic communities and cosmologies. For my Black American interlocuters, Islam was a holistic way of life that spoke to their intersecting experiences, concerns, and aspirations as people who were Black and Muslim. As they learned and sought to implement the teachings of Islam, they did so within communities in which they perceived that most people were Black and Muslim. Their perspectives pointed to the central role of Islam in cultivating African-diasporic communities and offering spiritually grounded paths of resistance against racial capitalism and white supremacy.

My formulation of collective care also situates Black people at the center of academic and religious discourses about what it means to be a Muslim. In so doing, it disrupts the myth that relegates Black people to the margins of Islamic intellectual networks and global Muslim communities. Some who read about this theorization of collective care as an Islamically informed way of being and belonging might interpret it to be synonymous with Muslim piety. Anthropological studies on Muslim piety tend to focus on how believers cultivate a Muslim subjectivity through personal ritual and embodied acts of ethical self-discipline, such as wearing *hijab* (women's head covering), making salat, or attending classes and listening to lectures on Islam (Fadil 2011; Hirschkind 2006; Jouili 2015; Mahmood 2004; Renne 2021). Less attention has been paid to social and relational acts that cultivate Muslim piety.[15] Centering the perspectives of Black Muslims in the Tijani tariqa draws attention to a different set of embodied acts that promote piety—those oriented towards collective care.[16]

This book's focus on collective care shows, for instance, how a Muslim's piety is cultivated when she volunteers to raise other people's children (Chapter 2), when she helps cook dinner for dozens of people (Chapter 3), when she recites the Qur'an and dedicates its blessings to those subjected to racial injustice (Chapter 4), when she seeks out opportunities to teach others (Chapter 5), and when she gives money to neighbors in need (Chapter 6). Most people would likely agree that these examples are acts of piety; they are, after all, practices that bring religious blessings and help mold people into "good Muslims." However, in many Muslim communities and in academic scholarship alike, acts such as wearing hijab tend to gain much more attention in discussions about piety than the aforementioned acts of collective care. This is why I use the language of care rather than piety. By definition, care is relational. It describes how people secure one another's basic needs of food, housing, health care, and education by developing systems of support that are better than what the state provides (Nadasen 2023). For Black Muslims in the Tijani tariqa, collective care is a way of being and belonging that challenges the dichotomies between the material and the spiritual. Instead, it points to a worldview in which caring for others is central to what it means to be a "good Muslim."

Theorizing a Black Muslim Radical Tradition

This book tells the stories of a community of Black Americans who recognized the revolutionary potential of Islam, learned from Sufi shuyukh and communities in Senegal, and strove to attain liberation in this world and the next. Their stories are part of much longer histories of resistance among Black Muslims in Africa and the Americas. Their stories represent contemporary expressions of the Black Radical Tradition and Muslim International.

In *Black Marxism*, Cedric Robinson develops the concept of the Black Radical Tradition to describe the history and legacy of a collective revolutionary consciousness among Africans on the continent and in the Americas who rebelled, resisted, and revolted against racial capitalism. Robinson locates the origins of the Black Radical Tradition in the transatlantic slave trade, a racist economic project that exploited African peoples to produce the global system of racial capitalism. Africans who were kidnapped and brought to the Americas carried with them their cultures, histories, and fundamental understanding of their humanity. Armed with this knowledge, many enslaved people revolted against the system of slavery which sought to obliterate their past and transform them into property. For many enslaved people, Islam was a core part of the African knowledge systems that shaped their Black radicalism. As Sylviane Diouf (1998) asserts, many enslaved West Africans in the Americas "brought with them a tradition of defiance and rebellion, because as Muslims, they could be only free men and women" (210). Robinson notes that some of these enslaved African Muslims led a collective rebellion in Bahia, Brazil in the nineteenth century (Robinson 1983, 154–155).

After European chattel slavery legally ended, Black people in the Americas and Africa endured evolving systems of racial capitalism through forced labor, European colonialism, and European imperialism. However, maintaining a long-standing tradition of Black radicalism, new generations of Black people opposed these global systems of exclusion, exploitation, and extraction. Thus, while the Black Radical Tradition emerged out of the knowledge and cultures of African peoples and their historical opposition to racial capitalism dating back to the transatlantic slave trade, it encompasses both a historical and ongoing revolutionary struggle that "cements pain to purpose, experience to expectation, consciousness to collective action" to achieve liberation (ibid., 317). As this book shows, the Black Radical Tradition continues through the ongoing efforts of Black Muslim youth, mothers, fathers, shuyukh, and everyday believers who contribute to the collective struggle for freedom and liberation.

In *Black Star, Crescent Moon*, Sohail Daulatzai shows how the Black Radical Tradition evolved and expanded during the twentieth century. At the time, activists in the U.S. Civil Rights Movement demanded legal and social reforms from the government. Daulatzai examines how, in contrast, Black American Muslims and other Black radicals drew inspiration from the people, places, and politics of the Muslim Third World. These Black radicals' search for freedom beyond the U.S. drew them to what Daulatzai terms the Muslim International—a critical contact zone where they engaged with and connected their struggles to pan-African and anti-colonial movements across the Muslim Third World, including in places such as Palestine, Algeria, Iraq, Egypt, and Indonesia. For Black Muslims and other Black radicals, the Muslim International therefore served as site "of contact and difference . . . where ideas about justice, agency, and self-determination take root and are given shape" (Daulatzai 2012, xxiv).

Taken together, the Black Radical Tradition and the Muslim International point to the relationship between Islam, Africa, and liberation—in the past, present, and future. The Black Radical Tradition and the Muslim International serve as reminders of the long-standing and persisting current among African and African-descended Muslims who drew strength from their religious beliefs, cultural traditions, knowledge systems, and lived experiences to collectively resist oppressive systems and seek liberation. As we will see, Black American Muslims in Shaykh Ibrahim's branch of the Tijani tariqa belonged to a revolutionary pan-African Sufi movement that carried forth the collective consciousness and modes of resistance that characterize the Black Radical Tradition and the Muslim International. They joined a historical and ongoing Black Muslim Radical Tradition of people who engaged Islam as a way of life that committed them to oppose oppression and struggle for liberation in this world and the next.

Historicizing Muslims in Africa and the Diaspora

The Black Muslim Radical Tradition points to the overarching themes that have characterized the histories of Muslims in Africa and the diaspora. While an in-depth examination of these histories is beyond the scope of this introduction, I will briefly outline the events and memories that are key to understanding the contemporary stories and dreams of the Black Muslims who are featured in this book.

The presence of Muslims in Africa dates back to the seventh century, well before it spread widely through the Arabian Peninsula. In the fifth year after Prophet Muhammad received the first divine revelations of Islam, he advised a group of his followers to escape religious subjugation in Mecca by making *hijra* (migration) to Abyssinia (in present-day Ethiopia and Eritrea). This group of women and men sought refuge under the protection of the righteous al-Najashi, also known as Ashama, the Christian king who ruled the Kingdom of Aksum. These migrants formed the first Muslim community in Africa. In the eleventh century, as Muslim merchants and clerics from North Africa began traveling to lands south of the Sahara, they spread word of Islam and created new Muslim communities on the continent (Lewis 1966; Levtzion 2000, 68; Kane 2016, 47).

In West Africa, Islam spread primarily through the efforts of African Muslim scholars (Kane 2016; Ware 2014; Wright 2015a). By the eleventh century, there were Muslims in the kingdoms of Ghana (in present-day Mauritania and Mali) and Mali (in present-day Senegal, Gambia, Mauritania, Mali, Guinea-Bissau, Guinea, Côte d'Ivoire, Burkina Faso, and Niger). In the thirteenth century, the Jakhanke, a Manding-speaking group of itinerant Muslim clerics and educators originating from Diakha-Masina (in present-day Mali) helped spread Islam throughout Senegambia (in present-day Senegal, Gambia, and Mauritania, as well as parts of Mali and Guinea). The Jakhanke were one of many clerical groups that helped spread Islam in West Africa primarily through service and education—including opening schools that brought in Muslims and non-Muslims alike (Sanneh 1989).

When Europeans began kidnapping West Africans for the transatlantic slave trade, many captives were taken from Muslim societies (Diouf 1998, 57–60). Some Muslim clerical communities challenged the African rulers who collaborated with European slavers. As a result, these Muslims faced harsh retaliation. For instance, in the seventeenth century, Muslim clerics associated with the Tuubanaan movement in and around the Senegal River Valley were sold into slavery by African kings as retribution for attempting to overthrow those unjust kings (Ware 2014, 103–109). In the nineteenth century, the Islamic scholar and Tijani leader Shaykh Umar Futi Taal critiqued the rulers who allowed Muslims to be enslaved and sold to the Europeans. He launched a successful jihad to establish the Umarian Caliphate (in present-day Mali, Senegal, and Guinea) (El-Sharif 2021; Robinson 1985; Ware 2014, 162). Also in the nineteenth century in Hausaland (in present-day northern Nigeria and Niger), Muslims who fought in the Islamic scholar and Qadiri Sufi leader Shaykh Usman dan Fodio's successful jihad against the ruler of the region were sold into slavery in the Americas (Diouf 1998, 52–55). Of course, not all African Muslims launched armed rebellions to protest the transatlantic slave trade or the predatory rulers who benefited from it. But the aforementioned examples point to the Black Radical Tradition among numerous Muslim (and often Sufi) communities in West Africa and comprise some of the histories that contemporary Black American Muslim Tijanis draw inspiration from.

In the Americas, enslaved West African Muslims maintained their revolutionary consciousness within a hostile society that was set on eliminating all traces of their humanity. In 1522 in Hispaniola (in present-day Dominican Republic), Muslims from the Wolof ethnic group from Senegambia led the first collective insurrection of enslaved peoples in the Americas (Diouf 1998, 211; Gomez 2005, 3). Enslaved African Muslims also played a prominent role in the Haitian revolution that began in 1791 and that resulted in the first independent Black nation in the Americas (Diouf 1998, 216–220). In 1835, during the last ten days of Ramadan, African Muslims from the Hausa and Yoruba ethnic groups led the Malê uprising in Salvador da Bahia, Brazil, which marked the largest revolt of enslaved Africans in the Americas (ibid., 221). Some of these Muslims had previously fought in the jihad of Shaykh Usman dan Fodio in Hausaland, which shaped their revolutionary consciousness and gave them combat experience. While some African Muslims launched uprisings, others escaped plantations and established maroon societies, or new communities where they governed themselves and audaciously enacted their own ideas of freedom (Diouf 2014).

In the U.S., even as white slave masters sought to eradicate the influence of Islam among enslaved people and forcibly convert them to Christianity, some African Muslims persisted in preserving their faith. During the nineteenth century on the Sea Islands off the coast of Georgia, enslaved Muslims prayed, fasted, wore Islamic clothes, refused to eat pork, wrote religious texts in Arabic, recited the Qur'an, distributed *sadaqa* (charity) to neighbors, and maintained semi-autonomous Muslim communities (Diouf 1999; Turner 2000). Yet by and large, within a white Christian hegemonic landscape that heavily policed Islam and deliberately sought to crush African peoples' memories of Islam, traces of the religion faded as subsequent generations of enslaved peoples were born in the U.S. (Austin 1984; Gomez 1998).

However, in the early twentieth century, Islam experienced a resurgence. Groups such as the Moorish Science Temple of America and the Nation of Islam asserted that Islam was the original religion of Black people (Weisenfeld 2017). Black Americans' engagement with Islam during this period was emblematic of the broader African American religious experience, in which Black Muslims, Black Christians, and Black Jews alike engaged in what Sherman Jackson (2005) describes as "holy protest against anti-Black racism" (4). Indeed, becoming Muslim meant asserting the ability to define oneself however one chose, to believe whatever one chose, and to live one's life and raise one's children however one chose—all in defiance of the spiritual, psychological, economic, and political systems that were designed to subjugate Black people.

Throughout the twentieth century, across the urban U.S., Black Muslims' community-building efforts contributed to public perceptions of Muslims as "disciplined, just, and God-fearing people who will stand up for the rights of others" (McCloud 2004, 81). These long-standing practices fostered a broader understanding that "the history of the [Black]

Muslim community in America is a history of consciousness. It is about the struggle to alter the perception blacks have about themselves and society" (Rouse 2004, 83). These scholarly observations point to the dominant impulse among Black American Muslims of engaging Islam as an ethical blueprint that shapes their ways of knowing and being and fosters individual and community-wide transformation (Chan-Malik 2018; Kashani 2023).

Also during the twentieth century, some Black American Sunni Muslims learned about the history of Islam in Africa. Like the Moorish Science Temple and Nation of Islam, these Black American Sunni communities similarly constructed sacred histories that presented more affirming accounts of Black Americans' religious past and situated them as inheritors of multi-century traditions of orthodox Islam on the continent (Abdul Khabeer 2017; Carter 2026; Mack 2018; Miller 2024). Being Muslim undermined hegemonic chronologies that began their stories as enslaved peoples in the U.S. Instead, it reconnected them to the African Islamic worldviews of the Black Radical Tradition. Some Black American Muslims traveled to Africa (Aidi 2014; Turner 2021), while others remained in the U.S. but cultivated relationships with the growing populations of African Muslim immigrants who arrived in the late 1980s onwards (Abdullah 2010; Babou 2021; Kane 2011; Stoller 2002). For many, being Muslim also meant seeing oneself as part of transnational moral geographies (Grewal 2014) that linked them to histories, ideas, people, and places in the Muslim International. Through these exchanges, Black American Muslims developed new understandings of their shared histories and ongoing struggles alongside African Muslims to achieve spiritual and material liberation.

The Politics of Global Blackness

This book centers the perspectives of Black American Muslims, a group whose experiences with international travel, pan-African exchange, and education in Africa have been largely overlooked within academic scholarship. Research on Black American and West African Muslims tends to focus on their interactions in the U.S. (Abdullah 2010; Babou 2021; Kane 2011; Stoller 2002) and works that discuss African Americans' engagement with Africa seldom focus on Muslims (Clarke 2004;

Gaines 2006; Holsey 2008; Umoren 2018). I focus on the experiences of Black American Muslims in Senegal to demonstrate how their spiritual and educational exchanges with peoples and a place in Africa created liberatory pathways beyond the U.S. and contributed to their revised understandings of Blackness in a global context.

Like Bianca Williams's (2018) ethnography of African American women who travel to Jamaica, I recognize that my decision to tell a story of pan-African exchange primarily from the vantage point of Black Americans "reinscribes the privileges and hegemony associated with African Americanness" (24). Williams's comment alludes to the hegemonies within African Diaspora Studies, where some scholars have argued that the experiences of African Americans are overrepresented and that understandings of race and Blackness in the U.S. are mapped onto analyses of dynamics in other African-diasporic contexts (Campt and Thomas 2008; de Sá 2025; Gilroy 1993).

Many of the Black Americans I spent time with articulated perspectives that could be seen as reifying U.S.-based notions of race. For instance, when describing their connection to Senegal, some invoked phenotypical definitions of Blackness ("Senegal is a place where everyone looks like me"), notions of African heritage ("This is where my people came from"), and fusions of religious and racial identities ("I'm learning Islam from my people"). However, these comments might be interpreted another way—not as an imposition of U.S. racial logics but rather as evidence of a pan-African consciousness that understands African peoples throughout the world to be a unified group. In either case, the Black Americans I spoke with acknowledged that some Africans shared their perspectives and others did not. This reality reflected the changing and varied meanings of Blackness, race, and pan-Africanism within an increasingly globalized, twenty-first century context in Africa and throughout the world (Clarke and Thomas 2006; Marable and Agard-Jones 2008; Pierre 2020). This reality also reflected the diversity among the Africans with whom Black Americans interacted in Medina Baye. Black Americans built relationships with Africans who had read *The Autobiography of Malcolm X*, learned about pan-Africanism and decolonization, and traveled outside of rural Senegal. They also interacted with people who had never left Medina Baye and whose formal schooling lapsed after a primary level of Islamic education. Variations in perspectives thus were not necessarily simply the result of many Black Americans' tendencies towards U.S.-based frameworks of race or investments in pan-African unity, but rather revealed the ways in which education, class, politics, mobility, and power differentials shaped peoples' worldviews.

Black American Muslims entered a Senegalese context in which Negritude and pan-Africanism held historical significance (Jaji 2014; Murphy 2016; Ratcliff 2014), but where contemporary discussions about race, racism, and Blackness were at times muted (de Sá 2025; Speciale 2021). While Black Americans' worldviews were refracted through U.S. racial logics and their experiences in the U.S., their time in Senegal troubled a simplistic view of Africa as primarily a historical and symbolic source of diasporic identity. Instead, by living and learning in Senegal, Black Americans experienced contemporary Africa as a dynamic and heterogenous site where they encountered a range of perspectives, where their understandings of Blackness, diaspora, and pan-Africanism were remixed, and where global processes of racialization persisted (Bedasse 2017; Jaji 2014; Pierre 2012; Young and Weitzberg 2022).

By focusing on Black American Muslims, this book illuminates the racial logics, experiences of racialization in the U.S., and pan-African politics that fueled their interest in Africa, and how their consciousness, coupled with their on-the-ground experiences with African Muslims, contributed to their revised understandings of what it meant to live in the world as Black Muslims. In this way, like Williams (2018), I use the experiences of Black American Muslims as a "starting point for the discussion about diasporic community" (24). By centering their perspectives, this book highlights their particular needs, experiences, and aspirations while simultaneously accounting for the ways in which their freedom dreams and lived experiences were forged in dialogue with African Muslims, from whom they gained new perspectives and questions that fueled their joint efforts to uphold a system of collective care.

Chapter Outline

This book examines how Black Muslims in the Tijani tariqa collectively care for one another as they pursue spiritual liberation alongside material relief.

Chapter 1 describes the prophetic lessons, Tijani Sufi teachings, and revolutionary pan-African orientation that has shaped members of this spiritual movement's commitment to pleasing Allah and working towards the liberation of people in Africa and beyond. Each subsequent chapter shows a different way in which believers apply these teachings to their everyday lives by collectively caring for each other.

Chapter 2 charts the origins of the pan-African Islamic educational exchange that has been sustained in Medina Baye over more than four decades. By focusing on the stories of four mothers, I examine why the first generation of Black American parents were interested in sending their children to AAII during the 1980s and 1990s, and how these young peoples' educational migration was made possible through the collective care practices of Black American and West African Tijanis.

Chapter 3 shifts to the contemporary moment. It examines the everyday Islamic education that Black American youth gain as they interact with the people, practices, and physical place of Medina Baye. I show how young people encounter a model of relational piety in which a person's spiritual esteem is linked to their willingness to serve their community with their time, physical labor, and material wealth. I argue that witnessing these day-to-day collective care practices shapes young people's own understandings of how they want to live in the world as Black Muslims, in the present and future.

Chapter 4 turns attention to Black American youths' experiences in formal educational settings. I argue that these youth experience Qur'anic education as a form of learning that is rooted in an axiomatic stance of Black Muslim brilliance. I show how this approach inculcates within students' discursive knowledge alongside religiously blessed habits of using what they learn to address the needs of their community.

Chapter 5 examines the long-term trajectories of Black American youth who studied in Medina Baye from the 1980s to the 2020s. I focus on three categories of young people, each of whom envisioned and enacted a different pathway once they finished their studies in Medina Baye. These three groups reflect the varied ways in which young people strove to collectively care for their community once as they moved into adulthood.

Chapter 6 considers the lasting impact of Black American Tijanis' engagement with African Tijanis in Medina Baye. I argue that

Shaykh Ibrahim's pan-African Sufi movement offers new paradigms of reciprocity and relational piety that enable Black American and African Tijanis to mitigate the impacts of racial capitalism and white supremacy.

The Epilogue summarizes the book's overarching argument and reflects upon the enduring lessons of Shaykh Ibrahim's spiritual movement at a time when global projects of exclusion, extraction, and elimination are being waged against Muslims and other communities of color throughout the world. It considers how the concept of collective care can help us freedom dream in this world and the next.

Research Methods

This book is based on a decade and a half of deep engagement with the Tijani community in the U.S. and Senegal, dating back to 2010 when I first visited the Tijani zawiya in Brooklyn. I conducted ethnographic fieldwork in Medina Baye, New York City, Atlanta, Detroit, Washington D.C., and online.

In Medina Baye, I conducted research during the summer of 2016, from 2017 to 2018, and during the summer of 2022, totaling 16 months of ethnographic fieldwork. Over a 12-month period from 2017 to 2018, I conducted classroom observations at the AAII School three days a week for two to three hours per day, totaling over 300 hours. Though I spent time in all classrooms at the school, the bulk of my observations occurred in the three classrooms that had the highest concentration of Black American students. I rotated consistently between these three classrooms. For an additional period each day, which lasted approximately 3.5 hours, I took on the role of a student and memorized the Qur'an. On weekends, I spent time with youth at their dormitory, took part in celebrations such as birthdays, supervised excursions to swimming pools and other local sites, and generally immersed myself in the social lives of the youth. I also collected field notes throughout Medina Baye. I accompanied Black Americans as they visited shuyukh, participated in wazifa and other Tijani activities, and attended religious and social gatherings.

In the U.S., I spent time in New York City, Atlanta, Detroit, and Washington D.C.—four cities with very active Tijani communities. In each city, I conducted participant observations at the local zawiya, special events, fundraisers, or other gatherings.

To elaborate on insights gathered through participant observation, I conducted open-ended, semi-structured interviews in Medina Baye and in the U.S. I spent time with Black Muslim Tijanis from 11 countries. In total, I interviewed 98 youth, parents, grandparents, teachers, shuyukh, alumni, and community members, 70 of whom were Black American, two of whom were Black British, and 26 of whom were Africans from Senegal, Nigeria, Niger, Gambia, Burkina Faso, Ghana, Côte d'Ivoire Guinea-Bissau, and South Africa.

I also participated in digital spaces where believers collectively studied and shared sacred knowledge from the Tijani intellectual tradition. This tradition includes writing and poetry from Shaykh Ahmad al-Tijani (the founder of the Tijani tariqa), Shaykh Ibrahim Niasse, Shaykh Hassan Cisse, and other Tijani shuyukh. Their works were either produced in Arabic or Wolof (the primary indigenous language spoken in Senegal) and later translated into English, or originally published in English. Some key sources include *Kashif al-Ilbas (The Removal of Confusion)* and *Ruhul Adab (The Spirit of Good Morals)*, two Arabic-language works by Shaykh Ibrahim that have been translated into English and are frequently studied among members of his fayda. The Tijani intellectual tradition also includes secondary sources, commentaries, and classes from other shuyukh and academics, as well as materials that Tijani murids find on the internet, such as YouTube videos of lectures given by their shuyukh and graphics featuring quotes from their shuyukh. Finally, Tijani murids contribute to this intellectual tradition as they discuss scholarly works written by their shuyukh and share the knowledge they gained from spending time with their shuyukh. My engagement in digital spaces attuned me to this vast intellectual tradition that informed Tijanis' quests for spiritual transformation. As such, throughout this book, I cite teachings from the Tijani intellectual tradition in order to bring to the forefront the rich milieu of ideas that shaped these spiritual seekers' ways of being and belonging in the world.

I approached this research as a Bangladeshi American Muslim Tijani woman and scholar writing about a community that I was connected to prior to beginning my academic work. As a racial outsider and religious and spiritual insider, I embraced the divergent and overlapping identities between myself and my interlocuters as a critical resource, rather than a liability that precluded rigorous analysis. This stance was informed by my understanding that objectivity is a myth rooted in white supremacist ideology. As Tukufu Zuberi (2008) argues, "We are not Martians from another time or place, thus we cannot study society as outsiders. We are part of the world and study society from the inside" (12).

Over 15 years of spending time in a community where most people espoused some form of Black liberatory politics, the salience of my racial identity as a South Asian faded for some as we had sustained conversations about our shared sociopolitical commitments. For others, my racial identity prompted silences and openings that I followed up on. On occasions where I wondered if people were tailoring their comments based on me being South Asian ("Them being Black didn't matter. If the shuyukh were from Pakistan, I would've gone to Pakistan!"), my racial identity emboldened me to frankly acknowledge the impact of South Asian and Arab hegemonies on U.S. Muslim communities and directly probe about the possibilities that emerged in a Sufi movement that centered and celebrated Black Muslims.

When I began my fieldwork, some of my interlocuters challenged the distance I had been taught to maintain during my doctoral coursework. When I first explained to Sayyida Kubra Askari-Cisse that I planned to conduct observations at the AAII School, she asked, "Why don't you memorize Qur'an? If you're going to sit there, you might as well get something out of it." She was responding to my religious identity and social performance as a practicing Muslim. Even though the majority of students at AAII were children and adolescents, the school always had a few adult students. In spite of my age as a then twenty-something year old, there was the social and religious expectation that I take advantage of the sacred educational opportunity, rather than merely observe it from a distance. And that I did.

Also, as I progressed in my research, I became a mother. This new role made me approach questions of education and liberation with greater urgency and deeper personal investment. When I interviewed parents and young people, I simultaneously mined their responses for advice because I had also begun making schooling choices for my own children. By then, the social distance between me and young people had expanded; I was no longer in the liminal period of youthhood

(Turner 1987); as a mother, I was treated by many young people as an aunty and full-grown adult who seemed to be in a similar generation as their parents.

Finally, over the course of this research, I became an organizer in the Tijani community. Among the efforts I contributed to were the annual Shaykh Hassan Cisse *ziyara* (visitation) in the U.S. and a digital project to document and preserve the history of Tijani tariqa. Because of these commitments, I deviated from the traditional ethnographic method of participant observation and instead became an observing participant (Cox 2015). The stories I share are thus from the vantage point of someone deeply involved in the work of envisioning, building, and sustaining a community on a daily basis.

To some, learning about my positionality may raise questions about the criticality of my analysis. However, I view my investments as intellectual and practical resources. The Black radical feminist and organizer dequi kioni-sadiki (2023) asserts,

> Chokwe Lumumba said, "If you don't love the people, you will betray the people." And you betray the people when you don't look at what you did that you could've done differently, when you don't assess . . . where you were, where you are, where you are going.

Lumumba was a member of the Republic of New Afrika and a co-founder of the Malcolm X Grassroots Movement, two organizations that were committed to the liberation of Black people and that included many Muslim members. Building upon the traditions of self-criticism among these Black radical formations, kioni-sadiki asserts that those involved in the work hold a meaningful vantage point from which to ruminate and assess. She frames critique as a necessary practice of reflection. Rooted in love for and accountability to one's community, critique propels the practical goal of charting a liberatory path forward. While some anthropological scholarship tends to take a critical stance towards its subject matter as a way of illuminating the contradictions and complexities of human behavior, such an emphasis on critique can crystalize our shortcomings without also presenting maps to a better future. In this book, in which I embrace desire-based research frameworks and build upon an anthropology of the good, I embrace a mode of subjective and reflexive inquiry that celebrates our wins while simultaneously offering analyses to enhance our future work. As you read this book, I hope you find within it valuable lessons that can inform your own work in the world.

1

The Prophetic and the Political

Islam, Sufism, and Revolutionary Pan-Africanism

In a *hadith* (narration) from Prophet Muhammad, he advised his companions: "The most beloved to Allah are those who are most beneficial to His creation. The most beloved deed to Allah is to make a Muslim happy, or remove one of his troubles, or forgive his debt, or feed his hunger. That I walk with a brother regarding a need is more beloved to me than that I seclude myself in this mosque in Medina for a month... Whoever walks with his brother regarding a need until he secures it for him, then Allah Almighty will make his footing firm across the bridge on the day when the footings are shaken."

While some might think that the most pious Muslims are those who spend their days worshipping Allah in solitude, this hadith indicates that Allah is most pleased with those who remain among the people and fill their time by helping others in need. This hadith invites Muslims to think expansively about what constitutes worship. It explains the sacred blessings that come with relieving another person's emotional, economic, and social burdens. This hadith highlights a model of relational piety that links the worldly to the spiritual. In other words, it teaches Muslims that the path to Allah's love is forged through acts of collective care.

This hadith is one of thousands from Prophet Muhammad that Muslims throughout the world have studied, shared, and strived to implement for centuries. The first part of this hadith—the most beloved to Allah are those who are most beneficial to His creation—was a teaching that numerous Black American Tijanis recalled that Shaykh Hassan Cisse frequently reminded them of. Shaykh Hassan's grandfather, Shaykh Ibrahim Niasse, invoked a similar hadith during a speech in Nigeria in 1966, when he advised his *murids* (disciples): "The creation is the family of God, and the most beloved to Him are those who provide for

His family" (as cited in Wright 2015a, 273). Shaykh Hassan and Shaykh Ibrahim's references to these hadiths reflect their Tijani Sufi community's distinct approach to spiritual transformation—it is a movement that emphasizes spiritual liberation alongside revolutionary sociopolitical action. For Black American Muslims who embrace Shaykh Ibrahim's branch of the Tijani tariqa, they join a pan-African Sufi movement that teaches people to follow the prophetic example by collectively caring for others.

The Prophetic

Islam was revealed to Prophet Muhammad during the seventh century in the city of Mecca (in present-day Saudi Arabia). At the time, the Quraysh, Mecca's ruling tribe, had abandoned *muruwah*, their historical ethical and social code that included "virtues like bravery, honor, hospitality, strength in battle, concern for justice, and, above all, an assiduous dedication to the collective good of the tribe" (Aslan 2005, 29). Instead, as a new economy emerged, the Quraysh became guided by individualism, competition, and greed (Armstrong 2006, 29–35). The city's wealth became concentrated among a few elite families, who hoarded their resources and exploited the vulnerable.

Islam represented a radical alternative that addressed the growing moral bankruptcy and socioeconomic inequities in Mecca. Among the first revelations that Prophet Muhammad received were the *ayats* (verses): "Read! And your Lord is the Most Generous; Who taught by the pen; taught humanity what they knew not" (Qur'an 96:3–5[1]). Another early revelation included the ayat: "And you are truly [a man] of outstanding character" (Qur'an 68:4). This was a reference to Prophet Muhammad's reputation as *al-Amin* (the trustworthy one). Yet another early revelation included the ayats: "And (surely) your Lord will give so much to you that you will be pleased. Did He not find you as an orphan then sheltered you? Did He not find you unguided then guided you? And did He not find you needy then satisfied your needs? So do not oppress the orphan, nor repulse the beggar. And proclaim the blessings of your Lord" (Qur'an 93:5–11). These early ayats laid out the foundational teachings of Islam: lessons about Allah's generosity, confirmation of Prophet Muhammad's praiseworthy character, and reminders that

Allah cared for all of creation and that Muslims ought especially to care for the marginalized. These teachings underscored Islam's core emphasis on love and justice, and the call for Muslims to seek internal spiritual transformation alongside external societal change.

As Prophet Muhammad continued to receive revelation, Muslims learned about the different dimensions of their religion. These dimensions are summarized in the hadith of Jibril,[2] which describes an occasion when a man came to see Prophet Muhammad and his companions. The man said, "Oh Muhammad, tell me about *Islam*." The Prophet explained that Islam meant adhering to the five pillars—the *shahada* (declaration of faith), *salat* (prayer), *zakat* (annual tax on wealth), *sawm* (fasting during Ramadan), and *hajj* (pilgrimage to Mecca). The man responded, "You have spoken truthfully." Then, he asked the Prophet about *iman*. The Prophet explained that *iman* meant having belief in Allah, His angels, His books, His messengers, the Last Day, and *qadr* (just, divine decree). The man replied, "You have spoken truthfully. Tell me about *ihsan*." The Prophet explained that *ihsan* was to worship Allah as if you saw Him, and if you did not see him, to know that He sees you. When the man left, Prophet Muhammad explained to his companions, "Verily, [the man] was [Angel] Jibril who came to teach you your religion."

The hadith of Jibril provides a framework for the primary dimensions of the religion: submission (*islam*), faith (*iman*), and excellence (*ihsan*). The first dimension corresponds to the five obligatory pillars of Islam, and the second dimension outlines the core theological beliefs in Islam. The third, ihsan, is the focus of Sufism, the inner, mystical dimension of Islam. Muslims who study the Islamic science of Sufism strive to achieve *marifa* (experiential knowledge of Allah)—thereby becoming those who worship Allah as if they see Him. They do so in part by perfecting their character such that they reach the highest level of human excellence. The goal of ihsan is to emulate the model of Prophet Muhammad, who is *insan al-kamil* (the most perfected human being) and therefore the best of Allah's creation.

In their pursuit of ihsan, Sufis place considerable emphasis on loving Prophet Muhammad, whose life "was a tireless campaign against greed, injustice, and arrogance" (Armstrong 2006, 13). Many Sufis formalize their spiritual journeys by joining a specific tariqa and taking *bayat* (an oath of allegiance) to *shuyukh* (spiritual guides). The shuyukh's "fundamental concern is to shape the character (*khuluq*) of the disciple so that it conforms to the prophetic model" (Chittick 2007, 28–29). These shuyukh serve as real-life examples for Sufi murids seeking to emulate Prophet Muhammad's historical model in contemporary contexts.

Different tariqas prescribe different approaches to cultivating ihsan. One common approach is to strive for asceticism, restrain oneself from worldly pleasures, and embrace material poverty. Doing so is intended to help one detach from the *dunya* (temporal world) and instead focus on the *akhira* (afterlife). A Sufi who undertakes this approach is often called a *faqir*, an Arabic word that literally describes one who is poor but figuratively reflects the Sufi's conscious acknowledgement of their neediness for Allah and His favors. The Tijani tariqa, however, outlines a different approach to cultivating ihsan—one that builds upon the hadith that opened this chapter, that those who are most beloved to Allah are those who are most beneficial to His creation.

The Tijani Approach to Emulating the Prophetic

In the Tijani tariqa's teachings, spiritual transformation occurs because of "God's action, not the result of the servant's efforts" (Wright 2020, 201). The Tijani tariqa prescribes that the best way to gain closeness to Allah is through *shukr* (gratitude). While numerous Sufi shuyukh have emphasized the importance of shukr, Shaykh Ahmad al-Tijani (1737–1815), the Algerian Islamic scholar who founded the Tijani tariqa in the late eighteenth century, asserted that shukr was especially important for the Muslims of his time because they lived in an age of "unprecedented corruption" (ibid., 198). Shaykh al-Tijani critiqued the corruption among individual Muslims of his time who pursued selfish desires as well as the corruption among the ruling Muslim Ottoman government and other Muslim societies that contradicted Islamic principles (ibid., 201). Living during an era when the transatlantic slave trade was ongoing, Shaykh al-Tijani also asserted, "Processed sugar is forbidden to eat or sell: it has been confirmed to me that it is mixed with blood" (as cited in Wright 2020, 60). Though processed sugar is not *haram* (forbidden) in Islam, Shaykh al-Tijani's efforts to prohibit it among his followers suggests that he was likely also critiquing the corruption among the European powers of his time, who forced Africans to work to death on sugar plantations in the Americas.

Shaykh al-Tijani reported that Prophet Muhammad visited him in a waking vision and informed him that he and his followers could achieve spiritual esteem without extreme *zuhd* (worldly asceticism) or *khalwa* (solitary spiritual retreats). In the Tijani tariqa, murids are therefore encouraged to remain involved in their community as they progress on their spiritual journey. In fact, when a young person stayed in the zawiya after joining the Tijani tariqa, Shaykh al-Tijani told him, "Learn a craft while you are still young" (as cited in Wright 2020, 205).

Shaykh al-Tijani's emphasis on being engaged in the world shaped his interpretation of the word *faqir*. Zachary Wright (2005) explains that Shaykh al-Tijani "spoke of the concept of the *faqir*, a word literally meaning 'the poor one' often applied to a Sufi disciple, but generally applied the notion of poverty to the state of the aspirant's heart before God instead of material renunciation" (125). Among the miracles attributed to Shaykh al-Tijani was the fact that he was known to give "great gifts the like not seen by people" (ibid., 124).[3] This included feeding people, of which Shaykh al-Tijani said, "The blessing (*baraka*) of feeding people is like the blessing of prayer in the mosque (*al-salat fi makaniha*)" (as cited in Wright 2020, 203). Addressing Shaykh al-Tijani's habits of charitable giving, Wright (2005) explains,

> This emphasis on wealth and generosity seems to indicate a clear attempt to implement the Sunna of the Prophet, concerning giving in the cause of God, in a very tangible manner . . . The Shaykh's concept of the Sunna of the Prophet and the Sufi's need to emulate this ideal model in both its external and internal attributes certainly contributed to his tendency to remain involved in society at its most tangible and pragmatic level: at the level of money and the basic needs of its members. (125)

Shaykh al-Tijani's understanding challenged dominant Sufi notions of wealth as a vice. His understanding also troubled capitalist conceptions of wealth as defined by individual accumulation. Instead, his actions and statements indicated a notion of wealth as a resource associated with an attitude of generosity, as including an ethical imperative for redistribution, and as fostering opportunities to receive sacred blessings on par with praying in a mosque. In striving to improve others' material conditions as a way of holistically emulating the prophetic model, Shaykh al-Tijani advanced a concept of relational piety. He taught his students to be like Prophet Muhammad by caring for, rather than separating from, their community.

This approach builds upon the ayat from the Qur'an that links ihsan to justice: "God commands justice (*adl*), doing good (*ihsan*), and generosity towards relatives and He forbids what is shameful, blameworthy, and oppressive. He teaches you, so that you may take heed" (Qur'an 16:90[4]). While many academic scholars emphasize the importance of love within Sufism (see for example Chittick 2007; Lapidus 1984; Lumbard 2020), few foreground justice as a manifestation of Sufis' love. In contrast, Omid Safi (2018) cites the above ayat to assert that ihsan, love, and justice are connected: "This radical love is one that moves inward and shows up as tenderness, and pours outward and shines as justice. To be a mystic of the path of radical love necessitates tenderness in our intimate dealings, and a fierce commitment to social justice in the community" (xxxvi). The Tijani tariqa's emphasis on collective care thus orients the murids towards cultivating ihsan through love and justice for others.

Emulating the Prophetic in Shaykh Ibrahim's Fayda

The Tijani tariqa spread from North to West Africa during the eighteenth and nineteenth centuries as individual Islamic scholars embraced the Sufi path and introduced it to Muslims in their local areas. In the twentieth century, the Tijani tariqa experienced unprecedented growth through the efforts of Shaykh Ibrahim Niasse. Like Shaykh al-Tijani, Shaykh Ibrahim urged his followers to strive for ihsan while bringing benefit to the world. In fact, in the early 1970s, Shaykh Ibrahim described his millions of Tijani murids as "among the best sons of Africa. We see their positive presence in the mosques and places of worship, in the farms and in the schools, in the universities and in the market, in political parties and parliaments, in the government and in courtrooms, in the factories and other sectors" (as cited in Seesemann 2011, 224).

While Shaykh Ibrahim was preceded by numerous notable Tijani shuyukh in North and West Africa—including his father al-Hajj Abdoulaye Niasse as well as Shaykh Umar Futi Taal—he was exceptional because he was seen to have been endowed with the *fayda* (flood) of divine knowledge. The fayda was a long-anticipated and highly coveted spiritual ranking understood to be associated with a Tijani Sufi master who would attract unprecedented numbers of murids to the tariqa and help them achieve marifa. As tens of millions of Muslims joined the Tijani tariqa and embraced Shaykh Ibrahim as their spiritual guide, he became the leader of the largest and most prominent branch of the Tijani tariqa globally.

The fayda is distinguished from other branches of the Tijani tariqa because of its emphasis on *tarbiya*, an Arabic word that is generally used to describe Islamic education and holistic development. Among Shaykh Ibrahim's movement, however, tarbiya refers to a specific form of spiritual training through which murids gain marifa. Through tarbiya, the opportunity to gain marifa—which is often portrayed in other Sufi contexts as high-level, esoteric knowledge that is restricted only to the most spiritually advanced people—becomes accessible to all, from the most socially marginalized to those of the most elite lineages (Seesemann 2011, 146; Wright 2015a, 99). As Tijanis do their tarbiya and gain marifa, they come to experientially know the divine presence, becoming among the esteemed group mentioned in the hadith of Jibril—those who worship Allah as if they see Him.

As Shaykh Ibrahim explains in his magnum opus *Kashif al-Ilbas* (*The Removal of Confusion*), tarbiya and the benefits of Sufism "can only be gained through serving (*khidma*) the people of spiritual distinction (*rijal*), and companionship with the perfected ones" (Niasse 2010, 22). Tijani murids strive to achieve ihsan and marifa not simply by studying books on their own, but also by spending time with shuyukh who emulate prophetic teachings. Through these interactions, sacred knowledge becomes ingrained not only in the murids' minds, but inscribed into their very beings and made manifest through their prophetically inspired way of inhabiting the world.

Like Shaykh Ibrahim, Shaykh Hassan underscored the significance of khidma: "It is said, 'The service (*khidma*) of the disciple (*murid*) is his ladder to attain his aspirations'" (as cited in Wright 2015a, 122).[5] For Tijanis, khidma is both a pedagogy that promotes spiritual transformation and a social practice that produces worldly benefit. During Shaykh Ibrahim's time, the most common form of khidma was farming, which he described as holding "one of the greatest secrets of tarbiya" (as cited in Seesemann 2015, 68). In fact, Shaykh Ibrahim's largest farm was known as *bustan al-'arifin*, or the Garden of the Knowers (ibid.). This name underscores the metaphysical and material dimensions of farming as khidma and a technology of tarbiya through which the murids come to know Allah. Shaykh Hassan addressed these twin dimensions of farming when he recounted a conversation with his father, Sayyidi Aliou Cisse:

> [My father] said, "Who told you that we are going to the farm to get money? We are going to the farm to worship God. Work is worship." My father used to say, "If you are in a place and you do nothing, you are spoiling that place. I don't know where a man can stay and get all that he needs without doing anything." (as cited in Wright 2015a, 122–123)

Sayyidi Aliou's comments reflected the understanding of the sacred and material aspects of khidma, as well as the ethical responsibility to benefit one's community.

During French colonization and even after Senegal became independent, farming enabled Shaykh Ibrahim's community in Medina Baye to grow its own food and generate revenue to help sustain residents. By 1971, Shaykh Ibrahim oversaw 264 fields in the Sine-Saloum region, where he and his murids raised cattle and grew peanuts, millet, beans, corn, cassava, tomatoes, and other crops (as cited in Wright 2015a, 102). Farming was thus a form of khidma that was key to tarbiya. It helped murids gain marifa while simultaneously empowering the community to develop autonomy from the state.

From the twentieth century into the twenty-first century, as Shaykh Ibrahim's community grew from a local to regional to transnational movement, and as agriculture became less central to Senegal's economy, Tijanis increasingly undertook other forms of khidma. This included domestic labor such as cooking, devotional labor such as making dhikr, and organizational labor such as fundraising. These evolving forms of khidma continued to index social and material practices that pushed the murids to attend to one another's needs as they strived to gain marifa and become most beloved to Allah.

In Shaykh Ibrahim's movement, *hadiya* (gift-giving) is a second key practice that fosters piety. As Shaykh Ibrahim (1941) advised in a letter to Sayyidi Aliou Cisse, "It is through proper belief that the inner state of the murid is rectified, but through khidma and hadiya that his or her outer state is rectified." In many Senegalese Sufi movements, hadiya describes monetary and non-monetary gifts that disciples offer their shuyukh (Villalón 1995, 191). The shuyukh tend not to treat monetary hadiya as gifts in the common sense of items that are enjoyed primarily by the recipient. Instead, as Shaykh Hassan explains in his commentary on Shaykh Ibrahim's didactic poem *Ruhul Adab* (*The Spirit of Good Morals*), the shuyukh have a moral obligation to redistribute hadiya. Shaykh Hassan describes the shaykh as a "balancing pendulum that everyone runs to, to receive blessings or be relieved of their distress. This is why a disciple should give freely out of his possessions of either money, strength, or health, to the Shaykh who redistributes these to the poor, weak and sick" (Niasse 2001, 31).[6]

Within Shaykh Ibrahim's movement, shuyukh and their murids jointly participate in what I call the hadiya economy, or the circulation of material resources that reflect Tijanis' everyday practices of collective care. As murids heed the advice to give hadiya as part of their spiritual journey to Allah, they assist the shuyukh in caring for the community's most vulnerable members. Just as farming historically helped Shaykh Ibrahim's community in Medina Baye attain a degree of self-sufficiency, the hadiya economy similarly allows the community to create its own social safety net, thereby reducing members' dependency on the government for financial assistance or social services.

Hadiya is both a spiritual pedagogy and an ethical economic redistributive practice that alleviates societal inequities. In contrast to approaches to Sufism that discourage spiritual seekers from pursuing worldly success, as well as capitalist conceptions of wealth as means of individual accumulation and hoarding, the Tijani tariqa's emphasis on hadiya reflects the idea that material wealth is not an inherent vice but ought instead to be leveraged as a communal asset. In fact, material wealth fuels the hadiya economy; the wealthier the murids become, the more they are able to give as hadiya, and the more money their shuyukh have to redistribute.

In Shaykh Ibrahim's *dua* (supplication) *Miftah al-Arab fi ma li al-'Abd mina al-Talab*, he asks Allah: "Place the world in our hands, but prevent it from entering our hearts."[7] Several Black American Tijanis narrated versions of this dua to me and explained that Shaykh Hassan had shared it with them. This dua reflects Shaykh Ibrahim's movement's approach to Sufism, which rejects the association between piety and poverty. Many Tijanis I spoke with interpreted the dua as affording them the license to accumulate worldly possessions so long as they did not lose sight of the responsibility to use their wealth in ways that were beneficial to the community and pleasing to Allah.

In the late 1960s or early 1970s, Shaykh Ibrahim gave a talk in Medina Baye during the *gamou* (an event commemorating Prophet Muhammad's birthday) in which he shared a hadith about Prophet Muhammad's wife, Sayyida Aisha, perfuming some clothes before gifting them to a person in need, because she knew the clothes would reach Allah first. Extracting a lesson from Sayyida Aisha, Shaykh Ibrahim commented:

> When you give even a penny to someone, it will surely reach Allah, the Creator. Anything a person does for another person is in reality done for Allah. If someone wants to work for Allah, he should first work for His servants; if someone wants to give to Allah, he should first give to His servants. (as cited in Wright 2015b, 97)

In asserting the "reality" behind giving money, food, and clothing, Shaykh Ibrahim centered Islamic ways of knowing, being, and belonging and pointed out the sacred dimensions of material and social practices. His comments reflect an Islamic worldview in which practices of collective care are also acts of worship.

Shaykh Ibrahim's comments align with a hadith reported by Prophet Muhammad's companion Abu Hurairah:

> Allah will say on the Day of Judgment, "Son of Adam, I was sick, but you did not visit Me."
> [The person will respond:] "My Lord, how could I visit You when You are the Lord of the Worlds?"
> [Then Allah will say:] "Did you not know that one of My servants was sick and you didn't visit him? If you had visited him, you would have found Me there."
> [Then Allah will say:] "Son of Adam, I needed food, but you did not feed Me."

[The person will respond:] "My Lord, how could I feed You when You are the Lord of the Worlds?"
[Then Allah will say:] "Did you not know that one of My servants was hungry, but you did not feed him? If you had fed him, you would have found its reward with Me."
[Then Allah will say:] "Son of Adam, I was thirsty, but you did not give Me something to drink."
[The person will respond:] "My Lord, how could I give a drink when You are the Lord of the Worlds?"
[Then Allah will say:] "Did you not know that one of My servants was thirsty, but you did not give him a drink? If you had given him a drink, you would have found its reward with Me."

This hadith reflects an Islamic worldview that recognizes the sacred relationship between Allah and His creation. It underscores the responsibility Muslims have to care for one another, and that doing so is a blessed and direct opportunity to deepen one's relationship with Allah.

Overall, in the fayda, murids are encouraged to emulate the prophetic model, cultivate ihsan, and gain marifa by engaging in acts that benefit Allah's creation, chief of which are khidma and hadiya. These teachings point to a notion of relational piety; one increases in religious esteem by being of service to others. This notion of relational piety is at odds with dominant, white Protestant Christian epistemological traditions and legal precedents of religion in the U.S., which frame religion as "a privatized system of individual beliefs" (Prickett 2021, 52). Such a framing confines religious expression to the private sphere, which in turn is intended to strip religion of its potential to spark societal transformation. In contrast, Tijanis understand that important forms of religious practice take place publicly and in community with others. The Tijani emphasis on collective care resonates with the Black Radical Tradition and Muslim International, which engage religion as a key source that fuels a revolutionary consciousness and leads to collective liberation. By learning and adopting prophetic practices of collective care, Black American Tijanis develop an orientation to the world that refuses U.S. society's legal and social project to sideline and silence religion. In Shaykh Ibrahim's movement, khidma and hadiya are among the social and spiritual practices of collective care that murids implement as they address the needs of their community, mold their character according to the prophetic example, and strive to know and become most beloved to Allah.

The Prophetic and the Political in a Pan-African Sufi Movement

In the late eighteenth century, when Shaykh al-Tijani founded the Tijani tariqa, he critiqued the corruption of his time. In the twentieth century, when Shaykh Ibrahim brought the fayda to millions of Muslims in Africa and beyond, he too responded to the ills of his time. This, in fact, was something that Shaykh al-Tijani had anticipated, as he predicted the context in which Shaykh Ibrahim would receive the fayda: "A flood (*fayda*) will overwhelm my companions to the point that people will enter our path in multitudes. This fayda will come at a time when mankind will be in a state of utmost difficulties" (as cited in Cisse 1984, 200).

Shaykh Ibrahim himself also asserted in *Manasik Ahl-al Widad*, a work in his *Dawawin al-Sitt* collection of prophetic praise poetry: "Through me, the great injustice (*jawr*) will be lifted! And through my fayda, the banner of *deen* (Islam) will be raised high." In Shaykh Ibrahim's time, one of the greatest injustices confronting Africans was European colonialism. Though the French presence in Senegambia dated back to the seventeenth century, the Berlin Conference of 1884 cemented Europe's partition and theft of almost the entire African continent (Uzoigwe 1984). European nations seized, divided, and distributed the lands of Africa among themselves, imposing new political borders and forms of governance as they exploited the continent's people and extracted its natural wealth and resources for European capitalist gain (Rodney 1972).

During the mid-twentieth century, as Europe's colonization and exploitation of Africa continued, Shaykh Ibrahim's branch of the Tijani tariqa became the largest Muslim movement on the continent. This was in an era when people throughout Africa waged successful liberation movements to overthrow European colonial powers. Between 1957 and 1960 alone, 19 African nations won their independence. Among them were many countries to which Shaykh Ibrahim's movement had already spread or would soon spread, including his home country of Senegal, as well as Nigeria, Ghana, Mauritania, Guinea, Burkina Faso, and Côte d'Ivoire. In 1960, Shaykh Ibrahim wrote a letter published in a Nigerian newspaper in which he applauded the revolutionary changes sweeping through Africa:

> We are the people of Africa, so Africa belongs to us, and we belong to Africa. Sooner or later every nation (*watan*) will come to be governed by its children whatever the schemes of the enemies of the African citizenry (*jinsiyya*). A current of freedom and nationalism (*wataniyya*) has burst forth in this twentieth century, and nothing can stop it. (as cited in Wright 2015b, 76)

Shaykh Ibrahim unapologetically embraced his African identity as he enthusiastically anticipated his peoples' success against the European colonizers. His letter was titled *Ifriqiya ila al-ifriqiyin*, an Arabic phrase that translates to "Africa for the Africans"—the exact slogan used by Edward Wilmot Blyden, Marcus Garvey, Kwame Nkrumah, and other Black intellectuals and leaders who promoted pan-Africanism. In addition to his 1960 letter, Shaykh Ibrahim penned a letter in 1961 in which he asserted that "Muslims and people of West Africa . . . should liberate themselves and raise the pan-African banner, so that they may practice their beliefs and traditions freely" (as cited in Wright 2015a, 270). These statements contributed to Shaykh Ibrahim's reputation as a proponent of pan-Africanism.

Pan-Africanism is a movement to unite and empower Africans on the continent and throughout the diaspora (Drake 1959; Shepperson 1962). However, the term pan-Africanism has held slightly different meanings based on when, where, and by whom it has been used. In the 1930s, when much of Africa remained under European colonial domination, one popular expression was cultural pan-Africanism, which emphasized the shared ancestry and cooperation among African and African-descended peoples (Mazrui 2005). Cultural pan-Africanism fueled the birth of Négritude, a movement to reclaim the value of Black and African cultures that was led by intellectuals including Léopold Sédar Senghor, who went on to become the founding president of Senegal. However, from the 1960s onwards, as people across Africa and the Caribbean launched anti-colonial movements, and as Black Americans linked their struggles to these international causes, revolutionary pan-Africanism became another popular expression.

Revolutionary pan-Africanism is part of the Black Radical Tradition of rebellion and revolt. Revolutionary pan-Africanism opposes the exploitation, oppression, and dispossession of African peoples and calls for their total liberation and unification, typically through scientific socialism (Robinson 1996; Touré 1974). In 1974, Guinea's founding president, the Muslim and African socialist Ahmed Sékou Touré explained the meaning of "revolutionary pan-Africanism" in his address to the Sixth Pan-African Congress. The Congress took place at a moment when competing factions of pan-Africanists were debating which expression was most empowering. Some, for instance, argued that pan-Africanism in post-independence Africa had actually given way to neocolonialism, with the ruling elites of many newly independent countries continuing to facilitate the exploitation of their country's people and resources (Rodney 1975). Touré (1974) addressed these tensions as he advocated for a revolutionary pan-Africanism that would "uphold the primacy of Peoples as against States" (27). He also asserted that revolutionary pan-Africanism situated Africans' efforts within the context of the "masses of all the countries of the world in their march towards a new world . . . in which justice will hold sway over injustice, equality over inequality, responsibility and sovereign power of the people over dictatorships by exploiting minorities; briefly, a world of redemption for Africa and all peoples" (ibid.). The General Declaration adopted by the Sixth Pan-African Congress further elaborated that the pan-African struggle for dignity "has always been one aspect of the world-wide struggle for human liberation," and asserted that revolutionary pan-Africanism's "fighting solidarity has been forged in the support for the heroic peoples of Indo-China struggling against U.S. imperialism; in the support for the Palestinian people and our Arab brothers struggling against Zionist annexation, aggression, and racism; in the support for the workers and the discriminated minorities in North America, in particular for the struggle of black people for the destruction of bourgeois society which is oppressing Blacks and Whites" (214, 217). Revolutionary pan-Africanism thus linked the liberation of African peoples to a global mass movement of oppressed peoples seeking to overthrow colonialism, imperialism, neocolonialism, racial capitalism, and white supremacy.

Shaykh Ibrahim's perspective aligned with revolutionary pan-Africanism's concern for the liberation of peoples in Africa and beyond. In *Ifriqiya ila al-ifriqiyin* (*Africa for the Africans*) and other writings, Shaykh Ibrahim called for an end to foreign domination and a restoring of Africans' right to self-rule. Moreover, as an African Islamic scholar deeply concerned about the Muslim *ummah* (global community of believers), Shaykh Ibrahim's commitments also invoked the Muslim International, a space and conscience that incorporated pan-African and anti-colonial ideologies and was anchored in the understanding that "Islam provided a pathway and a roadmap that led to the Muslim Third World of Africa and Asia" (Daulatzai 2012, 23). Reflecting this revolutionary pan-African, Muslim International perspective, Shaykh Ibrahim staunchly advocated for a free Palestine. On numerous occasions, he urged Arab heads of state and members of the Arab League to defend Palestine. Shaykh Ibrahim wrote a series of letters in which he forcefully condemned the global Zionist movement and the state of Israel and asserted that his people were "brothers in this [Palestinian] struggle and companions in this battle" (El-Sharif 2024). Thus, across his writings, Shaykh Ibrahim reminded his followers of Islam's core principles of justice while simultaneously endorsing specific, timely efforts to achieve African liberation.

Shaykh Ibrahim also had relationships with three of the most prominent revolutionary pan-Africanists and anti-colonialists of his time: Kwame Nkrumah, Gamal Abdel Nasser, and Ahmed Sékou Touré (Nyang 1993; Wright 2015a, 270). Shaykh Ibrahim's relationship with Nkrumah dated back to the early 1950s, when he visited Nkrumah in a British-controlled prison and shared that he received spiritual insight that Nkrumah would go on to lead an independent nation (Wright 2015a, 269). Shaykh Ibrahim's insights rang true, as Nkrumah was the first prime minister of Ghana at independence in 1957. Nkrumah pushed for pan-African initiatives such as the Organization of African Unity and the Akosombo Dam, a hydroelectric dam that would provide electricity for the country's aluminum industry and fuel Nkrumah's vision of African self-sufficiency. Though Nkrumah was Christian, he recognized Shaykh Ibrahim's spiritual esteem and asked him to pray for the success of these two pan-African initiatives (Daaru 2020). Nkrumah introduced Shaykh Ibrahim to Gamal Abdel Nasser, who led the Egyptian revolution of 1952 and served as Egypt's second president. Shaykh Ibrahim, Nkrumah, and Nasser shared a "common commitment to the betterment of African societies" (Wright 2015a, 269). In the 1960s, at Nasser's personal invitation, Shaykh Ibrahim sent several of his sons as well as his grandson, Shaykh Hassan, to pursue higher education in Egypt (Wright 2012, 61). In 1966, after Shaykh Ibrahim had a spiritual vision that Nkrumah might be in harm's way, he sent word to Nkrumah not to travel (Wright 2015a, 269). Despite Shaykh Ibrahim's warning, Nkrumah went to Hanoi, Vietnam, and during this time away from Ghana, he was overthrown from power by a military coup that was supported by the CIA (Department of State 1964; Nkrumah 1972). Nkrumah went into exile in Guinea, where he was welcomed by the country's president Ahmed Sékou Touré, who made Nkrumah his co-president. Shaykh Ibrahim sent a telegram to Touré in which he thanked the political leader for receiving Nkrumah (Wright 2015a, 264). The contents of Shaykh Ibrahim's message to Touré were shared on national radio, making the Shaykh's continued support for Nkrumah clear to the masses.

Overall, while Shaykh Ibrahim's religious prominence made him well-known to many heads of state, his relationship with Nkrumah, Nasser, and Touré in particular was indicative of their shared commitments to the liberation of peoples in Africa and beyond, as well as the political leaders' recognition of Shaykh Ibrahim's valuable contributions—as an Islamic Sufi scholar—to the causes of freedom and liberation.

Nkrumah and Touré were among the many African politicians who engaged pan-Africanism as a top-down approach to structure their new nations' systems of political and economic governance. Although Shaykh Ibrahim supported some of these state-building efforts, his role as a religious scholar rather than a politician enabled him to cultivate a revolutionary pan-African spiritual movement that was not beholden to a nation-state. Shaykh Ibrahim led a movement of what George Shepperson (1962) and St. Clare Drake (1993) describe as pan-Africanism with a "small p." They distinguish it from Pan-Africanism with a capital P, which refers to more formal political efforts. Drake (1993) describes small-p pan-Africanism as a "people-to-people approach to transatlantic relations among black people" as well as among Africans on the continent (463). Drake argues that small-p pan-Africanism "has had greater sociological significance than the small groups of intellectuals and politicians [of capital *P* Pan-Africanism], as important as they were in carrying forward the African revolt against imperialism" (ibid., 464). Small-*p* pan-Africanism therefore brings to light the broader landscape of non-state actors and activities geared towards fostering African unity from below. It describes everyday Africans' grassroots efforts to cultivate bonds of solidarity with one another independent of nation states in order to improve their collective condition.

Shaykh Ibrahim led a grassroots, revolutionary pan-African Sufi movement that unified tens of millions of Muslims across Africa and the world under a shared Tijani identity. His murids strived towards a shared goal—adopting prophetic modes of collective care to achieve spiritual and material liberation. The widespread reach of Shaykh Ibrahim's movement was noted in a poem by the Hausa scholar Malam Balaby, who observed how Shaykh Ibrahim was received during his 1950 visit to Hausaland (in present-day northern Nigeria):

> The greatest proof that Shaykh Ibrahim is the right person is that the Hausa of Kano, Katsina, Zaria, and Bornu submit to him. In that alone is evidence for a righteous person to believe in him. Return then to Kumasi and see Accra, and go up to Lagos, let alone Ilorin and Bida, not to mention Okene. Look there at the folk of Adamawa, Bauchi and Gombe; go then up to Sokoto and Gondo. Even in Sokoto [a center of the Qadariyya Sufi tariqa], so folk follow him. Look now at the happy reception at his landing in Kano, where a gathering of the cities walked in multitudes to greet him. He went to Mecca. Happy were they at his arrival. He went then to Medina, whose folk also accepted his leadership. The magnates and shaykhs all came to him and acknowledged that, in him, they had found a true spiritual master of the worlds. (as cited in Cisse 1984, 203)

Balaby asserts that Shaykh Ibrahim's movement appealed to members of Hausa, Yoruba, and Fulani ethnic groups across Nigeria and Ghana. Some embraced the Tijani tariqa even though they were from Saudi Arabia or regions of Africa that were historic strongholds for other tariqas. Shaykh Ibrahim's movement thus united Muslims in Africa and beyond who, despite their varying ethnic, national, racial, linguistic, and spiritual backgrounds, turned to him for guidance as they strove to know Allah.

In Africa, many of Shaykh Ibrahim's murids were those who would be considered "ordinary" believers (Seesemann 2011, 146)—those who, by virtue of their socioeconomic standing and primarily Islamic educational experiences, might be presumed to be unknowledgeable about, uninterested in, or unable to access the more elite spaces associated with capital-P Pan-Africanism. However, Shaykh Ibrahim fostered a people-to-people movement of millions of everyday Africans whose spiritual practices nonetheless contributed to some of the sociopolitical aims of capital-P Pan-Africanism. These Tijanis committed themselves to doing khidma, giving and recirculating hadiya, and engaging in collective care practices that fostered unity, solidarity, collaboration, and reciprocity. Mapped against the global structures that exploited and divided African peoples, Shaykh Ibrahim's grassroots Sufi movement guided believers to a radically different, spiritually liberated way of being and belonging that was anchored in the prophetic model and that enabled them to collectively resist the sociopolitical and economic ills that confronted Africans.

Shaykh Ibrahim urged his followers to make dhikr and dua to aid in anti-colonial and pan-African efforts. He and his murids waged what Zachary Wright (2013) describes as spiritual wars of liberation. In 1936, Shaykh Ibrahim instructed his murids to recite dhikrs with the intention of calling upon Allah to protect them from "the evil of the upheaval occasioned by the French state . . . And (protection from) all who have relations with them (the French)" (as cited in Wright 2013, 13). In 1957, following Ghana's independence from Britain, Shaykh Ibrahim advised Tijanis in the city of Kumasi to pray for Prime Minister Nkrumah after every wazifa and make dua that Allah bless Nkrumah to complete his plans, which were for the benefit of Africa (Ibrahim 2021). Similarly, in a dua in *Al-Kanz Al-Masun (The Guarded Treasure)*, a book of special prayers compiled by Shaykh Ibrahim that Tijanis recite for spiritual benefit, Shaykh Ibrahim includes the lines: "Save me and save on my behalf Kwame,[8] and save Sanusi[9] and likewise all my people" (282). In 1970, Guinea's president Ahmed Sékou Touré sent the following telegram to Shaykh Ibrahim: "I thank you warmly, and your students and companions in Islam, for all the prayers done for me for the sake of African progress" (as cited in Wright 2015a, 270). These examples indicate Shaykh Ibrahim's commitment to mobilizing esoteric Sufi knowledge against European intervention and in service of African liberation.

Shaykh Hassan expanded his grandfather's grassroots pan-African Sufi movement to include communities in the African diaspora. In 1976, one year after Shaykh Ibrahim returned to Allah, Shaykh Hassan took his first trip to the U.S., where immediately upon arriving he began introducing the tariqa to Black American (i.e., African American and Afro-Caribbean) Muslims. Hundreds joined the Tijani tariqa and took Shaykh Hassan as their spiritual guide. In the 1980s, Shaykh Hassan and many of his Black American murids collaborated, first to open an Islamic school and then to create a humanitarian organization, both of which they named the African American Islamic Institute (AAII). Under the banner of AAII, Shaykh Hassan and his murids also established a medical clinic and community radio station in Medina Baye and organized programs to feed the hungry, empower women and children, and promote peace throughout West Africa. AAII became another key vehicle that made it possible for Tijanis to sustain pan-African collaborations and implement prophetic modes of collective care.

By the late twentieth century and into the twenty-first century, greater numbers of Black American Tijanis journeyed to Medina Baye at the same time that West African Tijanis began immigrating to the U.S. With the multidirectional flow of believers moving between the U.S. and Africa, the fayda continued to foster grassroots pan-African exchange among Black American and African Muslims seeking spiritual liberation alongside material relief.

Overall, Shaykh Ibrahim sparked a pan-African Sufi movement from below where murids were taught to emulate prophetic practices of collective care by bringing benefit to, rather than withdrawing from, the world. Just as Shaykh al-Tijani pointed out the widespread corruption of the eighteenth century, so too did Shaykh Ibrahim critique the global systems of exclusion and exploitation that defined his time. From the twentieth into the twenty-first century, this was and still remains a time in which Black Muslims' lives are constrained by colonialism, imperialism, neocolonialism, racial capitalism, and white supremacy. Shaykh Ibrahim addressed such ills, in part, by mobilizing the rhetoric of one of the most popular liberatory theories in his time and place—pan-Africanism, an ideology and movement that he understood to be compatible with Islam. By embracing revolutionary pan-Africanism and encouraging his murids to support pan-African causes, Shaykh Ibrahim fostered a Sufi movement that remains, decades later, concerned about the liberation of peoples in Africa and throughout the world. Fusing Islamic teachings with pan-African ideologies, Shaykh Ibrahim's grassroots Sufi movement brings together Tijanis from across Africa and the U.S. who strive to foster transnational solidarity and collective action to benefit Allah's creation and become most beloved to Him.

2

Launching the Dream

Building Black Muslim Worlds from the U.S. to Senegal

In July 1988, Aminah Salah,[1] a 12-year-old Black American Muslim girl from Brooklyn boarded an Air Afrique flight from New York City's John F. Kennedy International Airport. Aminah had just finished sixth grade at a Muslim school in Jersey City, New Jersey. When I interviewed her in 2021, Aminah could still recall the thoughts that had raced through her young mind decades prior when she started her international journey: "I remember driving in the car and saying, 'Aminah, remember all of your scenery because you might not ever see this again.'" Aminah was moving to Senegal to attend the African American Islamic Institute (AAII) School, an international boarding school located in the city of Medina Baye. The school was born out of a collaboration between Shaykh Hassan Cisse and Hajjah Kareemah Abdul-Kareem, one of his Black American Tijani murids. They created the AAII School to provide Black American Muslim children with access to Qur'anic education, and hoped that these young people would achieve the blessed feat of becoming *huffaz*[2] (those who have memorized the entire Qur'an in Arabic).

Aminah boarded the flight with her five-year-old sister, Tauhidah. Their mother, also named Tauhidah, said goodbye at the gate; her daughters would be relocating without her. When Aminah and her sister landed in Senegal's capitol city Dakar, a Senegalese man met them at the airport. He drove the girls to see Shaykh Hassan, who was staying at a hotel that overlooked the Atlantic Ocean. Aminah recalled, "All this time, I was excited. I wanted to come, but I understood in that moment that my mother was all the way on the other side of this ocean that you couldn't see the end of. And I was just here in this country where I didn't speak the language, I didn't know anyone but Shaykh Hassan, and I had never been to this continent."

Up until that point, neither Aminah, her sister, nor her mother had ever left the U.S. Yet despite this, the mother Tauhidah sent her daughters nearly four thousand miles away. She trusted that her daughters would be cared for in Medina Baye. Two other adults—Shaykh Hassan, Tauhidah's spiritual guide in the Tijani tariqa, and Hajjah Kareemah Abdul-Kareem, whom neither Tauhidah nor her daughters had ever met—would collectively care for Tauhidah's children as they embarked on the sacred journey of Qur'anic education.

It had not been an easy decision for Tauhidah—financially or emotionally. It took her almost a year to save up $1400 to purchase her daughters' plane tickets. Rather than have the girls wait until she had enough money to buy her own ticket, Tauhidah felt an urgency for them to go ahead. It would likely be at least a year before Tauhidah could join her daughters. Until then, she would miss out on everyday moments and milestones in her daughters' lives, from the precious bits of joy to the inevitable bouts of sadness that would make the girls yearn for their mother. But these were the burdens that Tauhidah willingly endured as she arranged what she earnestly believed would be the best opportunity for her children. She was, after all, a freedom dreamer. She dared to "imagine something different, to realize that things need not always be this way" (Kelley 2002, 9).

For much of her daughters' upbringing in the U.S. during the late 1970s and early 1980s, Tauhidah was a single mother who moved her family frequently. Aminah recalled that it "wasn't really easy for an African American woman to get decent employment, so my mother did odd jobs, whatever jobs she could get her hands on," including working as a janitor, street vendor, and bus driver. Confronting anti-Black racism, sexism, and economic marginalization, Tauhidah desired for her daughters to access a new world that was radically different from the present.

In 1987, one year before Tauhidah sent her daughters to Senegal, she met Shaykh Hassan in New York City. She was deeply moved by their interaction and immediately joined the Tijani tariqa. Becoming a Tijani meant that Tauhidah had pledged to consistently complete extra worship beyond the basics obligated upon all Muslims. Once Shaykh Hassan returned to Senegal, Tauhidah continued gathering with fellow Tijanis for *wazifa* and *dhikrul jummah*, two devotional acts that Tijanis complete on a daily and weekly basis, and preferably aloud in congregation.

At these gatherings, Tauhidah met mothers and fathers who, like her, were trying to construct social worlds that would nurture their children's racial, religious, gendered, and moral development. The Tijani gatherings, where children were frequently present, were part of the emerging social worlds that Black American Muslim families cultivated as they sought refuge from a broader U.S. landscape marred by racial capitalism and white supremacy. As Tauhidah and her daughters spent time with other families at Tijani gatherings, they became introduced to their new friends' freedom dreams. Several parents spoke of an Islamic educational experience in Africa that offered seemingly unparalleled opportunities for Black American Muslim girls and boys. They were referring to the AAII School in Medina Baye, Senegal.

In the more than forty years since the AAII School was established, hundreds of Black American Muslim youth took the same international journey that Tauhidah's daughters embarked upon. For Tauhidah and her contemporaries, the decision to send their children to Medina Baye alone was neither the first time they pursued seemingly radical pathways nor made seemingly confounding sacrifices to achieve greater fulfillment and liberation. Rather, their decision marked an internationalization of their long-standing quests for racial, religious, and spiritual transformation as well as educational dignity. Parents like Tauhidah identified in Medina Baye the promise of more meaningful possibilities than what was accessible in the U.S. They embraced both the blessings and burdens that came with having their children embark on the sacred journey of becoming huffaz in Medina Baye.

To understand why Black American parents saw Medina Baye as an attractive educational opportunity, despite its significant distance from loved ones in the U.S., this chapter focuses on the perspectives of four mothers who were among the foremothers of the Tijani community in the U.S.—Hajjah Tauhidah Abedeen (1940–2022), Hajjah Kareemah Abdul-Kareem, Dr. Karimah Joseph (1949–2024), and Dr. Khadijah Askari.[3] These foremothers' stories offer a window into the shared concerns and aspirations among dozens of parents who sent their children to Medina Baye during the 1980s and 1990s.[4]

As we will see, these mothers' schooling decision represented freedom dreams informed by four factors: their interest in contemporary Africa and Africans; their journeys as striving Muslims; their commitment to

Figure 2.1. Shaykh Hassan Cisse (center) poses with Hajjah Tauhidah Abedeen (right), Dr. Khadijah Askari (second from the right), and Dr. Karimah Joseph (left) in Medina Baye in 2001. Photo courtesy of Aminah Salah.

looking beyond the U.S. public school system to provide their children with educational experiences that aligned with their sociopolitical and moral sensibilities; and their investment in leveraging collective care networks to offer their children liberatory possibilities. Medina Baye and the AAII School spoke to these mothers' overlapping commitments to Africa, Islam, and the pursuit of quality education. This opportunity promised to transport their children to a radically different societal and educational paradigm that would nurture their identities in ways that had been unattainable in the U.S.

Oral Histories of Everyday Black Women

Throughout U.S. history, Black women have been actively involved in Black community life. During the nineteenth and twentieth centuries, Black women started welfare organizations, religious groups, schools, and other institutions to improve their lives as well as those of their children, families, and community (Cash 2001; Davis 1996; Neverdon-Morton 1991). The women who are the focus of this chapter maintained this long-standing tradition of collective care among Black women, as they actualized freedom dreams that ushered in greater possibilities for themselves and those around them.

Deborah Gray White (2009) asserts that scholarship on Black women's contributions "directly challenged the contemporary wisdom that only men made and were the center of history" (9). Such misconceptions also pervade the literature on American Islam, where the perspectives of men dominate (Chan-Malik 2018, 2). Countering the emphasis on men as the most prominent actors in African American history and in the history of Islam in the U.S., this chapter focuses on four women to demonstrate the essential role that mothers played in actualizing and sustaining their community's freedom dreams.

Hajjah Tauhidah, Hajjah Kareemah, Dr. Karimah, and Dr. Khadijah's names are well-known among Tijanis in the U.S. and Senegal, and even among some Black American Muslims who are not Tijani and some Black Americans who are not Muslim. Yet there is little to no mention of them in newspapers, magazines, journals, and other archival sources.[5] This absence reflects the reality that public documents, written records, and other traditional primary sources of historical evidence rarely reflect the lives of everyday Black people, let alone Black women (Valk and Brown 2010, 5).

The lack of attention in the written public record to Black lives, and to Black women's lives in particular, underscores the immense value of oral histories in documenting people, events, and experiences. In this chapter, I retell Hajjah Tauhidah, Hajjah Kareemah, Dr. Karimah, and Dr. Khadijah's life stories using oral histories from three of these four women, as well as interviews and testimonies from each woman's adult children, who recounted memories of their mothers, how they made sense of their mothers' decisions, and how these decisions impacted them.[6] A few aspects of these women's life stories, such as major milestones, are corroborated by primary and secondary sources, while others are verified through the shared details recounted by multiple individuals. However, the epistemic erasure of everyday Black women from traditional archives, coupled with the nature of personal stories, makes it difficult to triangulate oral accounts alongside other data sources.

In *Women of the Nation*, Jamillah Karim and Dawn-Marie Gibson draw on oral histories with approximately 100 women who recollected their experiences as members of the Nation of Islam. Karim and Gibson (2014) approach these women's testimonies as "authentic accounts" that are "psychologically true," even though the contents may differ from scholarly analyses (33). Building upon Karim and Gibson's approach, I engage oral histories as authentic and instructive memories. In writing about real people who entrusted their stories to me or other community members, I consider it my ethical responsibility to center their self-representations. I acknowledge that people may misremember certain aspects of their life, or present other details in a particular light. I do not consider either of these tendencies to be deceptive. Instead, I accept and honor their narratives as reflections of how they want to be represented in the public record.

The Cite Black Women Collective argues that Black women are radical producers of knowledge whose contributions have been devalued in academia. The collective "understand[s] that knowledge emerges from all sectors of life: from people who are organizers, activists, and artists" (Smith et al. 2021, 12). Building upon the provocations of the Cite Black Women Collective, Su'ad Abdul Khabeer (2021a) examined the personal archive of her mother, Amina Amatul Haqq, who was neither an academically trained scholar nor a public leader whose life had garnered significant scholarly interest, but rather an "everyday black woman." Abdul Khabeer argues that Haqq's life demonstrates how everyday Black women are "people who know things we all need to know" (ibid.). Building upon the Cite Black Women Collective and Abdul Khabeer, I engage Hajjah Tauhidah, Hajjah Kareemah, Dr. Karimah, and Dr. Khadijah as everyday Black American Tijani women whose knowledge, analyses, and lives provide generative historical sources and theoretical insights that enhance our collective understanding of how mothers strived to actualize liberatory futures.

Four Mothers as Foremothers

Hajjah Tauhidah, Hajjah Kareemah, Dr. Karimah, and Dr. Khadijah were among the foremothers of the Tijani community in the U.S. They were born between the late 1930s and mid-1950s and were raised in segregated cities in the urban North. They became young adults during the Civil Rights and Black Power eras that transformed the racial consciousness, political orientation, and aesthetics of millions of Black youth. They also came of age in the aftermath of the pan-African and Third World movements of the 1950s and 1960s that connected the struggles of Black Americans to oppressed peoples throughout the world. Perhaps influenced by these movements, each of the four women had some interest in Africa. Their engagement ranged from wearing their hair in afros, donning West African clothes, and selecting Swahili names for themselves or their children, to befriending African immigrants, joining pan-African organizations, and visiting West Africa. They were part of an often overlooked contingent of Black women during the twentieth century who engaged communities and histories beyond the U.S. (Boyce Davies 2008; Burden-Stelly and Dean 2022; Ransby 2013).

These four women were born into Christian families. They embraced Islam when they were in their twenties and thirties, in an era when Islam was overwhelmingly associated with Black liberation, Black pride, and religious resistance to racism and white supremacy (Jackson 2005; Turner 1997; Weisenfeld 2017). They were familiar with the Nation of Islam, yet only Hajjah Tauhidah associated with it. The other three women were connected to Black American communities that embraced Sunni Islam independent of the 1975 mass transition of an estimated two million members of the Nation of Islam into Sunni Islam under the leadership of Imam Warith Deen Mohammed (Bowen 2017; Howell 2014; Miller 2019).

Hajjah Kareemah and Dr. Khadijah were already mothers by the time they became Muslim, while Hajjah Tauhidah and Dr. Karimah became mothers after they embraced Islam. In 1983, Hajjah Kareemah moved to Medina Baye with her daughter and stepson to open the AAII School. Her children became AAII's first Black American students. Hajjah Kareemah lived in Medina Baye until 1990. She served as the adoptive mother for the school's Black American and African boarding students, who added the Arabic word for mother to the beginning of her name and called her *Umm* Kareemah. In 1988, Hajjah Tauhidah sent her daughters to AAII, and in 1989, she moved there and began helping Hajjah Kareemah. To young people in Medina Baye, Hajjah Tauhidah was also affectionately called Umm Tauhidah. In 1989, the school welcomed its first students from Detroit when Dr. Karimah took her two oldest sons and her friend's son to Medina Baye. All of Dr. Karimah's remaining children eventually joined. In 1990, seven years after Hajjah

Kareemah cofounded AAII, her daughter Aminah became the school's first Black American hafiza, an achievement that also made her the first ever documented hafiza from the Black American Muslim community in the U.S. Also in 1990, Dr. Khadijah asked another mother in Atlanta to take her oldest son with her when she traveled to Medina Baye; a few years later, Dr. Khadijah's other children joined. In 2000, Dr. Khadijah's youngest daughter, Kubra, became the school's second Black American hafiza. In 2001, carrying forward the work of Umm Kareemah and Umm Tauhidah, hafiza Kubra (who by then had come to be known as Sayyida Kubra or Aunty Kubra) became the primary caretaker and adoptive mother for AAII's boarding students.

These foremothers' initial decisions thus laid the foundation for their families' multi-generational freedom dreams. Each had grandchildren who went on to pursue Qur'anic education in Senegal, and three of the four women had grandchildren who became huffaz. Beyond their individual family units, these foremothers were instrumental in facilitating this educational opportunity for their broader communities. They collectively cared for other people's children, financially supported the school, and spread word about it in the U.S.

Hajjah Kareemah Abdul-Kareem

Hajjah Kareemah Abdul-Kareem was born on February 2, 1937 in Harlem, New York City. Her mother was from Greensboro, North Carolina. Her father was from Memphis, Tennessee. Her parents were among the nearly six million Black people who moved northward as part of the first Great Migration in the early twentieth century. Kareemah's parents met and married in New York City. Her mother was a homemaker and her father worked on the railroads.

Hajjah Kareemah recalled Harlem in the 1940s as a "wonderful place to grow up in . . . it was like a village" where she felt a strong sense of community among African American residents.[7] Adults kept a watchful eye on the neighborhood's children. If they saw Kareemah in "some place that I had no business being in, they had no problem saying something to me or my mother."[8] Kareemah attended neighborhood public schools. She grew up around famous Black figures including tap dancer Bill "Bojangles" Robinson, jazz musician Lucky Millinder, and boxer

Joe Louis. These celebrities often hosted events for the neighborhood's youth. Harlem's strong sense of community began to disintegrate in the late 1940s and early 1950s, when the streets became flooded with heroin (Schneider 2008, 44). It was during this time that Kareemah entered junior high.

In 1958, Kareemah married Jamil Abdul-Kareem (1937–2001), a Black American man from the Bronx. The couple welcomed four children during their first four years of marriage. Jamil worked for the American Management Association while Kareemah stayed at home and took care of their children. She occasionally worked outside the house as a bookkeeper. Hajjah Kareemah recalled, "We were always fortunate. Jamil always had a good income. I don't know why my kids thought they was rich, but they weren't. [*laughs*] But we had more than a lot of people had."

Hajjah Kareemah explained that when Jamil came home from work "and started talking about being Black . . . I'm the one who started going out. I was going to Brooklyn for knowledge." She attended poetry readings and other Black cultural events throughout New York City. Kareemah and Jamil also owned Mother Blues Café, a jazz club located at 3855 Bronxwood Ave in the North Bronx (Palmer 1967, 1969). On one occasion, Kareemah organized a concert and cookout at the club during the Biafra war in Nigeria. Hajjah Kareemah recalled, "I didn't know who was the good guy and who was the bad guy, 'cause it was a lot of politics. . . . So we just raised funds and I just sent it to the United Nations for the children of Biafra in Nigeria, cause for me, the kids were the innocent ones."[9]

Jamil's job required him to travel a lot. During work trips to Chicago, he spent time with Black jazz musicians. During the mid-twentieth century, many Black jazz musicians became Muslim or were interested in contemporary African liberation struggles (Kelley 2012; Turner 2021). Through conversations with some of these musicians, Jamil grew interested in Islam. When Jamil told Kareemah, she initially "wasn't really excited about it. I just thought it was more restricted. I didn't really know too much about [Islam]," other than the Nation of Islam, which she was skeptical of.[10] Jamil bought her some books about Islam. On the back of one of these books, she found information for the Islamic Cultural Center, a mosque on the Upper West Side of Manhattan. Kareemah decided she would "call them up for classes" on Islam.[11] On February 6, 1970, at the age of 33, Kareemah took her *shahada* (declaration of faith) at the Islamic Cultural Center along with her husband. Kareemah and Jamil began raising their four children, by then aged 8 to 11, as Muslims. The couple had already started the process of legally changing their birth names to Swahili or Arabic names, an increasingly popular phenomenon among Black people in the U.S. during the 1960s onwards (Onaci 2015; Umoja 2013). When they took their shahada, the imam at the Islamic Cultural Center gave them Arabic names. They decided to use these as their new legal names.

Kareemah and Jamil were also in the process of making plans to leave New York. Jamil wanted to relocate to a place where he could raise cattle. Hajjah Kareemah recounted, "Jamil gave me a choice of Texas, Georgia, or Africa. And I said Africa." Growing up, Kareemah would get into wrestling matches with her brother. Seeing them, her mother would threaten that she was "going to leave us and go to Africa. To me, Africa was always a place to go." In June 1970, Kareemah and Jamil embarked on their journey. Their first stop was Dakar, Senegal. There, every morning, Hajjah Kareemah "heard all this singing. I said, 'Oh, what is this beautiful sound?' Later on, I found out that was the *adhan*."[12] After visiting several countries on the Western coast of Africa, the couple decided that they wanted to settle in Ghana.

Kareemah and Jamil returned to the U.S. to prepare. Shortly after they came back, they met a fellow worshipper at the Islamic Cultural Center named Ibrahim Yusuf. Ibrahim was a Ghanaian immigrant who had arrived in the U.S. earlier in the morning on the very day that Kareemah and Jamil met him. Having recently returned from Ghana, the couple was excited to talk to Ibrahim about his home country. The three became fast friends, and the following summer, they traveled to Ghana together. They stayed with Ibrahim's father in his hometown of Kumasi, a city in southern Ghana with a sizeable Muslim population—many of whom were Tijani. In Kumasi, Kareemah and Jamil attended their first wazifa and heard about Shaykh Ibrahim, who Hajjah Kareemah recalled learning "was a big shaykh who was known all over Africa . . . even though we as the Americans didn't know anything about him at all."[13]

In 1972, back in New York City, Kareemah gave birth to the couple's fifth child, a girl whom they named Aminah. Around August of that year, Kareemah and Jamil moved to Ghana with their children, who were by then between the ages of two months and 14 years old. The family abruptly returned to the U.S. after a few months when they received the devastating news that Jamil's mother had been diagnosed with cancer. Because the family had spent thousands of dollars to relocate to Ghana and then fly back, they could not afford another trip abroad.

At this point, Kareemah had only been Muslim for two years. She approached Dr. Sulaiman Donia, an Egyptian Islamic scholar from the famed al-Azhar University in Egypt who had become the imam at the Islamic Cultural Center of New York. Kareemah asked him to offer a class for new Muslim women like herself. Through these classes, Kareemah and dozens of Black Muslim women in New York City learned the basics of their religion. Together, they founded the Muslim Educational Action and Resource Committee (MEARC), an organization dedicated to *dawah*, or educating people about Islam (Abdul Khabeer 2021b). Through this organization, Kareemah hosted fundraisers, African-inspired Islamic fashion shows, and other initiatives for Black American Muslim women and children, thus continuing her long-standing efforts to promote pan-African cultural exchange in New York City.

Hajjah Tauhidah Abedeen

Hajjah Tauhidah Abedeen was born in York, South Carolina on July 15, 1940. She attended racially segregated public schools. In the early 1960s, Tauhidah moved to Brooklyn, New York. Around 1968, she met and married Abdullah Salah (1927–1985), a Black man who came to Philadelphia as a child, spoke Arabic fluently, and who family members later suspected had been born in Sudan or Somalia. Tauhidah and Abdullah were coworkers at a juvenile detention center in Brooklyn. Abdullah was a member of the Nation of Islam and introduced Tauhidah to Islam. Shortly thereafter, Tauhidah became Muslim. In 1976, Tauhidah and Abdullah had a daughter whom they named Aminah. As the years progressed, Tauhidah struggled to adhere to the strict discipline of the Nation; she had always been, as her daughter Aminah described her, a "free spirit." Around 1979, Tauhidah decided to move back to South Carolina. This marked the end of her marriage to Abdullah, who was not interested in relocating down South.

Figure 2.2. Hajjah Tauhidah Abedeen (1940–2022). Photo courtesy of Aminah Salah.

Tauhidah and her daughter stayed in South Carolina for approximately five years. During this time, Tauhidah remarried and gave birth to another girl, whom she named after herself. Around 1983, by which point that marriage had dissolved, Tauhidah and her daughters went back to Brooklyn. Even though the family moved around a lot, Aminah recalled that her mother "tried to always be around the Muslim community wherever she was." While in Brooklyn, Tauhidah learned about a Black American Shi'a community in Rhode Island. She decided to move her family there in order to immerse them in what appeared to be a nurturing Black Muslim social world. Mirroring other Black Muslim enclaves that emerged in the 1980s in places like Detroit, Harlem, Brooklyn, and Newark (Miller 2019; Nash 2008), Aminah recalled that the families in Rhode Island "were a very tight-knit community. Pretty much everybody lived in the same area. Everyone made all their *salats* together." It was in this community that Tauhidah became friends with Amina Muhammad, a fellow mother. The community had ties to Ayatollah Ruhollah Khomeini, the Shi'a scholar who became the first supreme political and religious leader of Iran following the country's 1979 Islamic revolution. Aminah recalled that several community members "were trying to encourage Ummi [my mother] to send us to Iran to study Islam," a decision that some Black American Shi'a families opted for beginning in the 1980s (El-Mekki et al. 2020; Rose 2016). Tauhidah declined the invitation. In 1986, Tauhidah decided to move her family to Jersey City. She stayed in touch with Sister Amina, who remained part of her family's extended network of care.

Dr. Karimah Joseph

Dr. Karimah Joseph was born in Knoxville, Tennessee on August 1, 1949. Her parents divorced when she was six years old. Karimah and her mother moved to Detroit, joining the wave of Black people who were part of the second Great Migration. When they arrived in Detroit, the city was in the process of a major demographic transformation; the Black population skyrocketed from 300,000 in 1950 to more than 660,000 in 1970 (Sugrue 1996, 23).

Beginning in the 1920s, Black people in Detroit clustered in the Black Bottom and Paradise Valley, two of the few areas they were confined to due to racist segregation. Paradise Valley was home to nearly 300 Black-owned businesses (Detroit Historical Society n.d.; Wolcott 2013, 165). Karimah witnessed the tail end of these neighborhoods' flourishing history. The residential segregation of the time meant that Black people of various class backgrounds lived among one another. Karimah's mother was employed as a domestic worker, one of the few occupations open to Black women back then (Walters 2021). While her mother's job made their family working-class, they also had middle-class and affluent Black neighbors, such as those who worked as teachers, lawyers, and doctors. Dr. Karimah recalled, "We felt safe. I never saw an abandoned house. I never saw a house that was burned out. Even our alleys were clean. The streets were clean. It was something you were taught in school—pick up litter and things like that. You always had a sense of community." She also recalled that Detroit was a hub of Black music and activism, particularly with the rise of Motown.

Karimah attended Detroit Public Schools, a system that was condemned by Black educators of the time for being "not organized for the benefit of black youth" (as cited in Thompson 2001, 151). During high school, she met a classmate named Salim Joseph (1948–2020). Karimah and Salim (who was later honored by community members with the title *Imam* Salim) graduated in 1967, just before the uprising that devastated the infrastructure of the community in which they had grown up (Kurashige 2017; Stone 2017). The 1967 uprising in Detroit was part of a wave of mass rebellions and collective actions that took place at the height of the Civil Rights Movement. In Detroit and cities across the U.S., these uprisings were led by Black people who were outraged at the persisting poverty, police brutality, and systematic repression that Black communities faced (Hinton 2021).

The next year, in 1968, Karimah and Salim married. Salim was a male of draft age, so he was conscripted to join the military and fight in the U.S. war on Vietnam. He was deployed for one year. During his time there, Salim met a Vietnamese Muslim who played him a recording of the Qur'an in Arabic. While Salim was away, Karimah became active with the Association of Black Students at Wayne State University. She was not enrolled there at the time, but she recalled that her friend "invited me to some of their meetings and programs, so I did work with them." Through the Association of Black Students, Karimah became friends with Sadiq Bey, an artist, musician, and activist who was one of several Black American Sunni Muslims in the group. At the time, Dr. Karimah recounted, most of the Sunni Muslims she encountered "either came out of the pan-African community or the kind of a revolutionary community, politically active and all of that. And they were artists and musicians and speakers."[14] These Black Sunni Muslims saw themselves as distinct from the Nation of Islam, which had started in Detroit but by then had grown into a widely popular nationwide movement.

One day, Karimah went to visit Sadiq. Dr. Karimah recalled that Sadiq was "throwing away some books that he had. And I love books. I said, 'Just give me the whole box.'"[15] Sadiq handed Karimah a copy of the Qur'an translated into English by Yusuf Ali, an Indian Muslim lawyer and civil servant. During the 1970s and 1980s, Ali's work was one of the most widely distributed English translations of the Qur'an. Dr. Karimah explained, "The first thing that I ever read in Qur'an, the first ayat was in Surah an-Nur, the surah of the light."[16] Reading the Qur'an and discussing Islam with Sadiq had a profound impact on her and Salim. Dr. Karimah recalled, "We considered ourselves Muslim after [Sadiq] told us and introduced us. We just decided we were Muslim."[17] The year was 1969 and Karimah and Salim were 20 years old.

Karimah and Salim joined a community of Black American Muslim artists and activists in their late teens and early twenties who called themselves the Beys. The Beys were known for their radical politics, knowledge of Arabic, and dedication to studying the Qur'an (Howell 2014, 241). After becoming Muslim, Karimah and Salim maintained their pan-African cultural aesthetics. Dr. Karimah reminisced, "The brothers used to wear dashikis, we used to wear a *geles* [head wrap associated with Yoruba women]."[18]

In the post-1967 landscape of Detroit that was marked by urban disinvestment, the Beys tried to cultivate a protective environment for their families. They rented apartments in the same building or close by each other. Karimah and Salim relocated to live among the community. In 1971, Karimah gave birth to the couple's first child, Yusuf. The next year, the couple welcomed a second son, Ansar. In the years to come, the couple had four more children—one daughter and three sons. As new Muslims and parents in their early twenties, Karimah, Salim, and others in the Bey community had virtually no elders in their midst from whom to receive religious guidance or parenting advice. Dr. Karimah reflected that "We were kinda learning as we went along." Like most mothers in the Bey community, Karimah stayed at home with her sons until they were school-aged. Her boys grew up with the other children in the Bey community. One of the mothers taught all the children how to read and do math. Overall, in her early years as a Muslim and a mother, Karimah leveraged the support of other families in her network as she and Salim did their best to anchor their children in a Black Muslim social world.

Dr. Khadijah Askari

Dr. Khadijah Askari was born in Philadelphia, Pennsylvania on July 20, 1955 to parents whom she described as freedom fighters. She grew up in a city where Black people encountered racism from white residents, the police, and the government. Because of this, Dr. Khadijah recalled, "Early on, I learned, this is who protects me—my people. This is who loves me—my people. These are the men who keep me from getting harmed. And these are the men who want to harm me . . . early on, I knew where my support lied, where my love was, had to be around Black people." Dr. Khadijah recalled that on her way to elementary school, she was regularly escorted by older Black men in her community who protected her from the harassment of white Philadelphians. At age 13, when Khadijah went swimming at a public pool with her younger sister and a friend, a white employee called the police to remove them. A SWAT team showed up. The officers put the three Black girls into a van and took them to the local precinct. Khadijah's parents leveraged their political connections and mobilized nearly 50 community members to show up to the precinct. This group included Wilson Goode, who went on to be Philadelphia's first Black mayor. Khadijah credited the impressive show of Black community solidarity for contributing to the three of them being released.

Throughout her childhood and adolescence, Khadijah attended Philadelphia Public Schools. She was very bright student. For junior high and high school, Khadijah attended highly selective academic magnet schools, where most of her classmates were white. In high school, she became more familiar with the Nation of Islam, which boldly championed Black empowerment. Khadijah did not join the organization, but she proudly decorated her bedroom walls with pictures that she carefully cut out from the pages of *Muhammad Speaks*, the organization's newspaper, because "there were no other real images of Black people that were positive any place else."[19]

After graduating from high school in 1973, Khadijah attended Harvard University, where until the 1970s, fewer than 12 Black undergraduates were admitted each year (Ojogho 2014). Khadijah studied at Harvard in an era when the university employed the likes of Daniel Patrick Moynihan, who authored the infamous *Moynihan Report* that was published by the U.S. federal government. In the report, Moynihan described Black people's culture as pathological and blamed their unstable family structures for causing an unending cycle of Black poverty and disadvantage. Khadijah took classes with professors who were likely influenced by these racist ideologies; they overtly questioned her and her fellow Black classmates' intellectual abilities. She experienced such intense racism from professors that she left after her first year. She transferred to Tuskegee Institute, the historically Black college in Alabama.

At Tuskegee, Khadijah was introduced to the writings of the Ghanaian intellectual and president Kwame Nkrumah, the Martinican political theorist Frantz Fanon, and the Jamaican scholar J. A. Rogers. Their works influenced her to start identifying as a pan-Africanist. Dr. Khadijah recalled becoming convinced that "we as a people will not be free until Africa was free."

A decade earlier, in the 1960s, on U.S. college campuses, "the very presence of African students . . . made the politics of decolonization immediate and concrete" to many African American students (Murch 2010, 96). Charles Cobb Jr., an activist with the Student Nonviolent Coordinating Committee (SNCC), reflected that during his time at Howard University in the 1960s, African students "were talking about their situation, and they knew what we were talking about and we knew what they were talking about, and there was something to share there" (as cited in Hall 2022, 12). Similarly, by the 1970s at Tuskegee, Khadijah befriended students from Nigeria, Ghana, and the Gambia. Her West African friends had witnessed their countries gain independence and brought these stories with them to Alabama. Khadijah's friendship with these students deepened her knowledge of contemporary African politics. In 1975, Khadijah married her classmate, a Black American engineering student and fellow pan-Africanist named Aminufu Askari. Over the course of their marriage, the couple had five children—two sons and three daughters. The parents, who during college adopted Swahili names for themselves, gave their children Swahili names as well.

While at Tuskegee, Khadijah attended a lecture by the pioneering African American historian John Henrik Clarke. She recounted the lecture, which was titled "The Black Radical Tradition":

> He said, "The problems that we face as a people will never be solved until we get really connected to who our creator really is, who our God really is." And I think he might've been thinking more like traditional African religions, but that just blew my mind. And it meant all the things that I had ever been exposed to about Islam just kind of came rushing back in. And so then I was on a quest to find out—how do you become a Muslim? What is a Muslim? What [do] the Muslims really, really believe, and can I do it?[20]

Khadijah's quest for religious clarity continued for several years. After graduating from Tuskegee, she started medical school. She had been accepted to a school in Ghana, but a professor cautioned her against taking up one of the more limited number of spots available there and instead encouraged her to take advantage of the resources she had access to in the U.S. Heeding this advice, Khadijah joined the first cohort of students at the Morehouse School of Medicine, another historically Black institution (*Atlanta Daily World* 1979; *Ebony Magazine* 1978).

In Atlanta, in addition to juggling motherhood and medical school, Khadijah was the Programming Chair for the local chapter of the All-African People's Revolutionary Party (AAPRP), a revolutionary pan-African organization founded by Kwame Nkrumah. The AAPRP was a political party comprised of Africans seeking to foster continental unity and achieve liberation from imperialism, capitalism, and other systems of exploitation. However, Kwame Ture (formerly known as Stokely Carmichael, a key Black Power and pan-African activist from Trinidad who moved to the U.S. in his youth and became a leader in both the Student Nonviolent Coordinating Committee and the Black Panther Party) reminded Nkrumah of the essential role of Africans in the diaspora in promoting revolutionary pan-Africanism. Ture gained Nkrumah's permission to spread the AAPRP among African-diasporic people in the U.S. (Ture and Thelwell 2005, 623). As members of the AAPRP, Khadijah and her comrades provided political education to college students, with the goal of building a base of young people committed to the liberation of Africans.

When Dr. Khadijah was in medical school, she recalled discussing a patient with one of the doctors:

> He was like, "Well, good thing [the patient] came here. Because God couldn't save her, but I can." And I was like, "This man is crazy. How did he get this arrogant?" And I was like, "I want to be a doctor, but I never want to be that arrogant. I know for sure, that [it] is only God who heals us."[21]

This encounter finally propelled her to embrace Islam. She approached a Muslim brother she knew in the nearby West End neighborhood, home to a Sunni Muslim congregation led by Imam Jamil al-Amin (formerly known as H. Rap Brown of the Black Panther Party and the Student Nonviolent Coordinating Committee). This brother took her to the Community Masjid of Atlanta, where in 1980 at the age of 25, she took her shahada with Imam Jamil. Once she graduated from medical school, Dr. Khadijah worked at a neighborhood health clinic in Atlanta, where she served as the pediatrician for many Black and Black Muslim families. Overall, through Dr. Khadijah's journey with motherhood and into Islam, she remained involved in efforts to cultivate revolutionary pan-African and Muslim social worlds for her family and others.

Raising Children in an Anti-Black Society

For Hajjah Kareemah, Hajjah Tauhidah, Dr. Karimah, and Dr. Khadijah, racism, sexism, and economic marginalization constrained their childhood and adolescence. Yet as they moved into adulthood, they were attracted to Black, revolutionary pan-African, and Muslim communities that promised them new pathways to liberation. Once they became mothers, they strove to immerse their children in nurturing social worlds that affirmed their multilayered identities.

In the 1970s, Hajjah Tauhidah, Dr. Karimah, and Dr. Khadijah became mothers, and Hajjah Kareemah gave birth to her youngest daughter. These mothers raised families in urban areas that were the targets of government-led wars on drugs and crime. These wars were rooted in myths of Black criminality, which Elizabeth Hinton (2016) explains "justified both structural and everyday racism through government policies" that resulted in increased funding for police and prisons alongside disinvestment in social welfare programs (19). During the 1970s, "the deliberate arrest and incarceration of young African American men became a strategy to prevent future crime" and resulted in the "calculated decision to remove low-income youth of color from their neighborhoods" (ibid., 22). The targeted removal of Black youth escalated during the 1980s under U.S. President Ronald Reagan's national punishment campaign. As crack cocaine was flooded into Black neighborhoods, residents expressed concerns about public health and safety. But rather than address the social ills that fueled crack cocaine usage, Reagan implemented punitive measures that "blamed the pathological culture of black and brown youth for the problems of poverty and urban divestment" (Murch 2015, 171). Urban Black neighborhoods were saturated with a militarized police presence, youth were subjected to frequent police sweeps, and drug charges were escalated to federal crimes with mandatory minimum sentences (ibid., 166). Throughout the 1970s and 1980s, anticrime and antidrug policies targeting urban Black youth stoked white fears that they were inherently dangerous, a notion that "reified the idea that youth needed discipline, not care or education" (Tilton 2010, 9).

These four mothers' educational upbringing had shown them that public schools could be sites of peril for Black students. While the U.S. Supreme Court's 1954 *Brown vs. Board of Education* ruling ended legalized racist segregation in schools and initially held promise that Black students would gain access to equal resources (Gadsden et al. 1996), public schools would continue to remain inequitable for decades to come. By the 1980s, when these mothers considered where to enroll their children, Black students—particularly those in inner-city neighborhoods—were still relegated to underfunded public schools. These inequities continued under the Reagan administration. In 1983, Reagan commissioned a report entitled *A Nation at Risk: The Imperative for Educational*

Reform, which documented the widespread failures in the country's public school system. The Reagan administration's solution was to propose cuts to the Department of Education (Todd-Breland 2018, 164) and introduce educational and social policies based on the assumption that "the government could do little to produce social progress" (Orfield and Ashkinaze 1991, 3).

Confronted by the dire conditions facing Black students in public schools, some families opted out. For decades, Black Muslims had been at the forefront of creating their own schools. From the 1930s onwards, the Nation of Islam operated the largest national network of independent Black schools. At these schools, Black children and youth were taught to have pride in their culture and develop the knowledge and skills to uplift their community (Essien-Udom 1962, 241; Lincoln 1961, 250). From the 1980s onwards, under the leadership of Imam Warith Deen Mohammed, Sister Clara Muhammed Schools nurtured students' identities as Muslims and African Americans (Muhammad and Rashid 1992, 183). Around this same time, other Sunni Muslim communities, including those associated with the Darul Islam movement, also opened their own schools, operating at least 17 part-time or full-time Muslim schools from Boston to Washington D.C. (Ali 1981, 84; Rahman 2025). These schools served families in inner-city neighborhoods and offered curricula that included Islamic studies, African and African American history, and other academic subjects (Abdur-Rahman 2021; Al-Islam 2010, 289; Dannin 2002, 243–247). Afrocentric and pan-African schools offered families additional educational alternatives (Lomotey 1992; Rickford 2016). These various independent institutions reflected Black people's willingness to look beyond public education and instead collectively care for and educate one another's children.

Overall, during the 1970s and 1980s, Hajjah Kareemah, Hajjah Tauhidah, Dr. Karimah, and Dr. Khadijah encountered urban policing and educational landscapes that criminalized rather than invested in Black youth. These four mothers grappled with how to educate and nurture their children in a racist society that seemed not to care about their well-being. As these mothers considered where, how, and with whom to educate their children, they had access to an educational landscape that included not merely neighborhood public schools but also Black Muslim community schools and independent Black schools. Deciding what kind of schools their children would attend thus became critical junctures in their efforts to build nurturing social worlds.

Motherwork and the Education of Black Muslim Children

These four mothers engaged in what Patricia Hill Collins (1994) defines as motherwork, or the labor of motherhood among women of color in the U.S. who navigate how best to raise their children within a racist society. Collins argues that for Black and other mothers of color, being a mother is defined by three dimensions: ensuring their children's physical survival, having the power to determine their children's education, and cultivating a meaningful racial identity for their children. Making decisions about how, where, and with whom one's children would learn are therefore important forms of motherwork (Cooper 2007). I draw upon Collins's concept of motherwork to illustrate the specific concerns, aspirations, and efforts of these four mothers. My goal is not to erase the contributions of fathers, who, as we will see, also played an influential role in their children's growth and development. Instead, by focusing on these women's motherwork, I chronicle how they actively searched for and helped to create affirming learning experiences as part of their lifelong efforts to care for their children.

When Kareemah and Jamil's four oldest children started school in the mid-1960s, the couple was not yet Muslim. They sent their children to a multiracial, private Catholic school that was within walking distance of their apartment in the South Bronx. Outside of school, Kareemah drew on the cultural resources of Harlem. At the time, Harlem was one of the epicenters of the Black Arts Movement, which was the "aesthetic and spiritual sister of the Black Power concept" (Neal 1968, 1). Members of the Black Arts Movement saw art and culture as central to Black self-determination. Kareemah made sure her children were connected to these dynamics. Hajjah Kareemah explained, "I kept them in the culture. They were one of the first kids walking around in Harlem with afros. Everybody was stopping them as they would go to the streets on 125th Street." Kareemah enrolled her children in classes at LaRocque Bey School of Dance Theatre in Harlem, which was founded in 1960 and was the oldest African dance school in the U.S. During the summers, Kareemah signed the children up for programs at the Harlem School of

Arts. There, they learned instruments, ballet, tap dancing, and had visits from members of the Alvin Ailey American Dance Theater, the famed African American modern dance troupe. Even though her children attended a Catholic school, these efforts ensured that they were immersed in a rich Black social world outside of school hours.

In 1970, when Kareemah and Jamil became Muslim, they no longer wanted their children to attend a Catholic school. Black Sunni Muslim schools did not yet exist in New York City—the first one in Brooklyn opened in 1974 and the first one in Harlem opened in 1980 (*Western Sunrise* 1979). Thus, Kareemah and Jamil put their children in public schools, where they remained for the rest of their educational upbringing, except for the brief time that they lived in Ghana. While in Ghana, the children split their time between an international, English-medium school and a Qur'an school where their first teacher was Shaykh Osman Nuhu Sharubutu, who has served as National Chief Imam of Ghana since 1993. Back in New York City, Kareemah was vigilant when her children attended public schools: "I was the kind of parent, if you call me into school and complained about my kids, you better have the documents." She took just that approach when the school claimed her oldest son hit another student. She went to investigate and concluded that he had been wrongfully accused. Incidents like this were why Kareemah made sure she "was always at the school because people just assume certain things about your kids." To build her children's knowledge of Islam, Kareemah took them to the Islamic Cultural Center on Sundays.

Hajjah Tauhidah also experimented with different schooling options. By 1988, when her daughter Aminah had finished sixth grade and was preparing to move to Senegal, the family had lived in New Jersey, New York, Rhode Island, Virginia, South Carolina, and Florida. Tauhidah often homeschooled Aminah, then enrolled her in public school long enough for her to take state exams, and then pulled her back out. Aminah recalled,

> Even as a young child, I was aware that we were in a bubble, but outside of that bubble wasn't very Islamic-friendly. 'Cause remember, I knew how people reacted when Ummi would wear her *chador* [veil] . . . I was fasting at six years old. I remember being in public school, and it's Ramadan and I'm the only one not eating, and all the other children are eating.

Tauhidah sought to instill within her daughter a commitment to Islamic practices even while Aminah attended public school. When they lived in the tight-knit Black Shi'a community in Rhode Island, Aminah remembered, "We went to public schools, but it was a lot of us, so we would go to school, and we knew everybody in the school." Having Black Muslim classmates made that public school experience more positive than her previous ones, where her religion set her apart.

When Aminah was in fourth or fifth grade, Tauhidah moved the family to northern New Jersey. Aminah attended a Muslim school in Jersey City where she was one of the only Black students among a predominantly Egyptian Arab population. Aminah recalled, "I would pass state exams, amongst the highest, so they couldn't deny my existence. But they didn't necessarily want to deal with Black people." Tauhidah struggled to afford the tuition. She worked as a janitor and bus driver for the school, and on weekends, she cleaned the principal's house. Juggling multiple service jobs was a sacrifice Tauhidah was willing to make to immerse her children in a Muslim world during school hours.

Like Hajjah Tauhidah, Dr. Karimah navigated public and private schools. She stayed at home with her children during their early childhood. Around 1977, when the two oldest boys reached first grade, the Josephs enrolled their sons in Detroit Public Schools and Karimah went back to school for her undergraduate degree. Karimah felt that the boys' principal "did not know how to relate to African American children." The children's instruction also varied based on their teachers. One of her sons' third grade teacher identified him as gifted, while the next year, a different teacher, a young white woman, informed Karimah that she felt that the boy needed to be placed in special education. These persistent issues prompted Karimah and Salim to ultimately pull their sons out of public school.

When the Joseph parents first withdrew their children from Detroit Public Schools, Karimah handled the homeschooling duties, a role that is most often fulfilled by mothers (Mazama and Lundy 2015). After some time, she transitioned them to a homeschooling collective run by another mother in the Bey community. In 1981, Imam Luqman Abdullah (1956–2009), a leader in Detroit's chapter of the Darul Islam Movement, founded Masjid al-Haqq as Detroit's newest Black American-led Sunni mosque (Howell 2014, 255). As was the Dar's model in other cities, Masjid al-Haqq was accompanied by a school created for the congregation's children. The Joseph children attended Masjid al-Haqq's school until it shut down. By then, Karimah still attended Wayne State University, first for her undergraduate degree, then for a post-baccalaureate program, and finally for medical school. Her studies made it difficult for her to homeschool the children, so she and Salim reluctantly reenrolled them in Detroit Public Schools.

At home, Salim was his children's first Arabic teacher. The oldest son Yusuf also recalled that his father supplemented their public school curriculum. Salim required his children to read the newspaper and books such as *Black Genesis: The Prehistoric Origins of Ancient Egypt*. Yusuf explained, "My father always made sure we were reading something, reading books about the history of African Americans and where we actually came from, and how our history did not start on the cotton field"—an erroneous narrative that Yusuf had encountered in his high school history class. Overall, in their search for quality education, Karimah and Salim thus experimented with public schools, homeschooling, a community school for and by Black Sunni Muslims, and like Hajjah Kareemah, supplemented their studies after school hours with content that celebrated their Blackness.

Finally, in Atlanta, Dr. Khadijah was also intentional about her children's schooling. She was a product of Philadelphia Public Schools in an era when private schools were predominantly white and too expensive for her parents to afford. But by the time Khadijah had her own school-aged children in the 1980s in Atlanta, she had access to more schooling options than her parents did in Philadelphia during the 1950s and 1960s. The Atlanta of the 1980s also had a different racial and socioeconomic landscape. Starting in the mid-1970s, Atlanta experienced an economic boom and became known as a Black Mecca because of its prominent number of successful Black business owners and politicians. However, the economic prosperity of the Black elite did not extend to working-class Black residents (Hobson 2017), nor did it result in widespread improvements for Black students. In 1985, in Atlanta Public Schools, a district where almost 90 percent of students were Black, the city's high schoolers scored the lowest on standardized tests in the state of Georgia (McGrath 1995, 871–872).

Dr. Khadijah described her family as being part of the "upper echelon of Atlanta." She was a physician and her husband was an engineer. They lived in middle-class neighborhoods and could afford private schools. They raised children in an era when independent Black schools had become a viable alternative to both Atlanta's failing public schools and predominantly white private schools. The Askaris thus opted out of public schools.

For Khadijah, the decision was informed by her analysis of the objectives of public education and her vision of the true purpose of education, which was shaped by her revolutionary pan-African perspective. Dr. Khadijah explained,

> Public education was basically to maintain the status quo. It was to educate people to get a job in corporate America. And nobody in corporate America was bringing things back to our community. So, I wanted our children to be educated, to be responsible and responsive to the needs of our community, of African people in this country or abroad. So that means we had to educate them.

The Askaris were in community with other families who felt similarly. These families reasoned, Dr. Khadijah's daughter Sayyida Kubra explained, that "if we pool our resources and have a committed person amongst the people who will educate the children, then we can get behind them and support them." Khadijah's sister Jaliwa volunteered for the role. Jaliwa opened a pan-African school called Freedom Institute (later renamed Atlanta Progress Academy), which she initially ran from the basement of Khadijah's house. She relocated the school to a new building as it grew and attracted more students, including the children of members of the All-African People's Revolutionary Party. Jaliwa's willingness to open the school was part of her motherwork to provide meaningful educational experiences for her own children, her nieces and nephews, and other children in the community. The school's theme song was, "Freedom Institute, we're learning about our roots!" During the early 1990s, when the school became Atlanta Progress Academy, it held an Annual African Village ceremony, had students perform at an African American History Month celebration, and received the Malcolm X Self-Determination Award from a local Black organization (*Atlanta*

Daily World 1992, 1993). The Askari children's pan-African education also extended outside of school hours. Sayyida Kubra recalled birthday celebrations during which there would be competitions to see "whoever could recite the most African countries and their capitals.... That was like normal for us."

As the Askari children got older, Khadijah decided that they needed to be in a bigger environment with more students their age. There were no pan-African schools that fit the criteria, so Khadijah enrolled them in the Sister Clara Muhammad School. Dr. Khadijah explained the similarities between the two schools: "It was still Black. They still were talking about building African communities. The Sister Clara Muhammad School in Atlanta was very vocal about Black economic support and opportunities. They were trying to establish a community for the African American Muslims here. And of course, you had that Islamic learning."

Overall, these four mothers engaged in motherwork to protect their children from an urban landscape that criminalized rather than cared for Black youth. Recognizing the politicized nature of schooling, these mothers looked beyond public schools and the traditional school day to create nurturing experiences. Their choices ranged from reluctantly accepting public schools but supplementing their children's learning, to opting out of public education altogether. Because these mothers understood that school was not the only place where children learned, they also sought out extracurricular programs. Their motherwork was shaped by their political analyses and firsthand experiences as students and/or parents of children in public schools. In choosing to enroll their children in independent Black and Muslim institutions, these parents sought schools that promoted sociopolitical, religious, and moral sensibilities that could or would not be taught in public schools. In this sense, these mothers' decision to withdraw their children from public schools was not simply based on a desire to escape the poor-quality urban educational landscape that most Black students were subjected to. Rather, for those mothers who sought alternatives, they saw Black and Muslim schools as places of possibility. Even for those mothers who toggled between public and private schools, their motherwork was marked by a commitment to providing their children with experiences that inculcated within them pride in their identities as Muslims and Black people.

Coming to America: Shaykh Hassan and the Tijani Tariqa

In an anecdote often repeated among Black American Tijanis and confirmed by Shaykh Hassan's brother Shaykh Mahy, it is said that Shaykh Ahmed Thiam, a renowned Islamic scholar and Arabic grammar teacher hired by Shaykh Ibrahim Niasse, stood in front of a crowded classroom in Medina Baye, Senegal. Shaykh Ahmed asked the attentive group of children before him, "Who will go to America for us? I would go, but I don't speak English."

The story goes that a little boy at the back of the classroom raised his hand. This boy was Shaykh Ibrahim's grandson, Shaykh Hassan, who would eventually become Shaykh Ibrahim's spiritual heir. As Shaykh Hassan got older, Shaykh Ibrahim encouraged his grandson to learn English. Shaykh Hassan took this task on with such enthusiasm and diligence that he earned the nickname "American" amongst his Senegalese peers before he ever traveled to the U.S. After Shaykh Hassan graduated from Ain Shams University in Egypt with a bachelor's in Arabic Literature and Islamic Studies, he received an offer to teach in Libya. He asked his grandfather for advice on what he should do next. Recalling their conversation during a television interview, Shaykh Hassan explained that Shaykh Ibrahim said to him, "Yes, fine, if you like, you can go. But if you like to do what I want you to do, you should go to London and study English" (Cisse n.d.). Several Black American Tijanis also narrated this story to me and explained that it was a testament to Shaykh Hassan's fulfillment of his grandfather's pan-African vision and desire to spread the tariqa to English speakers in the diaspora. Shaykh Hassan took his grandfather's advice and moved to London, where he received his master's from the University of London's School of Oriental and African Studies in 1974.

In 1976, one year after his grandfather passed away, Shaykh Hassan, then aged 31, took his first trip to the U.S. Shaykh Hassan arrived in New York City at a time when there were approximately only one thousand Senegalese immigrants there (Babou 2021, 250). Yet it was not Shaykh Hassan's country people who hosted him on his first trip. Rather, he was welcomed by the city's small community of Ghanaian Tijanis. Hajji Yusuf Anan, a Ghanian immigrant who lived in Staten Island, worked at the United Nations, and was Shaykh Hassan's classmate in Egypt,

Figure 2.3. Shaykh Hassan (right) answers questions from a reporter during a televised interview in Medina Baye, Senegal. Shaykh Hassan recounts his first trip to New York City, his travels throughout the U.S., the Tijani community in the U.S., and Shaykh Ibrahim's advice that he go study English in London. See the full interview at http://tiny.cc/ShaykhHassanTVinterview.

helped Shaykh Hassan secure a visa (Miller 2020, 212). Hajji Yusuf asked his friend, Hajji Ahmed Dimson, an accomplished soccer player who had migrated to the U.S. at the suggestion of Shaykh Ibrahim, to meet Shaykh Hassan at the airport. Hajji Ahmed lived in the Bronx with his wife Hajjah Halima and their children. After picking Shaykh Hassan up at the airport and taking him to Hajji Yusuf's place to make salat and wazifa, Hajji Ahmed took Shaykh Hassan back to his family's modest apartment in the Bronx. Hajji Ahmed and Hajjah Halima hosted Shaykh Hassan during his first stay in New York.

Another of the Ghanaian Tijanis in the city, Hajji Isa Mama Cisse, was friends with Hajjah Kareemah Abdul-Kareem. Hajji Isa called Hajjah Kareemah and asked her to invite her friends to meet Shaykh Hassan and learn about the tariqa. She obliged. Hajji Isa, Shaykh Hassan, and a group of at least four other Ghanaian Tijanis came to her apartment in the South Bronx to see her and her friends. They made wazifa in

Hajjah Kareemah's living room—marking the first time that a group of Black Americans attended a Tijani dhikr in the U.S. Hajjah Kareemah decided to join the Tijani tariqa. Soon, she was appointed as the first American *muqaddama* (woman in a position of spiritual leadership in the Tijani tariqa).

Shaykh Hassan recalled his first trip to the U.S. during a television interview:

> Before I left to New York, I knew only one person called Ahmed Dimson. But when I reached New York, and the people got to know that I was around, they used to come to where I was. During the first three weeks I spent in New York, many people were able to join the tariqa of Tijaniyya through me. (Cisse n.d.)

During his first and subsequent trips to New York, as well as to cities and states including Chicago, Detroit, Atlanta, Washington D.C., Newark, Philadelphia, Cleveland, Memphis, New Orleans, Rhode Island, and California, Shaykh Hassan met more Black American Muslims, including Imam Sayed Abdus-Salaam (1942–2017), who joined the tariqa and became the first American *muqaddam* (man in a position of spiritual leadership in the Tijani tariqa).

The next year, in 1977, Hajjah Kareemah visited Medina Baye for one day on her way to Nigeria. Imam Sayed and his wife Hajjah Salwa Abdus-Salaam (1952–1993) were also visiting. In 1982, the three of them, along with Hajji Ahmed Dimson, returned to Medina Baye to pay their condolences after the passing of Shaykh Hassan's father, Sayyidi Aliou Cisse, who had served as the Imam of Medina Baye since 1975, when Shaykh Ibrahim returned to Allah. Shaykh Ibrahim had left instructions in his will that he would be succeeded first by Sayyidi Aliou, and then by Shaykh Hassan. So, in 1982, after his father passed away, Shaykh Hassan became the new Imam of Medina Baye.

During Hajjah Kareemah's second trip to Medina Baye in 1982, she stayed longer. She recalled, "When I was there for the funeral, I just noticed the kids, everything was la illaha illallah. Everybody just spoke of Allah all the time. I said, this is what I would like for [my youngest child] Aminah."[22]

When Hajjah Kareemah returned to the U.S., she handwrote an eight-page letter to Shaykh Hassan, who was just transitioning into his new role as the primary spiritual leader of Shaykh Ibrahim's branch of the Tijani tariqa, both in Medina Baye and across the globe. Hajjah Kareemah told him that she wanted to bring Aminah to Medina Baye. She proposed the idea of setting up a boarding school where children from the U.S. could learn about their religion and culture as Muslims of African descent. She suggested that they charge $200 USD per month to feed, educate, and care for the children. Hajjah Kareemah offered to serve as the den mother, housekeeper, or whatever role would enable her to live there rent-free in exchange for her service.

Hajjah Kareemah envisioned an educational experience that benefited more than just her daughter. Reflecting on her mother's rationale, Hajjah Kareemah's daughter, hafiza Aminah Abdul-Kareem Niasse (2015), explained, "All children are her children, whether she has given birth to them or not. So plans began to brew." Hajjah Kareemah served as what Patricia Hill Collins describes as an othermother, or a woman who shares mothering responsibilities for other people's children. In contrast to capitalist models that assign biological mothers the sole responsibility to care for children in their nuclear family, the existence of othermothers reflects a cooperative approach (Collins 1990, 182). Othermothering was and remains common in Africa and the diaspora. It was a survival practice employed by enslaved Africans in the U.S. and one that African Americans continue to rely upon (James 1993; Stack 1974). In the 1980s, as the influx of crack cocaine, mass incarceration, and poverty assaulted inner-city, working-class Black communities and undermined biological parents' ability to raise their children, othermothers stepped in to care for Black children (Collins 1990, 181). The willingness of othermothers "to take responsibility for Black children illustrates how African-influenced understandings of family have been continually reworked to help African-Americans as a collectivity cope with and resist oppression" (ibid., 183). Othermothering practices were "powerful nontraditional resources utilized to intervene creatively in situations or conditions that threatened the survival of the community" (James 1993, 52). However, as Audrey Thompson (2004) notes, othermothering was not simply "an adaption to economic and oppressive conditions . . . but a valued caring

Figure 2.4. Hajjah Kareemah (back row, third from the right) stands with her daughter Aminah (middle row, first from the right) and other Black American, Senegalese, and Gambian women and children in Medina Baye in 1983. Most people in the picture were part of a group of Black American mothers and children from New Jersey, New York, and Ohio who came to visit Medina Baye a few months after Hajjah Kareemah moved there to set up the school. Photo courtesy of Majida Abdul-Karim, from the archives of Aliyah Abdul-Karim.

tradition that enriches the lives of children" (34). Hajjah Kareemah had the flexibility and means to move with her daughter to Medina Baye, something that other parents were unable to do. In seeking to open a boarding school and serve as an othermother to its students, Hajjah Kareemah offered parents in her community a cooperative caregiving and educational strategy. Her willingness to othermother not only offered Black Muslim families a means of circumventing the inequitable domestic public schooling landscape, but also offered young people access to enriching social worlds beyond the U.S.

Shaykh Hassan was compelled by Hajjah Kareemah's freedom dream. Together, in the summer of 1983, they founded a Qur'an school in Medina Baye. They initially named the school Nasrul Ilm, a reference to

"Jamiat Nasrul Ilm" (the community of beneficial knowledge), another of the names that Shaykh Ibrahim gave to his global Sufi movement. In 1988, the Qur'an school became absorbed as the first of many initiatives by the African American Islamic Institute (AAII), a pan-African Muslim, United Nations-recognized nongovernmental organization that Shaykh Hassan and his murids founded to promote education, health care, women's rights, and dialogue between communities in the U.S. and Africa. Following the establishment of AAII as an NGO, the school became the organization's flagship initiative and began to be referred to as AAII as well.

Educational Dreams of Medina Baye

The opening of the international Islamic boarding school in Medina Baye signaled the emergence of a new nurturing world for Black Muslim children and youth beyond the U.S. In the years that followed, word spread across the country about Shaykh Hassan, the Tijani tariqa, and the AAII School. As Shaykh Hassan visited different cities, his Black American, Afro-Caribbean, Ghanaian, and Senegalese murids took their friends to meet him. Based on the retellings of how Black Americans introduced their friends to Shaykh Hassan or how they themselves first met Shaykh Hassan, the characteristics that they most often mentioned were his race, religion, age, appearance, and scholarly achievements. They remarked on his identity as an African Muslim, his lineage as a member of a family that produced several generations of Islamic scholars, his complexion as a dark-skinned man, and his young age as a 30-something year old who possessed a deep knowledge of Islam and was eager and patient in sharing his knowledge with them.

By the time Hajjah Kareemah, Hajjah Tauhidah, Dr. Karimah, and Dr. Khadijah met Shaykh Hassan, each of them had been Muslim for at least six years. They were striving Muslims. They had developed a firm understanding of the foundations of the religion, continued to deepen their knowledge, and were involved in Muslim community life. They attended their local mosques, read Islamic books in their free time, took advantage of Islamic classes, and organized religious events in their community. As mothers, they often did all this with their children in tow.

In 1976, Hajjah Kareemah was the first of the foremothers to meet Shaykh Hassan and join the Tijani tariqa. The remaining three mothers followed in the years to come. In November 1987, Tauhidah and her daughters met Shaykh Hassan. In her nearly two decades of being a Muslim, Tauhidah had passed through numerous Muslim communities; she had spent time with the Nation, then identified as a Shi'a, and then considered herself Sunni. Tauhidah's daughter Aminah recalled her mother's engagement with Muslim communities and how she first heard about Shaykh Hassan.

> My mother was pretty open. I called her a floater . . . She was free as a bird. She would do whatever she wanted to do. She experienced life on her terms. By this time, we had already kind of been introduced to all types of shaykhs—shaykhs from India, shaykhs from Iraq, shaykhs from all over the place. And to be totally honest, it was a little confusing for me, but for her, I guess, that was just the journey that she was on. And so when Sister Amina said, "Well, do you wanna meet this African shaykh from Africa? He's from Senegal!" Of course, my mom was like, "Yeah, sure, let's do that." [*laughs*] And, you know, she was going through her, I guess, journey through Islam.

Aminah recalled accompanying her mother and Sister Amina Muhammad—her mother's friend from back in their days living in the Black Shi'a community in Rhode Island—to visit Shaykh Hassan at his Ghanaian murid's apartment in the Bronx. Aminah and her mother observed Shaykh Hassan and his murids make wazifa. Once the group finished, Shaykh Hassan invited Tauhidah to speak with him directly. Aminah accompanied her mother into the other room where they talked. Aminah recounted that first interaction between Shaykh Hassan and her mother.

> One of the things that I know about Shaykh Hassan is that he made Islam simple and easy to practice and understand. And he related to her, us on a human level. Like she had met other shaykhs and what have you. And it's not like they were living grandiose or whatever, but I don't think that they—and this is me talking from a child's perspective, but I'm also

looking at the way she behaved—I don't think they connected with her on a human level. . . . Here is Shaykh Hassan, a man who looked like her, who took the time to connect with her on a personal level.

That evening, Tauhidah joined the tariqa. Becoming a Tijani represented another milestone in her decades-long journey as a striving Muslim woman. Her daughters accompanied her on this journey, entering the pan-African Muslim social world that came with being a Tijani.

When Tauhidah's family attended Tijani gatherings, after the dhikr was over, people lingered for informal conversations. It was during these exchanges that Aminah, then aged 11, learned about the AAII School. She listened attentively to the stories of parents whose children lived under Shaykh Hassan and Hajjah Kareemah's care and studied at the school. The parents explained what it was like for their children to memorize the Qur'an in a Sufi city in West Africa. These stories represented a stark contrast to Aminah's experiences at her predominantly Arab Muslim school where she confronted anti-Black racism. These stories made Aminah want to go to Medina Baye. She recalled, "I told my mom, 'I want to go study Qur'an. This is something that I really want to do. It sounds interesting.' I would kind of repeat that back to her, over and over and over again." Tauhidah's membership in the Tijani tariqa had thus introduced her daughter to a new educational possibility, one in which Black American children could study in Africa and become huffaz. Aminah yearned to be part of that world.

The next year, as Shaykh Hassan came back and forth to visit, the young Aminah formed her own relationship with him. At the time, Aminah was aware of her family's economically precarious position; she was embarrassed by her mother's job as a janitor and even more displeased about how the Egyptian principal at her Muslim school treated her mother when she cleaned the principal's home on weekends. Aminah contrasted the principal's attitude with how Shaykh Hassan engaged her mother. Aminah reflected, "To see an African Black man who never belittled or demeaned my mom, I think had a huge impact on me. It made me want to go to Africa even more."

Finally, on another occasion, Shaykh Hassan encouraged Tauhidah to send her daughters to AAII. Aminah recalled,

> Shaykh formally invited my mom, like "Send your daughters to Senegal and study" and what have you. She said, "Yes Shaykh, I will, I will." He said, "Your children are my children. I'll treat them like my children." And she said, "Okay, Shaykh!" . . . They were having this conversation about her children from across the room, in between a million people . . . I was like, "Oh my God, this is so embarrassing!" [*laughs*]

Over the years, Tauhidah had leveraged her relationships with fellow mothers and Muslim communities to build social worlds that nurtured her daughters' identities. Joining the Tijani tariqa and forging a spiritual bond with Shaykh Hassan expanded the resources that Tauhidah could draw upon.

At the time, it was common for Black American parents to call upon family members to help raise their children. From the era of slavery and into the twentieth century, Black families turned to extended kin and community members for support in resisting the racist oppression, degradation, and violence that their children encountered (Gutman 1977; Martin and Martin 1978; Stack 1974). Othermothering was one of many cooperative strategies that Black parents drew upon to protect their children. During and after the Great Migration, it was also common for parents in the North to send their children to the South for extended stays with grandparents or other family members (Brown 1965). Some parents hoped that their children's temporary or permanent exile would shield them from the ills of Northern, inner-city neighborhoods and expose them to new possibilities (Richardson et al. 2014).

Tauhidah's spiritual bond with Shaykh Hassan allowed her to expand this practice beyond her biological family to a spiritual kinship network that extended across the Atlantic. In many West African cultures, it was also common for children to be raised by extended family members, esteemed community members, or those with greater financial means. This collective of people helped raise children, contributing to the commonly appropriated adage, "It takes a village to raise a child." Shaykh Hassan's comment that Hajjah Tauhidah's children were "my children" reflected this notion of a network of collaborative parenting, emotional labor, and collective care that extended beyond the nuclear family norm commonly practiced in the capitalist U.S.

Furthermore, Shaykh Hassan's comments pointed to a reestablishment of the kinship ties between West Africans and Black Americans that had been violently severed by the transatlantic slave trade. His comments represented what Todne Thomas describes as kincraft, or a relational ethos and community praxis among Afro-diasporic religious people who see and treat one another as spiritual kin. Writing about Black evangelical Christians in Atlanta, Thomas argues that kincraft forms the basis of their religiosity and sociality and shapes how they cultivate their religious identities and fashion their community. Thomas (2021) argues that community members' kincraft allows them to create sacred solidarities in order to "attend collectively to the moral and pragmatic demands of familial and religious life, as well as the material vulnerabilities that derived from antiblack racism, migration, and neoliberalism" (4). Through kincraft, Black evangelicals cultivate religious virtues and work together to address the material injustices that impact their community. Kincraft thus describes principles and praxes similar to those that I refer to as collective care, as both demonstrate how Black religious communities relate to one another in pursuit of spiritual transformation alongside worldly redress. Kincraft is a useful way to think about the specific acts of collective care that encourage believers to treat each other as family.

Shaykh Hassan positioned the experience at the AAII School as a form of pan-African Tijani kincraft. Just as Hajjah Kareemah pledged to serve as an othermother for the school's boarding students, so too did Shaykh Hassan promise to treat the children as his own. Shaykh Hassan and Hajjah Kareemah recognized the intergenerational responsibilities that came with kincraft; as parents themselves, they understood the care that children needed to thrive, as well as the reassurances prospective parents needed before they relinquished their children to other adults. Once young people arrived in Medina Baye, Shaykh Hassan and Hajjah Kareemah undertook day-to-day collective caregiving responsibilities. Their labor made it possible for young people to live and learn abroad while their biological parents remained in the U.S. Shaykh Hassan and Hajjah Kareemah's continued presence also offered solace to parents who struggled with the emotional strains of being physically separated from their children. While no assurance could fully make up for the heavy toll that parents endured, these mothers and fathers found comfort in knowing that their children were under the care of adults who treated them as family. In this way, everyone's shared commitment to caring for each other as pan-African Tijani kin helped ease parents' burdens and made it possible for young people to embark upon their sacred educational endeavors.

Like Tauhidah, Karimah had interacted with Muslims from other countries prior to meeting Shaykh Hassan. The Josephs belonged to social worlds beyond the U.S. Salim had been deployed to Vietnam, the couple had African friends, Karimah was involved in the Black student movement, and they had both spent their early years as Muslims in the globally oriented Bey community. Yet despite their Black internationalist leanings, their experiences with Arab Muslims in Detroit left them wary. Dr. Karimah recalled,

> Every time they came, they would want to teach us how to use a *miswaq* [a twig that Prophet Muhammad used to clean his teeth] and teach us how to make *wudu* [ablution]. The [Black American] brothers, when they would ask them questions, [the Arabs] didn't want to answer.... We were used to running into people who would ask us if we knew our *Fatiha* [the first surah of the Qur'an]. "Do you know your three pillars?" to see if you knew that there were five.[23]

The Josephs were striving Muslims, but their fervent commitment to Islam was questioned by Arab Muslim immigrants.

The Josephs' experiences made them reluctant to join a tariqa based overseas, even one from a country in Africa. However, two of Salim's Black American friends were Tijani—Brother Mahmoud Salaam and Brother Bilal Muhammad. Brother Bilal even lived in Medina Baye with his family from the late 1970s to the early 1980s. These brothers encouraged Salim and Karimah to learn more about the tariqa. In 1985, after several years of his own research and study with these friends, and 16 years after becoming Muslim, Salim was ready to join the tariqa. Brother Bilal, who was living in Chicago at the time, drove to Detroit to initiate Salim into the Tijani tariqa. Since Shaykh Hassan was scheduled to visit Detroit soon, Salim advised Karimah to wait and join the tariqa with him in person.

A few months later, Shaykh Hassan arrived in the Midwest. He stayed at Brother Mahmoud and his wife Sister Raqiba's place. Dr. Karimah recalled her and Sister Raqiba's interaction with Shaykh Hassan.

> We had never really met a shaykh that, well, that felt like he was a friend. . . . Shaykh Hassan was the first teacher, the first shaykh that we met that actually basically looked at us and said, "You're already Muslim. What can I do for you? How can I help you? What do you need? You're Muslim, you're practicing your religion. You're good Muslims. So this is how you can do better."²⁴

Unlike the Arab Muslims who viewed the Josephs through an anti-Black, deficit lens, Shaykh Hassan engaged them through a pan-African Tijani mode of kincraft. He approached them through a relational ethos anchored in the understanding that they were his brothers and sisters who had spent more than a decade striving for religious growth. Shaykh Hassan recognized their zeal for Islam and introduced them to Sufism.

After Salim and Karimah joined the tariqa, they regularly attended wazifa. The nascent Tijani community in Detroit did not have a formal gathering place, so they rotated between different families' homes, which included the Joseph residence and Brother Mahmoud and Sister Raqiba's place. The Josephs' oldest son Yusuf recalled that he and his siblings accompanied their parents to the dhikrs. In 1986, a year after his parents became Tijani, Yusuf, then aged 15, joined the tariqa as well.

Like in New York City, at the gatherings in Detroit, people made dhikr together, told stories, and shared their travel accounts. Brother Mahmoud encouraged the Josephs to visit Medina Baye. Others who traveled to Medina Baye also recounted their experiences. Their tales brought to life a new world that captured the interest of parents and children alike. Yusuf recalled,

> I had heard about the stories of them doing dhikr from Shaykh Hassan's house to the masjid for fajr in the morning, how beautiful the dhikr was. I had heard some recordings of it. I couldn't wait to go. . . . And [my parents were] just like, "You know what? We need to. Let's get 'em over there. Let's get them outta the country so they can see something different. Let them experience being in the school." Cause you know, Shaykh Hassan

opened up the African American Islamic Institute. That was also something else that no other community had done. The Pakistanis hadn't done it. The Arabs hadn't done it. The Bengalis and nobody else that anybody else was following had done that and had said, "We have a school that's open, dedicated to teaching the African American students, and they call it the African American Islamic Institute." Nobody else had done that. That was something else that our community was very impressed with.

Yusuf interpreted Shaykh Hassan's work in establishing AAII as indicative of Shaykh Hassan's explicit investment in Black Americans, a commitment that no other foreign Muslim community or scholar had shown. Yusuf and others were impressed that a Senegalese shaykh wanted to empower Black Americans by facilitating Islamic educational opportunities for them. Though not mentioned in Yusuf's commentary, the fact that the school actually emerged as a collaboration between Shaykh Hassan and Hajjah Kareemah further underscored the ways in which the Tijani tariqa fostered a close and unique partnership with Senegalese Muslims that had yet to be forged through Black Americans' relationships with Muslims from any other country.

Based on the stories and recordings he heard, Yusuf was also excited about the broader Muslim social world of Medina Baye. Yusuf looked forward to not only memorizing the Qur'an at AAII, but also experiencing everyday communal life in a city where most people were Sufi Muslims. He eagerly awaited the sights and sounds of residents reciting dhikr aloud together as they walked to the mosque for daily prayers. This was an everyday occurrence in Medina Baye, but it this was something that Yusuf had yet to experience. In the U.S., the urban geography, the militarized police presence in Detroit's inner-city Black neighborhoods, and Muslims' status as religious minorities were some of the many reasons why such public displays were difficult (Perkins 2015).

In December 1989, Karimah traveled to Medina Baye with her sons Yusuf, then aged 18, and Ansar, then aged 17. Karimah also brought along her friend's teenaged son, honoring pan-African Tijani kincraft and othermothering practices to facilitate an enriching opportunity for another young person in their community. At the time, Karimah was on her winter break during medical school, so she had the flexibility to travel. Salim, who was working full-time, stayed back to care for the couple's remaining children. Karimah was to stay for two weeks, while the three boys were to attend AAII for three months. However, shortly after arriving, Yusuf pleaded with his parents to extend his ticket. His three-month trip became a three-year stay. In the years to come, Yusuf's parents sent his remaining siblings.

Yusuf reflected on his parents' decision:

> Looking back at it, my parents couldn't have made a better decision. If you have an opportunity to save your children, and you see your children, that they have good hearts, that they have good natures, and that they have good manners, but you see that they're struggling, and you have an opportunity to save them—it's never an easy decision even if you know what you're getting into. To make the decision to say, you know what, I'm going to send my child somewhere to study and I know I might not see them for years—that's not an easy decision for a parent. There's always the internal decision, like, did I do the right thing? It takes a real certitude, a real fortitude, to understand that what you're doing is the best thing—especially when they're younger . . . you're always in a state of, okay, am I making the right decision? Even though you know you're making the right decision, it's always that emotional pull that's coming to get you.

Yusuf acknowledged that the gravity of physical separation required his parents to constantly reassess and recommit to their decision. Though the Joseph parents deeply felt their children's absence, Yusuf asserted that they nonetheless bore these emotional burdens because they saw in Medina Baye an opportunity to prioritize their children's well-being and nurture new possibilities.

Finally, in Atlanta, around the same time that Karimah took her sons to Medina Baye, Dr. Khadijah met Shaykh Hassan. Dr. Khadijah first heard about Shaykh Hassan around 1983 from Sister Safa Abdur Rahman, a Black Muslim mother who was part of a group of mothers and children who traveled to Medina Baye shortly after Hajjah Kareemah moved there to set up the AAII School. Sister Safa had pleaded for her children to stay with Hajjah Kareemah, but Hajjah Kareemah had insisted that she wait until AAII was fully operational. So when Sister Safa received word that the school was ready, she scheduled an appointment for her children to see Dr. Khadijah. Dr. Khadijah recalled,

Figure 2.5. Dr. Karimah and Imam Salim with two children in their laps—their youngest son (left) and their oldest grandson (right). Both boys, pictured here in the mid-1990s, ultimately studied at AAII. Photo courtesy of Yusuf Joseph.

> I was her kids' pediatrician. When they were getting ready to go, she came to me for their exam. And I was like, "Well, where are they going?" She was like, "They're going to Senegal. We have a shaykh over there and his name is Shaykh Hassan and they're going over there." And I was like, "Well, are you going?" And she's like, "No." I'm like, "Well, who sends their kids all the way to Africa and they've never been there and they're not going?" I mean, it was just blowing my mind. Just being an advocate for children, I was like, I have to find out what's going on. Too many people are sending their kids over there. I can't be giving them an exam and sending them someplace crazy, you know? It's like I'm giving them the okay to go. So I kind of wanted to find out more.[25]

As a pan-Africanist, Dr. Khadijah was invested in cultivating relationships with Africans. At the same time, as a mother and pediatrician, she was uncomfortable with the idea of sending young people to an unknown place, even if it was in Africa.

Sister Safa encouraged Dr. Khadijah to speak with Hajjah Kareemah's husband, Brother Jamil. He put Dr. Khadijah in touch with Hajjah

Kareemah, who eased many of Dr. Khadijah's concerns. Dr. Khadijah recalled, "I just thought that was just such a lot of faith that the mothers were showing, and actually going there and such a commitment on [Hajjah Kareemah's] part to take care of the children."[26]

In 1989, Shaykh Hassan came to visit the Sister Clara Muhammad School in Atlanta, the school that Dr. Khadijah's children attended at the time. Before Shaykh Hassan spoke, two students from AAII recited Qur'an for the audience. The students were the daughters of Sister Amina Muhammad, who, back in the Northeast, had first introduced Hajjah Tauhidah to Shaykh Hassan. Dr. Khadijah recounted her oldest son, Abubakr's, reaction to the girls.

> [He] heard them and he was challenged by them, that these girls knew more Qur'an than him, and could recite Qur'an. And he started telling me, "I want to learn Qur'an. I want to go to Africa and stuff like that." ... His sisters are close in age to him. And so him and [his sister] Badia had this really competitive spirit because they were both straight-A students. ... And so, when these girls came, he was just on me, like, "I want to go to Africa, I want to study Qur'an. I wanna be a hafiz, da da da." I was like, "Okay, we're going to see, we're going to see."[27]

For Abubakr, witnessing these two girls exhibit what they had learned in Senegal was impressive; he too studied the Qur'an at school, but these students were receiving an education that seemed unmatched. Seeing what they had learned sparked within him a desire to emulate, or perhaps exceed, their achievements. Though he was attending a Black Muslim school in the U.S., the African continent—and AAII in particular—held promise of a more appealing educational opportunity.

Later that month, Shaykh Hassan returned to the Sister Clara Muhammad School. Dr. Khadijah went to hear him speak. This marked their first meeting. Dr. Khadijah recalled,

> Just his whole charisma, it was just really obvious. He just flooded into the school. It wasn't that big of a crowd, but it was enough of a crowd. I asked him a question, like, "Why are you here? Why did you come?" He said, "I came for the sake of Allah to see my brothers and sisters." And it just really touched my heart. Because I was in the pan-African movement

at that time. Even as a Muslim, I was a really strong pan-Africanist at that time. It was always this question of, "If we were stolen from Africa, why didn't anybody come looking for us?" And he was here telling me, "I've come looking for you. And I got the answer for you!" So at that point, it was a no-brainer.[28]

Shaykh Hassan's response signaled a diasporic relationship unlike those she had previously experienced in pan-African spaces. Invoking the relational ethos and community praxis of pan-African Tijani kincraft, Shaykh Hassan asserted that West Africans and Black Americans belonged to one family, and that West Africans had a responsibility to find their siblings. For Dr. Khadijah, hearing Shaykh Hassan articulate and honor this mode of kincraft quelled a question that had lingered in her mind.

Shaykh Hassan's comments also opened Dr. Khadijah up to the educational possibilities in Senegal. After all, even though she considered going to medical school in Ghana, gave herself and her children Swahili

Figure 2.6. Hajjah Kareemah (center) with two other mothers in Medina Baye in the late 1980s. Photo courtesy of Hajjah Kareemah Abdul-Kareem.

Figure 2.7. Dr. Khadijah (first row, second from the left) with four of her five children in Medina Baye. Photo courtesy of Abubakr Askari.

names, was a leader in a revolutionary pan-African organization, enrolled her children in pan-African schools, and was in awe of the faith of Hajjah Kareemah and the many mothers who sent their children to AAII, she had been uninterested, up until then, in sending her children to Medina Baye. The fact that her worries subsided as she heard Shaykh Hassan's response revealed the emotional impact and practical outcomes of kincraft; it was both a reassurance and resource that mothers drew upon as they made decisions about how best to raise their children. In 1990, after years of being curious about the educational possibilities of Medina Baye, Dr. Khadijah enrolled the first of her five children at AAII. She arranged for her son to travel with her friend, Hajjah Ayisha Jeffries-Cisse, who like Dr. Karimah in Detroit, served as the othermother who made it possible for him to make the international journey without his parents.

By 1990, these foremothers all had children at AAII. Hajjah Kareemah and Hajjah Tauhidah had moved to Medina Baye to raise their own and other people's children. Dr. Karimah and Dr. Khadijah visited on numerous occasions, always bringing medical supplies with them and setting up pop-up clinics on the roof of the school to provide checkups to students and residents. In 1997, Dr. Karimah and Dr. Khadijah supported Shaykh Hassan in establishing Shifa-al-Asqam (Healers of the Sick) Socio Medical Center, Medina Baye's first health clinic.

While Hajjah Kareemah and Hajjah Tauhidah cared for young people in Medina Baye, Dr. Karimah and Dr. Khadijah worked, fundraised, and spread word about the school in the U.S. They shared stories about their children's experiences, their own visits to Medina Baye, and their

Figure 2.8. Hajjah Tauhidah (standing, second from the left) surrounded by Black American students in Medina Baye. Photo courtesy of Aminah Salah.

reflections about the blessings and burdens of having their children live and learn thousands of miles away from them. Moreover, as Shaykh Hassan continued to visit the U.S., as the Tijani community grew, and as Shaykh Hassan invited his new murids to visit and send their children to Medina Baye, more people became part of the pan-African Tijani family. As Black Americans and Africans saw and treated one another as kin, they collectively cared for one another and made it possible for Black Muslim youth to live, learn, and thrive in a new social world outside of the U.S.

Conclusion

The life stories of Hajjah Kareemah, Hajjah Tauhidah, Dr. Karimah, and Dr. Khadijah reveal the essential historical and sociopolitical contexts that attracted dozens of Black American parents to Islam, Shaykh Hassan, the Tijani tariqa, and the freedom dreams of Medina Baye. From their childhood and into their adult lives, these foremothers and their peers confronted racist segregation, anti-Black violence, sexism, inequitable public education, and other social and economic barriers. In their search for meaning, they embraced African cultural practices, joined pan-African and Black organizations, and became Muslim. Doing so expanded their worlds and connected them to a network of believers in Africa and beyond.

When these four women became mothers, their search for meaning turned into a family-wide endeavor. They pursued their own individual growth and simultaneously engaged in motherwork to nurture their children amidst an anti-Black landscape. These mothers brought their children with them as they entered into pan-African Tijani social worlds, where adults and young people alike participated in dhikr and fellowship. It was in these spaces that their children became interested in the educational prospects of Medina Baye, and urged their parents to let them to go. These foremothers identified within Shaykh Hassan, the Tijani tariqa, and AAII an opportunity to internationalize their longstanding search for educational dignity.

These foremothers anticipated that their decision would usher in immense blessings for their children, but they also worried that they would struggle in their children's physical absence. Their emotional burdens were eased in part by Shaykh Hassan's emphasis on pan-African Tijani modes of kincraft and his understanding of Black American students as members of his family. Shaykh Hassan became their African adoptive father. Othermothers like Hajjah Kareemah and Hajjah Tauhidah moved to Medina Baye, where they, along with Shaykh Hassan and other African adoptive fathers and mothers, collectively cared for everyone's children.[29] Othermothers like Dr. Karimah took her friend's son with her when she visited Medina Baye, while Dr. Khadijah relied on an othermother to take her son to Medina Baye. The willingness of Black American, Senegalese, and other African Tijani parents to engage in cooperative parenting and forge transnational spiritual kinship networks created pathways for Black American Muslim students to actualize the educational dreams of Medina Baye.

3

Pedagogy of Place

Everyday Islamic Education in Medina Baye

It was Thursday evening in 2017, which meant it was the weekend for Sadia and her fellow classmates at the African American Islamic Institute (AAII) School in Medina Baye, Senegal. Sadia was a 15-year-old Black American from the Anacostia neighborhood of southeast Washington D.C. Three years earlier, her parents had enrolled her and her younger brother, Aaqil, at the AAII School and entrusted them to the care of Shaykh Mahy Cisse and his wife Sayyida Kubra Askari-Cisse. That particular evening, Sadia decided to take advantage of her time off from school by walking to the Grand Mosque of Medina Baye to pray maghrib and make wazifa, a compilation of dhikrs that Tijanis recite aloud in congregation once a day.

Sadia and Aaqil were among the many Black American youth who were the second generation in their family to live and learn in Medina Baye. Sadia and Aaqil's paternal grandmother had been another beloved foremother of the Tijani community in the U.S. Her story was similar to those of the foremothers highlighted in the previous chapter. In the 1980s, Sadia and Aaqil's grandmother was a single mother raising three children in inner-city neighborhoods of Washington D.C. When I interviewed Sadia and Aaqil's father in 2022, he recalled, "[My mother] did her best to make sure that she imparted the lessons from the *deen* [religion] on us no matter what was going on around us. So we understood that while we were from this place, we didn't have to be of this place forever."

Sadia and Aaqil's grandmother's search for a positive schooling environment for her children initially led her to send them to an Islamic boarding school in another country. But in the late 1980s, her Ghanaian and Senegalese Tijani friends introduced her to Shaykh Hassan. She had previously belonged to a different Sufi tariqa, but she decided then

Figure 3.1. The Grand Mosque of Medina Baye, right before the sun sets and people arrive for maghrib, July 2022. Photo courtesy of the author.

to join the Tijani tariqa. In 1995, she convinced Sadia and Aaqil's father, who was nearing his sixteenth birthday, to take a three-week trip to Medina Baye. Sadia and Aaqil's father explained, "My mom just didn't want me to end up in a coffin or jail. She was doing everything she could to keep her babies out of the streets, and she knew that she couldn't do it alone. And that takes a lot for a single Black woman to say, 'I can't raise a man alone.'" She embraced the system of collective care that the Tijani tariqa offered, as she turned to Shaykh Hassan for assistance in helping raise her son. She arranged for her son to travel to Medina Baye with her Senegalese Tijani friend. By the end of the three weeks, Sadia and Aaqil's father called his mother and, much to her surprise, informed her that he wanted to stay longer.

Sadia and Aaqil's father explained his decision: "I hadn't felt love in a long time. There's this specific love that men give men that is missing in the world and it is missing at an astronomical rate in terms of Black folk. I'm not talking about just American [Black folk]—I mean throughout the diaspora.... All I saw in Medina Baye were scholars, world leaders, generals, presidents, kings following Shaykh Hassan, men following him and they followed him because of a defined love that Allah has put in men that we are supposed to share with other men. It was transforming." Sadia and Aaqil's father ended up attending AAII for several years. Later, when he became a father, he wanted his own children to have the same opportunity. In 2015, he asked his mother to take Sadia, then aged 12, and Aaqil, then aged 10, to Medina Baye, for what would be her final trip to the city before she passed away.

Back in Medina Baye, that night, Sadia ventured out alone. Her friends said they were too tired to join her. Sadia walked along the sandy streets from her dormitory, past her school and the corner store where she liked to buy snacks, and to the mosque. Sadia had changed out of the faded skinny jeans, knee-length cotton tunic, and stretchy jersey scarf she had on earlier. She donned a bright, tie-dye *melfa*, a neatly and elaborately wrapped garment stretching several yards of fabric that she had recently purchased from an elderly woman who brought in the latest stock from Mauritania. Sadia reserved her melfas for her visits to the mosque. Tightly looped around her right wrist was her dhikr beads—a hundred shiny, turquoise-colored stones threaded together on a thick, black string that she purchased from a Togolese vendor who had a stall in the mosque's courtyard.

Sadia had not yet joined the Tijani tariqa, so she was not obligated to attend wazifa or other Sufi gatherings that brought scores of Medina Baye residents to the Grand Mosque on a daily basis. Yet that was exactly what she wanted to do on her free evening. Sadia slipped off her plastic flipflops, smiled and nodded at the elderly women leaned up against the wall, and found an empty spot inside on the thick, maroon carpet. She sat down quietly, neatly folding her legs to leave space for latecomers. Body leaned forward, head bowed in concentration, Sadia let her beads rest on her lap, her thumb gently moving each stone on the string with every utterance of dhikr. In a soft voice that blended with those of the women around her, Sadia recited the Arabic phrases that she had memorized through osmosis over the years of growing up in a Tijani household. Joining in with the hundreds of people congregating inside the mosque and pouring out onto the courtyard, Sadia became part of a steady chorus of believers who took a pause from their day's activities to sit, be still, and reflect upon the meanings of the blessed phrases they recited.

Figure 3.2. A row of women seated inside the Grand Mosque of Medina Baye, holding dhikr beads and making wazifa, November 2023. Photo courtesy of the author.

After wazifa, Sadia stood up, stretched out her legs, grabbed her flip-flops, and walked out onto the courtyard. She strolled by several small groups of women, some praying, some reading Qur'an, and others reciting dhikr under the starry night sky while they waited to hear the adhan for isha. Sadia walked up to Shaykha Ruqayya Niasse, one of Shaykh Ibrahim Niasse's daughters who had been born on the very night that Shaykh Ibrahim moved his nascent community to Medina Baye (Niasse 2015). Shaykha Ruqayya was highly regarded as an Islamic scholar, educator, and advocate of girls' and women's empowerment. At the encouragement of her father, Shaykha Ruqayya wrote an Arabic treatise on the role of women in Islam, in addition to other works about the education of Muslim children and girls that have since been widely used as textbooks throughout West Africa (Marshall 2015). Shaykh Ibrahim had also asked his daughter on many occasions to deliver speeches on religious matters at gatherings with women and men alike in Medina Baye and elsewhere. Shaykha Ruqayya was spiritual guide to thousands of Tijani women and men in Senegal, Nigeria, Ghana, and the U.S.

An elderly woman in her late eighties, Shaykha Ruqayya moved about slowly, each of her tender steps seemingly weighted with time. Most nights when she came to the mosque, Shaykha Ruqayya was accompanied by two young men who had dedicated themselves to *khidma*, or acts of service for their spiritual guides. These young brothers clung to Shaykha Ruqayya's hands, attentively clearing her path and holding her steady as she walked. Whenever she came for wazifa, Shaykha Ruqayya tended to sit in the same place in the courtyard. Despite being renowned locally and internationally, Shaykha Ruqayya sat with fellow Tijani women. The two brothers laid down a velvety blue, cushioned prayer rug, then unfolded a black plastic chair and a thick, rose-colored pillow for her to sit and lean on.

Sadia greeted Shaykha Ruqayya, respectfully placing her right hand over her heart as she approached the shaykha. Shaykha Ruqayya smiled and asked Sadia in Wolof how she and her family were doing. Such a question might suggest a great closeness between the Sadia and Shaykha Ruqayya, but it was a common greeting among the Tijani shuyukh and residents of Medina Baye. Sadia assured her that everyone was doing well. Shaykha Ruqayya opened her palms to make a dua for Sadia. Sadia thanked her and departed, making space for the others waiting behind her.

Figure 3.3. Shaykha Ruqayya Niasse (center) seated with other Tijani women in the courtyard of the Grand Mosque of Medina Baye, August 2022. Photo courtesy of the author.

Sadia continued walking in the courtyard until she reached the *maqam*, the mausoleum where Tijanis make ziyara to the esteemed spiritual guides who have facilitated their journey on the Sufi path. Sadia methodically stopped at the gravesites of Shaykh Ibrahim Niasse (d. 1975), his closest murid and son-in-law Sayyidi Aliou Cisse (d. 1982), and his oldest grandson Shaykh Hassan Cisse (d. 2008). These were the three prolific figures who had facilitated Sadia's grandmother's introduction to the Tijani tariqa in the 1980s, her father's educational sojourn in Medina Baye in the 1990s, and now, her and her brother's studies there. She gently touched the soft fabric that covered each tomb. Sadia recited *salatul fatih* (the most blessed salawat on Prophet Muhammad used by Tijanis) and a specific combination of surahs that Tijanis recite when making ziyara to those who have passed away. Sadia ended by making a dua about her own needs, including that Allah make it easy for her to become a hafiza.

Sadia then walked the short distance to *keur Pa*, where Sayyida Fatima Zahra Niasse lived (d. 2020). Affectionately called Ya Fatou, she was Shaykh Ibrahim's oldest child, the wife of Sayyidi Aliou Cisse,

Figure 3.4. Women and men visiting the maqam to make ziyara after wazifa, May 2025. Photo courtesy of the author.

Figure 3.5. Sayyida Fatima Zahra "Ya Fatou" Niasse (d. 2020). Photo source unknown.

and the mother of Shaykh Hassan, Imam Cheikh, and Shaykh Mahy. Like her younger sister Shaykha Ruqayya, Ya Fatou was one of the most esteemed women in Medina Baye. Her sons, who were all formidable scholars, consistently sought her advice before they made important decisions. Many Black American students who studied in Medina Baye during the 1980s and 1990s, including Sadia's father, told me how Ya Fatou was particularly beloved to them. She had been their Senegalese othermother, looking out for them, feeding them, encouraging them, and caring for them as they lived and learned away from their parents. Several remarked, with deep admiration and pride, how Ya Fatou was a woman of khidma—always serving her community. Some years back, Ya Fatou had suffered a stroke that impeded her mobility and speech. Since then, she spent most of her days in her bedroom under the affectionate care of her children, grandchildren, and other Tijanis. Like the young men who did khidma for Shaykha Ruqayya, those who cared for Ya Fatou offered to do so out of love, respect, and honor for their spiritual mother.

Sadia pulled back the curtain that hung loosely from Ya Fatou's bedroom doorway and entered the modestly furnished room. Her final ziyara of the night would be to a living spiritual giant of the community. Kneeling closely next to Ya Fatou's bed, Sadia greeted her and asked Ya Fatou to pray for her. Sadia then quietly slipped out, rushing back to her dormitory to relax with her friends and scroll through Instagram before it was time to eat dinner. She wanted to be well-rested for the morning, when she would have to go in for an extra weekend session at school so that she could study the ayats that she had been struggling to memorize throughout the past week.

I interviewed Sadia the day before she flew back to Washington D.C. for a brief visit, her first trip back there in three years. I asked her if she had any reflections about her time in Medina Baye. Sadia explained,

> When I first came, my dad was always so on me about Islam and about my deen. He was like, "When you go there [Medina Baye], it should help you" blah blah blah. And I didn't even understand what he was talking about because he was always so strict about it. But when I came here, it was so much easier for me because of the people that are around me, and the environment that we're in, makes it easier because everybody is always going to the masjid, everybody is always dhikring, all this stuff, so that makes it easier. 'Cause you know, in America, you're around other people who aren't really doing all the stuff, so it's harder. But when you come here, everybody is doing the same thing so it's easier because you're so used to it, because it's a habit. And you see everyone doing it.

* * *

Both Sadia's father and grandmother had been drawn to the possibilities of Medina Baye, which promised to bring to life their freedom dreams of a Black Muslim social world where young people could live and learn freely and fully. Growing up, Sadia had heard her father share stories about Medina Baye, and she patiently listened whenever he strolled down memory lane. Yet it was only after Sadia arrived there that she developed her own understanding about the possibilities that came with studying in Medina Baye.

Over the past three years, Sadia had come to know Medina Baye as a place where she, as a young Black Muslim woman, felt comfortable walking to the mosque by herself. It was a place where she interacted with spiritually esteemed Black Muslim Tijani women. It was a place where she took part in congregational Tijani worship activities that were meaningful to her. It was place where she observed ethical behaviors and social practices that she incorporated as everyday habits. Though Sadia's formal Islamic education took place at AAII, the comments she made during our interview indicated that the broader Black Muslim Tijani world of Medina Baye was a major part of her education. For Sadia, the city was her classroom, the residents her teachers, and Tijani rituals her lessons.

When I asked Sadia how she had learned about the elaborate schedule of extra dhikr, ziyara, and worship that I observed her engaging in, she explained to me that she had accompanied her Tijani parents on the same routine while they were visiting Medina Baye. Now, on her own, Sadia participated in many of the key practices recommended for Tijanis seeking spiritual transformation in Medina Baye: offering khidma to their shuyukh and community; giving *hadiya* (gifts) to their shuyukh; attending wazifa and dhikrul jummah at the mosque; making ziyara to the spiritually esteemed; and spending time with their shuyukh. Such activities were deeply ingrained within the social fabric of Medina Baye and oriented daily life for the city's Tijani residents.

Sadia's experiences in and reflections about Medina Baye elucidate what I call its pedagogy of place, or the everyday moral education provided by the people, practices, and physical place of the Tijani hub that is Medina Baye. From Sadia's grandmother to her father, two generations of Black American Tijani parents sent their children to Medina Baye in hopes of immersing them in a nurturing Black Muslim social world that extended to an entire community and city. I use the term pedagogy of place to describe the educational possibilities that permeated throughout Medina Baye. Marking an approach to teaching that extended beyond formal places and sources of instruction, Medina Baye's pedagogy of place offered young people an Islamic education that was inherently relational and social. The city's pedagogy of place was anchored in the Tijani tariqa's distinct approach to Sufism, which emphasizes caring for, rather than withdrawing from, the broader society as a means of emulating the prophetic example and knowing Allah. In contrast to Sufi tariqas that emphasize worldly asceticism and social isolation, the Tijani tariqa encourages murids to engage in collective care. Medina Baye's pedagogy of place imparted lessons in relational piety that were learned, ingrained, and deepened through interactions with and observations of fellow community members. From Shaykha Ruqayya, to the young men who did khidma for her, to Ya Fatou, these people embodied what it meant to live as pious Muslims in community with others.

This chapter examines how Medina Baye's pedagogy of place shaped Black American Muslim youth's racial, religious, and gendered self-making. It shows how young people experienced the city as a liberating space of possibility that they juxtaposed to their previous experiences in schools, mosques, and neighborhoods across the urban U.S. In Medina Baye, they encountered an entire city of believers who strived to emulate the lifestyle of Prophet Muhammad. This ideal originated in the seventh century on the Arabian Peninsula but was brought to life by West African and Black American Tijani women and men in present-day Medina Baye. These figures' spiritual esteem was marked by a relational piety anchored in collective care. Day in and day out, morning and evening, from their homes to the mosque to the city streets, young people observed how Tijani leaders served the community with their time, physical labor, and material wealth. These leaders represented living mirrors—calling to mind the historic example of Prophet Muhammad and projecting out new possibilities for the Black American Muslim youth who observed them. As youth engaged Medina Baye's pedagogy of place, they encountered generative moral blueprints that they drew upon as they crafted their own understandings of what it meant to live in the world as young Black Muslims.

Medina Baye: A Maroon Geography

Medina Baye's pedagogy of place was informed by the city's history. Shaykh Ibrahim named the city after Medina al-Munawara, a place in present-day Saudi Arabia that Prophet Muhammad established in the seventh century. When Prophet Muhammad first received divine revelation, he lived more than 400 kilometers (or 250 miles) away in Mecca. As residents of Mecca embraced Islam, the city's ruling tribe, the Quraysh, feared Prophet Muhammad's growing influence. The Quraysh levied economic sanctions against the Muslims and barred them from openly practicing their faith. Recognizing the harsh conditions that his new community of Muslims faced, Prophet Muhammad urged some people to seek refuge by making *hijra* (migration). Hijra is an Islamic strategy of flight from hostile lands and is prescribed in the ayat: "Was not Allah's earth spacious enough for you to *migrate* to some other place?" (Qur'an 4:97, emphasis added). This group of Muslims made hijra from Mecca to the faraway lands of Abyssinia (in present-day Ethiopia and Eritrea). Most others remained with Prophet Muhammad in Mecca. However, 13 years later, as the Muslims who remained in Mecca continued to endure discrimination there, Prophet Muhammad encouraged more among his community to make hijra. This second group did not travel as far as the first. They went to Yathrib, an Arabian city known shortly thereafter as Medina al-Munawwara. It became a safe haven where they could live fully and freely as Muslims.

Approximately 1,300 years later and more than 3,000 miles westward, in 1929, Shaykh Ibrahim publicly announced he had been endowed with the *fayda* (flood) of divine knowledge, a long-anticipated, esteemed spiritual ranking that more than a century earlier Shaykh Ahmad al-Tijani had predicted a future Tijani leader would ultimately usher in. In 1930, Shaykh Ibrahim made hijra from the village of Kossi (in the Kaolack region of present-day Senegal) to a new, nearby rural area that he named Medina Baye. Baye is the Wolof word for father, and it is a title that many murids affectionately use to refer to Shaykh Ibrahim, whom they see as their spiritual kin and call Baye Niasse.

Like Medina al-Munawara, Medina Baye offered Muslims a safe haven where they could pursue spiritual transformation outside of the direct control of the French colonial administration, which ruled the region at the time. Medina Baye followed a model popularized by Islamic scholars throughout Senegambia (in present-day Senegal, Gambia, and Mauritania, as well as parts of Mali and Guinea) from the twelfth century onwards, who established communities in spatial isolation from lands perceived to be less hospitable (Kane 2016; Levtzion 1994; Sanneh 1989).[1] In these communities, Islamic scholars built a Qur'an school, a mosque, and a farm, thus developing the educational, religious, and economic infrastructure necessary for the community to sustain itself materially, fortify itself spiritually, and make it semi-autonomous from the state (Babou 2007; Seesemann 2015; Ware 2014). In Medina Baye, Shaykh Ibrahim similarly established these three institutions, laying the foundation for his Tijani community to survive and thrive on its own terms.

The founding story of Medina Baye—as a destination of fugitivity created by those who fled hostility, and as a place where a new community sustained itself—is also part of the Black Radical Tradition. In both its historical and contemporary existence, Medina Baye represents what Celeste Winston terms maroon geographies, or spaces of freedom where Black people sustain life-affirming communities. Such spaces originated among self-emancipated Black people who rebelled and resisted chattel slavery in the Americas by fleeing racial violence and creating liminal, spatially isolated zones of liberation (Diouf 2014; Roberts 2015). Winston argues that maroon geographies contain several key components. One is a fugitive infrastructure, or an alternative structure and ethic that allows residents to sustain everyday life in the face of state abandonment. A second is a radical Black praxis of community, in the form of cooperative living strategies through which residents fulfil their human needs and "survive and reproduce life on their own terms" (Winston 2023, 107). However, despite the more liberatory forms of community that exist in maroon geographies, these places are not fully independent. A third component of maroon geographies is therefore a strategic entanglement with the state, which forces residents to find methods of "crafting and enacting autonomy within a system from which one is unable to fully disentangle" (Bonilla 2015, 43).

Figure 3.6. The gate that marks the main entrance to Medina Baye, featuring a well-known picture of Shaykh Ibrahim Niasse smiling widely. Above Shaykh Ibrahim's picture are the words "BAYE NIASS"—the familial term of endearment that many Tijanis refer to him by. The words "There is no God but Allah and Muhammad is His messenger, peace and blessings upon him" are written in Arabic on both sides of Shaykh Ibrahim's picture, December 2017. Photo courtesy of the author.

Winston's concept of maroon geographies is useful in illuminating the ethical norms, social practices, and political economic arrangements that have sustained Medina Baye over the years and contributed to its pedagogy of place. From its founding until 1960, Medina Baye was within a broader territory that was colonized by France. During this period, Medina Baye was strategically entangled with the colonial administration, which heavily surveilled Shaykh Ibrahim's community but did not fully encroach on its semi-autonomous status or set up a permanent colonial outpost there (Kane 1997; Seesemann and Soares 2009). After Senegal became independent in 1960, Medina Baye became strategically entangled with the new government. Situated within an independent nation where 94 percent of the population was Muslim (Guend 2018) and where 58 percent of these Muslims belonged to the Tijani tariqa (Hill 2018, 7), Medina Baye was a major Sufi city that the government recognized as a site of power and pilgrimage.[2] During election seasons, politicians often visited Medina Baye to secure the goodwill and endorsement of the city's leaders. The government also helped to finance development projects in the city. For example, Senegal's president Macky Sall (2012–2024) subsidized costs for the construction of an amphitheater adjoining the Grand Mosque and *keur gan*, a large conference hall and guest house in the city. As Joseph Hill (2013) observed in his research in Medina Baye: "The hierarchy is ambiguous: Where politicians may see themselves as seeking religious leaders' political support, the religious community may see political leaders performing obeisance to religious leaders" (103).

Some high-profile investments and public gestures notwithstanding, the government's financial assistance was limited. The community maintained its own fugitive infrastructure. Shuyukh and their murids gathered funds to pave the few roads that existed in Medina Baye, install streetlights, and build a medical clinic, among other development projects. In 2019, Cheikh Ahmed Tijani Cheikh Ibrahim Niasse, the *khalifa* (administrative leader) of the community at the time, launched the Medina Baye Fund, an initiative to which residents could contribute in order to help finance public works projects such as building a water treatment center, an electricity plant, a new market, and a hospital (Camara 2023; Souleymane 2023). The fund reflected the community's commitment to advancing its own growth, rather than being at the mercy of a lackadaisical or inefficient government. In fact, Shaykh Mahy Cisse, who is the official spokesperson for Shaykh Ibrahim's movement, spoke directly to this impulse when I asked him to elaborate on whether Medina Baye received financial assistance from the government. He emphatically responded no, and asserted that the community tended to do things by itself. Shaykh Mahy then quoted his grandfather, Shaykh Ibrahim, who advised, "If you depend on the government, you'll always be last. But if you depend on Allah, you'll always be first." Similarly, in Shaykh Ibrahim's *Ifriqiya ila al-ifriqiyin* (Africa for Africans) letter, he contrasted African Muslims' well-known reputation for self-sustaining their institutions with those of Christian missionaries: "Are not the number of mosques, gathering places, and schools—in which [the Muslims] have always volunteered their learning—multiple times the number of churches (and missionary schools)? In all of this, there is no government support; the Muslims have always depended on Allah and themselves" (as cited in Wright 2015b, 81). In both Shaykh Mahy's response and Shaykh Ibrahim's letter were the rationale that reflected the community's theological emphasis on *tawakkul* (relying primarily on Allah to orchestrate all affairs), the political commitment to self-determination, and the maroon emphasis on maintaining a fugitive infrastructure.[3] At the same time, given the major costs associated with financing public works projects, as well as the innumerable needs that divided the community's limited pot of funds, the city's commitment to self-sufficiency left it dealing with several unaddressed issues, such as few paved roads, a poor water sewage drainage system, and ineffective modes of trash collection and disposal.

While these outstanding development issues revealed the long-term challenges facing Medina Baye, the city remained as a maroon geography in large part because of the community's emphasis on khidma and hadiya. Among Shaykh Ibrahim's movement, khidma and hadiya were understood to be essential practices that helped Tijanis gain *marifa* (experiential knowledge of Allah) and meet one another's basic needs. These two practices thus also contributed to the city's fugitive infrastructure and radical Black praxis of community. From the twentieth to the twenty-first century, as the centrality of farming waned, murids did other types of khidma that brought benefit to their shuyukh and the community at large, such as cooking, cleaning, doing security, driving, teaching, and translating. Their willingness to give monetarily also fueled the city's hadiya economy. In a community that long shied away from government support, and in a Senegalese cultural context in which leaders were expected to provide for their followers (Wright 2015a, 101), murids' contributions to the hadiya economy made it easier for shuyukh to fulfill their role as the primary social safety net for the people of Medina Baye. Many of these residents were among the 21 percent of households in rural areas of Senegal such as Kaolack (the region where Medina Baye was located) that experienced food insecurity (USAID 2018) and received little to no assistance from the government. While the hadiya the shuyukh received did not match the vast sums of money they spent to sustain the community (Wright 2015a, 101), receiving hadiya nonetheless helped alleviate the shuyukh's costs associated with caring for residents. The shuyukhs' collective care practices included regularly distributing money to residents in need; gifting cows, rams, and goats to residents during *gamou* (an event commemorating Prophet Muhammad's birthday) and *Tabaski* (the Wolof equivalent of the Arabic term Eid ul-Adha); allowing murids to live indefinitely in the shuyukhs' homes free of charge; providing daily lunches and dinners to dozens of murids; sending daily bowls of food to dozens of households in the city; paying for medicine for sick residents; and providing free schooling for murids and/or their children.

Overall, as Tijani shuyukh and their murids followed Shaykh Ibrahim's advice to do khidma and give and redistribute hadiya, residents maintained a fugitive infrastructure and radical Black praxis of community through which they cared for one another largely independent of the state. For Sadia and other Black American youth who came to Medina Baye, these aspects of the maroon geography shaped the city's pedagogy of place. It offered them lessons about how they should care for one another. Combined with the founding vision and ongoing legacy of the city as a haven, these dynamics helped forge Medina Baye into a nurturing, city-wide social world.

A Place of Safety

"My life here, it doesn't compare to my life in America. My life is way better here than it was in America. My mom just told me, 'America is changing.' People are getting shot. Young Black males like myself are getting

shot every day. And I just make dua for my family every day that I don't have to get one of those calls."
—Abdullah, a 14-year-old from Brooklyn who had lived in
  Medina Baye for one year

"In America, I just didn't have a lot of freedom. I couldn't even walk down to 7/11. Here I can walk all the way to the masjid. . . . That's pretty far compared to where I could walk in D.C. Because people are always paranoid that someone is going to do something to you because you're Black, because you're Muslim, because you're a *Muslimah* [Muslim woman]. Medina Baye is perfectly safe. It's not like they're running around like the police do [in the U.S.] and shoot teenagers that are our age because they're Black Americans. We're perfectly fine. I mean, the only people who are armed here are the police force, and they're all the way in Dakar, so we're perfectly safe!"
—Sadia, a 15-year-old from Washington D.C. who had lived in
  Medina Baye for three years

When I asked young people what made their life in Medina Baye so different from that in the U.S., many matter-of-factly described their greater sense of safety and improved quality of life. They talked about Medina Baye as a place where they need not worry about police brutality, racialized-gendered terror, or anti-Muslim violence. Coming from a country where driving, jogging, and sleeping were just some activities that resulted in the murder of Black people, young people experienced Medina Baye as the fulfillment of a freedom dream. They could lay down the heavy burdens that had long weighed on them, the fears that they might be harmed at any moment.

While Abdullah and Sadia framed the experience in Medina Baye as completely unlike that in the U.S., a few young people acknowledged the overlaps between their lives in both places. For instance, Musa, a 17-year-old from Atlanta, explained that his parents made sure he had lived "in a bubble" and Soraiya, a 15-year-old from Washington D.C., admitted that her parents had provided her with a "sheltered" upbringing around other Black and Muslim families. Yet even the phrases and words these youth used betrayed the fleeting nature of safety in the U.S.; if or when young people ventured outside of the nurturing social worlds that their parents had deliberately curated, they could fall into harm's way.

Moving to Medina Baye offered Black American youth a relief from the psychological burdens they carried in the U.S. In *The Pursuit of Happiness*, Bianca Williams (2018) similarly found that Black American women who vacationed in Jamaica experienced an "affective and seemingly physical transformation" as they spent time in a country "where they feel free to express themselves as Black American women" (113–114). Williams notes that not every tourist made meaning of Jamaica in this way. Black American women experienced Jamaica in this liberating way precisely because of their racialized and gendered subjectivities, national identity, and previous experiences in the U.S. Having battled stress, racism, and sexism, these women experienced Jamaica as a Black paradise where they could live out their fantasies of cultivating joy, emotional wellness, and belonging with fellow Black people.

Similarly, as Abdullah and Sadia explained why they valued their time in Medina Baye, they infused their own meanings and freedom dreams into the city's landscape. In contrast, for example, to an elderly Senegalese grandmother who traveled to Medina Baye from Dakar during the height of French colonization, or a middle-aged, newlywed Ghanian Tijani man who migrated to Medina Baye after years of living in the postcolonial urban center of Accra, Black American Muslim youth in the twenty-first century experienced the city through their distinct religious, racial, gendered, national, and aged vantage points. In Medina Baye, these youth asserted that they need not worry about police terror, vigilante violence, or premature death.

While Williams documents the nurturing possibilities that Black American women actualize in Jamaica, she points out that the women try to curate their experiences so as not to ruin "the sense of fantasy, freedom, and enjoyment Jamaica gave them" (114). The women recognized that they constructed utopic narratives of life in Jamaica, and they consciously worked to preserve such depictions. Sadia's comment that there were no police in Medina Baye could be interpreted as reflecting a similar impulse. Each year during gamou and other major events, police patrolled the area around the Grand Mosque and had authority to apprehend people. This arrangement reflected the maroon geography's strategic entanglement with the state; though it often activated its own security force, *Shabaab al-Fayda* (Youth of the Flood), the community was not fully autonomous and still enlisted the government assistance from time to time. However, Sadia found the police presence in Medina Baye to be negligible. Whereas back in the U.S. she instinctually feared and understood the police to be a highly dangerous and potentially deadly entity that neither protected nor served her community, she did not view them in that same way in Medina Baye. After all, there, the police were not known for the same overt, racist histories and legacies of anti-Black social control and violence that plagued their counterparts in the U.S. While it was indeed possible that police in Medina Baye could abuse their power and enact unjust harm on the city's residents, Sadia preserved her fantasy of Medina Baye as a safe haven by (consciously or subconsciously) erasing the few traces of the police that she indeed observed.

Williams acknowledges that some may call Black American women's narratives of Jamaica as fantasies, but she asserts that "illusions and fantasies that are fulfilled fleetingly are still powerful and productive. Illusions can provide hope and sustain one's soul" (118). The same could be said for Sadia. As someone who felt unsafe in the U.S., the vision of Medina Baye as a this-worldly Black Muslim paradise had been meaningful for her. Reflecting on the impact of her time in the city, Sadia concluded that living there had made it easier for her to practice her faith. Medina Baye symbolized a maroon geography where she was hopeful that she could pursue spiritual growth unfettered. This vision not only unburdened her of her worries but also emboldened her to participate in the Tijani communal life.

For Sadia, Abdullah, and other Black American youth I spoke to, they described Medina Baye as "way better" not only because of the absence of daily oppressions. They also emphasized the new possibilities they experienced there, such as the freedom to "walk all the way to the masjid." Such comments described the fundamental nature of fugitivity, which is "not running *from* something as much as it is running *to* a destination that is created and determined by those who are experiencing injustice" (Stovall 2020, 4, emphasis in original). This is not to overlook the violent circumstances that compel people to create maroon geographies, but rather to center the life-affirming ways of being and belonging they cultivate after satisfying the initial need to flee.

This dual dynamic—of an escape and a haven—has been evident throughout Medina Baye's history as a maroon geography. Medina Baye was founded as an escape and place of refuge where Tijanis could deepen their faith. By the 1980s, when Black American Tijani parents started sending their children there, they were not solely concerned with sequestering young people from harms in the U.S.; they were also attracted to the educational possibilities that the city promised. Sadia and Abdullah's comments similarly reflected this dual vision, pointing to an awareness of and desire to dream and live beyond anti-Black and anti-Muslim violence.

Their experiences of Medina Baye as a space of relief and possibility made it akin to what Sylvia Chan-Malik terms safe harbors. Writing about Muslim women of color in the twentieth century U.S., Chan-Malik (2018) defines safe harbors as spaces of respite from racism, sexism, poverty, and white supremacy where women could "protect and nurture their bodies, minds, and souls . . . while using Islam's teachings to navigate and find solace from urban life" (43). Chan-Malik documents how Muslim women of color found safe harbors in physical places such as mosques or homes, in social spaces such as their friends' or spouses' company, and in ideological spaces such as Islam itself. In these safe harbors, Muslim women of color disassociated from the violence and totalizing gaze of their oppressors. They were also able to fortify their emotional, physical, and spiritual well-being and construct "expansive identities beyond the U.S. nation-state, beyond the racist terrains that circumscribed their bodies and minds" (ibid., 59).

For Black American youth, the entire city of Medina Baye was a safe harbor, and nestled within it were smaller safe harbors. Sadia's safe harbors encompassed the streets that she felt comfortable walking alone on, the mosque and maqam that she felt welcomed to enter, the wazifa which she felt at ease participating in, and the shuyukh who prayed for her. These safe harbors were also key aspects of Medina Baye's pedagogy of place; they were spaces of Islamic education where Sadia learned how she should treat others and fill her time.

In Medina Baye's safe harbors, many Black American youth felt emboldened to independently roam about without adult supervision—a practice that was also a norm among Senegalese and other African children and youth. Young people went by themselves to visit the shuyukh at their homes. In the afternoon, if they wanted a little snack, they could visit the women who fried and sold fish *fatayas* (savory pastries) on the side of the road. And if there was nothing else to do, several young women told me they loved nothing more than to *doxee*—a Wolof word that meant walking, a simple but pleasurable pastime that allowed them to observe the sights, sounds, and action of everyday life. Youth explained to me that these seemingly mundane acts of movement were so memorable because such activities were seldom possible in the U.S., where they tended not to be allowed to venture out too far alone. Concerned about their safety, parents often restricted Black children's freedom of movement in order to keep them out of harm's way (Dow 2019; Thomas et al. 2014). Yet in Medina Baye, these same Black American parents encouraged their children's mobility. Parents who remarked that they generally accompanied their children everywhere in the U.S. readily asked their children in Medina Baye to run to the nearby *bitig* (corner store) to buy them cold bottles of water or credit for their cell phones. Such requests indicated that parents had not only relaxed their safety concerns in this safe harbor, but also that they recognized that their children had grown responsible enough to handle such duties.

Being in Medina Baye's safe harbors encouraged and enabled many young people to do khidma. Black American youth relished in their newfound sense of physical safety and freedom of mobility. They quickly developed the experience, cultural knowledge, and linguistic fluency to help orient newcomers to spiritual life in the city. When Black American and other English-speaking pilgrims entered the maqam, youth filled these guests in on what they should recite and who was buried where. In the courtyard of the mosque, as guests browsed through piles of kufis embroidered with designs ranging from simple stars and crescents to intricate geometric patterns, the youth helped them carefully sift through the goods to find the ones of the highest quality. Black American youth who had become fluent in Wolof helped guests converse with vendors, first translating queries about what stones a particular set of dhikr beads were made of and then haggling to get the best deals. Young people who had memorized the shuyukhs' schedules walked with guests to the shuyukhs' homes and patiently waited until they knew that the guests had an audience with the shuyukh. Some youth delivered piping hot steel bowls of rice, meat, and sauce from the shuyukhs' kitchens to the front door of guests staying several blocks away. In some instances, these acts of khidma were responsibilities assigned to young people by adults who saw them as having the street savvy, trustworthiness, and competence to carry them out. In other instances, youth volunteered with great pride and confidence. In either case, young people's ability and willingness to do khidma in public contributed to their everyday Islamic education. In Medina Baye's safe harbors, Black American Muslim youth took advantage of opportunities to learn from the city's people, practices, and physical place as they nourished their own identities, collectively cared for each other, and worked on becoming those who were most beloved to Allah.

Prophetic Practices

> "They follow extra sunnahs. If you're here, you just think that's the way of life, but actually, it's Islam. I see it all the time with anybody. They see something in someone else's way, they'll move it out of the way. That is sunnah. I feel like, they just grew up learning that. We didn't grow up doing that in the U.S., but that's sunnah! The things they just do in life here, that's the sunnah. If I was memorizing Qur'an somewhere else, I wouldn't learn that."
> —Hafsa, a 19-year-old from Atlanta who had lived in Medina Baye for five years

Hafsa made this comment as she pressed a large white onion against her palm. With quickness and precision, she diced the onion into what seemed like a thousand pieces using a small, thin, and deceptively flimsy yet incredibly sharp knife. As one of the oldest Black American female students at AAII, Hafsa had more latitude than her peers to do as she pleased in her free time. But she preferred to spend her time off from school reading or helping out in the kitchen at Sayyida Kubra Askari-Cisse's house—the place where Hafsa had lived for the majority of her time in Medina Baye. Hafsa had become quite efficient at cutting onions, potatoes, and carrots for the communal meals that the women in Sayyida Kubra's kitchen prepared for Shaykh Mahy's guests and neighbors. Hafsa sat on a wobbly wooden stool, hunched over as she chopped, blinking away the tears that welled in her eyes from the

Figure 3.7. A young person carries a plate of food on her head that she will deliver to a guest, May 2025. Photo courtesy of the author.

onions, somehow focused on the task at hand while also talking to me and chiming into the ensuing conversation in Wolof with Tijani women from Senegal, Guinea, Ghana, and Burkina Faso who had come to offer domestic labor as khidma to their shaykh's wife. These African Tijani women participated in cooperative living strategies, cooking for themselves and dozens of others as they enacted a radical Black praxis of community and pursued spiritual growth in their maroon geography.

The khidma and conversation in Sayyida Kubra's kitchen were part of the Islamic education Hafsa experienced as she interacted with people in Medina Baye. In her comments, Hafsa pointed out that their everyday practices—which at first glance appeared to be random acts of kindness—were patterned after the sunnah. In contrast to actions that were *fard* (obligatory), sunnah actions were blessed but voluntary. The sunnah encompassed innumerable daily practices that Prophet Muhammad upheld and recommended. It included preferences such as wearing green or white (the colors that were most beloved to and frequently worn by him), habits such as sitting down when eating a meal, ritual acts such as reciting Surah al-Kahf on Fridays, and behaviors such as smiling at others. In making the case that the people of Medina Baye had incorporated these sunnahs into their daily practices, Hafsa cited a relational act within the sunnah; the action that Hafsa observed was mentioned in the hadith: "Removing a harmful thing from the path is a charitable act." While there were of course numerous other aspects of the sunnah that Medina Baye's residents strove to uphold, the fact that Hafsa pointed to a relational act underscored the community's emphasis on emulating the prophetic example through practices of collective care.

Scholarship on Black Muslims in Africa and in the U.S. has often emphasized their seemingly syncretic religious practices, and as such, has depicted them as less orthodox than their co-religionists in and from the Middle East (Marty 1917). In contrast, Hafsa contended that people in Medina Baye not only adhered to the core tenets of Islam, but exceeded what was required. When people moved something out of the way, they embodied Prophet Muhammad's example. Rudolph Ware (2014) argues that such prophetic deeds are commonplace in Senegal, where the "goal of Qur'an schooling is not just to teach the book but also to fill children with the Word of God, allowing them to embody the Prophetic example" (8). Similarly, writing about Qur'an schools in Morocco, Helen

Figure 3.8. An intergenerational group of women do khidma and chat together in Sayyida Kubra's kitchen while they cook lunch, August 2022. Photo courtesy of the author.

Boyle (2004) found that while there were no explicit lectures on manners and that teaching about ethics was not part of the official curriculum, "children learned through watching and through practice how to embody community values in their behavior" (32). For Hafsa, her education extended beyond the walls of her school, the pages of the Qur'an, and the direct instruction from her teacher.

To be fair, though Hafsa asserted that she learned new morals that "we didn't grow up doing" in the U.S., she had actually arrived in Medina Baye with an admirable character. Even as she studied thousands of miles away from Atlanta, she still lived out the lessons she garnered in the devout Black Muslim home she grew up in, the elementary school she attended, and the mosque that her family was active in. However, in Medina Baye, the sources and scale of her moral inspiration were amplified. She learned from an entire pan-African community of Tijanis, who embodied the spirit of prophetic service and collective care not merely as they interacted with one another in confined settings but also as they engaged in everyday public life throughout the city and set the community's overarching social norms. Concluding that "if I was memorizing Qur'an somewhere else, I wouldn't learn that," Hafsa's comments illustrated Medina Baye's distinct pedagogy of place that was geared towards teaching everyone to emulate the prophetic example by consistently serving others and the community at large.

The idea that residents of Medina Baye emulated the prophetic lifestyle was one that I heard from many Black American youth. Sadia made a similar point during one of our interviews:

> SADIA: Here you are living in Islam. Because in America, you know, people don't really live in it. They just talk about the hadiths, "This is bad. Oh, he did this, that." But here, you're actually living in it. You're not just talking about how this happened, how that happened in the Prophet Muhammad sallallahu alayhi wa sallam's time. You're actually living, like, how he lived.
>
> SAMIHA: So you're telling me the Prophet sallallahu alayhi wa sallam had Netflix?
>
> SADIA: No, you know what I mean! Not technology-wise.
>
> SAMIHA: So the Prophet sallallahu alayhi wa sallam went to the pool? Got some *mburu* [bread] bun and *akara* [black eyed pea fritters]?

SADIA: Not the twenty-first century-wise!

SAMIHA: So then what part of it?

SADIA: The overall, the way the Islam works here. They're not just talking about hadith. They're actually living through—'cause like in America, they talk about, "This is *haram* [forbidden]! That is haram! All that is haram! Everything is haram!" But you know, if you actually go to ask your shaykh, they're going to say, "*Bismillah* [Go ahead]." Or if you actually think it's haram, they're going to ask you, "Do you think it's haram? Look at the research. You can go look it up. You can go look in the Qur'an. And if they say you can do it, then bismillah. Go ahead." It's not like everything is haram, like everything is so strict, blah blah blah because it seems so oppressive or whatever. You can do what you can, as long as it's not haram, and everything is not haram!

Sadia's perspective was one that I encountered from many Black American Tijanis, who compared the city and its residents to Prophet Muhammad's historic community in Medina al-Munawarra. But having hung out with Sadia and her friends, I knew that they enjoyed Netflix, swimming pools, and other modern amenities that Prophet Muhammad's early community did not have access to. Yet Sadia asserted that such discrepancies were insignificant, and in fact saw no issue with engaging with those contemporary forms of leisure. As I observed at other times, being a Qur'an school student did not preclude Sadia from being obsessed with the Korean pop boyband BTS, watching their music videos on YouTube on repeat, and memorizing and practicing their complicated dance routines. Nor did it preclude her from scrolling on Instagram for fashion inspiration as she sketched designs of dresses that fused West African, Black American, and South Asian styles. In Sadia's estimation, an adherence to the outer trappings of Medina al-Munawarra was not important; rather, what was significant was that the people of Medina Baye preserved the underlying spirit of Prophet Muhammad's community. In a place where the shuyukh encouraged their students to investigate and implement the essence of Islam, Sadia asserted that they gained a nuanced and balanced approach to their faith—something that was a welcome change from the approach of the scholars she was familiar with in the U.S., who seemed to categorically outlaw everything.

Seerah, a 14-year-old student, encountered a similar strictness at the Muslim school she previously attended in Chicago. There, Seerah had been one of a handful of Black students among a predominantly Arab and South Asian student population. She admitted that the racial demographics and school culture made her feel "as if I wasn't Muslim at all, like I was that much out of place." Seerah went on to explain,

> Everything was kind of restricted. Because they're kinda obsessed with little things! They'll be like, "You can't wear an *abaya* [long gown]. It shows your shape! You can't do this. You have to wear gloves and socks and everything. Women have to cover their faces and everything." Like, that's just the little things, so you're not getting the main benefit of the religion. It's not like you're getting any more knowledge because you decided to wear some socks or some gloves. . . . There they focused more on little things, like *fiqh* [Islamic jurisprudence] and stuff, like the outward things. But the Tijani tariqa, it starts from the inside and then goes outside.

Echoing Sadia's observation that Muslims in the U.S. would say that "Everything is haram!", Seerah recalled that her teachers in Chicago were fixated on Islamic legal rulings of what was forbidden or not. Religious leaders paid so much attention to what was haram that Seerah later jokingly referred to them as "the haramy shaykhs." Seerah critiqued the leadership at her previous school for its emphasis on legislating minor rules about external appearance, especially for young women.

Though not explicitly named as such, the Muslim leaders that Sadia and Seerah critiqued perhaps ascribed to Salafi interpretations of Islam. In the contemporary context, Salafism is a Muslim reform movement associated with literalist approaches to the religion. In the U.S., where Islam is not the foundation of the country's dominant culture, the growth of the Salafi movement has contributed to the idea that many aspects of everyday life fall outside of the bounds of Islam. While Sadia and Seerah took issue with the U.S. scholars who claimed absolute authority over what was religiously permissible, such scholars in actuality represented only one of numerous Islamically sound interpretations. In fact, often, Salafis took stances that were at odds with Sufi approaches and that stressed the types of injunctions that the two young women encountered in Washington D.C. and Chicago.

Seerah observed a different norm in Medina Baye, especially in regards to gender. She told me that she had been pleasantly surprised to find more open interactions between women and men, such as when they helped each other with their lessons in class or chatted during breaks. In addition, youth saw women and men regularly collaborate with one another for khidma. For instance, as Hafsa peeled onions, young men peeked their heads into the kitchen to help. Like their female counterparts, these young men had come to Medina Baye for spiritual transformation. Some, like Hafsa, studied formally and spent a portion of their free time doing khidma. Moving in and out of their shaykh's wife's kitchen, these men handwashed the large platters that the meals would eventually be served on, or delivered the last-minute ingredients that the women in the kitchen needed. Women and men also worked together to assemble plates of food for the shaykh's guests. The men carefully carried the heavy plates to the living room, holding them steady as they gently lowered them onto the floor in front of the women and men who had gathered to eat with their shaykh. After the guests finished eating lunch, the men doing khidma served them steaming hot, frothy glasses of *attaya* (Chinese gunpowder green tea mixed with fresh mint leaves). Afterwards, the men poured a fresh round of the very sugary, highly caffeinated drink for the women who cooked, equipping them with an extra jolt of energy to hold them over for when they would return to the kitchen in a few hours to finish preparing dinner. These interactions reflected the mundane, meaningful, and respectful ways in which young Tijani women and men engaged in khidma and upheld a radical Black praxis of community. These interactions were common within Shaykh Ibrahim's Sufi movement and offered a paradigm of gendered piety that challenged misconceptions of Islam as a conservative religion that imposed stringent regulations upon women (Hill 2018)—misconceptions that Seerah had often heard back in Chicago.

Seerah attributed the gender norms she encountered in Medina Baye to the Tijani tariqa's broader approach to cultivating piety, which she asserted "starts from the inside and then goes outside." Zachary Wright (2015a) argues that the goal of Islamic learning in Medina Baye and other West African Muslim communities was to "'root' (*rasakh*) disposition into the very bodily presence of students, thereby producing individuals

Figure 3.9. Eight steel bowls filled with dinner cooked by the women in the kitchen and waiting to be distributed by a few young men, July 2022. Photo courtesy of the author.

who personified the religion" (6). For Seerah, being in Medina Baye meant gaining an Islamic education that was less concerned with legislating, and often policing, others'—especially women's—external actions. Instead, given its Sufi orientation, it was a place where the pursuits of piety and religious knowledge began internally and were ultimately fused into one's entire being.

Observing these interactions between young women and men as they learned, did khidma together, and pursued spiritual transformation reaffirmed Seerah's conviction that the Islamic education at her school in Chicago focused on the wrong priorities. In contrast to her previous schooling experiences in which being Black made her feel as if she "wasn't Muslim at all," Seerah encountered in Medina Baye a form of everyday moral education and radical Black praxis of community that emphasized ideals that were more meaningful to her. It was a place where the pinnacles of religious knowledge and piety were those who were Black, Muslim, Tijani, and often women. Medina Baye was thus a place where Seerah learned how to emulate prophetic practices of collective care from people in whom she saw herself.

Living Mirrors: Models for Young Black Muslim Men

In my interviews with Black American youth, I asked who their role models were. A few mentioned athletes and musicians. Others listed their biological parents or older siblings. However, the three most frequent responses I received were Imam Cheikh Tijani Cisse, Shaykh Mahy Cisse, and Sayyida Kubra Askari-Cisse—three of the most prominent Tijanis in Medina Baye. After Shaykh Hassan passed away in 2008, Imam Cheikh was appointed as the Imam of Medina Baye. In 2017, Imam Cheikh was ranked the most influential Muslim from sub-Saharan Africa (Schleifer 2016). In 2018, Shaykh Mahy was given the title "Voice of the Fayda" and appointed as the official spokesperson and global representative of Shaykh Ibrahim's branch of the Tijani tariqa. Imam Cheikh and Shaykh Mahy often met with heads of state from Africa and the Middle East and received international dignitaries at their homes. Sayyida Kubra was the Director of the AAII Legacy Academy and married to Shaykh Mahy, which meant that she provided critical support for many of his efforts.

All three individuals were incredibly busy, but they nonetheless cared for young people in Medina Baye. Just as Shaykh Hassan had done for more than two decades, the three adults did the work of kincraft, or "making one another spiritual kin" by sharing parenting responsibilities for young people whose biological parents lived elsewhere (Thomas 2021, 15). Reflecting their understanding of kincraft as a familial ethos, religious imperative, social praxis, and pan-African sensibility, Imam Cheikh, Shaykh Mahy, and Sayyida Kubra served as these youths' adoptive Senegalese fathers and Black American othermother.[4] All three adults welcomed young people into their households. Since Shaykh Hassan's return to Allah, many older male students lived free of charge in guest rooms at Imam Cheikh and Shaykh Mahy's homes. Female students and the younger male students stayed at Sayyida Kubra's house,[5] and since 2017, in a new dormitory around the corner from her house that she managed. These modes of pan-African Tijani kincraft gave young people an intimate look into the daily lives of prominent leaders, both when they were at home and when they went out and about.

Many youth described how and why they aspired to be like Imam Cheikh, Shaykh Mahy, and Sayyida Kubra when they got older. Though female and male students alike expressed admiration for all three figures, there was a gendered pattern among the Black American youth's responses; male youth tended to cite Imam Cheikh and Shaykh Mahy, while the resounding answer among female youth was Sayyida Kubra.

Aaqil, Sadia's 13-year-old brother, cited Shaykh Mahy as his role model. In 2015, when Aaqil moved to Medina Baye, he shared a room with about five teenaged boys from the U.S., Senegal, and the Gambia on the first floor of Sayyida Kubra's house. When I interviewed him in 2018, he had moved to the dormitory. Back when he lived at Sayyida Kubra's house, the 20 or so students who were part of her household ate lunch and dinner together. However, on weekends, Aaqil and two of his roommates often sought permission from Sayyida Kubra to instead eat with Shaykh Mahy and his adult guests. Even after Aaqil moved to the dormitory, he would walk over to Sayyida Kubra's house after isha with hopes of joining Shaykh Mahy and the others for dinner.

One evening, I saw Aaqil bolt up to Sayyida Kubra's roof, taking the stairs two at a time. As had been my habit when Shaykh Mahy dined at Sayyida Kubra's house, I had come to eat with him and his guests. Aaqil slipped his leather sandals off at the edge of the colorful straw mat that we gathered on. He walked directly up to Shaykh Mahy. With his head bowed and hand outstretched to greet Shaykh Mahy, a grin peeked out of the side of Aaqil's mouth as he tried to mask his excitement. Shaykh Mahy asked Aaqil how far he was in his studies. Shaykh Mahy had been closely following Aaqil's progress, since Aaqil was projected to become the next Black American hafiz at AAII. Aaqil later told me that those exchanges with Shaykh Mahy were nerve-wracking. They served as a reminder of the heightened pressure placed upon him to finish. But Aaqil also admitted that those interactions were motivating. Shaykh Mahy had been in his same shoes, Aaqil explained, as he too had become a hafiz in his youth. Shaykh Mahy shared stories with him about all that he had to go through to finish memorizing the Qur'an. Aaqil said that hearing those stories reminded him that becoming a hafiz was indeed possible.

When I asked Aaqil to elaborate on why Shaykh Mahy was his role model, we had the following conversation:

> AAQIL: Shaykh Mahy is a role model to me more than anybody else. I feel like, he's the one that's really motivating me. . . . I want to be like him.
>
> SAMIHA: Did you know him when you were in America?
>
> AAQIL: Yeah, I did. I saw him four or five times. I went up to New York for his conference at Shaykh Hassan's ziyara. And then he came down to D.C. once to take a flight back here [to Senegal].
>
> SAMIHA: So would you interact with him back when you were in America?
>
> AAQIL: Yeah, a little bit, but I didn't really understand anything until I came here and I saw what he did. And then my dad was like, "Don't tell everyone how much he's paying for this hotel." Like it's so expensive. I would say, "How does he have so much money?" My dad would say, "I don't know. You gotta find out."
>
> SAMIHA: So what did you find out?
>
> AAQIL: Uh, I really don't know how he got all that money. [*laughs*]
>
> SAMIHA: So after you came here, what did you learn from him?
>
> AAQIL: His kindness, mostly kindness, and knowledge really. I never really wanted all that until I saw him because I saw how far it got him. Like, if you can walk into your house with a whole bunch of

people behind you, you're probably like, "That guy must be famous!" I was like, "Woah! How come Shaykh Mahy has all those people behind him?" And then I realized that it's because he's helping so many other people.

Aaqil's limited interactions with Shaykh Mahy in the U.S. left him with questions about the shaykh's wealth—namely how and why Shaykh Mahy stayed in four- and five-star hotels when he visited New York City. Aaqil was not alone in wondering about this. Several people whom we invited to visit Shaykh Mahy or Imam Cheikh in the city similarly questioned their lodging arrangements, as did some longtime murids whom we invited to contribute to the costs of hosting our shuyukh. As someone who helped plan the logistics of Shaykh Mahy's trips to New York City, I knew that any hotel in Manhattan that had a suite large enough to accommodate the shaykh and the dozens of people who would come to visit him (and some of whom would commandeer the hotel suite's living room floor as their place of rest each night) would be costly. These were the unique burdens that came with hosting the shuyukh and collectively caring for our fellow Tijanis in one of the most expensive cities in the world. These were hardships that we didn't contend with when the shuyukh visited more affordable cities like Atlanta and Detroit, where they and out-of-town visitors typically stayed at the homes of local Tijanis. In New York City, we paid not necessarily for the shuyukhs' luxury, but for a space that was convenient and accessible for the shuyukh and those who came to see them. Despite these logistical considerations and our efforts to collectively care for the community, for some onlookers, the idea of Sufi shuyukh staying at a high-end hotel contradicted the popular conception of Sufis as cultivating piety by maintaining ascetic lifestyles. For others, the scene triggered memories of Christian prosperity preachers and opportunistic religious leaders who lived lavishly off donations from financially struggling followers. Our modes of collective care were thus often illegible to those who had witnessed scenarios where material resources tended to be hoarded rather than redistributed. These realities were perhaps why Aaqil's father was wary of the external perceptions about the shaykh's relationship to money.

Some first-time visitors from the U.S. expressed similar concerns when they arrived in Medina Baye. They remarked about how heartbroken they were to observe boys who looked to be no older than nine years old plead with them for coins to buy bread or shoes while families living in houses nearby drove around in Mercedes Benzes. Of course, such inequities were also everyday realities in the U.S., where a weary mother could stand by the highway ramp holding her infant daughter in one hand and a "help wanted" sign in the other as drivers in Teslas zoomed past, or where unhoused people could try to rest on a concrete park bench while families grilled burgers, sipped soda, and munched on potato chips nearby. In the U.S., many were conditioned to see others' hardships as unfortunate but inevitable, seldom reflecting on how or why some people in the racial capitalist society would always have much less than others. However, for some Americans visiting Medina Baye, the juxtapositions of poverty and wealth somehow felt more jarring there than in the country where they were born and raised; they thus interpreted the lifestyle choices of the Senegalese shuyukh and other African residents as ostentatious consumption.

However, as Americans spent more time in Medina Baye and learned from its pedagogy of place, they gained a better grasp of how the shuyukh's relationship to their material wealth was informed by the community's system of collective care. For example, many shuyukh owned multiple homes. Each had two or more floors, finely decorated living rooms in which they dined with guests, and numerous bedrooms that they reserved for their murids to stay in indefinitely and free of charge. The shuyukh also built separate guest homes to accommodate their growing number of murids, who were bursting from the seams of the shuyukhs' existing family homes. For lunch and dinner, the shuyukh enjoyed extensive spreads featuring imported fruits and dates as well as expensive local fish or meat. They seldom if ever enjoyed these meals alone or solely with their spouses and children. Their consistent habit was to eat with no less than ten people. The shuyukh ate directly from the same communal platters as their murids who sat on the floor next to them. The shuyukh owned multiple cars, which they let murids use if they needed transportation for trips to the hospital or airport. These everyday lifestyle choices demonstrated how the shuyukhs' wealth was a communal, rather than individual, resource that fueled cooperative living strategies.

After Aaqil joined Shaykh Mahy's extended household, he gained more context about the shaykh's wealth and learned how it sustained Medina Baye's fugitive infrastructure of collective care. The scene Aaqil described of Shaykh Mahy entering his house was a daily occurrence. When Shaykh Mahy briskly walked the several block distance from his home to the mosque for salat, ten or more murids quickly assembled to accompany him. Crowds followed him throughout the city, such as when he attended *gentes* (naming ceremonies) for his murids' newborn babies or visited sick murids. Some in the crowd asked for and received money as they rushed to keep pace with Shaykh Mahy. Aside from these on-the-go requests, it was common knowledge among residents that there were designated times and places where Shaykh Mahy gave out hefty stacks of money. Every morning, after Shaykh Mahy prayed fajr at the mosque and made ziyara at the maqam, he pulled out a pile of cash so crisp it had most likely been recently withdrawn from the bank for the sole purpose of being redistributed. He spread the money out among more than a dozen women and men, some of whom were sitting in wheelchairs and others who were known to care for orphaned children. Every afternoon as Shaykh Mahy headed to *asr* (late afternoon prayer), he distributed more crisp notes to an even larger group of people—mostly elderly women—who had congregated in the foyer of his house. One of Shaykh Mahy's murids from Burkina Faso who often helped withdraw and distribute the money estimated that Shaykh Mahy likely gave out approximately 125,000 CFA (more than $200 USD) each afternoon and 200,000 CFA (more than $330 USD) on Fridays alone. These public offerings were in addition to the private offerings that he gave to the lines of people who came to his living room. Guests would lean in, stressed out, as they showed him bills for medical prescriptions they desperately needed to purchase, estimates for the cost to repair their leaking roofs before the downpour of the rainy season became more intense, or explained other financial debts that their family had been saddled with. On cue, Shaykh Mahy would reach into the pockets of his flowing garments and discretely pass them a bundle of money—money which, often, he had received just moments earlier as hadiya from other murids.

As a member of Shaykh Mahy's pan-African Tijani family, Aaqil witnessed these encounters on a regular basis and had developed an

Figure 3.10. A crowd forms around Shaykh Mahy Cisse (center, directly under the umbrella) as he exits the Grand Mosque, November 2023. Photo courtesy of the author.

up-close perspective of the hadiya economy in practice. Reflecting on what he had learned over his years of observing Shaykh Mahy's interactions with residents in Medina Baye, Aaqil concluded, "People here need money a lot and Shaykh Mahy gives it to them a lot. He gives whatever he can. I feel that I should do more of that, to be a better person."

For Aaqil, Shaykh Mahy was a living mirror that foreshadowed what he could achieve academically and offered lessons on how he ought to carry himself in the world. By witnessing Shaykh Mahy's example—which was informed by Islamic, Tijani teachings and Senegalese cultural norms—Aaqil learned how material wealth was a resource that should be redistributed. This conception of wealth challenged capitalist impulses towards individual accumulation and hoarding. Furthermore, seeing the shaykh's example demonstrated that partaking in worldly pleasures did not undermine a believer's piety; if anything, wealth was a test—would the believer use the wealth that Allah had blessed them with to engage in collective care, or would they abuse that wealth to flaunt their privilege and enjoy ostentatious consumption? In fact, this dilemma was one that Shaykh Ibrahim directly addressed. Understanding that material wealth could be either a resource or a test from Allah, Shaykh Ibrahim warned his murids during a public class he gave in Medina Baye on the *tafsir* (exegesis) of the Qur'an: "The Divine [Allah] says to the world, O material world (*dunya*), serve the one who serves me, and wear out the one who serves you" (as cited in Wright 2022, 257). Shaykh Ibrahim's comments underscored that the rewards of the dunya were promised to those who served Allah, rather than those saw success in the dunya as an end in of itself. Indeed, those who used their wealth in ways that pleased Allah would be rewarded with further material gain. Aaqil observed how Shaykh Mahy did just that by using his money to help others and serve Allah. It was this generosity that Aaqil hoped to replicate.

Shaykh Mahy's public displays of wealth coupled with his acts of collective care aligned with the Tijani tariqa's emphasis on holistically emulating the prophetic model. Tijanis were instructed to treat wealth as a resource, not a vice. In fact, Shaykh Ahmad al-Tijani, who founded the tariqa, was known to be "extravagant in spending in the cause of Allah and feeding the poor" and "gave as if he did not fear poverty, neither desiring increase (in his wealth) nor ostentation" (Wright 2005, 124).

Shaykh Mahy's practices thus reflected the recommendations outlined by the founder of the tariqa, who himself replicated Prophet Muhammad's actions. What Aaqil admired as Shaykh Mahy's everyday moral practices in Medina Baye was thus an emulation of the prophetic example in the contemporary moment.

Living Mirrors: Models for Young Black Muslim Women

Many of the young Black American women cited Sayyida Kubra as their role model. They noted that she exemplified the academic accomplishments that were within their reach. Like them, she had journeyed to Medina Baye from the U.S. as a teenager with dreams of becoming a hafiza. She succeeded after seven arduous years. Female and male students alike explained that Sayyida Kubra shared stories with them about the struggles she faced as she was memorizing Qur'an and the sacrifices she made in order to finish. When young people vented to her about how they felt that their teacher had wronged them, or how their motivation had waned, Sayyida Kubra lent an empathetic ear, advocating on their behalf or offering sage advice on how to reframe their perspective.

Several young Black American women also explained that they were impressed by Sayyida Kubra's ability to effortlessly juggle multiple responsibilities. In 2003, she opened Medina Baye's first preschool, which she started in her house and volunteered at as the sole teacher, and eventually expanded into two locations that she directed and that served hundreds of students and were staffed by dozens of teachers. From 2017 to 2018, she also served as the director of Shifa al-Asqam Socio Medical Center, a clinic in Medina Baye that was founded by Shaykh Hassan and supported by his Black American murids, including Sayyida Kubra's mother, Dr. Khadijah Askari. During her tenure as director, Sayyida Kubra reestablished partnerships with doctors in Senegal and the U.S. and organized free clinic days that served more than a thousand residents in and around Medina Baye. In 2017, after 16 years of housing Qur'an students in her own home, Sayyida Kubra used her personal savings to build a four-story dormitory. After the bulk of students relocated to the dormitory, Sayyida Kubra continued to oversee their daily needs, including arranging their meals and calmly resolving their inevitable interpersonal conflicts. In 2018, she opened the AAII Legacy

Academy, a school that carried forward Shaykh Hassan's commitment to Islamic education and soon became the primary Islamic school in Medina Baye that Black American boarding students attended (with most young people I interviewed ultimately transferring there). Sayyida Kubra oversaw all the affairs at AAII Legacy Academy, including hiring and supervising teachers for its Preschool and Qur'an programs and developing extracurricular programs. Several young women (Black American and African alike) remarked about how Sayyida Kubra did all this while balancing the responsibilities associated with being the wife of one of the most prominent shuyukh in the city. Furthermore, while her marriage granted her high social and religious ranking in Medina Baye, numerous young women explained to me that Sayyida Kubra's scholarly credentials as a hafiza and her expansive work to benefit the community underscored that she was admirable in her own right.

On any given day during 2017 and 2018, when I conducted my longest period of fieldwork in Medina Baye, young people would see Sayyida Kubra race around the city. She would go from the preschool to the clinic to the dormitory and then back home, balancing what might be considered several full-time jobs. Her various responsibilities represented what Judith Casselberry calls spiritual labor, or the essential work that women undertake to sustain their congregations. In *Labor of Faith*, Casselberry's ethnography about African American women in a Black Pentecostal community, she argues that women's spiritual labor is integral to their congregation. Casselberry shows how women believers religiously multitask across domestic and professional spheres. The same women may juggle several roles, including teaching, cooking, cleaning, managing staff, and organizing events. These women model "a religious posture and work ethic for girls and women" and contribute to the congregation's notions of Black religious female personhood (Casselberry 2017, 86).

While Sayyida Kubra's spiritual labor and religious multitasking were feats that female and male students alike observed, it was almost exclusively the young women who remarked about wanting to emulate her example. Challenging the notion that women's contributions ought to be confined to the domestic sphere, Sayyida Kubra's religious multitasking offered young women a blueprint of the boundless possibilities they might aspire to. Through her example, they gained an expansive conception of Black Muslim religious female personhood—it could include being a mother, wife, organizer, scholar, and educator, among many other simultaneous roles.

Moreover, because Sayyida Kubra served as their othermother and treated them as her family, young people had an up-close look into her personal life. They saw how she navigated the spiritual labor and responsibilities that came with being the wife of an important shaykh. Youth took note of how she, as a Black American, navigated Senegalese cultural norms while serving diverse members within their pan-African Tijani community. While intently watching episodes of the latest Senegalese soap opera on the TV in Sayyida Kubra's living room, youth saw people come to visit her at all hours of the day. They watched as she took a pause from whatever she was doing, whether it be reading or tending to her own affairs, to make time for others. They observed the emotional labor she expended as she counseled visitors on how to deal with various crises—an aunt seeking prayers of protection for her nephew who she worried was headed down a bad path, a mother struggling to find a upstanding son-in-law for her daughter, a neighbor praying that her husband would heal fully and return home from the hospital shortly. Given that Sayyida Kubra was married to Shaykh Mahy, young people also told me that they were convinced that she had a lot of money. Much like Shaykh Mahy and Imam Cheikh did, young people encountered through Sayyida Kubra's example a moral blueprint for how the wealthy ought to redistribute their material abundance. They witnessed how Sayyida Kubra constantly gave money to or agreed to help find jobs for the steady stream of women and men who came to her house in search of assistance.

Young people also saw the grueling labor Sayyida Kubra shouldered as she too did khidma. On the days that Shaykh Mahy was at Sayyida Kubra's house, youth witnessed the physical strain and exhaustion that Sayyida Kubra experienced as she oversaw the cooking of lunch and dinner for dozens of people, including Shaykh Mahy, his guests, and her neighbors. If Sayyida Kubra was cooking on a day that she had work to finish up at the school or clinic, they would observe her get up early in the morning to make headway in the kitchen, step out to take care of her other obligations, and return in time to put finishing touches on the meals. If Sayyida Kubra's cooking days coincided with students' weekends, young women like Hafsa did khidma in the kitchen. These glimpses of Sayyida Kubra in her home illustrated to young people the tremendous physical workload that came with the esteem of being a community pillar.

Young women also witnessed the glamorous encounters Sayyida Kubra had out in public. As members of her household, young women often accompanied Sayyida Kubra as she moved about Medina Baye, a vantage point from which they saw her celebrity stature. When they strolled with Sayyida Kubra from her house to the mosque, they stepped aside as Tijanis rushed to greet her, asked her to pray for them, or offered to carry her and sometimes even the young people's own prayer mats. Young women smiled sheepishly as they stood next to Sayyida Kubra during Tabaski and gamou events, when people snapped pictures of her as if they were paparazzi, or when women and men alike came up and took pictures with her that ended up as their profile pictures on social media.

Hanaan, a 13-year-old from Detroit, explained to me the admiration that she and her peers had for Sayyida Kubra.

> HANAAN: With Aunty Kubra, you're like, "Oh yeah, you know that lady, and she owns the clinic and she has the preschool and she has all those American kids that came here to study. And oh yeah, she's also a Sayyida. Yeah, she's also a Sayyida on top of that." I feel like Aunty Kubra is a big role model for all of us. Like even when we're doing something as small as picking out clothes, we're like, "Oh yeah, I saw Aunty Kubra wear a fabric like this. Oh yeah, I saw Aunty Kubra wear her outfit made like this before."
>
> SAMIHA: What does that mean to you? What is a "Sayyida" in your opinion?
>
> HANAAN: A Sayyida is, well, a shaykh's wife or a shaykh's daughter. And the way people look up to shaykhs, they also look up to their wives as well as their daughters and sons and stuff. But they look up to their wives, so they get the name of a Sayyida, like a queen or something . . . So, "Sayyida this, or Sayyida that." And I feel like Aunty Kubra just owns that name.

According to Hanaan, Sayyida was not a title that Sayyida Kubra merely inherited through marriage or birth. Instead, Hanaan cited Sayyida Kubra's many accomplishments as evidence that she had rightly earned such a lofty title. Hanaan's rationale was reminiscent of the esteem held for another famous Sayyida in Islamic history—Sayyida Khadijah bint Khuwaylid, Prophet Muhammad's wife. Coincidentally, when Shaykh Hassan first met Sayyida Kubra as a young girl, she was known as Bimkubwa, a Swahili name that her parents gave her at birth. Shaykh Hassan later suggested she instead take on an Arabic name that sounded like and bore similar connotations as her birth name. He recommended Khadijatou Kubra—which means Khadijah the Great and was the title ascribed to Sayyida Khadijah bint Khuwaylid. She agreed, and her name become shortened in everyday practice to Kubra.

Muslims affectionately refer to Sayyida Khadijah bint Khuwaylid as one of the *Ummahat-ul-Mu'mineen*, or Mothers of the Believers. Prophet Muhammad described Sayyida Khadijah as one of the best women among the people of paradise. Prior to marrying Prophet Muhammad, Sayyida Khadijah was a successful businesswoman in Mecca. During their marriage, in the early days of Islam, she used her own wealth to help propagate the religion. Having emulated many of the virtues, economic redistributive practices, and spirit of service modeled by the historic Sayyida Khadijah, Sayyida Kubra represented a modern-day version of an ideal Muslim woman leader, thus "owning," in Hanaan's estimation, the esteemed title of Sayyida.

Alongside the historical meanings associated with the title of Sayyida, Hanaan likened it to that of royalty. Having observed how Tijanis in Medina Baye treated Sayyidas, Hanaan concluded that these women were similar to queens. Hanaan's word choice was significant. To begin with, mapped against an anti-Black, white supremacist cultural hegemony in the U.S. that typically projected controlling, denigrating images of Black women as mammies and matriarchs (Collins 1990), Hanaan's words defiantly challenged these tendences and instead conjured up the bold image of a Black Muslim queen. Furthermore, Hanaan's assertion that there were actual living, Black Muslim queens represented a joyful proclamation that echoed contemporary pro-Black cultural expressions that sought to showcase the historical presence and futuristic visions of Black (often African) women as queens (see, for example, *The Woman*

King, the historical film that dramatizes an all-female warrior unit in the Dahomey kingdom in West Africa, and the *Black Panther* films featuring the Queen and Princess of Wakanda). In contrast to both these erasures and recuperations, Hanaan contended that she and her peers had access to real-life Black American and African women whom they saw as royalty. Young women drew inspiration from these Black Muslim Tijani queens.

Many young women sought to emulate Sayyida Kubra's example, from her scholarly accolades and tireless khidma down to her elegant style. Just as Hanaan indicated, I saw young Black American and African women request that their Eid dresses be tailored in a design that matched Sayyida Kubra's outfits. After events, I saw young women post pictures of her on social media, marveling at how elegant "our mother" looked. I also observed young Black American and African women style their headwraps in the same way that Sayyida Kubra did, with a long, narrow fabric that matched their dress tightly wrapped around the frame of their head and tied into a bun, and a larger and wider *kala* (scarf) loosely draped over their head and shoulders. These fashion styles were informed by the aesthetic enacted by Senegalese, other African, and Black American Tijani women in Medina Baye. Young women made fashion choices inspired by a pan-African Muslim aesthetic.

In *Muslim Cool*, Su'ad Abdul Khabeer similarly examines how Muslim youth draw inspiration from Black culture. For many of Abdul Khabeer's (2016) Black Muslim youth interlocuters, these cultural and aesthetic expressions serve as the "performative blueprint" of their sincere Black Muslim selves (131). As an example, Abdul Khabeer analyzes three ways that Muslim women cover their hair. She charts how each style conveys unique religious, racial, and sociopolitical meanings. Among the styles Abdul Khabeer analyzes is a headscarf wrapped in a bun, which she associates with an Afrodiasporic tradition. It is the same style that Sayyida Kubra adorned as the first layer of her hair covering. Abdul Khabeer finds that some young Black Muslim women embrace the style because it makes them "feel more Black" (ibid., 129). Within a multiracial U.S. Muslim community in which anti-Black racism persists, Abdul Khabeer argues that young Black Muslim women "reclaim the Afrodiasporic headdress as Islamic, in contradistinction to the hegemonic legitimacy often afforded solely to Arab and South Asian styles of head covering" as the religiously appropriate way that Muslim women should cover (ibid., 122). The Afrodiasporic headdress is thus a powerful symbol within a Muslim community in which Blackness is often misnamed and devalued (ibid., 131). It offers young Black Muslim women a model for self-making that is rooted in the intersections of Blackness and Islam.

For young Black American women like Hanaan, Sayyida Kubra offered a performative blueprint that similarly built upon the intersections of, rather than binaries between, their racial and religious identities. Sayyida Kubra's performative blueprint affirmed, rather than negated, the overlaps between these young women's Black and Muslim identities. Sayyida Kubra's own style had been informed by the cultural sensibilities of Medina Baye's diverse, pan-African Muslim community. There, unlike in the U.S., Black Muslim women were not pressured to justify their fashion choices to Arab and South Asian Muslims whose religious rubrics were likely anchored in their own cultural norms. Instead, in a city and country in which Black Africanness and Islam had for centuries formed the basis of the dominant culture, the validity and richness of their gendered performances of Black Muslimness were taken for granted. For young Black American women, many of whom had shared with me that they had previously encountered some form of anti-Black racism from Arab and South Asian Muslims in the U.S., coming of age in Medina Baye offered them a new opportunity to fashion their identities outside of an anti-Black gaze which often constructed Black and Black American cultural expressions as haram or un-Islamic. As these young women lived and learned in a nurturing Black Muslim Tijani social world that extended to a society-wide level, they encountered a pedagogy of place that fostered their racial, religious, spiritual, gendered, and national identities. Through examples of Black American women such as Sayyida Kubra, young women like Hanaan gained performative blueprints that weaved together the various aspects of their identities and commitments. For these young women, Sayyida Kubra not only served as their exemplar of religious knowledge, gendered piety, and community leadership, but also as their style icon. Merging the different aspects of their desired future selves, Sayyida Kubra was a living mirror and their exemplar of Black Muslim religious female personhood.

Overall, for Black American Muslim youth, the Black American and African Tijani women and men leaders who collectively cared for them were living mirrors. They saw in these adults not only the timeless character of Prophet Muhammad, but also gendered ideals of who, how, and what they might be in the future. What made Imam Cheikh, Shaykh Mahy, and Sayyida Kubra beloved and admired by Tijanis in Medina Baye was the fact that they gave generously of their resources and time, providing advice, emotional support, money, and prayers to thousands of people whom they cared for as their spiritual family. As young people observed these esteemed leaders at home and in public, they gained an everyday moral education. They learned, by example, how becoming revered as a role model, celebrity, or royalty required one to embody the prophetic lifestyle in the contemporary Senegalese context and serve one's community with one's time, physical labor, and wealth. This was a blueprint of relational piety that they, as Black Americans, hoped to carry with them both in the present and in the future when they left Medina Baye.

Conclusion

Black American Muslim youth lived and learned in a maroon geography where they felt safe from the racial terror, gendered discrimination, and anti-Muslim violence that was endemic to the U.S. Yet the nourishing possibilities of the place extended beyond physical safety. Throughout the safe harbors of Medina Baye, they described experiencing their own freedom dreams and realities as they learned lessons that nourished their identities as young Black Muslim women and men.

In Medina Baye's maroon geography, residents remained strategically entangled with the Senegalese government. At the same time, Tijanis maintained a fugitive infrastructure through the hadiya economy. They also enacted a radical Black praxis of community through their cooperative living strategies and commitment to doing khidma. Taken together, the people, practices, and physical place of Medina Baye coalesced to form a specific method of teaching Black American Muslim youth. Young people learned from Tijani leaders who were their spiritual kin, as well as from African Tijani pilgrims and residents who strived to emulate the prophetic example of service. Young people learned by doing khidma, observing the hadiya economy, participating in congregational dhikr, and spending time with spiritually esteemed people. Youth learned in classrooms, living rooms, kitchens, mosques, streets, and corner stores. They refracted the lessons they gained through their racial, religious, national, gendered, and aged lenses and their lived experiences in the U.S. Young people spoke about how they witnessed the historic exemplars of Prophet Muhammad and his community in Medina al-Munawara be brought to life by Black Muslim Tijani women and men. These adults served as living mirrors that informed young people's own notions of spiritual esteem, scholarly achievement, and leadership, and expanded their imaginative possibilities of how to live in the world as pious Black Muslims.

As Black American youth learned from Medina Baye's pedagogy of place, they grasped the spiritual and social significance of cultivating a relational piety. On a practical level, practices of collective care enabled Medina Baye to remain a maroon geography where Tijanis could survive and thrive somewhat independent of the state. Yet on a spiritual level, these practices helped residents perfect a relational piety that resembled the prophetic ideal. Collective care was both a pathway to and marker of one's spiritual esteem; believers emulated the prophetic model by caring for others, and because they cared for others. As young people interacted with Tijani women and men, they reflected upon how those who were most spiritually esteemed were those who collectively cared for others. Reviving the example of Prophet Muhammad, Senegalese Tijani leaders from Shaykha Ruqayya to Ya Fatou to Shaykh Hassan to Imam Cheikh to Shaykh Mahy, alongside Black American Tijani leaders like Sayyida Kubra, modeled for young people the lesson that being a pious Muslim meant caring deeply for others and giving generously and consistently of one's time, labor, and money.

4

To Be Young, Gifted, and Black

Qur'anic Education as Collective Care

"When Grandma came to Medina Baye, before she had left, she had told Shaykh Hassan that she was going to have someone in the family finish memorizing the Qur'an... Her wish was for her grandchildren to at least come to Medina Baye, at least try to finish the Qur'an, to at least get the experience, to at least study for a little while."
—Hanaan, a 13-year-old from Detroit

"My mom used to say, if you go home to the U.S., you're throwing away everything. And my sister Hafsa used to always correct her, like, 'No,' because we still have this experience. We learned something. We did something. It's not like all these years were just thrown away."
—Isra, a 15-year-old from Atlanta

The sky was still dark as Hanaan, Isra, Hafsa, and a few other Black American students rushed from their dormitory to the African American Islamic Institute (AAII) School. It was dawn and very quiet in Medina Baye. The majority of residents were still indoors, but these young people ventured out early each weekday morning to attend their first period at AAII. AAII's daily schedule centered around the times of *salat* (prayers). In lieu of bells, the *adhan* (call to prayer) was broadcast from the loudspeakers of the Grand Mosque. That, coupled with the changing colors of the sky, alerted students throughout the day about when they needed to be in class. The school day began at *fajr* (early morning prayer), which was around 5:30 am, and ended at *isha* (late evening prayer), which was around 9 pm. Their weekends were from Wednesday afternoon to Friday morning, with the new school week beginning after jummah. On each school day, students had a two-hour breakfast break, a two-hour lunch break, and an approximately one-hour break before *maghrib* (sunset prayer). Those breaks aside, students spent almost ten hours a day in the classroom.

Though arduous, it was a routine that the three young women had grown accustomed to. However, in 2018, after attending AAII for more than five years, Hafsa had become a bit weary—not necessarily of the schedule, but of how difficult her studies were. Hafsa was very close to becoming a *hafiza* (woman who has memorized the entire Qur'an in Arabic). She was "on review," which meant she had finished memorizing the Qur'an and was now reviewing it to ensure she still remembered it all; this was challenging because she had memorized all of her *surahs* (chapters of the Qur'an) over several years and had not regularly reviewed what she had previously learned. Hafsa doubted whether she had the willpower or desire to finish. She was proud of all that she had learned and was now eager to transition to a new educational dream: high school and college back in Atlanta, with hopes of eventually becoming a psychologist for Black girls and women.

Both Hanaan and Isra referenced the "experience" of memorizing the Qur'an in Medina Baye. According to Hanaan, her grandma had hoped that someone in the family would memorize the entire Qur'an, but then revised her expectations and asserted that she would still have felt fulfilled if her grandchildren were able to "at least try to finish the Qur'an, to at least get the experience." Isra and Hafsa's mother, Tahira, seemed to have a different perspective. Tahira reportedly warned Hafsa that she "would be throwing away everything" if she didn't finish. Yet, like Hanaan's grandma, Isra contended that she and Hafsa saw value in what they had learned at AAII along the way. The sisters contested their mother's claim by asserting, "We still have this experience. We learned something. We did something."

From Hanaan's grandmother, to Isra and Hafsa's mother, to the young people themselves, Black American Muslims understood the experience of Qur'anic education in Medina Baye in different ways. Some adults suggested that the experience hinged upon students becoming huffaz. Other adults and young people asserted that the experience encompassed many outcomes that included but were not limited to memorizing the entire Qur'an. Yet across the different perspectives, these Black

American Muslims were unified in their understanding that memorizing the Qur'an was transformative.

From the exciting prospects to the unexpected difficulties, this chapter examines how Black American youth made meaning of their Qur'anic education in Medina Baye. Building upon the previous chapter's argument that the people, practices, and physical place of Medina Baye offered young people an everyday Islamic education geared towards cultivating a relational piety, this chapter shows how Qur'anic education further ingrained within young people blessed habits of collective care.

There were many dynamics that shaped how Black American Muslim youth made meaning of their education. Their perspectives were shaped by their racial identity as Black people, their genealogy as the descendants of enslaved Africans who were likely from West Africa and who perhaps had been Muslim as well, their previous schooling experiences in the U.S., and their current experiences learning in what they perceived to be a predominantly Black Muslim society. Attentive to these dynamics, this chapter tracks how Black American Muslim youth experienced Qur'anic education as a form of learning that was rooted in an axiomatic stance of Black[1] Muslim brilliance. I define an axiomatic stance of Black Muslim brilliance as an ideological orientation and educational paradigm that recognizes and cultivates the inherent abilities and boundless potential of all Black Muslim youth. This stance was reflected in two aspects of the Qur'anic education in Medina Baye: peer-to-peer learning in the classroom and student participation in community-wide events. In the classroom, youth learned to teach and support one another as they memorized the Qur'an. Outside of the classroom, youth drew upon their Arabic reading skills and memory of Qur'anic surahs to complete devotional acts on behalf of their communities in Senegal and the U.S.

These two practices demonstrated the robust and relational nature of Qur'anic education in Medina Baye. It was not a form of learning through which students merely memorized divine scriptures;[2] rather, it was an intellectual, social, and moral educational experience that molded young people's ways of being and belonging. In a society where Black Muslim youths' brilliance was an axiom, where every young person was seen to have value, and where believers helped one another as a way of becoming beloved to Allah, Black American Muslim youth experienced Qur'anic education as yet another practice of collective care. As they memorized the Qur'an, they simultaneously cultivated the habit of using what they learned to care for their community.

The Etiquette of the Bearers of the Qur'an

According to Islamic belief, Angel Jibril delivered Allah's message to Prophet Muhammad. Prophet Muhammad preserved the literal words of Allah by committing the verses to memory and repeating them to his companions. Through this process of person-to-person transmission, some of the early Muslims became huffaz.

Huffaz comes from the Arabic verb *hifz*, which means to preserve, guard, or protect. Al-Hafiz, or the All-Preserver, is one the 99 names that describe Allah's attributes.³ This name and attribute are mentioned in the ayat: "It is certainly We Who have revealed the Reminder, and it is certainly We Who will *preserve* it" (Qur'an 15:9, emphasis added). Muslims who memorize the entire Qur'an in Arabic are honored with the titles hafiz (male), hafiza (female), and huffaz (plural). These titles reflect the epistemological understanding of and ethical responsibility placed upon huffaz, who preserve, guard, and protect the Qur'an in their minds, hearts, and bodies.

Imam al-Nawawi, the prolific thirteenth-century Syrian Islamic scholar of hadith and fiqh, wrote a book about the ideal behaviors and characteristics of those who memorize the Qur'an. This text, *An Exposition on the Etiquette of the Bearers of the Qur'an (al-Tibyan fi Adab Hamalat al-Qur'an)*, is heralded as a foundational work about Qur'anic education. It was also a book that Sayyida Kubra Askari-Cisse, the Black American Muslim youth's othermother in Medina Baye, recommended that parents get for their children. In the first chapter of the book, "The Merits of Reciting and Bearing the Qur'an," Imam al-Nawawi presents two ayats and thirteen hadiths. He does not elaborate on any of them, opting instead to simply list them in succession.

Imam al-Nawawi begins with two ayats: "Surely those who recite the Book of Allah, establish prayer, and donate from what We have provided for them—secretly and openly—[can] hope for an exchange that will never fail, so that He will reward them in full and increase them out of His grace. He is truly All-Forgiving, Most Appreciative" (Qur'an

35:29–30). These ayats identify three acts that Allah guarantees will bring benefit to the believers. Of the three, only prayer is obligatory. The fact that the other two acts—reciting the Qur'an and donating one's wealth—are included alongside prayer indicates how significant they are. Earlier we saw how charitable giving in the form of hadiya cultivated one's piety and sustained a system of collective care. We now turn attention to how the first act in the list—reciting the Qur'an—further promotes a relational piety and collective care.

Imam al-Nawawi follows up the two ayats with the hadith: "The best among you is one who learns the Qur'an and teaches it." This is the first of 13 hadiths that Imam al-Nawawi presents about the merits of reciting the Qur'an. While Qur'anic education is often construed as an act that offers student the knowledge necessary to worship Allah and raise their religious ranking, this hadith joins the act of learning the Qur'an with the responsibility to teach it. The fusing of these acts reflects a robust understanding of Qur'anic education—it is a mode of relational piety and ethical formation that is cultivated as believers heed the imperative to share what they have learned.

The second hadith that Imam al-Nawawi includes is: "The one who recites the Qur'an and is skillful therein will be with the obedient, noble, recording angels; and the one who reads the Qur'an stammering, it being difficult for him, has two rewards." This hadith indicates the high ranking awarded to all those who learn the Qur'an, but it emphasizes Allah's special pleasure with those who struggle in the process but persist. This hadith also suggests that the benefits of Qur'anic education are not limited to those who become huffaz, but rather are offered to all those who put forth sincere effort to learn the holy book.

Imam al-Nawawi goes on to cite additional hadiths that detail the blessings, ethical responsibilities, and transformative impact of Qur'anic education. Included in these is the hadith: "Whoever recites the Qur'an and acts according to what it contains, Allah will adorn his parents with a crown on the Day of Judgment, its radiance more beautiful than the radiance of the sun in the abode of this world. So what do you presume [the reward will be] for the one who acts according to it?" In the first part of the hadith, reciting and implementing the teachings of the Qur'an are bundled together. Considered in conjunction with the first hadith that Imam al-Nawawi cites, these hadiths indicate an expansive conception of Qur'anic education that includes learning, teaching, and implementing the divine message. This hadith also offers two additional dimensions that underscore the relational nature of Qur'anic education: it brings blessing to students and parents, and its blessings are associated with the students' ability to manifest the message through their actions. Taken together, the ayats and hadiths that Imam al-Nawawi presents bolster the idea that Qur'anic education is a form of learning that cultivates a relational piety and promotes collective care.

Sacred Studies: The Social Significance of Qur'anic Education

Those who memorize the Qur'an play an important role in Muslim communities. In the early decades of Islam, the Qur'an was preserved orally. But after Prophet Muhammad passed away and many huffaz of his time were killed in battles, Muslims grew concerned that the contents of the Qur'an might be lost along with those who memorized it. Sayyidina Abu Bakr as-Siddiq, the Prophet's beloved companion who became the first *khalifa* (caliph) of the Muslims after his passing, initiated efforts to compile the Qur'an in written form. The continued presence of huffaz in Muslim communities also meant that the divine word remained intact and accessible to all who could hear the huffaz recite it.

As Islam spread, the demand for Qur'an schools grew. These schools were formal sites where Allah's message could be learned, retained, and applied by those who were part of newly emerging Muslim communities (Bin Omar 1993). Paper and the other materials necessary to produce physical Qur'ans were scarce and expensive until at least the nineteenth century (Lydon 2011, 41), so huffaz and the schools where they were educated played integral roles in burgeoning Muslim communities. Moreover, in nomadic environments where physical manuscripts were hard to transport, the ability to recite texts from memory was of practical importance (ibid., 42). As embodied repositories of the Qur'an, huffaz utilized their knowledge to ensure that Allah's word could be spread to and followed by others.

In the eighteenth century in Senegambia (in present-day Senegal, Gambia, and Mauritania, as well as parts of Mali and Guinea), many African huffaz were kidnapped for the transatlantic slave trade. In outrage, some African Muslim communities launched revolutionary movements to abolish slavery (Ware 2014). In the Americas, enslaved Africans who were huffaz or had pursued Qur'anic education leveraged their knowledge to preserve and propagate Islam (Austin 1984; Diouf 1998). This occurred during an era when enslaved people faced violent repression if white slave owners discovered that they knew how to read or that they had physical texts in their possession (Williams 2005).

By the twenty-first century, Hanaan, Isra, Hafsa, and the other Black American youth at AAII thus received an education that positioned them to join a transatlantic lineage of Black Muslim huffaz. These young people traveled thousands of miles to memorize the Qur'an in Senegal, a place where generations of African Muslims had long ago studied the holy book before being kidnapped and sent to the Americas. Through their classroom instruction, these young people embarked on a sacred and communally significant endeavor that Black Muslims in West Africa and the Americas had carried out for centuries.

The Politics of Qur'anic Education in Senegal

Few if any students at AAII understood Arabic well. Instead, day in and day out, students diligently read and recited letters and words whose beautiful sounds penetrated their hearts but whose substance and meaning they struggled to comprehend.[4] The Qur'an contains nearly 80,000 words that are arranged into more than 6,000 ayats that are organized into 114 surahs of varying length, all evenly partitioned into 60 *hizbs* (sections) that students gradually memorized over time. As was the case for *daaras* (classical Qur'an schools) throughout Senegal, AAII's curriculum started with learning to recognize individual letters of the Arabic alphabet, then learning to read Arabic words and ayats from the Qur'an. Once students could read fluently, they memorized Surah al-Fatiha (the opening surah of the Qur'an) and then the remaining surahs of the Qur'an progressively backwards, starting with the shortest surahs at the end of the Qur'an. Instruction was individualized. Teachers assessed students' knowledge when they enrolled and determined where in the curriculum they should begin. From there, students progressed at their own pace, memorizing as much as they could, as quickly as their minds would allow.

For centuries in West Africa, Qur'an schools were the "first essential place in the creation of a Muslim subjectivity" (Brenner 2001, 19). Young Muslims gained not only discursive religious knowledge but also became socialized with the practices and virtues prescribed by their Muslim communities—thus reflecting an epistemology that combined intellect, embodiment, and habitus (Boyle 2007; Ware 2014; Wright 2015a).

In Senegal, Qur'anic education was and remains highly polarizing, even though daaras are the most widespread, accessible, and popular form of primary education (Loimeier 2002, 122). A cursory search of academic publications, archival sources, news articles, and popular portrayals of Qur'anic education reveals an overwhelmingly negative representation of daaras. From the French colonial administration, to some political leaders in independent Senegal, to some Senegalese Salafi Muslim reformers in the late twentieth century onwards, all viewed the pedagogies at daaras to be deficient (Loimeier 2002; Ware 2014, 40–41). They critiqued teachers for exploiting students by pressuring them to do farmwork, for physically abusing students under the guise of discipline, and for requiring students to beg for money in the streets. In turn, human rights organizations, government officials, and middle-class urban residents alike critiqued daaras as sites of child abuse (Hugon 2015; Perry 2004; Ware 2014). The term *talibe* (pronounced "talee-bay"), which is a Wolof derivation of the Arabic word for student (*talib*), became synonymous with the vulnerable children presumed to attend Qur'an schools (Lahti 2019). In Senegal, talibes provoked what Stanley Cohen (1972) terms a moral panic, or a mass hysteria that occurs when a "group of persons emerges to become defined as a threat to societal values and interests; its nature is presented in a stylized and stereotypical fashion by the mass media; the moral barricades are manned by editors, bishops, politicians and other right-thinking people; socially accredited experts pronounce their diagnoses and solutions" (1). Public, popular, and development discourses were all widely concerned with the plight of talibes—who were portrayed as neglected by their parents and teachers, forced to fend for themselves, and ultimately blamed for harassing everyday people and threatening the social order. This moral panic made talibes a stand-in for Senegal's entire system of Qur'anic education, which by extension, was seen as an unregulated system of exploitation.

While I do not dismiss or deny that abuses of talibes take place at some daaras in Senegal, my focus here is not in proving the merits of Qur'anic education to those who question its inherent value.[5] Instead, I center the perspectives of my Black American Muslim interlocuters, who engaged Qur'anic education in Senegal as a site of freedom dreaming and with the baseline understanding that it was a worthwhile endeavor. Parents saw the Qur'anic educational experience there as enriching and more attractive than schooling options in the U.S. Youth who attended AAII on a day-to-day, year-after-year basis also discussed the significance of their educational experience. For instance, Seerah, a 14-year-old from Chicago, asserted, "My American friends assume it's all so terrible here. But it's like, I wouldn't come here for all this, suffering as they say, just like for no reason, for no benefit, if I knew that I could do it in America, because I can't." Young people recognized the unique nature of their educational experiences in Senegal and thought deeply about the possibilities and constraints that came with studying there, even as outsiders made negative assumptions about it. Given Black American youth's experiences learning in the U.S. and Senegal, as well as their parents' conscious decision to move them out of the U.S. and transfer them to a daara in Senegal, these families approached Islamic schooling in Medina Baye with a distinct set of concerns and aspirations than what tended to characterize discourses about Qur'anic education in Senegal.

There were also other dynamics that made AAII and Black American Muslims' engagement with it distinct from the dominant narratives associated with daaras in Senegal. When Black American parents enrolled their children at AAII, they entrusted that their children would be cared for by Senegalese Tijanis whom they saw as their kin. These familial and spiritual ties, coupled with their shared commitments to collective care, fostered ethical modes of accountability about young people's well-being that were perhaps less salient at daaras where child abuse was known to be rampant. Furthermore, Medina Baye's hadiya economy, coupled with Shaykh Hassan Cisse's (and later his brothers, Imam Cheikh Tijani Cisse's and Shaykh Mahy Cisse's) investments in the school, ensured that AAII had the resources to provide a decent quality of education. This fugitive infrastructure thus represented another structural feature that made AAII distinct from daaras that were in financially dire situations and perhaps forced to compromise the quality of the educational experience.⁶ However, while it is important to note the aspects that made AAII unique, the school should not be viewed as an exceptional case that either redeems or deviates from the norm; doing so fuels the impulse to prove that Qur'anic education is just as acceptable as forms of schooling that are glorified within the white Western liberal secular imagination.⁷ Instead, following the perspectives of Black American Muslims, this chapter argues that the Qur'anic education at AAII was a site of freedom dreaming where students learned about the collective responsibilities and possibilities that came at the intersections of being young, Black, and Muslim.

An Axiomatic Stance of Black Muslim Brilliance

In Medina Baye, Black American youth experienced Qur'anic education as a form of learning that was rooted in what I term an axiomatic stance of Black Muslim brilliance. I build upon the work of scholars of Black education who hold the brilliance of Black children to be an axiom (Gholson et al. 2012; Leonard and Martin 2013). An axiom is an idea that does not need to be proved because it is already assumed to be true. Adopting an axiomatic stance of Black brilliance means recognizing Black students' inherent capacities for achievement as a self-evident truth. By operating from the undisputed understanding that Black students can succeed, educators can cultivate the brilliance that already exists within them (Muhammad 2020). I extend the theoretical insights about an axiomatic stance of Black brilliance to understandings of Muslim students. Similar to the ways in which some have challenged the merits of Qur'anic education and others have reacted by proving its value, so too have some questioned Muslim students' ways of being while others have responded by presenting counternarratives that prove their humanity. This impulse, albeit well-intentioned, runs counter to Islamic teachings, which hold all people's humanity to be an axiomatic truth. In direct opposition to the systems of racial capitalism and white supremacy, Islam teaches that all human beings, by virtue of being creations of Allah, have inherent dignity and value. To debate one's fundamental humanity is therefore to question the sacred nature of Allah's creation. Thus, building upon Black educational perspectives and Islamic teachings, this chapter operates from two related axiomatic truths: that Qur'anic education in Senegal offers meaningful possibilities to Muslim students, and that Black Muslim youth are brilliant. These truths, in turn, shaped how Black American Muslim youth made use of their education as a form of collective care.

For some students, attending a Qur'an school where their brilliance was treated as an axiomatic truth was a new experience, while for others, this perspective built upon the affirming approaches that they were accustomed to back in the U.S. Nonetheless, prior to enrolling at AAII, all youth had completed some years of schooling in the U.S., a country where racism was a permanent reality (Bell 1993) that structured all aspects of society (Bonilla-Silva 2003; Mills 1997), including in education (Kohli et al. 2006; Ladson-Billings and Tate 1995; Leonardo and Grubb 2018; Vaught 2011). From the comments of teachers, classmates, politicians, and community members to the depictions in the media, Black Muslim students in the U.S. frequently encountered racist messages about their achievement. Within educational discourses, Black students were understood primarily through deficit lenses that obscured the racist structures that produced a so-called "achievement gap" between Black and white students (Carey 2014; Ladson-Billings 2007; Milner 2013). These racist narratives also filtered into some multiracial Muslim settings such as mosques and schools, where Black Muslims experienced anti-Black racism and were presumed by co-religionists from the Middle East and South Asia to be less knowledgeable than them (Jackson 2005, 4; McCloud 2004, 73–83; Yakub 2024).

Classrooms were crucial sites where Black students developed their beliefs and attitudes about their racial identity. Black American students who enrolled at AAII previously attended public schools (including charter schools), community-based Muslim or Black Muslim schools, and homeschools in the U.S. (see Table 4.1 for more details). Over the course of their elementary, middle, or high school years, many students transferred between different types of schools (e.g. from a public school to a Black Muslim school, or from a homeschool to a Muslim school). Students had a range of experiences at these schools. Some spent time in secular and/or Muslim educational spaces where they experienced anti-Black racism. Hanaan, for instance, mentioned that her classmate at a Muslim school in Detroit made anti-Black comments during a class discussion and that her teacher did not intervene. Similarly, Seerah

TABLE 4.1 Black American Students' U.S. School Enrollment Prior to AAII (data from 27 students enrolled at AAII between 2016 and 2018)

Type of School(s):	Female	Male	Total
Attended only public schools	7	8	15
Attended only Muslim schools	2	0	2
Attended only homeschools	1	1	2
Attended both public and Muslim schools	5	1	6
Attended both Muslim and homeschools	1	1	2

reported that classmates at both her public school and Muslim school made racist remarks towards her. However, other young people attended secular and/or Muslim schools that centered, supported, and honored Black people. Isra and Hafsa, for example, attended a community-based Black Muslim school in Atlanta where their teachers offered culturally responsive education anchored in their histories and identities as Black people and Muslims. Soraya, a 15-year-old from Washington D.C., was homeschooled by her mother, who curated experiences throughout the city and in nature that nurtured her daughter's multilayered identities. Overall, from educational experiences that cultivated students' pride in their identities as Black people, to those that promoted the myth that Blackness and brilliance were mutually opposed, Black Muslim students encountered racialized messages about the limits and possibilities of their achievement.

In Medina Baye, Black American Muslim youth encountered new norms. They learned in a city where they made meaning of most residents as Black (African or African-descended), Muslim, and Tijani. As was the case in the U.S., the messages young people encountered were informed by the social, demographic, political, and historical context of the city. Medina Baye was part of a multi-century lineage of cities of Islamic learning in West Africa that predated the onset of European colonization, back in an era when the region represented the "foundation of literacy and learning in the Muslim world" (Lydon 2011, 36). In fact, "the West or modern civilization did not yet exist or was still in its infancy when the Islamic scholarly tradition was already flourishing in West Africa" (Kane 2016, 9). These dynamics persisted in the twenty-first century, as youth attended a school and lived in a community filled with African Muslims who exhibited impressive levels of Islamic knowledge.

At AAII, youth were taught by accomplished Senegalese and other West African teachers who were huffaz, and learned alongside peers whom they viewed as fellow Black Muslims. Outside of school, they regularly interacted with young Black huffaz. As Hanaan observed, "Most of the 17- [and] 16-year-olds in Medina Baye have already finished memorizing the Qur'an. Like if the Qur'an is playing from the loudspeakers, you can walk in the street and multiple people will be reciting [along] with the Qur'an playing from the masjid." In Medina Baye, most local children's first schooling experiences were at daaras. By the time they were teenagers, many had already become huffaz and moved on to other forms of schooling. As Hanaan's comment indicated, this meant that there were incredibly high levels of Arabic literacy and Qur'anic mastery among Medina Baye's youth residents. This offered Black American students a constant reminder that Black Muslim youth could be academically successful.

Medina Baye's founder, Shaykh Ibrahim Niasse, also spoke highly and openly about being Black. In *Ruhul Adab* (*The Spirit of Good Morals*), a book of poetry that he published at the age of 20, Shaykh Ibrahim directly addressed the significance of his identity as a young Black Muslim man. *Ruhul Adab* is a foundational, introductory manual for Tijanis, and one that is widely studied and well-known among members of Shaykh Ibrahim's fayda. Shaykh Hassan even advised his murids that it was "the most important book after the Holy Qur'an and Hadith literature" (as cited in Dimson 2016, 1). Several Black American Tijanis referred me, with pride, to a collection of lines towards the end of *Ruhul Adab*, when Shaykh Ibrahim cautions, "Do not be prevented from memorizing this poem by my being a young man from the land of non-Arabs" (Niasse 2016, 26). Two lines later, Shaykh Ibrahim quotes Shaykh Amadu Bamba (1853–1927), the Senegalese Sufi scholar who founded the Muridiyya tariqa. Shaykh Ibrahim writes, "As has been said by the illustrious servant of Taha [Muhammad], Ahmad [Bamba] the Maliki [scholar]: Black skin cannot be associated with immature foolishness or deficient understanding" (as cited in Wright 2018, 180–181). Both Shaykh Ibrahim and Shaykh Amadu were aware of the ageism and anti-Black sentiment that plagued some Muslims. However, rather than prove why they were indeed knowledgeable, they implicitly critiqued the ageist and racist mindsets that prevented people from benefitting from their work. As Black Americans encountered these lines nearly a century later, the message stuck out to them.

Similarly, on another occasion which is included as an appendix in *Kashif al-Ilbas* (*The Removal of Confusion*), Shaykh Ibrahim reminds his murids: "Indeed, blackness of the skin does not prevent entry among the rank of those drawn near (to their Lord)" (Niasse 2010, 253). In yet another instance, Shaykh Ibrahim asserts, "Black Africa (*al-Sudan*) has gained preeminence in love for our Prophet, and white people have been humiliated in their hatred for him" (as cited in Wright 2022, 247–248). These were some of the many statements that reflected Shaykh Ibrahim's embrace of his Blackness as a source of Islamic virtue, and that I frequently heard from Black Americans as they discussed the racialized significance of being Tijani.[8] Furthermore, just as Shaykh Ibrahim spoke openly about being Black, so too were the French colonizers fixated on his race; the French feared that Shaykh Ibrahim would create "a state for the black race with a Muslim political and social structure" (Kane 1997 as cited in Wright 2022, 239). Taken together, these perspectives demonstrated a widespread awareness among members of Shaykh Ibrahim's spiritual movement and outsiders alike of the racialized dimensions and potential of African Muslims' achievements.

During the twentieth century, Shaykh Ibrahim encouraged his followers to embrace their Blackness. These racialized messages remained instructive and accessible to Tijanis who embraced the tariqa in the decades after Shaykh Ibrahim's passing; by reading his writings and through the oral tradition preserved among the community, I heard countless Black Americans discuss the significance of being in a spiritual movement that celebrated the intersections of Blackness and Muslimness through their scholarly achievement and piety. The contemporary shuyukh also carried forth Shaykh Ibrahim's spirit of racial consciousness. For instance, when Imam Cheikh Tijani Cisse, Shaykh Ibrahim's grandson and the current Imam of Medina Baye, was asked about Allah's wisdom in blessing Shaykh Ibrahim with immense spiritual insight and a massive following, Imam Cheikh responded, "If you mean, what was God's wisdom in giving the *fayda* [the flood of divine gnosis] to

Shaykh Ibrahim as a Black man in Senegal? Then, the reason is perhaps because God is just" (as cited in Wright 2022, 246–247).

Thus, in Medina Baye, Black American Muslim youth learned in a Sufi community and city where they constantly encountered affirming racialized messages. From seeing, learning from, and interacting with Black Muslim scholars, to hearing statements that celebrated their identities as Black Muslims, young people lived and learned in a place that took the brilliance of Black Muslims to be a self-evident truth. These truths shaped AAII's approach to Qur'anic education, and in turn, impacted Black American Muslim youth's understandings of themselves and their responsibilities to others.

Peer-to-Peer Learning in the Classroom

It was Tuesday afternoon in early January 2018, and I was out of breath as I crossed the threshold into the courtyard of the AAII School. I bolted up the narrow stairs of the building, onto the third floor, and into Ustadh[9] Taal's classroom. Ustadh Taal was a Senegalese hafiz in his midthirties, a slender man who smiled as often as he scolded. He had been teaching at AAII for the last few years. When I entered the room, Ustadh Taal was nowhere to be found. I was greeted by the sounds of more than twenty students energetically reciting aloud, each from a different part of the Qur'an, their voices somehow melding together to form one sacred soundtrack. Their voices bounced off the light blue walls of the building, with the open windows carrying the students' recitations down to the streets below and into the ears and hearts of passersby. Interspersed with the sounds of Arabic were the laughter of other students who relaxed in the last minutes before Ustadh Taal showed up.

That day, I was joined by Samira, a 19-year-old Black American college student who was visiting me from Philadelphia during her winter break. During her childhood, Samira's parents had enrolled her in a weekend Qur'an class where she memorized the last two hizbs of the Qur'an. Samira admitted that because she seldom reviewed what she memorized back then, she had forgotten much of what she learned. She was eager to come to AAII with me, in part to get a refresher on what had faded from her memory, and in part because she was curious about

Figure 4.1. Entrance to the African American Islamic Institute (AAII), July 2016. Photo courtesy of the author.

whether Qur'anic education in Senegal looked different from what she encountered in the U.S.

Samira came to class with a leatherbound notebook, blue ink pen, and hardcover copy of the Qur'an. When Ustadh Taal entered the classroom a few minutes after us, he was intrigued and seemingly pleased that I had brought a visitor. But after greeting us, he turned to apologize. He explained that his wife had called him to take care of an important matter. He assured me that he would return shortly. As I had observed in the past, it was not unusual for teachers to momentarily step away from their classrooms. In their absence, they trusted that their students would continue learning independently.

As Samira looked around wondering what to do, 11-year-old Aziza struck up a conversation with her. Aziza was the youngest Black American student in the class. She was from Detroit and had attended AAII since she was eight years old. Aziza's parents met as classmates at AAII during the 1990s. Her grandparents were among Shaykh Hassan's earliest Black American Tijani murids and among the first group of parents to send their children to AAII. From both her maternal and paternal sides, Aziza was the third generation in her family to come to Medina Baye. Aziza informed Samira that she could fill in for Ustadh Taal. Before Samira could respond, Aziza huddled over an open page in Samira's notebook and began writing each letter in the Arabic alphabet with careful precision. When Aziza finished, she pointed the tip of the pen under each letter, opening her mouth dramatically to model for Samira the correct way each letter ought to be pronounced. Samira thanked Aziza, and then began quietly practicing to herself, recalling the sounds of letters that lingered on the tip of her tongue, years after she learned them as a child.

Once Samira recalled how to decipher each letter, she gently opened her copy of the Qur'an. She flipped through the thin, onion-skinned pages until she reached Surah an-Naba, the first surah of the last juz, which she had once known by heart. As she began reciting in a low tone, Samira started, stopped, and restarted, stumbling here and there. Seeing

Figure 4.2. Two female students at AAII sit in the classroom, memorizing verses from the Qur'an, March 2018. Photo courtesy of the author.

and hearing her, Aziza closed the copy of the Qur'an that she was memorizing from and leaned over to Samira.

"See this small mark above that letter? It's easy to miss. But it means you have to make the letter longer when you say it. Like this. *Laaaa*, not *la*," Aziza explained as she slid her right index finger over a line of black ink on the green-and-gold bordered page. Aziza continued scanning the page, running her eyes and finger past each letter. She stopped again in the middle of the page.

"Okay, now you see how there is a *noon* followed by a *ya*? That means you don't pronounce the *noon*. So not *manya*, but *maaya*," Aziza added matter-of-factly.

Aziza paused to read Samira's facial expression. She continued once she saw Samira had unfurrowed her brows and began nodding. Aziza went on to explain the meaning of each grammatical mark on the page, which syllables should be elongated, and the correct way to pronounce particular words. She then returned Samira's copy of the Qur'an. As Samira began reading aloud again, Aziza listened intently. A few times, Aziza quickly interrupted to correct Samira's pronunciation before warmly encouraging her to continue.

These moments of peer-to-peer learning were part of AAII's formal pedagogy. Students were placed in mixed-age, mixed-level classrooms in which each student progressed through the memorization of the Qur'an at their own pace. On one end of the spectrum, students were learning to decipher letters and words in Arabic. On the other end, students had finished memorizing the entire Qur'an and were reviewing it. Students' progress along this continuum did not correspond to their age or the amount of time they had been at the school. There were younger students who were more advanced than older students who were only starting their studies. Samira and Aziza's interaction typified these dynamics.

The pedagogical model of individualized learning, coupled with the staffing model of one teacher per classroom, meant that students were not always able to seek assistance from a teacher. And, as was the case when Ustadh Taal stepped out, the teacher was not always available. In part by necessity and in part by design, peer-to-peer learning constantly occurred. Samira and Aziza's interaction was just one instantiation of a common phenomenon. For example, if a student could not decipher how to pronounce a word according to proper *tajweed* (rules of Qur'anic recitation), she might nudge the student next to her and ask for help. Before a student recited her lesson to the teacher, she might ask her peers to test her for accuracy. If a student was struggling to memorize a lesson, she might strike up a conversation with a more advanced classmate to gain tried-and-true tips for success.

While these interactions unfolded organically, other instances of peer-to-peer learning were formally integrated into the pedagogy. The teacher might designate one student to model the recitation of a new lesson to a classmate. The teacher might also stipulate that students should recite to him at periodic benchmarks and that all interim testing should be done with specific, more advanced students. If the teacher had to leave the classroom for any reason, he might appoint one student to supervise their peers' learning. Such students were called *maagi daara* (an older or advanced student who assists the Qur'an teacher).

These peer-to-peer exchanges gave students practice in explaining concepts and skills, offering emotional support to one another, and collectively navigating the rigors of their education. They acknowledged their shared difficulties and also encouraged each other to persist. Juxtaposed to the rigors of their academic task at hand and the individualized pace of instruction, peer-to-peer interactions fostered a nurturing climate of collaboration.

Layla, a 19-year-old Black American student who had previously attended a public school and a community-based Muslim school in upstate New York, reflected on the significance of these dynamics.

> Here, no one's at the same level as you. . . . I'm what, 19? But I was going to, like, a five-year-old or a six-year-old to listen to the surah I'm at because she passed me in her memorization of the Qur'an. It wasn't a discouragement or anything because I knew they were here longer than me. . . . It was just like, "Masha'Allah, you're here, and masha'Allah, I'm here." . . . When it comes to school in America, it's like, "Oh, you don't get it. You don't understand it." And it's just like a lot of bullying that takes place there if you're not on the same level. I know when I was first in school, I wasn't on the same level as everybody else, so sometimes I got pulled out of classes. So that was a lot of discouragement 'cause it's like, "Why am I getting put out of class to learn something different?" So it's just like I'm not on the same level. I felt dumber. I felt less educated.

Despite being older than most students at AAII, Layla remarked that neither she nor her classmates saw their age difference as a deficiency or source of embarrassment. This was unlike what she was used to in the U.S., where the norm was for all students in a class to be around the same age, and the expectation was that all students would meet the same benchmarks around the same time. Those who were younger were seen as outstanding. Those who were older were presumed to be lagging behind and made to feel bad. For Layla, receiving extra support by being pulled out of a classroom where there was one age-based rubric of success had been a jarring reminder that she did not measure up.

At AAII, students learned from each other, and it was not uncommon for younger students to teach older students. This emphasis on peer-to-peer learning contributed to the sentiment that all students could assist one another. Far from being understood as deficient in their knowledge and abilities, Black Muslim youth were viewed through an axiomatic stance of Black Muslim brilliance. They were valued as experts by peers and teachers alike.

AAII's mixed-age, mixed-level classrooms mirrored the set-up at daaras in Senegal and across Africa for centuries (Boyle 2004; Eickelman 1978). At such institutions, the "emphasis on students learning at their own pace, free from notions of uniformity and failure" was geared towards guiding all students to develop individual mastery (Boyle 2004, 14). However, once the French colonized parts of West Africa, they opened their own schools in the region and began teaching students according to their own methods. Robert Launay (2021) contrasts the methods at European colonial schools and West African Qur'an schools:

> [In colonial schools] learning was structured by cohorts, organized into grade levels. Performance was evaluated by formal examinations, explicitly structured to be competitive. Quranic schools, by way of contrast, were frequently characterized by collaborative learning, with more advanced or simply more gifted students assisting others to master their assigned tasks. (98)

As Layla's comments about her demoralizing learning experience in public school indicated, this European colonial method remained the dominant approach in contemporary U.S. schools. However, just as West

African Qur'an schools emphasized collaboration, so too did many of the educational institutions historically run by Black people in the U.S. encourage students to help one another as they learned. Gholdy Muhammad (2020) describes the approach utilized in African American literary societies in the nineteenth century U.S.

> It was an intentional practice to galvanize young people of different ages and 'abilities' in literacy together . . . Although most school classrooms today are organized by students' ages and reading abilities, this practice was not common historically. It was a practice, however, to use others' experiences and abilities as resources to teach and learn from one another. (34)

This approach harkened back to the time of slavery, when enslaved people honored and practiced the concept of "each one, teach one"—each enslaved people who learned to read made the commitment to teach another person how to read as well. Even after slavery was abolished, from the nineteenth all the way to the twenty-first century, the ethic of "each one, teach one" remained salient for many Black communities who viewed education as a pathway to collective, not merely individual, liberation (Givens 2021; Payne and Strickland 2008).

At AAII, students were thus encouraged to relate to their education and one another in ways that were radically different from how students tended to be organized and socialized in European colonial schools and in the contemporary U.S. schooling system. Whereas those educational institutions promoted and reproduced capitalist norms such as competition and hierarchy (Bowles and Gintes 1976), AAII adhered to a transatlantic tradition of schools that inculcated within Black and Black Muslim students the importance of collaboration and reciprocity. At AAII, students were aware that they were at different levels, but along with the knowledge of their differences came a sense of responsibility rather than a feeling of inadequacy. As students ventured on their own individual memorization journeys, they developed the skills, confidence, and ethical obligation to support their peers. This made Qur'anic education a relational process of learning, teaching, and self-making that oriented students towards collective care.

Aziza's eagerness to teach Samira surprised me. In my other conversations with Aziza, she often expressed frustration about her progress.

When I asked Aziza if she thought she would become a hafiza, she responded, without hesitation, "Nope! It's obvious. I'm too slow!" Aziza pointed out that in her nearly three years at AAII, she had only memorized seven of the 60 hizbs of the Qur'an. If she continued at that rate, it would take her more than 25 years to finish. I reminded her that it was more likely, however, that her pace of memorization would get faster over time. As we had both observed, students tended to develop stronger habits of memorization as they settled into the cognitive groove of the task; the more they memorized, the easier it became and the faster they went. However, Aziza was not optimistic about that outcome.

Aziza mentioned several classmates who were older than her or joined the school later than her. She matter-of-factly cited how many more hizbs each of them had retained. In that moment, it became evident to me that an emphasis on peer-to-peer learning had heightened Aziza's awareness of everyone else's performance and made it easier for her to monitor her growth in relation to others. While she was not denigrated because of her academic performance, as Layla had felt in a U.S. classroom organized by age and grade, AAII's peer-to-peer environment made Aziza doubt whether she would become a hafiza.

Yet even though Aziza claimed that she was "too slow," we both knew that there was no such thing as being "too slow." We knew students who finished in less than four years and others who finished after seven years. Aziza had also seen at least a few students at AAII who became huffaz when they were in their late forties or early fifties. These examples bore testament to the fact that people memorized at their own pace, and that neither age nor time dictated students' abilities to become huffaz.

Despite our shared knowledge that Aziza could become a hafiza, she sighed heavily and concluded, "My whole family is counting on me to finish but it's too hard. I just want to go home." Her family's high hopes did little to extinguish her desire to quit. All the hadiths that Aziza had heard about the blessings of Qur'anic education did not quell her feelings either. There was, for example, the hadith that promised that Allah would adorn the huffaz's parents "with a crown on the Day of Judgment, its radiance more beautiful than the radiance of the sun in the abode of this world." There was also the hadith that the person "who reads the Qur'an stammering, it being difficult for him, has two rewards," in contrast to those who learned with ease. Aziza, as a student who considered memorizing the Qur'an to be "too hard," would surely be rewarded for her persistence. There was also a hadith promising that "Whoever recites one letter from the Book of Allah has one reward, and rewards are [multiplied] by ten of their kind. I do not say that '*Alif Lam Mim*' is a [single] letter, rather '*Alif*' is a letter, '*Lam*' is a letter, and '*Mim*' is a letter."[10] If there was immense blessing promised to those who learned even the smallest excerpts of the Qur'an, then the merits of Aziza's accomplishment of memorizing seven hizbs were plentiful.

These hadiths were among the many religious proofs that teachers, shuyukh, parents, and concerned adults alike marshalled when students expressed defeat. Nonetheless, such assurances did not always quell young people's in-the-moment impulses to give up. Even though Aziza learned in a classroom environment that affirmed her brilliance, her comments reflected the frustration of focusing day in and day out, year after year, on one goal without observing significant progress.

However, as I watched Aziza teach Samira, I noted how different her vibe was than in the past. In their interaction, Aziza was a confident, competent instructor. She took initiative to use what she had learned to help someone else. Aziza neither belittled Samira nor drew attention to their age gap—which, as she had learned at AAII, did not determine one's ability, expertise, or potential to achieve. Aziza leveraged her knowledge and experience as a peer educator to show patience, kindness, and concern towards Samira, emulating an ethos of collective care.

Observing Aziza teach Samira cast her feelings of frustration in a different light. Even though there were moments when Aziza wanted so badly to give up and go home, she experienced other moments that brought her joy, stoked her confidence, and filled her with a sense of purpose. This range of emotions is something all of us experience as we go through challenging but rewarding experiences in school, work, and life. Aziza's Qur'anic education similarly included struggles and setbacks alongside satisfaction and successes. Her experience also underscored the many facets of Qur'anic education. It was not simply an individual process where Aziza memorized divine scriptures; it was also a relational process of character development and self-making through which she shared her knowledge and cared for others. While the ethical responsibilities and dispositions of the Qur'an student were affirmed in the hadith that "the best among you is one who learns the Qur'an and teaches it," Aziza did not need to wait to become a hafiza before she strove for that status. Immersed in a school and city where Black Muslim youth's brilliance was axiomatic, Aziza internalized the view that she was a knowledgeable resource. Through the classroom emphasis on peer-to-peer learning, Aziza had countless opportunities to fulfill that role.

Three years after I observed Aziza teach Samira, Aziza's parents withdrew her from AAII. Their decision perhaps reflected their realization that Aziza was unlikely to become a hafiza in the near future. Still committed to Aziza's education, her parents planned to enroll her in an online program that would allow her to get her GED while remaining in Medina Baye. Aziza admitted that she was relieved by her parents' decision; like Hafsa, she looked forward to transitioning to a new educational experience. Despite Aziza's eventual departure from AAII, her interaction with Samira that afternoon was a reminder that Aziza found meaning in her studies along the way. Aziza had gained a level of proficiency in reading Arabic that enabled her not only to recite the holy text with ease but also made her a teacher to others. Her experience echoed Isra's assertion that "we learned something. We did something. It's not like all these years were just thrown away."

Each One, Teach One

The classroom emphasis on peer-to-peer learning informed many of the young people's future aspirations to teach others how to read and memorize the Qur'an. Hanaan was one such person. Back in the U.S., Hanaan attended public school from pre-kindergarten to second grade in Kalamazoo, Michigan. After that, she and her mother relocated more than a hundred miles eastward to Detroit to be close to Hanaan's grandma and other relatives. In Detroit, she went to a Muslim school for third through fifth grade. Then, following the footsteps of her brother and cousins, she fulfilled her grandma's wish by coming to Medina Baye. Hanaan recalled:

> When I go back, I want to teach Qur'an at my school in Detroit. Actually, before I came here, I was one of the people who knew the least amount of Qur'an in my Qur'an class. It was mostly Arab girls [in the class], and they knew a lot of Qur'an. And they would always be teaching me. Sometimes, I'd be like, "Let me hurry up and learn this and I'll be teaching her over there and her over there."

Hanaan contended that there was a racialized hierarchy of religious knowledge at her school in Detroit, such that Black Muslims were situated below Arabs. In another interview, Hanaan shared that an Indian student at that school had said to her during a class discussion, "Indian people are supposed to be Muslim, but African Americans aren't really." Hanaan heard such false comments even though Islam had a long history among African Americans in the city. Detroit, like other urban centers such as Chicago and New York City, boasted several African American Muslim communities that dated back to the early twentieth century (Curtis 2002; Howell 2014; Turner 2003). Like Aziza and many Black youth in Detroit, Hanaan was a third-generation Muslim. Hanaan's classmate had likely encountered many Black American Muslims at school and in the city.

Hanaan's awareness of the racialized classroom dynamics, coupled with her classmate's comment, illustrated how Black Muslims were often viewed by their non-Black co-religionists (specifically Arabs and South Asians) as "Muslims-in-training" (Abdul Khabeer 2017, 41). Cast as "Muslims-in-training," Black American Muslims were assumed to be relatively recent converts to Islam and therefore lacking in their mastery of religious knowledge. In contrast, Arab and South Asian Muslims, by virtue of originating from regions with large, centuries-old Muslim populations, were assumed to be more well-versed about Islam.[11] They were seen to have achieved the status of full Muslims, a ranking that gave them a "virtual monopoly over the definition of a properly constituted 'Islamic' life in America" (Jackson 2005, 4).

Hanaan encountered a different paradigm in Medina Baye, which shaped her commitment to teaching in the future:

> I feel like, after you finish Qur'an, even the blessings of when you teach someone something, and they teach someone else something. And whoever taught the teacher, the teacher teaches me, I want to keep that line going. And to teach someone and be like, "You teach your kids when you grow up! Don't stop the chain." That's going to be my saying.

The concept of the "chain" (*sanad* or *silsila* in Arabic) is of central importance in classical Islamic education and Sufi epistemology. It reflects the notion that Islamic knowledge is transmitted directly from person to person and can be traced all the way back to Prophet Muhammad. Hanaan envisioned joining this long lineage of teachers and encouraging her students to do the same. Hanaan also referred to the Islamic concept that a teacher would be rewarded for the good deeds completed by all those whom they educated, as well as all those whom their students educated, and so on. Though teaching others was not necessarily Hanaan's primary motivation for pursuing Qur'anic education, her aspiration underscored how such an outcome was central to her understanding of the purpose of a Qur'anic education. Hanaan sought to transmit what she had learned to those who remained in the U.S. Hanaan's schooling experience in Medina Baye thus not only offered her a concrete way of addressing the marginalization and feelings of inadequacy she had previously experienced, but also sparked her commitment to help educate the next generation of Black Muslims in the U.S.

Participating in Community-Wide Events

The axiomatic view of Black Muslim youth as holders and transmitters of knowledge extended beyond the classroom. This view informed teachers' and adults' decisions to invite youth to participate in community-wide events in Medina Baye and in the U.S. In Medina Baye, this was most prominently evidenced by students' participation in *jangi kamil*. Jangi kamil was an annual, three-day event during which the city's thousands of residents collectively completed as many *khatms* (recitations of the entire Qur'an) as possible.

For Muslims, reading the Qur'an is a sacred act. I asked Shaykh Mahy Cisse—the Director of Studies at AAII, the global spokesperson for Shaykh Ibrahim's movement, and an adoptive father to most Black American youth in Medina Baye—why residents organized jangi kamil each year. He explained that reciting the Qur'an was an explicit way to ask for divine intervention. Himself a hafiz, Shaykh Mahy quoted the ayat: "Your Lord has proclaimed, 'Call upon Me, I will respond to you'" (Qur'an 40:60). Allah also states: "We send down the Qur'an as a healing and mercy for the believers" (Qur'an 17:82). These ayats support the idea that reciting the Qur'an is what N. Fadeke Castor (2017) describes as a spiritual technology, or practices "to access sacred knowledge and solve problems" (165). For Muslims, reciting the Qur'an is a spiritual technology that enables them to enlist Allah's assistance in addressing their needs.

In Shaykh Ibrahim's movement, murids used this spiritual technology to seek individual and collective aid. Shaykh Ibrahim wrote and spoke extensively about the value of congregational acts of worship such as dhikr and reading the Qur'an. In *Kashif al-Ilbas* (*The Removal of Confusion*), Shaykh Ibrahim devotes an entire chapter to the merits of communal worship. He quotes Shaykh Umar Futi Taal, the nineteenth-century West African Islamic scholar and Tijani shaykh who fought the French colonizers and established the Umarian Caliphate (in present-day Mali, Senegal, and Guinea), who cited the statement of the ninth-century scholar Sidi Ali al-Khawas,

> [The disciple] should also perform the remembrance with a congregation.... The Exalted Lord of Truth [Allah] has likened the heart to rocks, and it is well known that the rock cannot be shattered except by the combined strength of a group. The hardness of the heart is likewise impenetrable, except by the congregational remembrance of people gathered as a single heart. This is because the power of the congregation is stronger than one individual. (Niasse 2010, 46)

Later in the chapter, Shaykh Ibrahim cites the hadith: "Whenever a group of people are seated together remembering Allah the Exalted, the angels surround them, mercy envelopes them, tranquility descends upon them, and Allah the Exalted mentions them to those who are in His presence" (Niasse 2010, 44). Shaykh Ibrahim marshals these proofs to encourage his murids to commit themselves to communal worship.

Jangi kamil was a congregational practice and spiritual technology that Shaykh Ibrahim inaugurated in 1966. In a letter to Sayyidi Aliou Cisse, Shaykh Ibrahim outlined his vision for the event and instructed the people of Medina Baye to participate in jangi kamil. Shaykh Ibrahim concluded his explanation of the rationale for jangi kamil by making a dua on behalf of his community. He asked that Allah accept the community's efforts, make it easy for them to complete the construction of the Grand Mosque, and bless the mosque to be a place that remained busy with *ibada* (worship) forever. Shaykh Ibrahim also asked that Allah preserve Senegal

Figure 4.3. With the Grand Mosque of Medina Baye and its courtyard filled to capacity for jummah, some brothers pray on the street, May 2025. Photo courtesy of the author.

in the *dunya* (the temporal world) and *deen* (matters of religion), preserve Islam in the country, and protect its people from their enemies.

In the more than half century after Shaykh Ibrahim organized the first jangi kamil, his community continued to hold the event. Each year, jangi kamil ended with the imam at the Grand Mosque making a dua for those who participated in the khatms and for the community at large. The final dua was made after jummah—the most well-attended gathering of the week. The more than one thousand people who congregated inside the mosque, the courtyard, and the nearby streets were all present for the dua and therefore promised the blessings of the collective ibada. The Senegalese Tijani scholar Ustadh Barham Mahmud Diop mentioned the significance of this practice in his introduction to Shaykh Ibrahim's *tafsir* (exegesis) of the Qur'an. He cited the hadith, "Whoever witnessed a khatm, it is as though one were witnessing the distribution of the *maghanim* (spoils of war)" (Niasse 2014, 39).

Though anyone could participate in jangi kamil, Qur'an school students were a critical population who helped ensure that a high number of khatms were completed. Each year, jangi kamil began after fajr on Wednesday, the last day of the school week. On the Wednesday that I observed, teachers informed students that they would take a break from their regular schedule. Hundreds of students flowed out of the school, some walking hurriedly and others casually as they journeyed to the courtyard of the mosque. It quickly filled up as students sat on straw mats, shaded by massive black tents that had set up to provide some relief from the sweltering desert heat.

I sat with Ustadh Diallo's class. Ustadh Diallo had pledged that his class would complete 30 khatms of the Qur'an. He divvied up the total in a way that would maximize participation and efficiency. Reflecting the view of Black Muslim youth as knowledgeable resources in the here and now, Ustadh Diallo appointed Jamal to help him. Jamal was a 14-year-old student from Lagos, Nigeria, a kindhearted, serious young man whose love for football was on hold for the next few months while he was on review—by Ramadan, Jamal hoped to be ready for the

Figure 4.4. Hundreds of students assemble in the courtyard of the Grand Mosque of Medina Baye for jangi kamil, May 2018. Photo courtesy of the author.

final recitation that would certify him a hafiz. Ustadh Diallo appreciated Jamal's progress and dedication and chose him to be a *maagi dara* (Qur'an teacher's assistant). In the classroom, Jamal took occasional breaks from his studies to test other students on their lessons. Jamal's responsibilities extended outside of the classroom as he helped organize his peers' contributions to jangi kamil.

In Ustadh Diallo and Jamal's hands were 30 thin, paperback books, each containing one juz (or two hizbs) of the Qur'an. Together, they walked through the narrow rows of students. Crouching down to be eye level with one boy, Jamal asked his classmate, "Do you know this part very well?" To another, Jamal stared intently as he asked, "Which part do you know really, really well?" Each student, regardless of how far they had progressed in their studies, was assigned portions of the Qur'an that they had memorized and could read easily. Students read their assigned portion ten times per period. I watched as students started, their mouths moving with swiftness, their bodies rocking back and forth with momentum, their eyes only occasionally scanning the page as they recited primarily from memory.

The scene I observed was akin to activities in other West African Muslim societies. Writing about a Dyula community in Korhogo, Côte d'Ivoire, Robert Launay (2021) describes,

> Funeral ceremonies for adult men in Korhogo included a session held on the third day after burial that involved the recitation of an entire (long!) book of the praise of the Prophet, in the form of formulaic phrases. The book was literally disassembled into component pages that were handed out to all men in attendance capable of reciting them from the printed text; each participant would have a few pages to recite. Once they were told to start, everyone would recite their allotted pages. The recitation as such was unintelligible, at least to human ears, but in a relatively short interval, the entire book was recited. In other words, the ability to recite which men acquired in the course of their Quranic education was a considerable religious and social, rather than practical, utility. (95)

Like these men in Côte d'Ivoire, youth in Medina Baye were able to work strategically, collaboratively, and efficiently to complete the khatms because of their classroom education. While Launay concluded that the speedy recitation was "unintelligible, at least to human ears" and therefore bore "religious and social, rather than practical, utility," such a metric obscured the useful advantage that students brought to jangi kamil. Rather than work individually, they coordinated their efforts so as to increase the number of khatms and thereby offer their Lord a greater number of devotional acts. The Qur'an school students' expertise thus provided practical, religious, and social benefit.

During jangi kamil of 2019, the community rejoiced when it was announced that they had completed 75,461 khatms. The hundreds of students who dedicated three days to reciting the Qur'an were instrumental in helping reach this number. These youth were able to make significant contributions because of the strong Arabic reading skills and memorization they had acquired in the classroom. Adult residents celebrated the students' crucial role by distributing delicious homemade snacks. The adults filled small plastic cups with *bissap* (hibiscus), ginger, and other ice-cold drinks. They passed out cellophane bags bursting at the seams with freshly fried beignets and sealed containers of *chagri* (millet with sweetened yogurt and fruit). This distribution of food and drinks underscored the appreciation community members had for these young people who had labored for days in the hot weather to undertake a task on behalf of Shaykh Ibrahim's global movement. Students took pride in their participation as well, arriving for jummah in anticipation of the final announcement dressed in their finest, custom-tailored outfits.

That AAII suspended normal instruction during jangi kamil and required everyone to participate—rather than only those closest to becoming huffaz—was indicative of its axiomatic stance of Black Muslim brilliance. It was expected that all youth could and would contribute. After all, their classroom instruction had provided them with the necessary skills to assist with the collective effort. Moreover, for the duration of jangi kamil, as residents walked through Medina Baye, they inevitably saw or heard hundreds of youth sitting outside the Grand Mosque reciting the Qur'an. The scene, though striking, was not unusual. Khatms were everyday practices in the city. When I asked Shaykh Mahy to elaborate on the origins of jangi kamil, he explained, "Shaykh Ibrahim didn't just point to this one occasion, saying that this is the one time you have to read Qur'an. It can be anytime. . . . Here in Medina Baye, every day we read and complete the Qur'an." Shaykh Mahy noted how, historically, murids gathered at Sayyidi Aliou Cisse and Shaykh Hassan Cisse's houses each day to complete a khatm. Ahmed Sufi Muhammad (2018), who in 1989 became the first Black American hafiz at AAII, also recalled seeing people walk to Shaykh Hassan's house each morning after fajr, divide the Qur'an amongst themselves, and read the entire text. At Shaykh Mahy's house, I similarly observed the older male students who lived in his guest rooms read Qur'an together on behalf of the household. They read Surah Yasin every day after asr and started and completed the whole Qur'an every Friday morning. These gatherings included at least a dozen or so students from different African countries, a few who were huffaz but the majority of whom were not. The group welcomed participation from anyone who chanced upon them in Shaykh Mahy's living room.

Shaykh Mahy further elaborated on the idea of Qur'an recitation as a spiritual technology and an everyday form of collective care: "If people need something, they read the Qur'an." In Medina Baye, if someone moved into a new home, they would invite a group of Qur'an school students to complete a khatm and ask Allah to protect the residents of the new space. If a person was sick, someone would ask a Qur'an teacher to organize their students to complete a khatm and plead with Allah to restore the person's health. If someone passed away, those who remained brought students together to complete a khatm and ask Allah that the reward of the blessed act be bestowed upon the deceased, thus expiating their sins. As young people participated in these khatms, they drew upon their Qur'anic education to engage in acts of collective care to address the needs of their community.

Sayyida Kubra Askari-Cisse, the Black American Tijani and hafiza who served as the othermother for Black American youth at AAII, often gathered young people in her living room to complete khatms. During the summer 2020 uprisings following the police murder of George Floyd in the U.S., Black American and West African youth completed a khatm for all those suffering under racial injustice. Their efforts were part of a long-standing tradition among Shaykh Ibrahim's community, as he similarly authorized his followers to "use all that you have at your disposal in terms of the weaponry of (Divine) supplication" against the French colonizers (as cited in Wright 2013, 214). Zachary Wright (2013) argues that such recommendations were part of the "spiritual war of liberation waged by the community of Shaykh Ibrahim," and in particular, Shaykh Ibrahim's practice of "marshaling of disciples against colonialism" (213–214). As Black American and West African youth recited the Qur'an for people in the U.S., they adapted the religious and political practices of their spiritual community to address contemporary injustices.

In August 2020, after the passing of Mallam Muhammad Barayah Niasse Cisse, Sayyida Kubra gathered all the Black American and West African students under her care to complete a khatm in his honor. Barayah, as he was affectionately called, was a Tijani brother from Togo who served as an adoptive father for the first generation of American students at AAII. Aziza, Hanaan, Isra, and Hafsa had heard about Barayah from family members who had fond memories of him caring for them decades ago. Lastly, on many Friday mornings during the year, Sayyida Kubra organized the students to do a khatm for Shaykh Hassan, whom some had met as young children, whom several had been

Figure 4.5. A thirty-book set of the Qur'an in Sayyida Kubra Askari-Cisse's living room that students distribute among themselves for a collective khatm, November 2024. Photo courtesy of the author.

named after, and whom all had heard countless stories about. They dedicated their ibada to the person who had laid the foundation for their sacred learning.

Jangi kamil thus represented the most prominent instantiation of a common practice in Shaykh Ibrahim's movement. Tijanis understood Qur'anic recitation as a means of invoking Allah's assistance in addressing their material and spiritual needs. From Shaykh Ibrahim's time to the contemporary moment, people gathered in schools, at the mosque, and in their homes to recite the Qur'an and call on Allah on behalf of their community. As young people attended Qur'an schools, they received the formal instruction and knowledge needed to participate in these endeavors. Their involvement in jangi kamil and other khatms were not romanticized as token gestures towards activities primarily undertaken by adults. Rather, the enlistment of and reliance upon their expertise showed how the contributions of Black Muslim youth were appreciated but not unexpected. These young people were treated as knowledgeable resources who contributed to the community throughout the multi-year process of memorizing the Qur'an. The emphasis on student participation in community-wide events pointed to a collectivist understanding of the purpose of Qur'anic education; learning how to read, recite, and memorize the Qur'an entailed an ethical imperative to use that knowledge to benefit others. All Black Muslim youth were called upon to use their education to engage in religious acts of collective care.

Brilliance on the Move

It was Sunday evening in early May 2016 in downtown Atlanta, Georgia. I sat in a crowded conference room at a hotel, awaiting the start of an event commemorating Shaykh Ibrahim's birthday. Many in the audience had made ziyara to Shaykh Ibrahim's tomb at the maqam in Medina Baye, but this event in the U.S. was another form of ziyara. Organized by Black American, Senegalese, and Ghanaian Tijanis in Atlanta, the event was also considered to be a ziyara—an opportunity for Tijanis to be in one another's company as they paid honor to their departed shaykh.

The event's keynote speaker was Shaykh Mahy Cisse. Tijani attendees came from throughout the sprawling Atlanta metropolitan area, as well as from Detroit, New York City, Washington D.C., and other cities across the U.S. During the event, 15-year-old Musa was called up to recite Qur'an for the crowd. Musa had recently returned from AAII, which he had been attending since the age of nine. Musa and his parents were considering whether he should continue studying to become a hafiz, or if it would be better for him to enroll in a different type of Islamic school in Medina Baye. The event's host introduced Musa as someone who exemplified the impressive knowledge that characterized the Black American youth who studied in Medina Baye. Dressed elegantly in a three-piece, Senegalese grand bubu, Musa stood tall, exuding confidence as he recited a surah in a steady voice. Many in the crowd were familiar with Musa. Some were family friends who had known Musa since he was a baby. Others were AAII alumni who had studied alongside Musa's father in the 1990s. Others were parents whose children had been Musa's classmates in Medina Baye. A few in the audience were parents and young people who had heard about Musa but had yet to meet him personally. Once Musa finished reciting, the host awarded him a cash gift of a couple hundred dollars on stage. The host explained that this was a token of appreciation and encouragement given to Musa on behalf of the community for his academic feats.

The event organizers—who attended AAII during their teenaged years and were now in their thirties and forties, and two of whom had daughters at AAII—shared with me that calling upon young people like Musa was an obvious and practical choice; it was a task that youth in Medina Baye were trained for and entrusted to fulfill by virtue of their education. But they also acknowledged the important representational image that their choices projected. Even in Medina Baye, one alumnus recalled how Shaykh Hassan would bring some of the Black American students to the front of the crowd during large ceremonies at his house and ask them to recite from the Qur'an (Muhammad 2018, 6). Sayyida Kubra also recounted that Shaykh Hassan asked her to do the opening Qur'an recitation at a conference in Senegal. She was initially intimidated by the request, but agreed to do so after Shaykh Hassan explained how significant it would be for the Senegalese audience to see a young American woman fill the role. Similarly, in the U.S., the organizers explained that they invited young people to recite in order to inspire Black Muslim children and youth in attendance and to highlight the talent and resources that existed within

Black Muslim communities. From Senegal to the U.S., the presence of Black American Muslims who recited the Qur'an with confidence and ease to major crowds was impactful; their race, age, and nationality all projected meaningful messages to audience members.

As was the case when I observed Aziza help Samira, I was struck by Musa's public display of academic expertise. Having paused his studies in Medina Baye, Musa appeared to be at an impasse in his hafiz journey. I interviewed him two years later, at which point he had withdrawn from AAII and enrolled in an Islamic studies program in Medina Baye. I asked him to reflect on his Qur'anic education. Musa explained,

> What I was doing [at AAII] was just enough to flow under the radar and not get [physically] beat. . . . But I wasn't really going above and beyond to become, like, that kid that the teacher knows, "Oh this kid studies all the time, I don't have to [physically] beat him." We had kids like that, where they always knew their lessons every day, the first person to recite. . . . The good students are the ones who are actually trying to do extra. I was kinda doing just enough.

Musa reflected on how he was far from an outstanding student. He admitted doing just enough not to be subjected to corporal discipline—something that teachers at AAII had been explicitly instructed by administrators on numerous occasions not to use, with Shaykh Mahy, the Director of Studies at AAII, even explaining to me and others, "We want students to love the Qur'an, not to hate the Qur'an." Some teachers abandoned the practice, and others did not; some teachers used it on some students but not on others. Yet in Musa's case, because his teacher defiantly used corporal discipline against him, its looming threat shaped Musa's efforts. Musa's strategy was similar to the minimax principle, wherein a learner is motivated not by the pursuit or attainment of knowledge but rather by an extrinsic reward. As a result, the learner seeks to do as little as possible to attain the highest possible reward (Blum 2020, 56). In Musa's case, his extrinsic motivation was not a reward but rather the desire to avoid a consequence. Recognizing that this fear propelled his academic engagement, in contrast to some of his peers who wanted to go above and beyond, Musa concluded that he was not one of the "good students."

Despite Musa's self-assessment of his shortcomings, that night Musa was handpicked to fill a prominent public role. In fact, the organizers chose him over other huffaz from AAII who were in attendance. Musa recited a surah from memory and with accuracy, confidence, and grace. His recitation was met with an enthusiastic reception from the audience, who erupted in applause, cheers, and heartfelt calls of "Takbir!" followed by "Allahu Akbar!" (Allah is the greatest!). Much like Aziza, who exuded confidence in teaching Samira even though she doubted whether she would ever become a hafiza, Musa demonstrated competence and mastery despite the fact that he left AAII. The warm reaction, public praise, and monetary reward Musa received suggested that he had accomplished something noteworthy in the eyes of his community.

Since 1983, several hundred Black American students memorized the Qur'an in Medina Baye, but the majority of these young people did not become huffaz. Between 1983 and 2025, AAII and its partner school, the AAII Legacy Academy, graduated 19 Black American huffaz—nine young women and ten young men. The remaining memorized some (and often a quite significant) portion of the Qur'an but left the school before they finished.[12] As was the case with Aziza, Musa appeared to be a confident and celebrated student who nonetheless recognized that he struggled with memorizing. It was certainly true that becoming a hafiz or hafiza would have granted him a much greater degree of cultural capital (Eickelman 1978, 495), but Musa's performance revealed how students at varying points in their education possessed meaningful cultural capital. All students gained skills that were worthy of celebration and brought religious benefit to their community.

This contributed to the experience that Hanaan and Isra alluded to in their comments cited at the opening of this chapter. While the final benchmark of the Qur'an memorization program was becoming a hafiz or hafiza, the program entailed a more robust process. It built upon the religious understandings of the abundant blessings that permeated the entire process of learning the divine scripture, and the axiomatic stance that harnessed all students' inherent potential. Reflecting an understanding of piety as relational and cultivated through collective care, the Qur'anic educational experience also instilled within students the responsibility to contribute to their community.

Figure 4.6. The flier advertising the monthly Qur'an khatm for Ya Fatou, featuring a vintage photo of her.

This was further evident in the efforts led by alumni in the U.S. These alumni, some of whom were huffaz but the majority of whom were not, preserved the practice of Qur'an khatms that had been commonplace for them in Medina Baye. For example, starting in the fall of 2020, after the passing of Ya Fatou, the Senegalese Tijani woman who was the mother of Shaykh Hassan, Imam Cheikh, and Shaykh Mahy and an othermother to the Black American youth who studied in Medina Baye from the 1980s onwards, an intergenerational group of Tijanis gathered for several hours on Zoom each month to complete a khatm in her honor. By 2025, these khatms were still ongoing and led by hafiz Ahmed Sufi Muhammad and hafiza Sayyida Kubra Askari-Cisse, two alumni who had fostered deep relationships of care with Ya Fatou over their years of studying in Medina Baye.

During these khatms for Ya Fatou, the organizers tried to recruit as many people as possible to make sure that the khatm would be done quickly. On numerous of the khatms I attended, the organizers asked Musa and Isra, who by that point had both moved back to the U.S., to join. Of the 16 people who showed up to one of these Zoom khatms, the majority had studied at AAII between the 1980s and 2020s but only five were huffaz. As was the case with jangi kamil, each person volunteered to read a portion of the Qur'an. Unmuting their microphones and reciting aloud in a manner reminiscent of what they used to do at AAII, each alumnus contributed to the collective effort. A select few had neither studied at AAII nor had yet learned how to read Arabic, but they too attended the Zoom meeting. During the first monthly khatm, after the final dua was recited, one such elderly woman named Hajjah Muneera unmuted her microphone. Hajjah Muneera regretfully explained that she didn't know how to read Arabic, and that this prevented her from being able to read Qur'an for the khatm. She thanked the group for their work and for allowing her to be present and reap the benefits of the collective effort. In the following months, Hajjah Muneera took initiative to contact group members and remind them to plan the upcoming khatms, thus indicating her recognition of the alumni as critical and knowledgeable resources who brought religious benefit to the community.

Conclusion

In the whole world you know
There's a million boys and girls
Who are young, gifted, and Black
And that's a fact.
—Nina Simone, "To Be Young, Gifted, and Black"

Black American Muslim youth who attended AAII carried with them the racialized messages that they encountered in the U.S., where Black and Muslim students' inherent capacities were often questioned. As they made meaning of their Qur'anic education in Medina Baye, their perspectives were refracted through U.S. racial logics and their lived experiences with anti-Black racism in the U.S. In Medina Baye, they experienced Qur'anic education as a site of freedom dreaming, where community narratives, classroom pedagogies, and congregational worship reflected an axiomatic stance of Black Muslim brilliance. The place-based cultural norms that undergirded Qur'anic education in Medina Baye were anchored in the foundational truth that the African American singer and civil rights icon Nina Simone describes in her song—that "there's a million boys and girls who are young, gifted, and Black." Though this notion could be questioned in anti-Black discourses that undergirded public education and multiracial Muslim schools in the U.S., in Medina Baye, it had always been "a fact."

In a society in which Black Muslim brilliance was axiomatic, all students—regardless of how far or fast they progressed in their Qur'anic education—learned to read, memorize, and teach the holy book. As they engaged in peer-to-peer learning, young people developed the confidence and experience to support one another in memorizing the Qur'an. Outside of the classroom, both in Medina Baye and in the U.S., young people recited the Qur'an at events and completed khatms on behalf of others. They experienced Qur'anic education as a form of learning that cultivated their relational piety as they participated in communal activities that were socially meaningful and religiously blessed. Furthermore, their contribution to these communal activities bore practical benefits—they shared the load of the work needed to complete khatms. Through the emphasis on peer-to-peer learning and student participation in community events, all Black Muslim youth gained experience utilizing their Qur'anic education to engage in collective care—developing the ethical imperative and expertise to address the needs of their community.

5

Time to Work

Living, Dreaming, and Doing Khidma

It was Friday afternoon in October 2018 in Washington D.C. at Masjid Muhammad. Founded in 1937 by the Nation of Islam, Masjid Muhammad was known as the first mosque built in the U.S. by the descendants of enslaved Africans. Once the Honorable Elijah Muhammad passed away and Imam Warith Deen Mohammed brought members of his father's organization into Sunni Islam, Masjid Muhammad became a hub for Imam Mohammed's national community.

That Friday, jummah was led by a special visitor, Imam Cheikh Tijani Cisse—Shaykh Ibrahim Niasse's grandson, Shaykh Hassan's younger brother, and the current Imam of Medina Baye. Imam Cheikh, as most people called him, had just arrived from Senegal a few days before. Once jummah ended, several dozen women and men remained in the *musallah*, the expansive room with a soft carpet patterned in a beige and blue geometric design, where women and men listened to Imam Cheikh's khutba and then prayed together. Many in the audience were Tijanis, some who lived in the area but most who had traveled by car, bus, train, or plane to come see their shaykh.

As people enthusiastically exchanged light kisses, tight hugs, and firm handshakes, an older man with a gray beard walked to the *mimbar* (pulpit). It was Imam Johari Abdul-Malik, a Black American Muslim religious scholar, who, among other prominent roles, was the first Muslim chaplain at Howard University, the historically Black college and university (HBCU) located less than a mile away from Masjid Muhammad. Imam Johari addressed the crowd.

> Some of our young people [who studied overseas], they came home and their mind wasn't right. They went overseas to study, to learn the

Qur'an, and to learn Arabic, and when they came back, they loved the Qur'an but they hated themselves. [*Several people call out "mm'mmm" to voice their disapproval and disappointment.*] I'm saying to you now, we have a relationship with the Shaykh and his community of people, who when they come back, they love Islam, they love the Prophet sallallahu alayhi wa sallam, and they love themselves! [*Several people make jubilant sounds. One brother exclaims, "Takbir!", an Arabic command that means "Proclaim that Allah is great." Others respond, "Allahu Akbar!", or "Allah is the greatest!"*] . . . But to live in an environment, where they live the environment of the Qur'an, they live the environment of the companions, they learn to love Islam and love themselves and love their people, and come back and do service to this community. [*One brother affirms, "That's right!"*] Some of them come back home from good schools and then go serve some other community. Am I right? [*Multiple people call out, "Yes!"*] You can't find them once they learned the Qur'an because somebody offered them a few dollars and they go off somewhere. But with this school, we're talking about people from our community who would love to come back to Masjid Muhammad and teach us.

Imam Johari had not, to my knowledge, joined the Tijani tariqa. He had neither attended AAII nor enrolled his children there. Yet his narrative mirrored the testimonies and aspirations that I heard repeatedly from Black American Tijani parents, community members, and alumni when they spoke about the educational experience in Medina Baye, the religious and racial imperative it inculcated within students, and the types of work that alumni undertook once they returned to the U.S.

In March 2021, I heard Shaykh Mahy Cisse emphasize a similar narrative in Medina Baye. His remarks were captured in a video produced by a Senegalese news outlet that covered the graduation ceremony for a 12-year-old Black American student named Kamal who had just become a hafiz in Medina Baye. The title of the video listed Kamal's name, preceded by the descriptor *l'Americain* (French for "the American"). I came across the video because several Black American and West African Tijanis shared it on Facebook and WhatsApp. Within two days, the video had almost two thousand views.

In the video, several dozen people were tightly packed onto Sayyida Kubra Askari-Cisse's rooftop. I spotted members of Kamal's family who had flown in from New Jersey, his Senegalese teachers, his Black American and West African classmates, and a few Black American adult residents of Medina Baye, among many other nicely dressed women, men, young people, and children whose smiling faces I did not recognize. Seated at the front of the crowd, with bright lights shining onto them, were Shaykh Mahy and Kamal. After Kamal recited the final surahs of the Qur'an, Shaykh Mahy addressed the audience.

> The Prophet sallallahu alayhi wa sallam said, "The best among you are those who learn Qur'an and teach others." So now, today, you learned it. Make sure that you carry this light wherever you go. Carry it to America. Because when they took people to America, they thought that they separated them from the *deen* [religion], they separated them from Qur'an, but the Qur'an came back to our brothers and sisters. We thank Allah for that.

Shaykh Mahy invoked the hadith that fused the acts of learning and teaching the Qur'an as he urged Kamal to use his education to engage in collective care. He asserted that doing so would not only make among those who were most beloved to Allah, but would also mark an act of defiance against European slave traders who centuries earlier attempted to sever Africans' connections to Islam.

From Washington D.C. to Medina Baye, Imam Johari and Shaykh Mahy's comments reflected a pan-African Tijani worldview that held high hopes for Black American students. Earlier iterations of Black Muslims' freedom dreams had brought young people to Senegal. Now, Imam Johari and Shaykh Mahy spoke of the next phase of these dreams. They eagerly anticipated that young people would return as scholars who would educate their communities. According to these widely circulated narratives, Black Americans striving to deepen their knowledge of Islam could turn to young people in their own community, who would provide a religious education that nurtured rather than negated their racial identities. Ultimately, adults anticipated that these young people's efforts would help challenge essentializing myths of Islamic scholarly authority as incompatible with Blackness and repair the harms enacted upon their ancestors whose access to Islamic knowledge had been violently suppressed centuries ago.

Many adult Tijanis echoed the vision of young people returning to the U.S. and getting to "work." They often used the word "work" interchangeably with the Arabic word khidma and its English equivalent, service. These three words—work, khidma, and service—did not refer to formal jobs associated with waged labor. Instead, they described activities through which alumni could leverage their education to bring benefit to themselves, their shuyukh, and their people. In contrast to notions of Islamic piety as an individualistic endeavor, and capitalist conceptions of education as a route to individual socioeconomic mobility, ideas about work, khidma, and service encouraged Black American Muslim youth to collectively care for others as they moved into adulthood.

This chapter examines the trajectories of Black American youth who studied in Medina Baye from the 1980s to the 2020s. It asks: How did young people take up the often-repeated imperative to do work, khidma, and service? How did they balance this imperative with the need to economically sustain themselves in the U.S.? To answer these questions, this chapter focuses on three categories of young people. Each category envisioned and enacted a different pathway into adulthood. The first was young people who, true to Imam Johari and Shaykh Mahy's narratives, were committed to Islamic educational work. The second was young people who leveraged their education as a sociopolitical and moral compass that anchored their subsequent work and life choices. The third was young people who went to school or worked in the U.S. but ultimately returned to Medina Baye during their twenties with hopes of rebuilding their lives there. These three groups reflect the varied ways in which young people strived to live out new freedom dreams after their studies in Medina Baye. These three groups' trajectories demonstrate the possibilities and foreclosures of sustained pan-African Tijani Islamic educational exchange in offering Black American Muslims resources for transforming themselves and their communities.

Living, Spending Time, and Working as a Tijani

At the core of young people and adults' dreams were existential questions about what it meant to be Muslim. As we saw in the previous chapters, in Medina Baye, young peoples' education had been oriented towards collective care. For the next phase of their lives, what type of work would enable them to continue collectively caring for others? How should they spend their time in this *dunya* (temporal world)? Imam Johari and Shaykh Mahy's remarks offered some answers to these questions. However, their answers pointed to conceptions of piety, work, and time that were in tension with ideas promoted in the racial capitalist, white supremacist society of the U.S.

In her study of an African American Muslim congregation in Los Angeles, California, Pamela Prickett (2021) asserts the need for a broader conception of piety that "examines expected rituals (i.e., prayer, veiling) but also social, political, and economic practices that believers engage in together with the intent of deepening their faith" (12). In contrast to understandings of Islamic piety as a project of individual subject formation focused on personal virtues such as modesty and practices such as wearing hijab, Prickett found that her interlocuters held a different ideal for how they ought to live out their faith. For these Black Muslims, Islamic piety "involves the cultivation of virtues that must be achieved through engagement with others" (ibid., 13). Addressing poverty, racism, and other structural inequities in their neighborhood were essential activities through which "members of the mosque strive to deepen their piety and, in turn, their relationship with Allah" (ibid., 21). This understanding of Islamic piety as linked to community transformation was shared by many Black Muslim congregations in the twentieth and twenty-first centuries in the U.S. (McCloud 2004; Rouse 2004). Imam Johari's comments reflected one such example.

For Black Americans who were raised in such communities before moving to Medina Baye, the notions of piety they had been accustomed to were reaffirmed in the ideals articulated by Shaykh Ibrahim and the contemporary Tijani shuyukh they interacted with. Thus, from the U.S. to Senegal, many Black Muslims understood that work in and for their community would propel them to become most beloved to Allah.

Progressing towards that goal required one to make the most of one's time on earth. A person had to fulfill their divinely ordained purpose, which Allah identifies in the Qur'an: "I did not create jinn and humans except to worship Me" (51:56) This ayat explains that the purpose of a person's time on Earth is to engage in activities that allow them to worship, praise, or show gratitude towards Allah. Showing gratitude is of central importance in the Tijani tariqa, which is characterized as a path of *shukr* (gratitude). In *Jawahir al-Ma'ani* (*Precious Meanings and Attainment of Hope*), Shaykh Ahmad al-Tijani explains, "Gratitude is the greatest door to God, and His straightest path" (as cited in Wright 2020, 200). Shaykh al-Tijani also advises, "You will find all promises in God's revelation associated with gratitude: *If they are grateful, We will increase them* [Qur'an 14:7]" (ibid., 201). One commentator explained that this promise relates to the specific thing that a person shows gratitude for. If a person uses their time to engage in acts intended to show gratitude towards Allah, then Allah will increase the *baraka* (blessings) in their time (Suleiman 2021). As evidence, this commentator spoke of Muslims throughout history who accomplished significant feats in seemingly short amounts of time. Their achievements called into question literal notions of time and instead underscored how Allah could imbue greater baraka and value in a person's time. Any action could be done with the intention of showing gratitude for time, from fasting to feeding someone. Acts of collective care thus expanded and added baraka in one's time and constituted work that fulfilled a person's divinely ordained purpose on Earth, which was to fill their time with activities that allowed them to show gratitude to Allah.

Shaykh Hassan Cisse offered advice to his murids on how they should spend their time. Speaking at a Tijani zawiya near Cape Town, South Africa in 2003, Shaykh Hassan asserted:

> Islam is a religion of brotherhood. We should help our brothers and sisters. We should give assistance and help to anyone of the brothers who needs it. We should not even wait for him to say, "Oh brother, help me. Oh sister, help me." If you know your brother or your sister is in trouble, is in need, you should hurry up and help him. In Islam, to maintain the relationship between the brothers and sisters, to maintain the unity, to maintain the friendship, to maintain the connection between us, is more important even than salat and *siyam* [fasting] and *sadaqa* [charity]. This is a hadith of the Prophet sallallahu'alayhi wa sallam. We should work day and night to be together.

I initially heard Shaykh Hassan make these remarks in a video that an AAII alumna forwarded to me on WhatsApp. Shaykh Hassan's remarks were part of a 48-minute lecture, which I later found on YouTube. That

Figure 5.1. Shaykh Hassan Cisse (seated in the center) addresses attendees at the Tijani zawiya in Gugulethu, a township near Cape Town, South Africa in 2003. Watch his full speech at http://tiny.cc/ShaykhHassanCapeTown.

this short snippet had been extracted and shared on social media demonstrated the relevance and appeal of this message, especially among the U.S. Tijani community; the clip widely circulated in the days after I received that initial message. Summarizing what he framed as a core principle of Islam, Shaykh Hassan underscored the imperative for Muslims to foster relational bonds and assist others. He discussed the urgency of time and explained that Muslims should be very quick to help one another. Citing a hadith that underscored a notion of relational piety, Shaykh Hassan asserted that collective care practices could be even more meaningful than the five pillars of Islam. Finally, Shaykh Hassan explicitly used the word "work" to frame such religious acts of collective care as so important that they could even occupy all of a Muslim's time.

Shaykh Hassan offered an ethical representation of time as a resource that entailed "an explicit working on yourself, the world, and social relations" (Bear 2016, 494). Such a representation was at odds with capitalist conceptions of time as an entity that was "stripped of its meaning in order to make it a technique for assessing our worth according to market criteria and to accrue capital" (ibid., 492). In a capitalist society, one was seen as a valuable person if they focused all their time on activities that generated money. Under capitalism, because time was "reduce[d] to a tool to create and increase capital," then helping a sister in need, cleaning up a neighborhood, or teaching someone how to read the Qur'an—all activities that did not promise clear economic gains—were a waste of time (ibid., 496). As Julius Nyerere (1968), the pan-Africanist and founding president of Tanzania argued, education in European colonial and capitalist societies taught students values that "led to the possession of individual material wealth being the major criterion of social merit and worth" (416–417). If the usefulness of schooling was measured according to a capitalist rubric that placed value on a person's ability to make money, Qur'anic education—a type of learning that was not explicitly geared towards upward socioeconomic mobility—was a waste of time.

However, Black American Muslim students who moved between the U.S. and Senegal encountered a pan-African Islamic Tijani idea of collective care that offered them conceptions of human value, time, and work that were radically different from the ideals promoted by racial capitalism and white supremacy. They learned that they were valuable because they were creations of Allah, not because they could make money. They were taught that their purpose on this Earth was to do work that showed gratitude to Allah, and that engaging in such work would expand their time and make them most beloved to Allah.

A focus on collective care thus elucidates an alternative framework for understanding Black American alumni's long-term pathways beyond the ideal trajectories promoted through racial capitalism and white supremacy, which measured the outcomes of schooling and employment in ways that called into question the value of these young peoples' experiences in Medina Baye. At the same time, the majority of alumni ultimately returned to the U.S. as they transitioned into adulthood, a shift which forced them to consider how to reconcile the contrasting blueprints of success as they developed new understandings of what it meant to live, spend time, work, and dream in the world. Each of these three groups of young people grappled with how to leverage their educational experiences to do work for their community amidst the economic pressures of the U.S.

Group One: Learning to Teach

Back in Washington D.C., many in the audience were familiar with or were themselves the alumni who fulfilled Imam Johari's vision of youth who returned from Medina Baye with the religious knowledge, racial pride, and sociopolitical commitment to work for their people, regardless of the financial tradeoffs. Throughout the country, at Tijani zawiyas and predominantly Black Muslim mosques, many male alumni served as imams, gave the jummah khutba, and led taraweeh during Ramadan. Several female and male alumni taught Qur'an classes to children and adults, as well as classes on Sufism and Islamic texts written by Tijani shuyukh. These women and men substantiated Imam Johari's vision of "people from our community who would love to come back to Masjid Muhammad and teach us."

At the same time, these efforts were not enough to fuel a financially viable career. One alumnus put it frankly: "I would love to just teach things, but I have to feed my family and on the Day of Judgment I'm going to be held accountable for taking care of my family in a proper way." One mother whose daughter and son were enrolled at AAII similarly explained that she wanted her children to eventually teach Qur'an but clarified, "but for that to be their career, no! Unfortunately, we don't really see that Islamic knowledge has such a high value placed on it in the States. You're not really able to feed your family in that way. You always have to have that plus another job."

Another alumnus explained that his shaykh objected to the idea of charging people for Islamic classes. The objection was bolstered by a warning from Shaykh al-Tijani, who cautioned a student, "You must avoid seeking knowledge for the sake of leadership or worldly sustenance, in this is surely found the destruction of this world and the next" (as cited in Wright 2022, 87). A similar warning is found in the hadith: "Recite the Qur'an. Do not eat from it; do not be averse to it; and do not exceed proper bounds with it" (al-Nawawi 2013, 27). While being a Qur'an teacher was typically financially compensated work in Senegal, these teachings indicated the tenuous relationship between Islamic education and material gain. As such, they represented a stark contrast to the dominant, capitalist understandings of education in the U.S. and across the world, where schooling was marketed as a path to upward socioeconomic mobility, particularly for those who were most marginalized (Baum and McPherson 2022; Fong 2011; Jeffrey 2010; UNESCO 2015). However, Islamic teachings signaled an ethical endeavor in which financial compensation ought not be the primary driver for receiving or providing an Islamic education. Thus, in practice, most alumni pursued other full-time employment in the U.S. while they balanced their Islamic educational work as khidma.

One alumnus who worked as an electrician and taught Qur'an classes on weekends explained:

> When I do teach, I don't get paid. I do it for free, right? You know, you ask somebody for money, they say, "*Astaghfirullah* [I seek forgiveness from Allah], you charge for the deen?" [I say] Come on! I'm charging for the time that I have to take out my life so that I can be able to put food on my kids' plates, right? "Well, they don't in Saudi." Okay, you're right, 'cause they have a government job. The imam in Saudi is a government job. They get a salary from the government. The imams in Turkey are paid. These are government jobs. It's also why they can't tell you the truth all the time.

His comments indicated the economic pressures facing Islamic educators in the U.S., who were not supported by the type of state-sponsored infrastructure that sustained but also surveilled religious educational work in Muslim-majority countries. In the U.S., Muslim educators enjoyed the freedom to teach what and how they pleased, but also bore the burden of knowing that such work would likely not be enough to sustain themselves and their families.

Some current students dreamed of following in the footsteps of alumni who had undertaken Islamic educational work. Mahmoud was the most prominent example of this type of student. Mahmoud was a Black American from Brooklyn, New York who moved to Medina Baye in 2012 at the age of 19. He had just completed his first year at Howard University. Mahmoud intended to double major in performing arts and philosophy and aspired to become an actor or dancer. He navigated a higher educational landscape in which Black students graduated with the greatest student loan debt of any group, and in which 50 percent of Black student borrowers reported that their net worth was less than what they owed (Espinosa et al. 2019, 6). Mahmoud didn't receive enough financial aid to pay for his second year of college. Other students in his predicament might have either taken time off to work a low wage job, reduced their courseload and divided their time between work and school, or remained in school but gone into debt. However, Mahmoud's mother Ruqiyyah presented him with another option. Ruqiyyah was married to a Black American Tijani who had sent his daughters to AAII years before. Ruqiyyah tapped into her blended family's tradition and encouraged Mahmoud to study in Medina Baye. Mahmoud recalled,

> I wasn't really interested in religion at that point in my life. So my mother essentially had to bribe me to come here. She suggested I come for one year and within that year, she would save up money so that she could pay for my tuition after a year of me being away. . . . I thought it would be a pretty sweet deal. I would get a new experience in a new country, in a new continent, and when I came back home, I would be able to return to Howard and continue my studies. So, I decided to come.

About seven months into his time at AAII, Mahmoud learned to read, write, and speak a little bit of Arabic. Mahmoud described these early days: "I thought to myself, *hmmm*, if I can accomplish this much in only seven months, how much more can I accomplish if I stay here a bit longer?" He extended his trip by a few months, and then a few more months, "until I finally decided, you know what? I'm going to pursue this avenue of Islamic knowledge and mastery of the Arabic language."

When I formally interviewed Mahmoud in 2018, what was intended to be a gap year had extended to six years. Mahmoud told me he hoped to attend an Islamic university in Egypt after he finished in Medina Baye. After that, he would return to the U.S.

> MAHMOUD: I have a responsibility to go back and help my people, you know? Even Shaykh Mahy tells me that. He says, "Keep studying and go back and help your people." Stuff like that. He said that to me recently, actually, like a couple of days ago, because my mom was complaining to Shaykh Mahy about me still being here. He called me, and he said, "Did your mom tell you about our conversation?" and I was like, "Yeah." She's like, "When is my son coming back?" And

"Shaykh Mahy, you gotta let him go! You gotta let him come back!" Shaykh Mahy was like, "Come back and let him do what? Work or something?" She's like, "Yeah, he has to come back and work! He's 25!" Shaykh Mahy was like, "What? No!"

SAMIHA: Like what work? Like work in an office?

MAHMOUD: Shaykh Mahy was like, "Let him keep studying. When he's ready, he'll come back and help his people." So, yeah, I have an obligation to go back.

While Mahmoud's mother Ruqiyyah offered her son a path away from student debt and economic precarity in the U.S., she eventually came to believe that he had obtained more than enough Islamic knowledge in Medina Baye and needed to "come back and work!" As Shaykh Mahy and Ruqiyyah contrasted "work" and "study," they alluded to a definition of work as waged labor, rather than as synonymous with khidma. Shaykh Mahy contended that after prolonged study, Mahmoud would be ready to "work" to "help his people." Whether or not such work could double as Mahmoud's source of livelihood was unclear. Over the years, I had observed Ruqiyyah beam as Tijanis told her how hopeful they were about Mahmoud's future. However, with no end in sight to her son's studies, Ruqiyyah had grown apprehensive about the economic possibilities that might be foreclosed if he continued on that path.

Early on in Mahmoud's stay in Medina Baye, Ruqiyyah sent $300 USD a month to cover her son's expenses. Eventually, Mahmoud explained, "Shaykh Mahy was saying, 'No, you don't have to pay anything. You can stay in my house. You can eat with me whenever you want. Just go study.'" Mahmoud also sporadically received hadiya from Tijanis who wanted to encourage him in his studies. These monetary forms of collective care helped Mahmoud survive as a full-time student.

Mahmoud looked at me earnestly as he explained his future plans.

> In each nation, in each tribe, in each country, you have to have some sort of Islamic leadership that Allah raises up, that is able to speak the language of the people. Now, speaking the language of the people doesn't mean speaking English. Speaking the language means that you know and understand the customs and culture of the people. You know how to speak to them, you know? So, I'm not saying that I'm that guy that Allah

is raising up for the Americans. I'm not saying that at all, but I do feel like it is my duty to go back. Because one of the things, in hadith, *Nabi* [Prophet] sallallahu alayhi wa sallam says that on the Day of Judgment, a slave of Allah is not able to go forward until he is asked four questions . . . the last one, on his knowledge. How did he use the knowledge that he acquired? How did I use the knowledge that I'm acquiring here? I gotta go back and help my people. I have to. I have to. I have to at least try.

For Mahmoud, Islamic education was not simply an instrumentalist endeavor to gain the knowledge necessary to complete ritual acts, nor was it only an individualistic endeavor to learn personal piety. Instead, weaving together Qur'anic verses and prophetic teachings, Mahmoud emphasized the communal obligations that came with the privilege of being Islamically educated.

Adding further gravity to the sense of accountability that Mahmoud articulated, in another hadith, Prophet Muhammad said, "Whoever is asked about knowledge and conceals it, will be bridled on the Day of Resurrection with reins of fire." Though not mentioned by Mahmoud, this hadith underscores the obligation to share knowledge. Familiar with Islamic conceptions of time and his shaykh's encouragement to engage in work that benefited others, Mahmoud aspired to spread rather than hoard his knowledge. Perhaps in acknowledgement of the grandeur and gravity of his ambitions, Mahmoud clarified that "I'm not saying that I'm that guy" but nonetheless repeatedly reminded himself and me of the responsibility he had to share what he learned.

By 2024, twelve years into his studies, Mahmoud had become a husband and father. His wife was a Black American Tijani woman from Atlanta who had relocated to Medina Baye shortly after finishing high school. Like Mahmoud, she had access to Medina Baye as a postsecondary pathway because of her father, who attended AAII in the 1990s. Mahmoud's transition from a single youth who was dependent upon his mother, his shaykh, and his Sufi community to a family man marked his entry into social adulthood. This came with new responsibilities. By then, Mahmoud had become fluent in Wolof and Arabic, so he made money on the side by translating and teaching Arabic. He also took on a part-time remote job doing online marketing for a start-up established by a Black American Muslim brother in the community. These and other gigs gave Mahmoud a modest stream of income that came in handy as a married man and later a father, allowing him to give some hadiya to his shaykh, become slightly more financially independent, and mitigate the economic constraints associated with living out his and his community's freedom dreams.

Mahmoud's transition into social adulthood did not quell his dedication to his studies. His wife's family admired his ambitions, and he became a beneficiary of a more expansive network of collective care that included his in-laws and their extended community. Mahmoud, currently in his thirties, is still pursuing the collective dream that he will come back to teach his people. But rather than wait until then, Mahmoud began in 2023 to teach an online class based on a book of poetry by Shaykh Ibrahim. The book had yet to be published in English, so Mahmoud offered his own line-by-line translations and commentary on the work, providing English speakers first-time access to the poetry. At the end of the first class, he explained to the more than 30 people in attendance that he was teaching this class as khidma.

Overall, as students and alumni encountered a pan-African Tijani worldview that called them to benefit Allah's creation and saw education as a practice of collective care, they committed themselves to serving their people. For Mahmoud, who was among the growing number of students who were priced out of a college education in the U.S., a subsidized Islamic education abroad offered new possibilities. And for those alumni who juggled paid employment with khidma, their financial struggles nonetheless allowed them to do work that made them beloved to Allah and that contributed to their community's freedom dreams of religious autonomy in a U.S. context where Black Muslims' scholarly authority was often called into question.

Group Two: A Compass at Work

By 2024, I remained in contact with 31 Black American youth who studied in Medina Baye between 2012 and 2022. Of the 31 youth, 10 had remained in or moved back to Senegal, while 21 lived in the U.S. Five of the 21 were still in middle or high school, and the remaining 16 had by then graduated from high school (see Table 5.1 for more information). Among the 21 who returned to the U.S. for middle or high school, some

TABLE 5.1 School and Employment Status of Black American Alumni in the U.S. (data from 21 students who attended AAII between 2012 and 2022)

Current Status of Alumnus	Female	Male	Total
Enrolled in middle school or high school	0	5	5
Enrolled at a secular university	7	1	8
Enrolled at an Islamic university	2	0	2
Enrolled in a technical or trade school	0	1	1
Working and not enrolled in any school	1	2	3
Enrolled in graduate school	2	0	2
Total:	12	9	21

rejoined at their appropriate age-grade level, unimpeded by the several years of instruction they missed in math, language arts, and science. Others were placed in a lower grade, becoming the oldest students in their class but explaining their situation by sharing exciting memories of their international education. A few alumni sought out tutors to help them keep up with the rigors of their new schools. Overall, most alumni readjusted to the U.S. educational system within a few years.

Of the 16 alumni who graduated from high school, 12 of them (or 75 percent) went on to college, outpacing the 56.5 percent of Black students nationally who enroll in college immediately after high school (Espinosa et al. 2019, 5). Of these 12 college-going alumni, two young women had already obtained their bachelor's degrees and started graduate school. Eight were enrolled in a secular college, where they took on majors such as business, psychology, nursing, and Africana Studies. Another two, both of whom were women, enrolled at Islamic universities. Of the four out of 16 alumni who opted not to go to college after high school, one went to a trade school, and three others took on service sector jobs while they figured out their next moves.

Alumni who attended AAII in earlier times (between the 1983 and 2012) had similar trajectories. Some had gone on to college and graduate school, while others opted to end their schooling after earning a GED. Some started their own businesses after or without graduating from college or a trade school. Their formal employment ran the gamut— they were entrepreneurs, real estate project managers, graphic designers, electricians, construction workers, behavioral health specialists,

IT professionals, filmmakers, non-profit employees, lawyers, and stay-at-home mothers. At least eight adult alumni lived or worked transnationally. Such alumni leveraged their Wolof skills, Senegalese cultural knowledge, or relationships with Africans to create opportunities on the continent. Some started import-export businesses, sourcing clothing, dhikr beads, kufis, and other goods from West Africa that they resold in the U.S.

Across the different generations of alumni, their years in Medina Baye did not hamper their re-entry into the U.S. educational system or labor market. I learned that this was a primary concern among parents who considered sending their children to Medina Baye in the twenty-first century. One prospective parent informed me in a casual but matter-of-fact way that there was "a lot of racism in Muslim schools in Washington D.C." and that she wanted her seven-year-old son to "be in a place where he can see Black scholars around him." Yet like Ruqiyyah, this mother also inquired about how her son's schooling abroad might affect his long-term academic trajectory. She was among the many parents who acknowledged the economic demands of the U.S. and envisioned that their children would go to college. They worried about the foreclosures that might emerge if or when their children returned to the U.S. but still hoped that the educational experience would transform their children's lives.

Even as the school built up an online presence, most people learned about the educational experience in Medina Baye through word-of-mouth. Some who were on the fence about sending their children sought advice from alumni, who helped assuage prospective parents' concerns. Maimouna, a 24-year-old Black American Tijani woman from Detroit, was one such example. Maimouna attended AAII from 2005 to 2011 and returned to the U.S. for high school. After graduating, Maimouna attended a public university in Michigan. She majored in Middle East Studies because her university did not offer African Studies or Islamic Studies—the majors that she would have preferred. After graduation, she started an entry-level job at an educational non-profit. In 2018, when Maimouna came back to visit Medina Baye, I asked her to reflect on the impact of her time there. Maimouna explained,

> The little six years I had here, it completely changed my identity. . . . Mentally everything I was learning between nine and 15, it stays with me

throughout everything I do, the values that I have, and ideals that I have that shape and structure the way I am. That can never be changed. . . . In America, you get a lot of people who are like, "I have to find myself." Luckily, that's something I can't relate to them about because living here and growing up in Medina Baye, I had a culture to identify with. It filled in all those blanks for me that as African Americans in America, we can't fill on our own. So, it definitely gave me a culture, a set of principles. It gave me Islam.

Maimouna's travels and education helped her circumvent the self-doubt and the desires for self-discovery that she observed many of her peers struggling with. Maimouna's experiences in Senegal anchored her identity as a Black Muslim woman—an outcome that countless parents expressed that they hoped would be in store for their own children.

Maimouna's reflections resembled what Helen Boyle describes as the moral compass that Qur'anic education imbues within students. Boyle (2006) explains,

> Even without comprehension, the embodied Qur'an is believed to provide moral direction by virtue of its being the word of God, thus sacred and holy. A person carries it, and it provides direction, much like a compass. A compass is an apt metaphor for the embodied Qur'an. A compass will seek north because of its magnetic attraction; one orients oneself with a compass by finding north. However, one can go in any direction. Like a compass, the embodied Qur'an does not negate free will and the process of making choices about which direction to follow. Rather, it provides a point of reference from which to make choices. With a compass, the pull toward magnetic north can be interfered with by other magnets—smaller ones perhaps that pull the compass needle in the wrong direction away from magnetic north. Likewise, the Qur'an, because of its magnetic attraction, which comes from its divine essence, will pull the learner in the right direction as he or she grows; it is stronger than other magnets, although other magnets can interfere and lead one off course. It is possible that the student will go astray, but learning the Qur'an is one way of giving the child a compass—a moral compass—to help him/her find the desired path. (492–493)

Though many parents and alumni weighed the academic and economic trade-offs associated with the schooling opportunity in Medina Baye, Maimouna's comments underscored a rich immaterial outcome—the magnetic pull. As Maimouna finished college and got a job, her moral compass grounded her in her ideal values while still creating space for her to carve out her life's work in accordance with her own passions.

Rudolph Ware (2014) similarly argues that the purpose of Qur'anic education historically in West Africa was to transform a "lump of flesh into God's living word," an embodied process through which students were remade into walking Qur'ans who implemented Islamic teachings and lived the prophetic example (8). Their educational experiences prepared them to "shape and reshape the world around them in the face of any contingency," which beginning from the eighteenth century onwards included resistance against the transatlantic slave trade and European colonization (ibid., 14). Similarly, Zachary Wright (2015a) asserts that Islamic learning in Shaykh Ibrahim's movement inculcated in murids a religious subjectivity that enabled them to "respond to the social and political upheavals associated with colonialism, decolonization, and globalization" during the twentieth century (248). In Medina Baye and many other West African Muslim societies, Islamic education thus imbued within students' knowledge, a relational piety, and an emphasis on collective care that guided their work to resist the sociopolitical crises facing their communities.

This was an approach to Islamic education, which, "still alive in West Africa," dated back to the seventh century (Ware 2014, 253). Just as the divine revelation of the Qur'an offered the first generation of Muslims the religious knowledge, ethical framework, and call to action to address the injustices of their time, so too did Islamic education in West Africa offer students the moral compass to manifest religious teachings by caring about and for others and improving the world. In this sense, though Islamic education is generally associated with the timeless ethic of engaging in work that brings benefit to Allah's creation, Islamic education in West Africa in particular offered students a moral compass that pulled them to respond to the specific sociopolitical conditions of their time and place. For Black Americans attending AAII in the twentieth and twenty-first centuries, their moral compass was calibrated to the concerns that confronted Black Muslims on both sides of the Atlantic.

Fusing structural issues with the pan-African Tijani imperative to serve one's community, the compass that Black American alumni held on to could attune them to efforts to resist anti-Black racism, anti-Muslim racism, racial capitalism, European colonization, neocolonialism, imperialist extraction, and white supremacy as they cultivated their self-worth and helped their community attain autonomy.

Maimouna's moral compass ensured that she developed a strong sense of self that quelled doubts about who she was as a Muslim of African descent. Aside from her day job at an educational non-profit, Maimouna often modeled in Muslim women's fashion shows. She also helped organize a school supply drive for students in Medina Baye. Though less overtly political and not necessarily aimed at structural change, Maimouna's moral compass had thus compelled her to participate in cultural events that increased the visibility of Black Muslim women and lead pan-African humanitarian efforts to redistribute material resources from communities in the U.S. to those in Senegal.

Like Maimouna, several of the young people who returned as high school students remained guided by their moral compass and found their own ways to uphold the pan-African Islamic Tijani expectations to serve their people. Some activated their religious knowledge. Ismail (from the Introduction) led his classmates in salat at the Black Muslim school that he attended in Atlanta, and for his senior project, he taught a Qur'an class. Another young brother named Habib led taraweeh in his Bronx apartment for his father and grandfather. Isra (from Chapter 4) started a clothing company to "inspire you to follow the words from the book of Allah, highlighted and referenced in every design." Drawing upon the Qur'anic ayats she had memorized, Isra's designs were intended to "remind you to do great things and trust in Allah."

Others, swayed by their moral compass, charted their own paths to engage in work that was meaningful to them. Hanaan (from Chapters 3 and 4) contributed to a digital community history project by helping conduct oral life interviews with African and African American Muslim elders in Detroit. Layla (from Chapter 4) finished her associate's degree and continued on to a bachelor's, with plans of studying Africana history and eventually pursuing a career in film and television. During breaks from college, Layla returned to Medina Baye and interviewed Black American students with the aim of making a documentary about their and her own experiences. Hammad, a young brother from Brooklyn, joined along with adult Tijanis in New York City as they distributed food and clothing to unhoused people on a monthly basis. Hafsa (from Chapters 3 and 4) organized a program for young Muslim women aged 12 to 18 at the Tijani zawiya in Atlanta. According to the Instagram account, the goal of the program was to "support, inspire, and build young ladies" and part of the broader efforts of her organization, whose acronym spelled out "freedom." The caption accompanying the flier for the first event explained, "This is an effort by young women, for young women. This is the next generation taking their place and leading by example."

Many in the earlier generations also did work in and for their community. In 2007, a group of Shaykh Hassan's adult murids, most of whom were alumni of AAII, started an organization named Nasrul Ilm America. Shaykh Hassan recommended that name, which was a derivation of "Jamiat Nasrul Ilm," an Arabic term that translated to "the community of beneficial knowledge"—another of the names that Shaykh Ibrahim used to refer to his global community. Nasrul Ilm America's mission was to promote service through education, humanitarianism, and cultural exchange. The organization's website elaborated upon the name.

> In the Islamic tradition, knowledge, or *ilm*, is not simply information. Rather, knowledge is predicated on action. In other words, to possess real knowledge implies that a person act on that knowledge. Sound knowledge is, in turn, considered a prerequisite for correct action. Nasrul Ilm America is informed by this holistic understanding of what constitutes knowledge. We believe, therefore that the true "benefit" of knowledge is to assist humanity beyond just the dissemination of facts. As leader of the community of beneficial knowledge—Shaykh Hassan Cisse worked tirelessly to feed people, to provide them with access to medical care, and to facilitate moral and Islamic education, as well as secular education, for scores of students from around the world. Following Shaykh Hassan's model, itself patterned from the model of the Islamic Prophet Muhammad (SAW), Nasrul Ilm America is an organization that is dedicated to the core principle of service to humanity.

For alumni who joined Nasrul Ilm America, their compass propelled them to work that extended beyond their Qur'anic education. Nasrul

Ilm America's flagship event was the annual Shaykh Hassan Cisse ziyara, which highlighted Shaykh Hassan's enduring legacy of humanitarianism. The organization also distributed food, clothing, and other necessities to unhoused people in New York City, Atlanta, and Detroit. In 2016, during the Flint water crisis, where residents of the majority-Black city in Michigan found their water sources contaminated with dangerous levels of lead, Nasrul Ilm America distributed clean water to the city's residents. Shaykh Mahy, who was visiting from Senegal, joined in on the efforts, coming with a caravan of Tijanis who road-tripped an hour north from Detroit. At the start of the COVID-19 pandemic, Nasrul Ilm America organized a mutual aid fund to recirculate thousands of dollars to fellow community members in need.

Just as Shaykh Hassan and his early Black American murids conceptualized of the humanitarian organization AAII as a pan-African effort, so too did Nasrul Ilm America serve communities in the U.S. and Senegal. Through an initiative called Help for Humanity, the organization collaborated with Senegalese Tijanis in Medina Baye to distribute rice, oil, sugar, and dates to residents in need. Finally, the organization raised funds to support repairs and renovations at the AAII School, and sponsored the tuition of some local students.

Nasrul Ilm America had no paid staff members. One short-lived grant from a private foundation aside, they organized online crowdfunding campaigns for tens of thousands of dollars and rallied for members to pay $30 USD a month in dues. As they cobbled together funds from various sources, and carved free time out of their job and family schedules, members of the organization continued to work to serve their communities when they could.

Maimouna and others in this second category of alumni were thus those who, despite not becoming religious scholars and educators, matched Imam Johari's description of individuals who, "when they come back, they love Islam, they love the Prophet sallallahu alayhi wa sallam, and they love themselves!" Such alumni had spent years studying in a Black Muslim social world where they learned from Tijanis who strived to cultivate piety through collective care. These alumni developed a deeper sense of self and concern for their community, which they actualized by doing work for their people. They contended that benefitting the community extended beyond providing an Islamic education.

Fortified by their compass and building upon their individual passions, these alumni worked to address the challenges facing their people.

Group Three: Returning to Medina Baye

It was around 10:30 pm in Medina Baye in August 2022. It was the height of rainy season, when torrential downpours were known to flood the streets of the city, trapping people indoors or forcing them to wade through pools of water as they walked to their destination. But that evening's surprisingly dry skies meant that we could enjoy the breeze that came at the end of a long day in the desert heat. We gathered on Sayyida Kubra Askari-Cisse's rooftop. I sat with four Black American Tijani women residents of Medina Baye, three of whom were alumni of AAII—Sayyida Kubra, Maimouna (who by then had moved back to Medina Baye), and Nasira.

Nasira was a 20-year-old from Detroit whom I had last seen when she attended AAII from 2015 to 2018. I remembered Nasira as a student who often looked glum, dragging her feet as she walked slowly to school, shoulders slumped as she sat in class with her head down but eyes wandering just beyond the pages of her Qur'an. Back then, Nasira constantly reminded me that she was miserable in Medina Baye. When some of her classmates returned to the U.S., Nasira told them that she wished she could have gone with them. In 2019, Nasira's wish came true. Her mother brought her back for high school. In 2020, I reconnected with Nasira. As we updated each other on our lives, she wrote, "I think I like Senegal better than the U.S. (laughing-crying emoji). I guess I just never realized that Senegal is my real home." Her comment threw me for a loop. I reminded her of how eager she had been to leave. I asked her why she had such a change of heart. She explained, "Senegal makes me feel safe and it's peaceful. Everything there has something to connect with Allah. Here in America . . . not so much." She told me about the online high school that she attended, which she found to be hard and frustrating. She explained that her mother was trying to find her an alternative program that would enable her to get a GED. A year after our conversation, Nasira moved back to Medina Baye. Since she was already enrolled in an online school, the plan was for her to finish up while in Senegal.

Nasira was part of a cohort of Black Americans in their twenties who had studied in Medina Baye during their childhood or adolescence, and had returned there after some years in the U.S. This group had yet to achieve the conventional markers of social adulthood, such as moving out of one's parents' home, graduating from college, getting married, or becoming financially independent. They were not, however, the only ones. Such milestones had become increasingly out of reach for millions of Black youth who dealt with racist inequities in higher education and the job market.

On the Free Application for Federal Student Aid (FAFSA), 64.5 percent of all Black college students who applied identified as "independent," which likely meant that they did not receive assistance from their parents but instead financially supported themselves by working while going to school (Cruse et al. 2018, 7). Having to juggle work and school impacted their graduation rates. Black students completed college at lower rates than students of any other racial group (Causey et al. 2022). They continued to confront racist disparities as they searched for employment. Between 2007 and 2022, which included the period in which Nasira lived in the U.S., Black youths' unemployment rate was roughly double that of white youth (Austin 2022, 4). During the COVID-19 pandemic, which disproportionately harmed Black communities, Black youth who were employed were at greater risk for contracting the virus, as Black people comprised the largest racial group of essential workers, or those whose jobs required them to work in-person and come in close contact with others (Dubay et al. 2020, vi). It was against this grim backdrop that Nasira left the U.S.

In Medina Baye, Nasira was joined by several other alumni. Another of these alumni was Ismail, the 24-year-old from Atlanta whom I had met ten years prior during my first trip to Medina Baye in 2012, when he had just become a hafiz. When I interviewed Ismail in 2022, he recounted what he had been up to over the last decade. After finishing his education in Medina Baye, Ismail returned to the U.S. for high school. Next, he attended a public college in Georgia. He withdrew after his first year because "I didn't really like that school. I just felt like what they were learning was too slow and what I wanted to do, like computers and coding and stuff, I could learn more of that by myself or online." Ismail was interested in doing something that felt more relevant and practical, so he decided to work for his uncle's computer company. But when that opportunity fell through, he started working in construction with his father. After some time, Ismail looked up and assessed his options—work indefinitely in construction or return to school. Unenthusiastic about either one, Ismail decided instead to leave the U.S. and move back to Medina Baye. Similar to Nasira, Ismail described Medina Baye as "peaceful. It's a lot of Muslims around. Going to the mosque is nice." Once there, he contemplated briefly returning to the U.S., just "to work and save my money so I can come back here and live . . . before I come back, if I can get an online job where I can work from here, then that's what I want to do."

Asiya was a third, 20-something year old alumna whom I was pleasantly surprised to find living in Medina Baye in 2022. We last saw each other three years prior during the Shaykh Hassan Cisse ziyara in New York City, which brought together hundreds of Tijanis from throughout the U.S. for a week of fellowship. On that trip, Asiya had always been eager to do khidma. Several evenings, she carefully assembled platters of food for the guests, set aside individual bowls for elders, and passed out water to those who were thirsty. This is how she had seen others do khidma in Medina Baye and at the Tijani zawiyas in Detroit and Atlanta.

Asiya lived in Medina Baye for part of her childhood, and returned to the U.S. for middle and high school. After her first year at a public university in Georgia, she relocated to Detroit with hopes of transferring to a school there. Asiya didn't receive enough financial aid to enroll, so she put her plans on hold and found a job. She then moved back to Georgia to re-enroll in college. Once again, she wasn't granted enough financial aid. Asiya was unwilling to take out private student loans, so she couldn't afford to go back to school. Like Ismail, Asiya's short-lived experiences with higher education reflected the barriers facing low-income and first-generation college students, who were often pushed out of the higher educational landscape and forced to find alternative routes to economic survival. Once Asiya realized that college was out of reach, she reasoned, "I really did try to go back and clearly this is not something that Allah wants for me right now, so what am I gonna do next? And Allah led me to a software engineering bootcamp." As part of the growing industry of alternatives to college degrees in computer science, the bootcamp promised a job in a field that she had assumed she needed a bachelor's to enter. After that, Asiya said, "Something was just pulling me, like, it's time to go to Senegal. [*laughs*] And it was like, well, you just finished this coding bootcamp and it'll be a lot easier to be in the States to get a job as an entry-level developer, but I just was getting this feeling like, it is time to go back to Senegal." And so, 15 years after she left, Asiya returned to Medina Baye at the age of 25. Asiya played out what might have happened if she had she stayed in the U.S.

> I would probably be working as a [software] developer somewhere, dealing with the American culture of working and dealing with the racial bias and your work environment. Yeah, it would've been drastically different. You know, when you started to get into the fold of just the daily life of living in America, you don't always have time to make salat on time. You don't have always have time to go to wazifa. A lot of the focus is work, make money, pay bills, work—or work, make money, go to school, pay bills. And you have to want to remember Allah. Otherwise, you'll forget because you get so caught up in the daily life in America.

Asiya suspected that she'd confront racism on the job and would struggle to prioritize her Islamic and Tijani practices within the grind culture of the U.S. Tricia Hersey (2022) describes grind culture as a sinister collaboration between capitalism and white supremacy that normalizes and celebrates constant labor, making money, and overworking to the detriment of a person's well-being and liberation. Grind culture consists of the everyday practices and internalized mindsets that require "we ignore anything that is not centered on labor and doing" (ibid., 93). Grind culture frames rest as a luxury that people cannot afford to make time for because it will not help them make money. Asiya added salat and wazifa to the list of activities that became sidelined within grind culture's conception of time. Hersey argues that reclaiming rest is a radical act of resistance against capitalism and white supremacy because it disentangles a person's inherent worth from their economic production. By insisting on rest as a valuable activity, Hersey challenges the capitalist conception of time. For Asiya, the decision to leave the U.S.—where she could have made decent money as a software developer—was an act of resistance and a form of rest that would allow her to recalibrate her life to an Islamic conception of time.

Nasira, Ismail, and Asiya all remarked that they were drawn to Medina Baye because of the Islamic conceptions of time that they recalled had oriented daily life there. Yet in the past month that I had been in the city, I had not seen Nasira at wazifa or other Tijani gatherings. As we sat on Sayyida Kubra's roof, Nasira was glued to her cell phone for much of the conversation. Every few minutes, a chime rang out, notifying us that Nasira had just received a direct message on Instagram. Nasira's absence from the city's Sufi gatherings made me curious about how she spent her days. I wondered and asked aloud, was she reclaiming her time to rest and prioritize her religious and spiritual growth? At first, Nasira chuckled but didn't say anything. In a cheeky tone, I persisted, "Do you scroll on your phone all day? You could be doing that from Detroit! What's the point of being here?" Maimouna jumped in to correct me, "No, she couldn't be doing that all day in Detroit. In Detroit, she'd probably have to work."

Maimouna's comments pointed to the reality that most youth in the U.S. had three choices after high school: postsecondary education (the path that Ismail and Asiya pursued but struggled to finance), work (the path that Ismail and Asiya took after they left college), or both. As Black youth searched for schooling and employment options that might enable them to actualize their ideal futures, they were confronted with the reality that they lived under a state of precarity, or the "politically induced condition in which certain populations suffer from failing social and economic networks of support and become differentially exposed to injury, violence, and death," thereby being subjected to maximized vulnerability (Butler 2009, ii). Precarity is often understood as a recent phenomenon associated with the rise of neoliberalism, the globalization of capitalist production, the expansion of informal economies, and the shrinking of state welfare provisions from the 1980s onward (Han 2018). However, precarity is not new to Black people in the U.S., who have been treated as a perpetual precarious class since the first enslaved Africans arrived during chattel slavery (Hill 2017). Black students' status as a perpetual precarious class is the reason why they have been deemed disposable by the country's mainstream system of schooling (Stovall 2020). Subjected to politically induced conditions of uncertainty, exceptional vulnerability, and organized state abandonment (Gilmore 2007), many Black youth who finish high school remain unsure about whether any of the three choices in front of them will lead to employment, economic mobility, entry into social adulthood, or dignity.

Black youth in the U.S. are not alone in their experiences of precarity. Youth across the Global North and South confront politically induced vulnerabilities and structural barriers that make it difficult for them to transition into social adulthood. Neoliberal capitalism, structural adjustment, poverty, and massive unemployment even among those who graduate from college represent some of the numerous politically induced vulnerabilities that prevent young people from turning their dreams into realities. As a result, youth experience precarity as what Daniel Mains (2012) describes as a temporal problem that blocks them achieving life improvements and progress over time. Anthropologists have offered various concepts to describe young people's experiences with the standstill of time, such as waithood, timepass, boredom, killing time, and being stuck (Honwana 2012; Jeffrey 2010; Masquelier 2019; Ralph 2008; Sommers 2012). Whereas grind culture promises that overworking will allow a person to have social worth, the stalled relationship between precarity and progress exposes the myth of capitalist conceptions of time. Faced with politically induced vulnerabilities, young people find limited employment opportunities, and even if they figure out their own ways to make money, their efforts are unlikely to offer the financial independence necessary to transition into social adulthood.

Since Senegal became independent in 1960, the country's youth have mobilized against their politically induced precarity (Bathily et al. 1995; Diouf 1996). In the 1980s, Senegalese youth expressed outrage against their country's political, economic, social, and cultural institutions, which failed to deliver on the promises for their generation (Diouf 2003, 7). In the 2000s, confronted with the growing informal economy, the scarcity of income-generating opportunities, and the struggle for social and political recognition, youth in Senegal responded to their precarity in various ways, including redirecting energy to their dress and physical fitness, buying and marketing clothes that projected a cosmopolitan identity, and cultivating community through tea-making practices (Prothmann 2020; Ralph 2008; Scheld 2007). These strategies marked Senegalese youths' attempts to carve out dignity within a social, political, and economic landscape that robbed them of it. During Senegal's presidential elections in 2007, 2012, and 2024, young people were at the forefront of demanding leaders who would bring forth substantive change in the country's economic and political landscape.

Many Senegalese youth also put their hopes in migration. Starting in the 1980s, with the onset of the International Monetary Fund's structural adjustment policies that devastated the country's agricultural sector, as well as other political economic transformations, large numbers of youth left rural areas and migrated to the urban center of Dakar (Estruch et al. 2019). By 2009, 60 percent of all internal migrants in Senegal were youth (World Bank 2009). According to one study, the primary reason why youth migrated out of Kaolack, the region where Medina Baye is located, was the desire for employment opportunities (Ba et al. 2017, 2). While many youth migrated to Dakar, others migrated to other African countries, Europe, or the U.S. Many Senegalese youth saw international migration as the "only way in which the future could be envisaged" (Rodriguez 2015, 335).

Just as significant numbers of Senegalese youth identified migration as a solution to their precarity, so too did Black American youth like Nasira, Ismail, and Asiya seek out migration—but in the opposite direction. These youth hoped that relocating to Medina Baye would give them a break from the perpetual precarity they experienced. In this sense, while most U.S. high school graduates weighed the possibilities and limitations of going to school, working, or doing both, Nasira, Ismail, and Asiya had a fourth option: international migration. As alumni of AAII, they had the social ties, cultural knowledge, and linguistic familiarity to return to Medina Baye. In contrast to the U.S. where Black youths' precarious status meant that they would be subjected to crumbling, state-sponsored networks of support, in Medina Baye these youth encountered an infrastructure of collective care where community members sustained one another religiously, educationally, socially, and economically. These alumni's return was motivated by different reasons than what their parents had envisioned when they initially sent them to Medina Baye. These young people's interest in relocating there pointed to their own visions of what it meant to seek out radical pathways beyond the doomed rat race that had trapped so many of their peers in the racial capitalist, white supremacist society of the U.S.

In Medina Baye, Black American alumni were joined by Tijani youth who had migrated from rural and urban areas of Senegal and from countries across Africa. Like their Black American peers, African youth hoped that living in Medina Baye would offer them better prospects. Most of these African youth were not alumni of AAII, but their membership in Shaykh Ibrahim's pan-African movement had similarly facilitated their migration to Medina Baye. Once they arrived, they became incorporated into their Senegalese shuyukh or fellow country members' households, receiving food, housing, and other necessities that relieved their concerns of everyday economic survivalism. In exchange, though the exchange was far from even, young people offered khidma to help maintain the expansive households that they joined. Because khidma was a spiritually meaningful practice among Tijanis, it imbued their time with meaning. Furthermore, because Shaykh Mahy and Imam Cheikh's households fed and sustained more than a hundred people daily, these youths' khidma also brought practical benefit by helping maintain Medina Baye's system of collective care.

Many Black American and African youth had clearly defined work. Ismail helped supervise the younger male students at the dormitory, and on Fridays, he shepherded a boisterous group of approximately ten boys to jummah, watching them sternly during the khutba to make sure they remained quiet and attentive. Every so often, Ismail helped handwash clothes, swept sand off the hallway floors, or served food to guests. Asiya built and maintained the school's website, and from time to time, tutored some of the teenaged students. While it was not khidma to her shaykh or the broader community, Nasira babysat her niece. Among the African Tijani youth, Zakariya, a 19-year-old from Lagos, Nigeria, explained to me with pride that he took it upon himself to mop all the floors of Sayyida Kubra's house each morning. I also observed him helping out with whatever other random tasks he would be asked to do. Musa, a 31-year-old from Niger's capitol city Niamey, had become Shaykh Mahy's right-hand man. Musa made sure empty guest rooms were clean and ready to be occupied by the latest spiritual seeker who had arrived. Musa also distributed money to people in need, served dishes during lunch or dinner, and did whatever else was needed. Tariq, a 28-year-old from the urban port city of Abidjan in Côte d'Ivoire, stood guard at Shaykh Mahy's door to monitor how many people entered and exited the room throughout the day. When it was time to eat, Tariq laid the *maidas* (mats) out smoothly on the floor, carefully poured water for guests to wash their hands, and vigorously swept up the stubborn breadcrumbs that lingered on the carpet after the guests left. Siddiqa, a 21-year-old from a rural village in Senegal, went to the market each morning to buy the herbs and vegetables she would need to cook lunch for guests at Sayyida Kubra's house and students at the dorm. In Medina Baye's largest households, where dozens of people lived under the care of their shaykh, a significant portion of the essential daily work was handled by young people who did khidma.

Khidma seldom translated to the time-equivalent of a full-time job. Relieved of the concerns of everyday economic survival, young peoples' days opened up as they regained the time and peace of mind they had previously spent laboring or stressing about how to make ends meet. They found new time to rest, make dhikr, and carve out imaginative space to dream about their futures and how to transform those dreams into realities.

Back on Sayyida Kubra's rooftop, I asked Nasira about her dreams.

"I want to be a midwife," Nasira declared without hesitation.

Hearing this, Latifah jumped in. Latifah was a Black American Tijani woman in her fifties. A month prior, Latifah had materialized her own freedom dream. She had spent decades working as a nurse in the U.S., often enduring back-to-back 12-hour shifts that made her feet ache and soul weary. She had plotted, planned, and saved up enough to retire. She sold most of her belongings and moved to Medina Baye, where she hoped to regain her peace of mind as she lived modestly on a fixed retirement income. Latifah said, "Well, if you want to be a real midwife with real power, you know you have to get a master's, right? You can't just get an RN. You need to get a master's. That's how you will make the real money."

Latifah then outlined all the steps that Nasira would need to take to become a midwife: get an advanced degree, do clinical rotations, and pass a licensing exam.

"You can't do that online. You have to be in-person," Latifah stressed. Latifah gave Nasira the low-down on how to obtain her dream job, not-so-subtly pointing out the practical foreclosures of living in Medina Baye. I noticed Nasira avert her gaze and grow quiet.

Soon, the topic of the conversation changed, but I brought it back up a little later. I told Nasira about a study that one of my colleagues had conducted on college students' internship experiences. Many students reported that the most helpful part of an internship was realizing that they did not want to be in that line of work.

"If you want to be a midwife, maybe you can volunteer at Shaykh Hassan's [Shifa al-Asqam Socio Medical] clinic and get some experience to see if this is actually what you want you want to do," I suggested.

During the 1990s and early 2000s, the clinic was a key institution where Shaykh Hassan directed his murids to do khidma. Some Black Americans served as translators when English-speaking doctors came to volunteer. Others did administrative work such as tracking inventory in the pharmacy. Shaykh Hassan's son Sulaiman Amadi Cisse explained his understanding of his father's rationale for encouraging murids to do khidma. Using the example of one particular Black American student who lived in Medina Baye during his late teens and early twenties, Sulaiman explained,

> [The student] could have just been here doing dhikr and learning, but it's like, no, you can do that and can help in building some social and economic infrastructure that we need here. So that's the way [Shaykh Hassan] did it. He mobilized people into positions under this organization [the African American Islamic Institute] that he had established towards productive good. And that is the way he helped to raise their human capital.

Sulaiman asserted that Shaykh Hassan encouraged young people to benefit themselves and others by doing khidma for a portion of their time in Medina Baye. Shaykh Hassan's advice reflected the pan-African Tijani worldview that linked time to piety and collective care. While youth experienced precarity as a temporal problem that barred them from progressing in life, khidma was a solution that allowed them to achieve personal growth and "raise their human capital" in the present. Khidma pointed to ways of being and belonging that were in direct opposition to capitalism, which alienated people from their labor and reduced work to a form of exploitation. Instead, young people who engaged in khidma imbued their time and labor with purpose by leveraging them as ethical resources that brought benefit to themselves and their community.

In a 1941 letter that Shaykh Ibrahim wrote to Sayyidi Aliou Cisse, Shaykh Ibrahim offered a cautionary tale of murids who abstained from khidma.

> They have accompanied us in terms of belief, and gained the greatest *maqam* [spiritual ranking] in the shortest period of time, but they neither took up khidma nor did anything else—and that is why they have been delayed in outwardly accomplishing what they wanted to. If all of them committed to a certain kind of khidma to persist in, and obligated upon themselves a certain amount of hadiya that they can manage, at all times, they would see things go their way outwardly as well as inwardly.... Starting today, every murid who wants to learn must commit to two days' worth of khidma and accustom themselves to it.... Truly, it can be no other way, for today's dunya is not like the dunya they used to know. Living without being engaged in some type of work is not something that happens in this new dunya.

Shaykh Ibrahim acknowledged that khidma had to be attuned to the specific conditions of the era in which people lived. Writing in 1941, the "new dunya" of Shaykh Ibrahim's time was French colonization. Shaykh Ibrahim reappropriated the dominant conceptions of labor of his time and instead proposed a radically different paradigm that helped mitigate these modern ravages. Rather than be alienated from one's labor to maximize profit and generate value for an external entity, as occurred in capitalism, Shaykh Ibrahim presented khidma as a type of labor that grounded murids in the material world while simultaneously orienting them towards the metaphysical world. By coupling khidma with ritual practice, murids would witness growth in their spiritual ranking and material conditions. Through khidma, community members shared in the collective work of caring for one another at the same time that they experienced inward transformation. As a form of labor done for one's faith community, khidma also facilitated a way for murids to self-consciously cultivate ideals of religious personhood and piety (Casselberry 2017).

I encountered Shaykh Ibrahim's letter during an online course taught by Sidi Kaba Abdul-Fattaah, a Black American Tijani alumnus who attended AAII from 1988 to 1992. Sidi Kaba was among the first category of alumni—those who came back and served as religious leaders. Like many in that group, his primary occupation, however, was as a filmmaker. In 2019, Sidi Kaba started teaching weekly classes on *Kashif al-Ilbas* (*The Removal of Confusion*), Shaykh Ibrahim's magnum opus that Sidi Kaba had personally studied with Shaykh Mahy. During multiple sessions of the class, Sidi Kaba paused from offering his commentary to read from Shaykh Ibrahim's 1941 letter, which had been translated from Arabic into English by another American Tijani and which Sidi Kaba had found online. During a session in February 2023, he explained that the letter was a reminder that we should all commit ourselves to consistent khidma. Bringing Shaykh Ibrahim's discussion of the "new dunya" to our twenty-first century context, Sidi Kaba explained that khidma could mean making a website, organizing a fundraiser for a hospital, giving hadiya, or using whatever skills people had to bring tangible support and practical assistance to their shuyukh's humanitarian efforts. Yet speaking from experience, Sidi Kaba elaborated upon the immaterial benefits of khidma. He reflected upon how doing khidma trained a person's ego, catalyzing the internal spiritual transformation that was an essential goal of Sufism. His reflection was similar to Saba Mahmood's analysis of veiling among Muslim women in Egypt. Mahmood argues that Muslim women cultivated piety by veiling and consciously deliberating upon the religious significance of that physical act. Bringing together external action and internal reflection, veiling was understood by those women as "an entire process through which a pious individual is produced" (Mahmood 2004, 56). Yet as Tijanis spent time doing khidma and contemplated on the spiritual significance of their labor, they cultivated a relational piety that called them towards collective care.

The paradigm of everyday khidma that Shaykh Ibrahim laid out in the mid-twentieth century, that Sulaiman described Shaykh Hassan as encouraging murids to follow in the late 1990s and early 2000s, and that Sidi Kaba urged Tijanis to uphold in 2023 was neither a widespread requirement nor an explicit expectation for young residents of Medina Baye in the twenty-first century. While many youth did khidma, several Black American and West African Tijani adults I spoke with expressed great frustration that many other young people benefited from the system of collective care while contributing little in exchange. Given the size of the Shaykh Mahy and Imam Cheikh's households, these youth slipped under the radar—eating, sleeping, and surviving without dedicating some of their time to assist in the khidma necessary to keep their households going. The adults I spoke with gave examples of youth who neither pursued Islamic education, engaged in consistent khidma, generated an income, nor gave hadiya. They asserted that such young people were largely idle. Even though young people's social standing was not measured by their economic earnings, these adults' frustrations revealed a hope that young people would engage in work that elevated themselves and their community. Yet in a city where individuals' contributions to the collective were encouraged but not enforced, the onus ultimately fell on young people to decide whether they wanted to use their time to work on themselves and for their community.

Yahya, a 24-year-old Hausa brother from Zamfara State in Nigeria, alluded to the sense of idleness as he told me how he ended up in Medina Baye.

> Even if you don't do nothing here, it's better to be in Medina Baye than in Nigeria. In Nigeria, if you don't have nothing to do, it's not good for you to stay long. It's not like I hate Nigeria or something like that. I'm Nigerian and I still love Nigeria up to now. But if you don't have nothing to do, if you stay there, it's not good for you. Because you can spoil it and then you can spoil another person—because if you don't have nothing, you start smoking or stealing something, or bad, bad stuff. So that is why, before that happened, my mother sent me here.

Yahya's mentions of "nothing to do" and "having nothing" alluded to the sense of precarity as a temporal problem in which young people felt that their lives were stalled and that they had no hopes of improving their prospects in the future. Yahya acknowledged that young people might feel a sense of "nothing" both in Medina Baye and Nigeria, but he asserted that "nothing" was experienced differently in Medina Baye.

Back in Nigeria, Yahya had been enrolled at a public, government-run secondary school. But each morning, Yahya skipped school. He met up with his friends who played games, sports, and smoked. Yahya's mother was outraged when she found out what her son had really been up to. She immediately contacted an older Nigerian Tijani man who had grown up in Medina Baye and pleaded with him to take Yahya there.

The man agreed to take Yahya during gamou. He chartered a bus for Yahya and 26 other Nigerian youth. After many days on the road, they arrived in Medina Baye. The man divided the young people into smaller groups. He brought each group to the house of a different Tijani shaykh or shaykha, who took them in as members of their extended household. Yahya ended up under Shaykh Mahy and Sayyida Kubra's care.

Yahya soon befriended some fellow young Hausa men from Nigeria and Ghana who helped him adjust to the daily rhythm of life in Medina Baye. Initially, Yahya attended AAII. Yahya's new friends told him about the baraka that came from doing khidma. Yahya was not familiar with the concepts of baraka or khidma. Yahya recalled, "I asked, 'If you study, you can't have baraka?' They said, 'Yes, if you study, you have a baraka, but what you can have in khidma, you can't have it in study. What you can learn in that khidma, you cannot learn it in school.'" While this insight was likely intended to encourage Yahya to do khidma in his free time, Yahya (who even in Nigeria had been reluctant to go to school) decided to drop out of AAII. At that point, neither a full-time student nor working a formal job, Yahya "had nothing to do." But instead of entering a self-imposed period of idleness that in Nigeria had led him to seemingly destructive behaviors that alarmed his mother, Yahya observed in Medina Baye how youth in his position filled their time. When he noticed Siddiqa, a young Senegalese woman, handwashing buckets of dirty clothes belonging to her and the dozens of other people who were part of Sayyida Kubra's household, he identified an opportunity for khidma. Yahya volunteered to share Siddiqa's workload and began washing clothes with her. From then on, Yahya remained consistent in his khidma at Sayyida Kubra's household, ultimately becoming one of the main people she relied upon to take care of tasks for the household and Shaykh Mahy's guests.

Yahya, Nasira, Ismail, and Asiya's stories revealed how Medina Baye offered Black American and African youth some relief from politically induced precarity. For Black American alumni, their ability to return to the place they fondly remembered meant that they could enact freedom dreams in isolation from the systems that constrained their lives in the U.S. Having a place to go also meant that they could withhold their human capital from a society that had always exploited Black people's labor.

Figure 5.2. A young man gets ready to handwash clothes using the faucet in Sayyida Kubra's courtyard in Medina Baye. This is his khidma as a member of her household, July 2022. Photo courtesy of the author.

In Medina Baye, young people found a society where networks of social and economic support were generally intact. Medina Baye was a city oriented towards Islamic conceptions of time and where khidma was central to how Tijanis sustained one another and became more pious. With the local system of collective care ensuring that young peoples' basic needs were met, youth were freed of the pressures of economic survival that often prompted people to fill their time with work that was unfulfilling, exploitative, or dangerous. Living in Medina Baye without the necessity of working or the financial burdens of postsecondary education also presented a luxury that tended only to be accessible to socioeconomically well-advantaged youth. Like those whose family's generational wealth enabled them to take a gap year to meander through the world and explore their hearts' desires, living in Medina Baye held promise of a chance for Tijani youth to have the time and space to rest, prioritize their spiritual development, and explore new freedom dreams.

When asked what he wanted to do with his life, Yahya was stumped as he remarked, "You know, no one has ever asked me that." Yahya's response pointed to the fact that dreaming did not always come naturally. Instead, it took time, effort, and initiative. In fact, as Tricia Hersey (2022) argues, "Our imagination and sense of invention no longer exist in an abundant way when we are tied up in the shackles of grind culture" (112). Dreaming had to be intentionally cultivated. Dreaming was hard for those who had long spent their time just trying to make it to the next day and could finally bask in the comforts of not having to work. For Yahya and other Black American and African youth who had found relief from precarity in Medina Baye, dreaming required them to make a mental and temporary shift, to not simply be satisfied with an absence of economic responsibilities but rather to imagine a life filled with boundless possibilities. Rather than bask in their stable, day-to-day life, they had to give themselves permission to dream of and work towards an extraordinary future.

Nasira had started dreaming of being a midwife but had yet to fully sketch out the roadmap to her ideal future. Similarly, for Yahya, living in Medina Baye allowed him to have his basic needs met, purposefully fill his time with khidma, and grow closer to Allah, but he had yet to determine what he wanted his future to look like. Relieved of precarity, both Nasira and Yahya seemed to have become content with their present, somewhat ordinary lives. On the one hand, this was a radical, liberatory new reality. They could reject the racial capitalist, white supremacist norms of a grind culture, where a person's worth was defined by their labor, where work tended to be exploitative, and where making money was the primary objective. Instead, they could take break and just be.

At the same time, while young people were relived of the burdens of waged labor and economic survival, they were not obligated to fill their free time and reappropriate their labor in meaningful ways. After all, contributing to the city's system of collective care was a blessed recommendation, but not a strict requirement. As young people worked to unlearn capitalist modes of survival, they had the opportunity to dream up new relationships to work and time. By doing khidma, they could add baraka in their time in the present and freedom dream of the future. Or, young people could delve into idleness, developing a sense of complacency in their current state of rest without trying to contribute to their community or reach their highest potential. Medina Baye's infrastructure of collective care thus fostered generative conditions for young people to imagine the next phase of their freedom dreams. However, the onus fell on them to determine if, how, and when they would honor their divinely ordained purpose to worship Allah by engaging in work that brought benefit to their community.

Conclusion

From the 1980s to the 2020s, hundreds of Black American Muslim youth traveled from the U.S. to Medina Baye. Migrating to a Black Muslim Tijani maroon geography allowed young people to be physically separated from the racial capitalist, white supremacist society of the U.S. They had the opportunity to learn more liberatory ways of being and belonging in the world. As they moved between the U.S. and Medina Baye, they heard parents and other adults in the community express high hopes that young people would utilize their education for collective care. They constantly encountered a pan-African Tijani worldview that called them to orient their time towards work that brought benefit to others.

These ideas left a lasting imprint on young people, who followed but also remixed adults' expectations as they forged their own pathways into adulthood. Some, like Mahmoud, aspired to become religious leaders. Others like Maimouna were pulled by the moral compass and sense of self they strengthened in Medina Baye. These alumni heeded the call to address the sociopolitical concerns of their time and strove to serve their people. A third group confronted the precarity of Black youthhood in the U.S., and in search of greater meaning, returned to the place that had anchored them in their adolescence. Joined by those who experienced precarity elsewhere in Africa, these young people gained the luxuries of time, rest, and space to dream of their next steps. In the interim, they could seize opportunities to do khidma and contribute to Medina Baye's system of collective care.

While the educational experience in Medina Baye offered Black American Muslims new resources for transforming themselves and their communities, the three groups' trajectories also exposed the reality that it was quite difficult to fully extricate oneself from the effects of racial capitalism and white supremacy. Some who returned to the U.S. grappled with how to preserve their passions for religious educational and humanitarian work within a society that did not value such efforts, and that required them to take on additional employment to keep a roof over their heads and food in their bellies. Those who returned to Medina Baye faced challenges as well. They struggled with how to free themselves of the fiction that a human being's purpose and value was tied to their ability to make money. While young people found relief from politically induced precarity in a Black Muslim Sufi society rooted in collective care, truly unlearning these myths would mean embracing ethical Islamic conceptions of human dignity, time, and labor. It would mean resisting the impulse to become complacent and idle in a society where they were not forced to work in order to survive. Instead, they were tasked with implementing the pan-African Islamic Tijani teachings that held that all human beings were inherently valuable simply because they were creations of Allah, that human beings were created to show gratitude to Allah, that khidma constituted work that fulfilled Muslims' divinely ordained purpose, that Black American Muslims had a responsibility to empower their people, and that Muslims should constantly strive to reach their highest potential by emulating the prophetic example. By internalizing these teachings, alumni could birth new freedom dreams, based not simply on the absence of precarity, but rather on the boundless possibilities that came with working and spending time in ways that were most pleasing to Allah.

Overall, these three groups' trajectories demonstrate the possibilities and foreclosures of a sustained pan-African Islamic Tijani educational exchange in offering Black American Muslims resources for transforming themselves and their communities. These three groups demonstrated the multiple pathways that Black American Muslim youth carved out once they ended their studies in Medina Baye. Their educational experiences equipped alumni with religious teachings, racial sensibilities, a moral compass, and the sociopolitical imperative to undertake meaningful work in their communities. Across these three categories, young people drew upon their prior educational experiences as part of the resources and networks of care that enabled them to attain greater purpose, dignity, and piety. As alumni embarked on their own pathways, they engaged in ongoing freedom dreaming about what it meant to live, thrive, and work in community.

6

From American to Cisse

The Tijani Tariqa and the Making of Pan-African Families

"American, give me money!" demanded Usman, a nine-year-old Senegalese boy, to Kareem as we stood under the beaming sun in the courtyard of the Grand Mosque of Medina Baye after jummah. Kareem was a 29-year-old Black American Tijani who had moved to the city three years prior from Washington D.C. Usman gave Kareem no customary Islamic greeting of "Assalamualikum" that the other Muslim women and men around us exchanged. Nor did Usman extend a handshake as he zeroed in on us from the hundreds of immaculately dressed children, youth, and adults who milled around. Instead, after making his request in perfect English, Usman grinned widely, his right palm cupped and arm outstretched, a determined look on his face as he inched closer.

"Give you money? What? I'm a *talibe* [student] just like you. Give *me* money!" Kareem countered in frustration. Usman shrugged his shoulders, hesitating for a moment. Then he laughed, shook his head, and reached into the pocket of his light blue cotton trousers. Usman pulled out *cent franc* (a 100-franc coin).

"*Amm*," Usman said, which meant "here [you go]" in Wolof. The coin was just enough for Kareem to buy a 100-millilitre bag of filtered water or half a baguette.

"*Jerejef*," Kareem responded, thanking Usman in Wolof.

This was not the first time I heard an African resident call out in English "American, give me money!" to those they perceived to fit the label. Almost always, the "American" was a Black American Muslim, or in a few instances, a Black Muslim from the U.K. The racialized trope of the (Black Muslim) "American" was used to indicate those who, by virtue of their perceived U.S. citizenship, were assumed to be wealthy. Often, as was the case with Usman, the African resident who made the demand

Figure 6.1. A crowd of believers exit the Grand Mosque after jummah and disperse in different directions of the courtyard, May 2025. Photo courtesy of the author.

knew few additional phrases in English but had memorized and repeated this one expression in hopes that it would encourage, or perhaps compel, the "American" to give.

Usman and Kareem actually knew each other, though not well. They both attended AAII but were in different classes. Usman was not someone whom I had previously observed begging for money—a practice associated with talibes, or students who attended *daaras* (Qur'an schools) in Senegal such as AAII. In Senegal, talibes have sparked a moral panic (Cohen 1972). They are portrayed in the dominant imagination as vulnerable children forced to fend for themselves (Lahti 2019; Loimeier 2002). When Usman approached Kareem, he engaged the stereotypes of the talibe and the American, perhaps in hopes that the tropes of the destitute local student and wealthy foreigner would work to his advantage. Kareem was tired of being solicited for money from neighbors who approached him with no pleasantries but simply with the expectation that he must give because he was American. In contending that he, as a talibe, was also in need, Kareem challenged the notion that his nationality was what defined his interactions with his neighbors. Kareem signaled his knowledge of Senegalese cultural norms of charitable giving towards talibes, in which the whole community felt obligated to care for them (Ware 2014, 240). Usman entertained Kareem's attempt to flip the script, parting with some of his own money perhaps in acknowledgement of the reality that he and his American peer were not so different after all; they were dealing with a similar financial plight. I observed such a role reversal on more than one occasion. In these instances, there was a humorous recognition that the African and the Black American were more similar than dominant narratives would suggest.

This chapter focuses on the experiences of Black American Tijanis living and learning with African Tijanis in Medina Baye. From those who traveled from the U.S. to Medina Baye in the 1970s onwards, to young adults like Kareem who migrated there in 2015, Black American Tijanis across generations envisioned Medina Baye as a place where their freedom dreams would come to life. They came at the personal invitation of Shaykh Hassan Cisse and later his brothers Imam Cheikh Tijani Cisse and Shaykh Mahy Cisse—who all cared deeply about them and treated them as their spiritual family. But Black Americans' time in Medina Baye included interactions with a much larger community of people, including those who did not necessarily share the shuyukh's explicit commitment to collective care towards Black Americans.

This chapter interrogates the tensions between Black Americans' freedom dreams of Medina Baye and their on-the-ground experiences in the city. It examines the assumptions, expectations, and misunderstandings that characterize relationships among members of the pan-African Tijani movement. It shows how Black American and other diaspora Black Muslims' membership within the Tijani tariqa ultimately integrates them within the local system of collective care, which provides an alternative script of relationality between Muslims from Africa and the diaspora. Complicating narratives that tend to differentiate and hierarchize the economic hardships facing African and African diasporic communities, I argue that Shaykh Ibrahim's pan-African Sufi movement offers new paradigms of reciprocity and relational piety that enable Black Muslims on both sides of the Atlantic to mitigate the impacts of racial capitalism and white supremacy.

Legacies of Underdevelopment

The transatlantic slave trade and the forced labor of enslaved Africans fundamentally shaped the development of the modern world. Through the system of racial capitalism, Western European nations and the U.S. exploited Black peoples' labor and land to achieve white capitalist accumulation (Robinson 1983). Enslaved Africans' labor enabled those countries to become major political economic powers (James 1938; Williams 1944). In the U.S., white slave-owning families also accumulated personal wealth by exploiting enslaved Africans. Such wealth was passed down over generations and fueled the success of numerous corporations and universities (Oliver and Shapiro 1995; Wilder 2013). In the twenty-first century, even though many legal barriers facing Black Americans have been removed, Black people continue to confront stark inequalities across U.S. society, including in education, healthcare, housing, and employment (Bonilla-Silva 2003; Hinton 2016; Ladson-Billings 2006; Roberts 1997).

Africans on the continent also experienced dispossession and displacement. From the period of European colonization to the post-independence era, Western European countries and later the U.S. exploited the people, land, and natural resources of Africa, resulting in what the Walter Rodney describes as the deliberate underdevelopment of Africa. Connecting this long-standing and ongoing process of unequal exchange, Rodney (1972) points out, "In the first place, the wealth created by African labor and from African resources was grabbed by the capitalist countries of Europe; and in the second place, restrictions were placed upon African capacity to make the maximum use of its economic potential" (25). Once African countries achieved independence, they saw their progress be deliberately stunted by European powers. Europeans often retained ownership of African countries' means of production. They also imposed hefty international debt service payments, structural adjustment policies, and other predatory economic practices. When newly independent African nations articulated socialist visions to redistribute wealth (Nkrumah 1965; Nyerere 1974), neocolonial and imperial projects ensured that Western capitalist exploitation continued. Even into the twenty-first century, the impact of Europe's underdevelopment of Africa is widely evident—from individual countries' precarious national economies to the everyday lives of generations of Africans who experience inadequate healthcare and education.

Once Senegal became independent from France, it pursued economic development by rapidly modernizing its agricultural production and financially investing in rural farmers (Oya 2006). Yet France continued to exercise control over Senegal's economy, ensuring that "existing French investments in industry would not be threatened by the transition to self-rule" (Boone 1990, 345–346). In the 1980s, under pressure from the International Monetary Fund and the World Bank's structural adjustment programs, the Senegalese government reluctantly initiated a process of market liberalization and began withdrawing the direct economic supports it previously provided to farmers. In a country where more than 70 percent of the population worked in the agricultural sector, the removal of these policies was felt widely. In 1994, France devalued the West African CFA franc currency used in Senegal, resulting in price increases for food, medicine, and other necessities. If underdevelopment is a framework for revealing relationships of economic exploitation between nations, the impact of the underdevelopment of Senegal is exemplified by the wealth and socioeconomic privilege held by white French people and other Europeans who continue to find work and success in Senegal, as well as many Senegalese people's perceptions of the abundant economic opportunities accessible in Europe and the U.S. Overall, the processes that enabled the exploitation of Black people in the U.S. thus similarly fueled the extraction of wealth from Africa.

Connecting Dots and Building Bridges

Throughout the twentieth century, pan-Africanism was an ideology and movement that built bridges between people in Africa and the diaspora by emphasizing their shared experiences of racism and economic exploitation. After attending the Second Pan-African Congress in 1921, W.E.B Du Bois (1921), the African American scholar and pan-Africanist, criticized the "imperialistic schemes to enslave and debauch black, brown, and white labor" throughout the world (7). He argued:

> If we are coming to recognize that the great modern problem is to correct maladjustment in the distribution of wealth, it must be remembered

that the basic maladjustment is in the outrageously unjust distribution of world income between the dominant and suppressed peoples. (Ibid.)

Du Bois pointed out the global system of racist economic exploitation that divided the world into two groups: the haves and the have-nots. He contended that Black people—both in Africa and in the U.S.—had been forced into the second group, alongside colonized people throughout the world.

Decades later, Malcolm X, the Black Muslim revolutionary pan-Africanist, similarly drew attention to the persistent divisions that characterized the world's population. During his famed "Message to the Grass Roots" speech, Malcolm shared his reflections from the Asian-African Conference in Bandung, Indonesia in 1955, which was in the vein of the pan-African conferences of previous decades but was expanded to include attendees from across the Third World who together represented half of the world's population at the time (Daulatzai 2012, 25). Malcolm (1963) recounted what the conference attendees collectively realized:

> The same man that was colonizing our people in Kenya was colonizing our people in the Congo. The same one in the Congo was colonizing our people in South Africa, and in Southern Rhodesia, and in Burma, and in India, and in Afghanistan, and in Pakistan. They realized all over the world where the dark man was being oppressed, he was being oppressed by the white man; where the dark man was being exploited, he was being exploited by the white man. So they got together on this basis—that they had a common enemy. And when you and I here in Detroit and in Michigan and in America who have been awakened today look around us, we too realize here in America we all have a common enemy, whether he's in Georgia or Michigan, whether he's in California or New York.

Malcolm delivered this speech at the Northern Negro Grass Roots Leadership Conference, which was intentionally planned as a response and alternative to a convening organized by leaders in the Civil Rights Movement. At the time, many Civil Rights activists focused their efforts on addressing racism in the U.S. However, as a revolutionary pan-Africanist, Malcolm saw Black people's struggles against racism in the U.S. as part of, rather than unrelated to, an international movement for justice led by people in Africa and beyond. Malcolm urged Black Americans to reject narratives that sought to divide their struggles from those of oppressed peoples abroad, and instead called upon Black Americans to be in solidarity with these international communities and join the collective global movement against racist oppression and economic exploitation.

From the 1970s onwards, as Black American Muslims met Shaykh Hassan, joined the Tijani tariqa, and began traveling to Medina Baye, they had opportunities to live out the pan-African principles articulated by Du Bois, Malcolm, and Shaykh Ibrahim himself. In Shaykh Ibrahim's pan-African Sufi movement, Black Americans and Africans could not only unify based on their shared experiences and struggles, but also could collectively care for one another and develop new paths to spiritual and material liberation. These modes of solidarity could take place through everyday, informal interactions between Black American and African Tijanis, or through formalized efforts such as the African American Islamic Institute (AAII), the school and pan-African humanitarian organization that Shaykh Hassan and his Black American murids founded in the 1980s.

Back in Medina Baye, Usman's comments raised questions about whether, in the twenty-first century, Shaykh Ibrahim's movement was still a space of pan-African exchange. In the new millennium, were Black people still connecting the dots between their struggles, or was pan-Africanism no longer a meaningful ideology to build bridges? This question also persists in contemporary anthropological scholarship on the experiences of diaspora Black people who travel to Africa. Such works have revealed the perceived socioeconomic inequalities between the two groups and the divergent ways in which they interpret the impacts of the transatlantic slave trade and European colonialism (Holsey 2008; Pierre 2012). This and other recent scholarship on the African diaspora emphasizes the hegemonies that emerge as different communities of African descent engage with one another (Campt and Thomas 2008; de Sá 2024; Williams 2018). Contrasting this perspective with earlier scholars and activists who held pan-African perspectives and emphasized the connections between people of African descent, Maureen Mahon (2008) argues, "Much of this turn-of-the-millennium scholarship highlights differences within the African Diaspora and the impossibility of defining what constitutes authentic or representative blackness" (116).

To be fair, the global political economic order had changed enormously since when pan-Africanists like Du Bois, Malcolm, and Shaykh Ibrahim were active. By the late twentieth century, many pan-Africanists came to terms with the fact that African independence had shifted from an exciting possibility to an often-disappointing status quo. In the U.S., many of the Black liberation movements of the twentieth century had been violently repressed by the government. Some of these movements were co-opted by Black politicians who merely served as "Black faces in high places" (Taylor 2016). From 2001 to 2024, from the offices of Black secretaries of state, a Black vice president, and a Black president, these politicians not only struggled to drastically improve the life opportunities for the masses of Black people in the U.S. but also led the Global War on Terror and oversaw military punishment campaigns against Black people across Africa and the Caribbean. Thus, in contrast to earlier eras when pan-Africanists recognized the overlapping processes that left diaspora Black and African communities in similar positions of racist economic marginalization and called for collective modes of unity to resist global systems of injustice, Usman's comments reflected the distinct landscape of the twenty-first century which had perhaps muddied the potential for pan-African solidarities.

This chapter thus also tracks how the pan-African ideologies and praxis of Shaykh Ibrahim's Sufi movement shifted from the twentieth to the twenty-first century. On the one hand, the shuyukh and some murids continued to emphasize collective care and contribute to pan-African humanitarian efforts. On the other hand, Usman and Kareem's interaction raised questions about the varying material burdens endured by different subgroups within the Tijani community, as well as the ethical responsibilities they had towards one another. This chapter traces ideas and expectations about money and wealth among Tijanis in Medina Baye to examine the potential of Shaykh Ibrahim's pan-African Sufi movement for mitigating tensions that often characterize contemporary African diasporic exchanges. It asks: how have the changing but also enduring global structures of injustice that confront Black Muslims in the U.S. and Senegal aided and constrained their efforts to care for one another? How has Shaykh Ibrahim's pan-African Sufi movement facilitated opportunities for African and African diasporic Tijanis to sustain dialogue, exchange information, and build solidarities in the twenty-first century?

The Finances that Forge Community

Senegal is a popular destination for heritage tourism, a type of travel in which tourists from the African diaspora visit the places and people that are significant to their histories as communities of African descent. In Senegal, the most well-known site of heritage tourism is the House of Slaves (*Maison des Esclaves*) and its Door of No Return on Gorée Island. Now a museum and memorial, it was once one of the final exit points on the African continent for millions of people who were kidnapped and taken to the Americas. Scholarship on heritage tourism has illustrated the moments of disconnect that emerge at places like Gorée Island as Black Americans and other tourists from the African diaspora interact with West Africans, who often treat the former as wealthy foreigners whose diasporic longings can be commodified (Ebron 2002). These interactions between tourists and locals belie the narrative of presumed kinship between people of African descent, and call into question the basis of solidarity that undergirds pan-Africanism.

Among the Black American Tijanis I spoke with, many had gone to Gorée Island. However, numerous others who traveled to Medina Baye repeatedly or lived there had never visited—either because they had not made the time or because they chose not to. Kareem, for instance, had yet to visit Gorée Island. Most Black Americans came to Senegal (often directly from the airport in Dakar, as was the case for Kareem) at the personal invitation of their Senegalese shuyukh, to make ziyara to their shuyukh, and/or to pursue Islamic education and spiritual transformation. This dynamic meant that these Tijani murids differed from the dominant portrait of diaspora Black people who came to Senegal. For those Tijanis who visited Gorée and for those who did not, their time in Senegal did not center on the country's most prominent heritage tourism site.

Hajjah Najah Abdus-Salaam, an elder Afro-Puerto Rican woman from Harlem, New York spoke to this dynamic. Since 2000, Hajjah Najah had visited Medina Baye more than a dozen times, and she had enrolled all of her children at AAII. During a speech she gave in Harlem in 2019 at the annual Shaykh Hassan Cisse ziyara hosted by Nasrul Ilm America, Hajjah Najah explained to the packed crowd of predominantly Black American and West African Tijanis, "Alhamdulillah, because of Shaykh Hassan, I was able to return home to the motherland, not as a guest or a tourist, but to reconnect with my ancestry, my history through Gorée Island and Medina Baye." For Hajjah Najah and countless other Tijanis from the African diaspora, Senegal was both a site of historical significance given their heritage as Muslims of African descent and a site of contemporary relevance where they were embraced by Senegalese Tijanis.

Since the early years of AAII, many of the Black Americans who attended the school came from working-class families. Parents were expected to send $200 USD a month to cover their children's expenses. It was not uncommon for families to fall behind on tuition. Shaykh Hassan often made arrangements with families to reduce the tuition to a more manageable amount. During the 1990s, Shaykh Hassan enlisted Hajjah Ashaki Taha-Cisse to help collect tuition. Hajjah Ashaki was a Black American murida from New York and a *muqaddama* (woman in a position of spiritual leadership in the Tijani tariqa) whose khidma included serving as the pro bono executive director of the humanitarian organization AAII. Hajjah Ashaki frequently called parents in the U.S. to remind them of how much they owed and to urge them to send funds to cover their children's expenses—a task that she told me did not always result in more tuition payments. Her husband, Papa Khari Taha, also collected donations from attendees who gathered for wazifa at the Ghanaian murid Hajji Isa Mama Cisse's place in the Bronx. Each week, the 35 or so Tijanis in attendance—which included Black Americans, Ghanaians, Senegalese, and Nigerians, but only a minority of whom were parents of students at AAII—each chipped in five dollars. Papa Khari would send all the money raised to Shaykh Hassan to help fund the school.

Several alumni who attended AAII during the 1980s and 1990s confirmed that their parents struggled to consistently send funds. One alumnus estimated that if there were 20 Black American students at any given time, likely only about five of their parents paid the full tuition on a consistent basis. Many parents, particularly those who were working-class and head of single-income households, struggled to raise just enough money to purchase their children's international plane tickets; continuing to send money was quite burdensome.

With tuition coming in inconsistently and seldom covering the full expenses, Shaykh Hassan filled in the gaps. He paid the teachers' salary, provided a dormitory for Black American students (which was known as Yellow House) and covered the electricity and other expenses related to its operation; and later, he housed many students in his own home. After 1997, when Shaykh Hassan opened the Shifa al-Asqam Socio Medical Center, he used the revenue from the clinic to help pay the teachers' salaries. Several Black American adults I spoke with remembered the frustration of some Senegalese residents, whom they claimed did not understand why Shaykh Hassan spent out of his own wealth to care for these students. However, the adults remembered Shaykh Hassan explaining the importance of doing so. They recalled that Shaykh Hassan characterized his decision as a form of reparations owed to them by their African sisters and brothers. Thus, Shaykh Hassan's pan-African Tijani kincraft[1] and praxes of collective care enabled a predominantly working-class community to participate in international travel and study abroad, opportunities that were typically inaccessible to economically marginalized Black people from the urban U.S.

Although some Africans were reportedly less enthusiastic about Shaykh Hassan's financial sponsorship of Black Americans, others were remembered as being more receptive. Cheikh Diery Cisse, a Senegalese Tijani who was the general secretary of the NGO AAII, explained:

> The fellow residents of Medina Baye were very happy, even I might say proud, to have their American brothers and sisters come to Medina Baye and study the religion of Islam. Because Islam is worldwide, and they could have gone to any other place in this world, but Allah made them choose Medina Baye. And the population of Medina Baye was very proud to have one of their sons, Shaykh Hassan, go to America, talk to them, explain to them Islam and the tariqa, and they accepted it and came to join him here.

Ahmed Sufi Muhammad, who attended AAII from 1984 to 1989 and was the school's first Black American hafiz, described a similar sentiment.

During his first six months in Medina Baye, he became fluent in Wolof—the primary language spoken there but one that was not formally taught at AAII. Yet despite the close friendships he developed with local youth, many of which remained strong decades later, Hafiz Ahmed explained, "They knew about Muhammad Ali . . . but I don't think they knew the history of Islam in the U.S. For them, they felt that Shaykh Hassan brought Islam to the U.S." In actuality, many Black Americans, including Hafiz Ahmed's parents, were Muslim long before they met Shaykh Hassan. However, Cheikh Diery's and Hafiz Ahmed's comments suggested that, for some African residents, the presence of Black Americans served as a testament to Shaykh Hassan's pathbreaking efforts. Notably, this was in an era in which information about life for Black people in the U.S. was not as accessible as it was by the time Kareem and Usman interacted, when intensified globalization, social media, and increased Senegalese migration to the U.S. fueled consistent information exchange between Tijanis from different places.

Cheikh Diery, who has a near photographic memory, also described a conversation that Shaykh Hassan had with his father Sayyidi Aliou Cisse. Cheikh Diery recounted:

> SHAYKH HASSAN told me when he first came from America, his father called him one day and said, "Hassan."
> [SHAYKH HASSAN] said, "Yes?"
> [SAYYIDI ALIOU] said, "Do you owe some people money in America?"
> [SHAYKH HASSAN] said, "No."
> [SAYYIDI ALIOU] said, "Then why are these people . . ."—because at that time there was only one phone [in Medina Baye] and that was the phone of Sayyidi Aliou—". . . then why are all these people calling you?"
> [SHAYKH HASSAN] said, "They are calling me just because of Islam. Some of them accepted Islam because of me. Some of them joined the tariqa because of me. And whenever they have things that they want to discuss or questions which they want to ask or to clarify, they call me. This is the only reason they are calling me, but I don't owe them any money."

Sayyidi Aliou reportedly assumed that the relationship between Shaykh Hassan and the Black Americans was fueled by financial factors. Yet, as Shaykh Hassan explained, Black Americans were drawn to him and the tariqa because of their desire for Islamic knowledge and spiritual transformation. Shaykh Hassan recognized that they were striving Muslims, and he cultivated their burgeoning interests by answering their questions and making it feasible for them to study in Medina Baye. Through practices of collective care, Shaykh Hassan served as young people's adoptive father and financially subsidized their education.

After Shaykh Hassan passed away in 2008, Imam Cheikh, Shaykh Mahy, and Sayyida Kubra continued his work. They experimented with new ways to sustain young peoples' education. This included opening a short-lived shoe store whose profits were directed to the school, receiving a *daara moderne* (a French-Wolof term for "modern Qur'an school") designation from Senegal's Ministry of National Education which brought in government funds to pay teachers' salaries, partnering with a Turkish Islamic NGO that offered some financial assistance, and organizing online fundraisers to solicit support from the global Tijani community. These initiatives helped alleviate the financial burdens placed upon Imam Cheikh, Shaykh Mahy, and Sayyida Kubra, who otherwise used their own money to fill gaps, just as they had seen Shaykh Hassan do.

As had been the case among earlier generations of students, many Black Americans who came to Medina Baye from 2012 onwards were from working-class families. One family whose three children attended AAII for four years owed almost ten thousand dollars in back-tuition, a debt that became so difficult to repay even after the children ended their studies that it was ultimately forgiven. In 2020, after decades of the tuition hovering between $200 and $300 USD, rates were increased to $400 USD a month per child to account for increased living costs and inflation, and to address the fact that the school was operating from a deficit. While on paper the tuition was a fixed rate, in practice the amount was still determined on a sliding scale. As had been the case during Shaykh Hassan's time, administrators lowered the rates for families who could not afford to pay $400. The majority of Black American families whose children currently study in Medina Baye do not pay the $400 rate.

While parents of adolescent students were expected to send money for their children, the shuyukh covered the basic needs of older students who were not financially supported by their families. Kareem, for instance, didn't pay a monthly tuition to attend AAII, nor did he pay to live in the room he shared with Ghanaian murids in Imam Cheikh's guesthouse. Kareem humorously referred to the financial support that he and others received from Imam Cheikh and Shaykh Mahy during a conversation with a fellow Black American resident named Abdul-Hakeem:

> ABDUL-HAKEEM: We Americans think we have such high living standards here. But in America we get food stamps. We come here and we get what?
> KAREEM: African food stamps!
> ABDUL-HAKEEM: In America we get Section 8. We come here and get what?
> KAREEM: African Section 8!

They had this back-and-forth as we ate lunch together at Abdul-Hakeem and his Senegalese wife Kalima's house. Kareem and Abdul-Hakeem argued that the same people who received food and housing assistance from the U.S. government similarly benefited from social welfare programs in Medina Baye. The African version, however, was not funded by the government, but by Medina Baye's community-led system of collective care. Kareem and Abdul-Hakeem were thus clear that many Black Americans struggled financially and required assistance even after they migrated to Medina Baye. However, they took ownership of the fact that "we" refused to connect the dots and instead acted in ways that fueled Africans' perceptions of Black Americans as different from, and wealthier than, them.

Some Black Americans openly admitted that they benefited from Medina Baye's system of collective care. In an interview for a vlog hosted by a Black British Tijani murida, a Black American student in his early twenties named Anwar explained,

> I was impressed by the shuyukh, to be honest, their generosity. I'm from America. I'm from Washington D.C. I'm from Black America, you know?

You don't invite strangers into your home, but you know, Shaykh Mahy met me once at the airport on Christmas [in the U.S.], and then I got here. He put me in his house with the rest of the talibes, so that blew my mind. 'Cause he has his wife and children in the same house with all of his talibes. That was just mind-blowing to me, on top of just paying tuition, food, you know, all expenses paid.

Anwar was taken aback by Shaykh Mahy's collective care practices, which he observed was something that the shaykh offered to all talibes whom he embraced as his spiritual kin. A Nigerien brother who was one of the main murids who did khidma for Shaykh Mahy told me that he estimated that Shaykh Mahy likely cared for nearly a hundred male students in his homes. The largest group was Senegalese, but others were from countries including Togo, Côte d'Ivoire, Burkina Faso, Guinea, Nigeria, Niger, Ghana, and the U.S. Black Americans comprised only a small minority of the total students whose education Shaykh Mahy facilitated.

However, just as some Senegalese residents during Shaykh Hassan's time expressed frustration with the financial burden that the shaykh carried on behalf of his Black American murids, so too were Black Americans who were close to Shaykh Mahy and Imam Cheikh wary of the public narratives about their generosity. In fact, I came across Anwar's testimonial because a few Tijanis shared it with me. They were frustrated about how narratives of an "all expenses paid" experience undercut the very real burden that the shuyukh and school administrators faced in finding enough money to sustain young peoples' education. Such murids worried that people misinterpreted the shuyukh's generosity as relieving them of the responsibility to contribute whatever was in their means to finance their international education. Such murids had inside knowledge about the financial burdens placed on the shuyukh but were also cognizant of the fact that the shuyukh were committed to making it economically possible for spiritual seekers to remain in Medina Baye. Given the rising cost of living and inadequate financial support from families, one administrator wondered how much longer they could afford to operate a program for American students. Privy to the inner financial workings of the system of collective care, such murids' concerns pointed to some of the tensions within it and raised questions about its sustainability.

Some older students were also mindful of the economic responsibilities that sustained Medina Baye's system of collective care. Djibril, a young brother from rural Burkina Faso who lived in Shaykh Mahy's house for years, explained, "You can't just rely on the shaykh for everything. One thing I learned from my parents, I never want to be someone with my hand out." Though the financial support provided by Imam Cheikh and Shaykh Mahy meant that older students did not feel as strong a pressure to hustle to survive, youth like Djibril still felt compelled to make some money. In a city with few formal employment opportunities, many young people took on side hustles. Djibril started a part-time business raising and selling chickens, while Kareem translated and edited Islamic speeches, and both gave hadiya when they could. However, with their basic needs met, older Black American and African students alike had the luxury of treating their education and khidma as their primary work.

Kareem could dedicate his entire day to studying without having to worry about how to make ends meet, a sharp contrast to his experiences in the U.S, where he had been underpaid and overworked. After graduating high school, Kareem attended a university in Ohio. He studied international business and then international studies, but ultimately "kinda got, I guess, bored with that, and money was an issue." As had been the case for Ismail and Asiya—two of the AAII alumni from Chapter 5 who returned to Medina Baye in their twenties—Kareem was priced out of a higher education in the U.S.

For years after leaving school, Kareem worked full-time and juggled multiple jobs. He occasionally attended Islamic classes at the mosque if his work schedule permitted him to do so, and if he could muster up the energy after a long day of physically taxing work. These short periods of study did not allow Kareem to advance as quickly or as deeply as he would have liked. He explained, "I got to a point where I was kinda stagnant. It was too much, working all the time, two jobs. I was cooking, I was doing urban agriculture, but nothing was satisfying. I felt like I just needed to move forward."

Like the Black American and African Tijani youth we met in Chapter 5, Kareem experienced precarity and felt that time stood still. His frustration in not being able to dedicate himself to his studies, coupled with the stressful burden of constantly working only to make enough money to survive, and the daunting feeling that he just could not progress in life, propelled him to leave the U.S. Kareem had regularly attended Tijani gatherings in Washington D.C. There, he became friends with Black American, Senegalese, and Gambian Tijanis who arranged for him to study in Medina Baye. Kareem's membership in the tariqa and his relationship to the Cisse family opened the door for him to receive an international Islamic education that he could not otherwise afford.

Kareem, Hajjah Najah, Anwar, and most other Black Muslims who traveled from the African diaspora to study in Medina Baye thus varied from the stereotypical portraits of heritage or wealthy tourists. Tijanis from Africa and the diaspora converged in Medina Baye for similar reasons. They understood it to be a spiritually significant site where they would be cared for by the Cisse family as they pursued Islamic education and spiritual transformation.

Assumptions, Expectations, and Perceptions of Tijanis from the African Diaspora

Kareem's closest friends in Medina Baye were English-speaking Tijanis from Nigeria and Ghana. Late at night, as they sipped tea and enjoyed a slight breeze, they often traded stories about their shared experiences of precarity in Washington D.C., Lagos, and Accra. They reflected with gratitude on how they had been able to come to a place where their primary focus was cultivating their spiritual growth. However, even though Kareem found resonance with these African friends, he still encountered natives of Medina Baye who yearned to relocate to the U.S. Kareem recounted one interaction with a Senegalese classmate:

> I kept asking, "Why do you want to go to America?" He says, "There's money there! We're poor here! We need to come back and build homes and stuff!" So there's a Ghanaian brother Jabbar in the class who speaks very good English. I told him, like, "Look, this is what's going on in America. Black people are being killed, being shot, poverty, you know, the history of America in terms of slavery, what was done to African American males, in terms of being castrated, mutilated. African women were being raped in America, enslaved. They were subjected to constant rape, their daughters at early ages were raped." And some of them, their

jaw dropped because they actually don't know what we've been through in America, to be hanging from trees, these types of things. They actually don't know that, so to tell them that, they become more aware. But I know that they still do want to go to America to make money, because they feel like there's no other possibility. I tell them, "Donald Trump is no good. He made it tough for people. The economy is no good." But they just have it in their mind, "I want to go to America or Europe to make money so I can come back and build a home." Or, "I need money. There's no money in Africa!" All that stuff. I can't figure out how people build homes in Senegal then. I ain't build no home here [in Medina Baye]!

Kareem knew some Wolof, but not enough to clearly explain the horrors of U.S. history. He relied on his Ghanaian friend Jabbar, who spoke English and Wolof, to translate. Because of their language barriers, nuances articulated by both Kareem and his Senegalese classmate were likely glossed over, misunderstood, or lost in translation.

Nonetheless, according to Kareem, at least some of his Senegalese classmates imagined that life in the U.S. afforded all residents greater opportunities than were accessible in rural Medina Baye. Implicit in this perspective was the assumption that the U.S. was the land of prosperity regardless of one's race, and, as such, that Senegalese migrants could become rich and successful there. Some of Kareem's classmates reportedly insisted that international migration would enable them to accumulate the wealth necessary to build their own homes in Senegal. His male classmates' aspirations were likely linked to gender norms in Senegalese culture, where being considered a man was often defined by one's ability to build a house (Babou 2008, 13). Such aspirations were widely evident in Dakar, where migrants living abroad sent money to build family homes in Senegal as a way of maintaining their ties to the country and positively contributing to its growth (Melly 2010). His classmates' interest in migration to the U.S. therefore did not necessarily indicate their investment in a country built on the exploitation of Black people. Rather, their perspectives seemed to be informed by their assessment of the limited opportunities for economic mobility in their rural context and their desires to stake out more prosperous futures outside of Senegal—aspirations that were also increasingly prevalent among Senegalese youth in rural and urban areas (Ba et al. 2107; Rodriguez 2015), as well as youth in other African countries (Bleck and Lodermeier 2020; Yeboah 2021).

Grappling with the devastating effects of the legacy of European colonization, predatory economic arrangements imposed by European countries and corporations on independent African nations, and Europe's underdevelopment of the continent at large, Kareem's classmates reportedly "feel like there's no other possibility" than to leave. International migration might then be understood as a long-term strategy that allowed Africans to collectively care for their family back home. Senegalese migrants could send remittances from abroad and enhance the quality of life of their loved ones who remained behind (Hannaford 2017).

At the same time that these classmates envisioned, according to Kareem, a path to home ownership in Senegal, Black Americans in the U.S. struggled to purchase homes because of racist practices such as redlining and predatory lending (Taylor 2019). Kareem's claim that home ownership was easier in Medina Baye underscored his view of the persistent barriers confronting Black people in the U.S. and his perspective that there were greater economic opportunities in Senegal. In fact, during the 1990s, Shaykh Hassan encouraged his Black American murids to build their own enclave in Kossi Atlanta,[2] a sparsely occupied town close to Medina Baye. While extensive construction in Kossi Atlanta never materialized, to date, approximately ten Black Americans own land or homes in or around Medina Baye. Although the cost of real estate has skyrocketed in recent years, due in part to the influx of wealth from Senegalese people who send remittances from abroad, one could purchase land in Medina Baye in 2022 from around $15,000 USD—with the understanding that construction might cost at least $60,000 USD but would take place piecemeal as the owner provided cash funds. This made home ownership in and around Medina Baye more feasible for some Black Americans than it would be for them in the U.S., though in reality, most Black American Tijanis were still unable to own their own homes—a trend that mirrored patterns in the U.S., where fewer than 45 percent of Black people owned homes and where the Black homeownership rate was below the rates of any other racial group (Yun et al. 2025).

In addition to the longer conversations that Kareem attempted to navigate in the classroom, he confronted requests for money from people he interacted with only briefly. Kareem explained,

They look at the TV and that's like their information source now, so now they see America and they automatically see you as a *toubab*, or that you have a dollar sign on your forehead. They don't know the social, economic, political circumstances in America, that some people are actually living a bit worse than they are. . . . As shack as it might look, you actually have a four-walled home. You have food that's being prepared for you, even if it's your neighbor preparing a big bowl. Some people don't have that in America. They're on the street, no place to go, and then when they do go to the shelters, they get disrespected.

Toubab is a Wolof word that describes a person who is perceived to be culturally different from and socioeconomically more advantaged than the average Senegalese person. Toubab is primarily used to refer to white people or Senegalese people who are deemed to have become Europeanized. The word holds similar connotations as *obruni*, a word used in Ghana to describe not only white people but also Black American heritage tourists, much to their diasporic disappointment (Hartman 2008). Kareem expressed frustration that he and other working-class Black Americans were called toubabs, when their daily experiences and economic struggles were similar to those of their African neighbors.

Unlike a heritage tourist who might travel to Senegal only briefly, Tijanis from the African diaspora sought to regularly visit if not stay for extended periods. While Kareem faulted the media for broadcasting distorted narratives, the fact that diaspora Black Tijanis lived with Africans suggested that they had opportunities to develop more nuanced understandings than appeared on television. However, whether this potential was actualized varied on a case-by-case basis. While Kareem was still learning Wolof, others of his Black American peers had become fluent. I also knew at least three Senegalese Tijanis, one Nigerien Tijani, and two Tijanis from Burkina Faso who had become fluent in English over their years of befriending Black American and other English-speaking Tijanis. Having a shared language thus deepened bonds among neighbors and classmates who interacted regularly, making it possible for them to learn about one another's experiences and histories.

While Kareem faulted television portrayals for warping Africans' perceptions about life in the U.S., social media held potential to foster more nuanced conversations. Mariama, a young Senegalese woman who grew up in a village near the border of Gambia and moved to Medina Baye at the age of 17, explained,

> Me, I'm here with Americans, and I watch the news every day and I'm on the internet all the time. I know what's going on. Some people don't know, but most of the people here, they know. Now everybody is active on social media so everybody knows what's going on around the world.

Indeed, I observed African Tijanis ask their Black American friends about the horrific videos they saw of police murdering Black people in the U.S. In contrast to the 1980s, those who studied in Medina Baye during the twenty-first century interacted with African residents within an increasingly interconnected world in which information about anti-Black violence and other contemporary crises often went viral.

To deepen spiritual kinship ties and pan-African bonds, the Cisse shuyukh encouraged marriages between Black American and African Tijanis. They facilitated unions between Black American women and African men as well as between Black American men and African women. A Black American named Myiesha who married a Senegalese Tijani shared that conversations about police brutality used to be a "heated topic" with her husband. She reported that, early in her marriage, her husband made comments such as "Black Americans, y'all don't listen to the police and that's why people get killed," but that his perspective shifted over the years. Myiesha concluded, "It's conversation. I think the more we have these conversations with not just our own people but people all over the world, the truth is told. I think the perception changes." Myiesha's comment and other moments of nuanced engagement between Black American and African Tijanis demonstrated the impact of having a shared language and intimate relationships. While perhaps more conducive among peers in classroom settings, opportunities for dialogue were less likely to occur during brief, chance interactions between relative strangers such as Usman and Kareem and in public spaces such as the mosque's courtyard.

Nonetheless, conversations did not always lead to fully transformed perspectives. Among Black American–African Tijani couples, I heard several Black Americans explain that they would have preferred to stay in Medina Baye, but that their spouses insisted on moving to the U.S.

because they anticipated there would be greater economic opportunities there—a notion that the Black American partners had not been able to disabuse them of. As one young Black American woman knowingly remarked regarding her Ghanaian husband whose U.S. visa application was pending, "Oh, he'll see when he gets here that it's not all that great."

Mariama, the young Senegalese woman who reported being globally informed, was also married to a Tijani she met in the city—a Ghanaian American alumnus of AAII. Through conversations with her husband and her other Black American friends, Mariama learned a lot about life in the U.S., where her husband had spent the bulk of his life. However, Mariama pointed out the limits of dialogue in altering peoples' perceptions. She explained,

> Some people, no matter what you tell them about America, they're not gonna listen. They just wanna go, 'cause in their mind, it's easier to make money in America. And it's true too. It's easier to make money in America 'cause you can get a job and make some money. But here, you can study, have all your diplomas, and it's even hard for you to get internships. So, you know, it's not easy out here.

Mariama acknowledged the power of experiential knowledge in shaping peoples' perceptions. Yet even Mariama, who had a rather detailed understanding of realities in the U.S., contended that life was easier there—perhaps because she had never actually lived in the U.S. As someone who had pursued advanced degrees in Senegal, Mariama was intimately aware of the realities of her country's higher educational landscape, where students questioned the value of a college degree, as it did little to guarantee post-graduate employment (Garcia and Fares 2008, 42). Mariama's critiques of higher education bore resemblance not only to the disappointments articulated by students throughout Africa (Herrera 2010; Mkwananzi 2018) but also to the experiences of Black college graduates in the U.S. There, Black college graduates experienced higher rates of unemployment than their white college-educated counterparts, and Black graduates who found work still confronted discrimination, segregation, and unequal pay on the job (Weller 2019).

Like Mariama, Kareem compared and contrasted life in Senegal and the U.S. Kareem pointed out that he observed how residents in Medina

Baye generously shared whatever they had with their neighbors. Doing so was part of Senegalese culture, where the emphasis on *teranga* (hospitality) was a major source of pride among Senegalese people and even led to the country's reputation as *Pays de la Teranga* (a French-Wolof phrase meaning "the country or land of hospitality"). Kareem argued that the cultural norms of teranga and ethics of collective care were absent in the U.S., where unhoused people were "disrespected" even when they sought help at homeless shelters. Kareem's comments suggested that the effects of poverty were less devastating for residents in the maroon geography of Medina Baye than for Black people in the capitalist U.S.

On numerous occasions, when I walked by residents gathering in a circle to eat, each person's right hand reaching into the bowl to scoop the rice directly in front of them, their instinctual reaction would be to pause and call out, "American, *kaay lekk!*"—a Wolof invitation that meant "American, come eat!" It would not be unusual for an "American, *kaay lekk!*" invitation to come from the same person who had demanded the previous day, "American, give me money!" While these seemingly contradictory expressions could be interpreted as an indication of the Americans' status as outsiders, they actually reflected the radical Black praxis of community and deeply ingrained nature of collective care in Medina Baye, where all residents were expected to share rather than hoard their resources.

Another dimension that likely shaped some Senegalese residents' expectations and misunderstandings about Black Americans' wealth was their experience living in a country where approximately 39 percent of people lived in poverty and 75 percent of families dealt with chronic poverty (Seck and Terki 2020). Furthermore, 21 percent of households in rural areas of Senegal (such as Medina Baye) experienced food insecurity, in comparison to 9 percent in urban areas (USAID 2018). The heightened challenges facing people in rural Senegal were not unlike those of Black people in the U.S., where the poverty rate among Black Americans was greater than among any other racial group except Native Americans (Shrider 2024). Like families in rural Senegal, Black families in the U.S. confronted a disproportionately heavier impact of poverty.

Yet Black Americans and Africans did not always connect these dots. Instead, just as Kareem concluded that people in the U.S. were "actually living a bit worse" than residents in Medina Baye, Mariama asserted that it was "easier to make money in America." Their commentaries reflected a tendency among marginalized communities to compare and rank one another's plight, each one ultimately casting itself as less privileged than the other. Jemima Pierre (2012) similarly recounts how a Ghanaian man perceived an African American woman visiting Accra to be "one of the lucky ones" because she had escaped the poverty and hardships that he and his peers remained subjected to in Africa (154). Despite the fact that the African American woman's ancestors were ripped from their homelands and taken against their will to the U.S., the Ghanaian man nonetheless asserted that she ultimately had a better outcome than him. By recounting how slavery shaped the experiences of Black people, Kareem sought to illustrate the racist economic challenges that some Africans presumed existed only in Africa. By pointing out the bleak employment prospects for students who attended university, Mariama alluded to the crises that mired postcolonial Senegal's labor market and higher educational landscape—crises that she presumed did not exist in the U.S. Obscured from both of their conclusions was the recognition of the "links through the historical arc of slavery and colonialism—and the overlapping history of Blacks from the diaspora and those left behind on the continent" (ibid., 156). Similar processes of structural exclusion and underdevelopment resulted in the disenfranchisement of Black Americans in the U.S. and Africans in Senegal. However, despite this, and despite the fact that Tijanis from Africa and the diaspora could learn from one another, the impulse to contrast meant that the potential for forging pan-African solidarities was not always actualized.

Family Ties

In 2012, a group of Black American and West African Tijani alumni of AAII started Help for Humanity (HFH), a service initiative led by Nasrul Ilm America (which was discussed in Chapter 5). These alumni raised funds to distribute rice and other food to people in Medina Baye on a monthly basis. HFH was led by a Black American named Hajji Ajib Abdus-Salaam and his Senegalese wife Sayyida Ya Bilquis Cisse, who was also Shaykh Hassan's daughter. In their younger days in Medina Baye, Hajji Ajib and Sayyida Ya Bilquis witnessed firsthand Shaykh Hassan's consistent commitment to feeding people. Hajji Ajib, Sayyida

Ya Bilquis, and other alumni carried forth Shaykh Hassan's work and sought to repay the community who had cared for them when they were students.

Most months, HFH's distribution events were staffed by Black American and Senegalese residents. However, in February 2018, the monthly distribution event coincided with Journey to Africa, a cross-cultural travel experience to Senegal led by three Black American alumni from AAII who were leaders in HFH—Hajji Ajib Abdus-Salaam and his younger brothers, Hajji Hassan Abdus-Salaam and Hajji Dooley Abdus-Salaam (1978–2020). Journey to Africa, which they intentionally scheduled during Black History Month, brought out a group of ten or so Black Americans—Muslim and non-Muslim, Tijani and non-Tijani alike. The Abdus-Salaam brothers had deep roots in Medina Baye; in 1977, Shaykh Hassan had invited their parents, Imam Sayed (1942–2017) and Hajjah Salwa Abdus-Salaam (1952–1993) to visit Medina Baye, and during the 1980s, Shaykh Hassan encouraged the parents to enroll their children at AAII. Journey to Africa was part of the brothers' numerous efforts to continue Shaykh Hassan's work of building bridges between Black Americans and Africans. With two of the brothers married to Senegalese women, and all three speaking Wolof, being Tijani, and having spent years of their adolescence and adulthood in Medina Baye, the organizers served as knowledgeable mediators between Black American tourists and Senegalese residents.

The organizers did not market the Journey to Africa trip as a Sufi retreat to Medina Baye. Instead, the backdrop of the flier advertising the trip was a photo of the African Renaissance Monument in Dakar, a 49-meter-tall statue of a man, woman, and young child unveiled in 2010 by then Senegalese president Abdoulaye Wade. Explaining the symbolism of the statue, President Wade stated, "Africa has arrived in the 21st century standing tall and more ready than ever to take its destiny into its hands." The choice of the monument as the backdrop of the flier invoked a triumphant journey to the continent, one defined not by memories of slavery but one focused on the contemporary moment and the exciting possibilities of the future. The final stop of the trip was Medina Baye, where the group staffed that month's HFH distribution. Eager to assist, some group members tucked t-shirts, toys, and candies into their luggage to give out alongside the food.

Figure 6.2. Flier for the 2018 Journey to Africa trip.

Most months, the food staples were distributed in front of a store on the bustling main road that led into Medina Baye. But when the Journey to Africa group came, the distribution took place in the courtyard of AAII, a more logistically convenient location given the extra fanfare surrounding that month's event. The group of volunteers distributing the items would be much larger, and they had planned a special ceremony prior to the distribution. Beyond these logistical considerations, selecting the AAII courtyard was a nod to Black Americans' roots in Medina Baye. The distribution would take place in a space that Shaykh Hassan had created with them in mind and that many of their children continued to benefit from. The space bore testament to the multigenerational ties and collective care practices between Black American and Senegalese Tijanis.

During the ceremony, the Journey to Africa group stood at the front of the crowd. One by one, each person took the microphone, sharing impromptu, heartfelt words about what the initiative meant to them. Some in the group were Tijanis who frequently visited Medina Baye. They were delighted that they recognized the faces and remembered the names of several of the residents who had come to receive rice. These Journey to Africa participants recounted their memories over the years of building community with people in Medina Baye and promised to maintain these bonds in the future. There were other Black Americans in the group who were coming to Medina Baye, and in some cases, to Africa for the first time. Amaal, a Black American Muslim woman who was not Tijani, shared, tearfully, how she was in awe of the people in front of her, how so many of them reminded her of her own Black American family members, and how privileged she felt to be welcomed by local residents.

Later that day, I interviewed Rashida, a Tijani woman who was part of the group but also had come to Medina Baye to drop off her teenaged son to resume his studies at AAII. Rashida explained,

> For us, African Americans, people of color, it's knowing where we come from. And so for my son, building on those roots, to reestablish his roots with where his people are from is also important. Because we grow up in the States, as man without country. I feel that only Blacks and Puerto Ricans have that issue. Nobody else has that issue. But being here gives him a chance to do that. And as you saw today, you know, it's different what

Figure 6.3. A Help for Humanity volunteer prepares to distribute 50-kilogram sacks of rice, small bags of sugar, and packets of dates in Medina Baye. Photo by Hajji Hassan Abdus-Salaam.

Help for Humanity is doing, and not so much what they're doing, but who's doing it. It's people who have come back, established, reestablished their connections with their people and their land, and building on that. It's not, "Oh, I lived in this country for X amount of time, and I just want to give back because I was here doing whatever."

Like many other humanitarian efforts, HFH delivered essential resources to communities in need. However, Rashida asserted that HFH was distinct because of the people involved. It was run primarily by those whose connections to the people and place of Medina Baye fueled their desires to serve. Some of these participants, like Amaal who was a first-time visitor, possessed what Bianca Williams describes as a diasporic heart. Writing about Black American women who traveled to Jamaica, Williams (2018) argues that these women's diasporic hearts propelled their desires to use their economic privilege to "give back" to Jamaicans whom they recognized as diasporic kin (66). Similarly, Amaal had yet to build intimate relationships with residents, but she felt emotionally connected to them because of their shared racial identity. Others, like Rashida and her son, engaged HFH as a form of sustained kincraft (Thomas 2021). They saw themselves as connected to the people and place of Medina Baye. They had forged this relational and familial ethos decades prior and renewed their connections over the years. Just as remittances allowed family members who migrated abroad to economically support those who remained in Senegal, so too did HFH enable Black American Tijanis to uphold the responsibility they felt towards their spiritual family in Medina Baye. HFH was a formalized way to maintain their bonds and collectively care for one another.

Rashida's assertion that HFH was different because of "who's doing it" resonated with me when I went to another of the organization's monthly distribution events. This particular one had no extra fanfare. It was run by the usual on-the-ground representatives of the initiative. As I stood at the periphery of the growing crowd of people, a middle-aged Senegalese woman named Maam Fatou strolled over to me and asked if I knew Tahanee. I did indeed know Tahanee, a Black American Tijani woman whom I had spent time with in Detroit, New York City, and later in Medina Baye when she had come to visit her daughter Aziza, whom

Figure 6.4. A line of people, mostly women, stand and wait to receive items from Help for Humanity. Photo by Hajji Hassan Abdus-Salaam.

we met in Chapter 4. Maam Fatou told me that she had known Tahanee since she was student at AAII in the 1990s. Maam Fatou recounted fond memories of Tahanee, and asked about Tahanee's husband, parents, and those of Tahanee's siblings and children that she knew. Maam Fatou shared memories of how she used to watch Tahanee's youngest sibling, nephews, and nieces, and cook for Tahanee's parents when they visited. As Maam Fatou rattled off the names of countless people in Tahanee's family, I was reminded of their deep roots in Medina Baye. Tahanee's family was one of many Black American Tijani families who had been coming to Medina Baye for decades. Several people in her family had become fluent in Wolof, married Senegalese residents, and lived between Senegal and the U.S. After Maam Fatou finished checking in on Tahanee and her family, she looked around and sighed at the sight of the large crowd of residents who had gathered under the sun, hoping to get a 50-kilogram bag of rice to feed their family. But then she locked eyes with me, smiled, and asked, "Where's my bag of rice? Tahanee is my sister."

Each month, the number of people who showed up and patiently waited to receive food was greater than what HFH had been able to fundraise for. Each month, the distribution event ended not with a sense of satisfaction and relief, but instead with a palpable feeling of frustration among both organizers and recipients that there was not enough to serve everyone. Aware of this disappointing, common finale, Maam Fatou signaled her family ties to Black Americans as she did her best to ensure that she did not miss out on her bag. Her request could be interpreted as a way of circumventing a fair process of humanitarian relief and instead requesting preferential treatment. But, just as Rashida asserted that volunteers with HFH were different from those associated with a conventional humanitarian aid effort, so too did Maam Fatou's comments reveal her shared perception on the unique nature of the initiative. Maam Fatou implied that she should be treated not as a random aid recipient, but rather as a relative who was entitled to her kin's resources. Family ties recast the power dynamics inherent to both international humanitarianism and relationships between African and Black American Tijanis and reframed their exchange from foreign aid to remittances. Family ties offered an alternate way of making sense of social and moral obligations among spiritual kin. As Maam Fatou's request suggested, within a pan-African Tijani family, having differential access to privilege need not devolve into competitions about who had it worse. It could, instead, foster relationships anchored in concern, responsibility, and reciprocity and that ensured that all family members were collectively cared for.

From American to Cisse

Early one Friday morning, I walked with Bayyinah, a Black British Tijani woman, to the Western Union located near the towering gate that greeted people when they first entered the city of Medina Baye. We aimed to beat the crowd of residents, who, like her, would come to collect funds from family members scattered throughout Senegal and the world. For the last nine months, Bayyinah had given up lucrative paid gigs and had instead opted for a spiritual retreat away from the hustle, bustle, and struggle of urban life in London. Bayyinah stayed in a guestroom on the second floor of Imam Cheikh's house. As was the case for Kareem, Imam Cheikh voluntarily covered the bulk of Bayyinah's expenses, from the daily plates of lunch and dinner that he had delivered to her room to the medication he paid for when she got malaria. Bayyinah often gave hadiya to Imam Cheikh, but her hadiya was simply a small token of appreciation. After all, what most murids gave did not compare with the amount the shuyukh spent in housing, feeding, and educating them (Wright 2015a, 101).

While Bayyinah had to spend very little to live comfortably in Medina Baye, she occasionally received money from her family. That morning, Bayyinah's mother had sent her a small sum—not much by U.K. standards but enough to buy juicy mangoes, pineapple-flavored soda, and other snacks that brought Bayyinah joy. As Bayyinah exited the Western Union, she was stopped by an elderly woman.

"Cisse, Cisse!" the woman repeated, bowing her head and smiling at Bayyinah.

Repeating the family name of the person one meets was a common part of Senegalese culture. In Medina Baye, having the last names Cisse or Niasse meant that a person was associated with the two most regarded families in the city. The Cisses and Niasses were honored in everyday practice. They were greeted with physical deference from Tijani murids, asked to pray for others, given hadiya, and publicly acknowledged at the start of gatherings. Due to their status, the Cisses and Niasses were also expected to contribute significantly to Medina Baye's system of collective care.

As Tijanis who became part of their shuyukh's spiritual families and households, Kareem and Bayyinah had become intimately familiar with the communal obligations that the Cisses upheld. As we saw earlier, Tijanis from the African diaspora witnessed the large groups of people who expected and received money from the shuyukh at the mosque, on the street, and in their homes. They observed the stream of women and men who came to visit Imam Cheikh and Shaykh Mahy and asked for help in paying for their children's school fees, their travel expenses to go visit sick relatives, or overdue utility bills. Kareem and Bayyinah watched as the shuyukh reached into their pockets, and person after person, passed out money to those who asked.

In the U.S., in the 1960s and onwards, as part of the influence of Black consciousness movements, many Black Americans (including Muslims) eschewed their legal last names which bore the history of enslavement. They adopted Swahili and Arabic names to assert their African and Muslim identities. In the decades to come, many Black American and Black

British Tijanis in Shaykh Ibrahim's movement renamed themselves as well. Some cast aside their European-origin last names and took on the last name Cisse. Others hyphenated their last name, joining their given or chosen Arabic last names with the name Cisse.

The decision to rename oneself was not limited to those whose last names bore the legacies of enslavement and erasure. In Shaykh Ibrahim's movement, it was also common for Africans to take on the name Cisse. Numerous African and Black American Tijanis alike explained to me that they took on the name Cisse because they saw their shaykh as their adopted father. They said the sentiment was mutual, as Shaykh Hassan, Imam Cheikh, and Shaykh Mahy cared for them like members of their family, and in many instances explicitly referred to them as such. Similarly, Senegalese Tijanis and other Wolof speakers commonly referred to Shaykh Ibrahim as Baye, the Wolof word for father.

I also heard another explanation for why many African Tijanis chose the last name Cisse. At the start of my interview with Naeem, a Hausa brother from Lagos, Nigeria, I asked him to introduce himself. Naeem stated his full name at birth and then immediately clarified, "But because I was with Shaykh Mahy Cisse, I changed my name to Naeem Cisse." He explained that that was something done by

> [a]nybody who comes from whatever part of the world to make khidma in Medina Baye. So if you're in the Cisse house, they call you Cisse. If you live in the Niasse house, they call you Niasse. . . . Even before I told them I was Cisse, people already called me, "Cisse, Cisse, Cisse." That's how people call me because I make khidma in Shaykh Mahy Cisse's house.

Naeem's perspective was shared by several African Tijanis whom I interviewed. Cisse was both a name that was socially conferred upon them by others who recognized their immense service to their shuyukh, and a name that murids themselves adopted with pride as they signaled a Tijani mode of kincraft.

Bayyinah did not know the elderly woman who greeted her, yet the woman saw her as a Cisse. As was the case when Usman summoned Kareem, African residents attempting to get the attention of diaspora Black residents tended to call them American. Bayyinah, though a Black Brit, had been called American on many occasions. However, in this instance, by addressing Bayyinah as a Cisse, the older woman communicated her sense of respect and esteem for Bayyinah. As had been the case among those residents who recognized Naeem's dedication to his shaykh and called him a Cisse before he even self-identified as one, the elderly woman recognized Bayyinah's position within the community.

"Maybe she meant it, or maybe she knew that calling me Cisse would get to me, but I had to give her something," Bayyinah admitted to me. She took out a few bills from her newly acquired money and handed them to the woman.

In this interaction, instead of being seen as an American heritage tourist unfamiliar with local customs, Bayyinah was treated as a Cisse. When Tijanis from the African diaspora were called Cisse rather than American, they became incorporated into a pan-African Tijani mode of kincraft and the community's system of collective care. Having spent extended time in Medina Baye, Bayyinah was expected to be knowledgeable about and responsible for honoring the financial responsibilities and ethical obligations modeled by the Cisse shuyukh. This was ironic, given that Bayyinah and other Tijanis from the diaspora received financial assistance from their shuyukh. Nonetheless, even if it was a bit of a hardship and even if she was unable to provide the woman with a substantial amount of money, Bayyinah pushed herself to uphold the practices of collective care that came with being regarded as a Cisse.

Conclusion

Medina Baye represents a unique site of pan-African Islamic exchange. During the twentieth century, Medina Baye was the meeting point for Tijanis from across Africa who saw Shaykh Ibrahim as their spiritual leader and heard his calls for revolutionary pan-African unity in solidarity with Muslims throughout the world. After Shaykh Ibrahim returned to Allah, Shaykh Hassan, Imam Cheikh, and Shaykh Mahy spread word of the Tijani tariqa to Black Muslims in the diaspora. Like many African Tijanis, diaspora Black Tijanis came to Medina Baye at the personal invitation of the Cisse shuyukh, who echoed their grandfather's pan-African consciousness. These shuyukh carved out space for their murids in their schools, homes, and families. Such support was part of their broader responsibility as religious leaders of Medina Baye to help alleviate the financial hardships of the city's residents. Thanks to the financial sponsorship of their shuyukh, African and African diasporic Tijanis embarked on the shared pursuit of spiritual transformation.

In the twenty-first century, Shaykh Ibrahim's fayda marked fertile grounds for a continued pan-African Sufi movement. Challenging the narratives that differentiated and hierarchized the economic hardships facing African and African diasporic communities impacted by the overlapping legacies of slavery, colonialism, racial capitalism, and white supremacy, Medina Baye was a contemporary contact zone where African and African-descendent Tijanis could connect the dots between their struggles and imagine new futures. In a world that was increasingly interconnected through social media and globalization, Medina Baye was also as a rare, in-person space of sustained pan-African exchange where ordinary Black Muslims could learn from one another. It was a place where working-class Black Americans like Kareem, who lived most of his life in the urban U.S., could spend years in community with residents like Usman, who was from a rural area, did not attend a French-language school, and instead had spent the entirety of his educational upbringing at a Qur'an school.

Since Black Americans first began visiting Medina Baye in the 1970s, they laid the foundation for freedom dreams that gave them tangible paths away from anti-Black violence, anti-Muslim racism, and economic precarity in the U.S. As they pursued Islamic education and spiritual purification in Medina Baye, they reconstructed what it meant to live and practice their faith in community with others. The Black American Tijani community included people who permanently resettled there, became fluent in Wolof, built their own homes in Medina Baye, married African Tijanis, enrolled their children and grandchildren at AAII, led local humanitarian efforts, lived between there and the U.S., and facilitated opportunities for other Black Americans to visit. Within the Black American Tijani community were also people who expressed frustration about encountering some African residents who held misinformed assumptions and expectations about Black Americans. The irony aside that Kareem and many diaspora Black Tijanis hailed from working-class backgrounds and were beneficiaries of the Cisse shuyukhs' collective care practices, they were often accosted with the demand "American, give me money!" Despite the decades-long presence of Black Americans in Medina Baye, as well as the Cisse shuyukhs' significant commitment to incorporating Black Americans into their spiritual family, such a statement seemed to indicate Black American Tijanis' status as outsiders.

When Kareem retorted that he too was a talibe in need, he tried to connect the dots between his and Usman's experiences. Although his comment momentarily shifted the dynamics of their interaction, it did not spark an in-depth conversation about the realities confronting Black people in the U.S., nor did it foster the space to explore their overlapping experiences and develop a pan-African consciousness. Such outcomes were unlikely to unfold during brief and impromptu encounters among residents who knew little about each other, who interacted only briefly as they stood in public spaces, or who were not fluent in one another's languages.

Conversations between spouses or among friends held greater potential. So too did the classrooms at AAII, where students learned together. However, in the case of Kareem, he reported that some of his African classmates were unfamiliar with the transatlantic slave trade and its lasting impact. As they experienced the everyday impacts of structural adjustment and the underdevelopment of Africa, coupled with the romanticized depictions of life in the U.S. and Europe that they were bombarded with on television, some Africans presumed that Tijanis from the diaspora held socioeconomic privilege by virtue of their former residence in the U.S. or Europe. As evidenced by the mediation of Kareem's interactions through his Ghanaian friend, language barriers made it difficult for diaspora Black Tijanis who did not yet have a firm grasp of Wolof to engage fellow residents. Struggling to develop a full understanding of each other's experiences, members of both groups reportedly compared and ranked one another's plight, claiming that each was in a more precarious position than the other. And even in cases where shared language, social media, and intimate relationships meant that Black Americans and Africans had a greater understanding of one another's experiences, the tendency to differentiate persisted.

But because diaspora Black Tijanis tended to be residents rather than tourists, they had greater opportunities to build relationships with Africans and learn local norms. Black Americans observed how the Cisse shuyukh spent their own resources to ensure that their murids could pursue spiritual advancement. These Tijanis received the invitation

"American, *kaay lekk* [come eat]!" and observed neighbors of all socioeconomic levels insist on sharing their food. They saw how caring was not simply a burden placed upon those with the most resources; instead, they observed how those who one day might be in need could on the next day generously give to others. Through these observations, they learned how the system of collective care sustained the people of Medina Baye, softening the effects of poverty and economic marginalization in rural Senegal while bringing them closer to being those who were most beloved to Allah. For Tijanis coming from the African diaspora, these experiences generated within them a sense of financial and ethical responsibility informed by local economic and social norms. Although diaspora Black Tijanis may not have been as wealthy as the stereotype of the "American" might suggest, they nonetheless acknowledged that they were blessed with means and understood that they had a responsibility to share their resources. In honoring this local norm, Tijanis from the African diaspora became seen in new ways by African residents of Medina Baye, and became integrated into the community's system of collective care. They forged new family ties, shifting from American to Cisse.

In the twenty-first century, membership within Shaykh Ibrahim's pan-African spiritual movement thus altered relationships between African and African diasporic Tijanis—relationships which were often overdetermined by misinterpretations of each another's socioeconomic privilege. It transformed understandings of economic and social reciprocity between the two groups, whose experiences were interconnected through their sustained, familial relations of care as murids in Shaykh Ibrahim's fayda. While language barriers and differences in firsthand experiences meant that a pan-African consciousness and analyses of their overlapping experiences were not always realized, expectations about money and wealth revealed another way in which they could relate to one another. Shifting away from the tendency to compare and hierarchize the economic hardships facing people in Africa and the diaspora, these newly emerging social relations among Black Muslims in Medina Baye pointed to the ways in which the Tijani tariqa continued to foster a pan-African movement.

Of course, given the varying sociopolitical contexts, economic conditions, and cultural norms in the U.S. and Senegal, there were critical differences that shaped the assumptions and perceptions held by diaspora Black and African Tijanis. To grow a pan-African movement, it is important to identify opportunities for solidarity without flattening the varied hardships that members face. As African and African diasporic Tijanis recognized that they belonged to a shared system of collective care, they identified their differential resources and called for modes of relationality that addressed these differences in positionality. In a twenty-first century context in which pan-Africanism appeared to be eclipsed by diasporic tensions, when U.S. hegemony loomed large, and when international migration gave the allure of greater economic opportunities for those struggling to survive in a deliberately underdeveloped Africa, Shaykh Ibrahim's pan-African Sufi movement held potential for shaping new understandings of the responsibilities and possibilities of being Black and Muslim. For those seeking to be most beloved to Allah, the Tijani tariqa represented a space where they could learn new paradigms of economic and familial reciprocity that helped ease the weight of the racist economic exclusion facing Black Muslims in the U.S. and Senegal.

Epilogue

Freedom Dreaming in Frightening Times

In November 2023, I touched down in Senegal and opened my cellphone to find a WhatsApp message with a flier advertising a pro-Palestine rally that would be taking place later that afternoon outside of the Grand Mosque of Medina Baye. The rally was being organized by a group of young Tijani residents who, like millions of people throughout the world, were outraged by Israel's ceaseless violence against Palestinians. The rally invoked the long-standing tradition of their spiritual leader, Shaykh Ibrahim Niasse. Back in the 1960s, Shaykh Ibrahim inaugurated al-Quds Day in Medina Baye—an annual event referring to the Arabic name for Jerusalem and held in support of the global movement to liberate Palestine. Al-Quds Day had historically taken place on the eve of the *gamou* (the celebration of Prophet Muhammad's birth)—the occasion that brought out the largest number of people to Medina Baye each year.

The November 2023 rally attracted more than one hundred students, adult residents, and religious leaders in Medina Baye. Among them were many of the Black American and African youth who I had come to know over the years. Several showed up with kaffiyehs wrapped around their heads, necks, or faces. Some wore the t-shirts that organizers made specifically for the rally—green and red shirts with a giant fist emblazoned in the center, in the color and design of Palestine's flag. Attendees listened as speakers took to the stage to recite Qur'an and deliver impassioned speeches about the need to liberate Palestine. The next day, Sayyida Kubra Askari-Cisse called the Black American and African students from the dorm to her living room to see a film. With the lights turned off and the fan humming quietly, she screened *Born in Gaza*, a documentary that examines how Palestinian children were impacted by Israel's

2014 war on Gaza. Nearly a decade had passed since the events captured by the film had transpired, yet the footage looked eerily similar to the horrific videos that youth in Medina Baye could not peel their eyes away from as they scrolled through social media.

These were among the many moments of consciousness-raising and Palestine solidarity that I observed during my 2023 trip to Medina Baye. Each time I entered the courtyard of the Grand Mosque, I was greeted by Palestinian flags shimmering in the sun, waving in the wind, high in the sky. When I went to buy dhikr beads in the mosque's courtyard, I saw that several vendors had fastened Palestinian flags to the front of their stalls. In the weeks, months, and years to come, these visual signs of support were coupled with blog posts and archival photos documenting Shaykh Ibrahim's staunch support for Palestinian liberation, opposition to Zionism, and visit to Masjid al-Aqsa in Jerusalem. This content quickly circulated among Shaykh Ibrahim's global Tijani movement and beyond—popping up over and over again in WhatsApp groups, Instagram stories, and Facebook posts, even generating curiosity from people who were encountering Shaykh Ibrahim and the Tijani tariqa for the first time. As for those who were part of the fayda, learning about Shaykh Ibrahim's position was a reminder and affirmation of their own obligation to support efforts to liberate Palestine.

During Israel's genocide in Gaza—which is ongoing and livestreamed to the world as I complete this epilogue in late 2025—we have witnessed the awe-inspiring resistance and faith of Palestinians. We have seen videos of Muslim mothers and fathers who stood amidst the rubble, surrounded by death and destruction deliberately inflicted upon them by other human beings. Between tears and anguish, they defiantly exclaimed, "*Hasbunullahu wa ni'mal wakeel.*" These Arabic words are found in the Qur'an and translate to "Allah is sufficient for us and the best disposer of affairs." It is a dhikr that Shaykh Ibrahim advised his murids to recite when in need, and that many Tijanis recite daily. From Palestine to Senegal to the U.S., this dhikr is a source of comfort and spiritual fortification for those who believe—even in the face of ceaseless violence and inexcusable injustice—that Allah will grant them the most perfect outcome, either in this world or the next. This dhikr is a form of collective care—a spiritual technology that Tijanis and many

Figure E.1. A Palestinian flag hangs near the entrance of the *maqam* (sacred burial grounds), located in the courtyard of the Grand Mosque of Medina Baye, November 2023. Photo courtesy of the author.

Figure E.2. A Palestinian flag hangs from a vendor's stall in the courtyard of the Grand Mosque of Medina Baye, November 2023. Photo courtesy of the author.

other Muslims recite in their struggles for worldly liberation and justice in the afterlife.

Israel's genocide of Palestinians in Gaza is part of a global, long-standing, and ongoing project of exclusion, extraction, and elimination against Muslims and other oppressed peoples throughout the world. From the West Bank to Sudan to Haiti to Congo to Lebanon, people have been brutalized by imperialism, neocolonialism, racial capitalism, and white supremacy.

Yet at the same time, we have witnessed, by the millions, people refusing to surrender. Throughout Africa, we have recently borne witness to incredible moments of transition. In 2022, in Burkina Faso, we witnessed the rise of Ibrahim Traore as the country's leader. Traore's vows to fight imperialism and neocolonialism reminded people of their country's celebrated former president, the revolutionary pan-Africanist Thomas Sankara. In 2023, we witnessed the leaders of Burkina Faso, Mali, and Niger create a united front against neocolonial intervention by establishing the Alliance of Sahel States. In 2024, in Senegal, we witnessed the election of Bassirou Diomaye Faye, a self-described pan-Africanist who became the country's youngest-ever president. Alongside Faye, Senegal's new Prime Minister Ousmane Sonko directly referenced Shaykh Ibrahim's letter, *Ifriqiya ila al-ifriqiyin* (*Africa for the Africans*), in a televised interview in which he stressed the importance of pan-Africanism.[1] President Faye and Prime Minister Sonko pledged to remove all French soldiers on Senegalese soil, close all foreign military bases, remove the names of French colonial administrators from streets and public squares and rename them in honor of Senegalese national leaders, and rewrite Senegal's textbooks to more accurately portray the nation's history. The Senegalese leaders' plans came on the heels of moves from Chad and the Alliance of Sahel States to end European military intervention and reassert their national sovereignty. In 2024, we also witnessed youth-led, anti-government protests in Kenya and Nigeria. Only time will tell if and how these movements will deliver on their liberatory promises, but for now, these forms of collective resistance and rebellion give us hope that the Black Radical Tradition lives on through the efforts of African Muslims. These events remind us that wherever there is injustice, there are people who resist and fight to create the world we deserve.

In *Freedom Dreams*, Robin D. G. Kelley describes how the events on and after September 11, 2001 compelled him to revise what he had initially drafted as the book's epilogue. Kelley (2002) wondered,

> Where are we heading? How do we begin to dream ourselves out of this dark place of death and destruction and war, from this suffocating place where anyone who is not down with the war plan could be labeled a traitor? (196)

As militarism and the violence of imperial nation-states continue to engulf the world, these difficult questions become timeless. In the U.S., we have witnessed university professors, students, workers, and people of conscience punished by the powers that be for daring to demand an end to genocide. Throughout the globe, we have long witnessed children, youth, adults, and elders locked up, beaten, and killed when they flooded the streets in protest of unjust governments. With these fires of repression likely continuing to grow in the years and decades to come, how do we go about freedom dreaming of better worlds while living in frightening times?

Shaykh Hassan Cisse asserted that his grandfather, Shaykh Ibrahim, was "the best example of the description: 'The Sufi is the son of his hour (*ibn waqtihi*).' He will respond to the needs of the time and deal with the requirements of every moment" (Cisse 1984, 207). As we look around the globe and collectively bear witness to seemingly insurmountable suffering alongside fierce defiance, we can take lessons from Shaykh Ibrahim. He led a movement that emerged in a West African, anti-colonial context in which Islamic scholars were at the forefront of building self-determined, semi-autonomous communities in which Muslims cared for and about one another in resistance to state violence, oppression, and intervention. Shaykh Ibrahim's fayda gained traction in an era when Islam, Sufism, pan-Africanism, and revolutionary politics were seen as inextricably linked frameworks that would bring forth freedom and liberation. By the twenty-first century, the fayda grew into a global community of believers who studied, taught, engaged in collective ibada, gave hadiya, and did khidma. They did all this in hopes of following the most perfect example of Prophet Muhammad, bringing worldly relief to their people, and becoming those who were most beloved to Allah.

Shaykh Ibrahim's revolutionary pan-African Sufi movement disrupts narratives that seek to strip religion and spirituality of their emancipatory potential by limiting them to systems of personal beliefs and practices that are divorced from societal transformation. Shaykh Ibrahim's fayda defies the critique that religion is an opiate that placates the masses into delaying justice until the afterlife. Instead, it is a movement that understands Islam and Sufism as instilling Muslims with the internal fortitude and spiritual arsenal to achieve liberation, both in this world and the hereafter. This understanding—which offers critical lessons to academics, practicing Muslims, and secular leftist organizers alike—comes to us from West Africa, a region that is not always at the forefront of people's minds when thinking about Islamic intellectual networks or contemporary movements for Black liberation. Yet Shaykh Ibrahim's revolutionary pan-African Sufi movement highlights ways of being and belonging that all justice-oriented people—across race, religion, and geography—ought to take heed of.

The Black American Muslims who embrace the fayda belie both instrumentalist framings of Black religion in the U.S. as merely a coping mechanism against racism, and myths that Black American Muslims possess a rudimentary knowledge of Islam when compared to immigrant Muslims. Since the 1970s, the generations of Black American Muslims who have joined the Tijani tariqa have been attracted to and transformed by a spiritual path that teaches experiential knowledge of Allah, Qur'anic education, and prophetic practices as it physically transports them to a new social world thousands of miles away from the U.S.

Being able to experience this new world has allowed Black American Muslims to flee the racist, religious, gendered, and economic oppression endemic to U.S. schools and society. For parents and education scholars who are disillusioned by the country's schooling system, these families' choices illustrate the possibilities that come with internationalizing the seemingly elusive quest for educational justice.

Yet these Black American Muslims are not simply running away from something, nor do they abandon their ties to the U.S. Instead, they plug into a Sufi path that nurtures young people's holistic well-being and instills within them the ethical obligation and Islamic knowledge to serve others, here, there, or wherever their people are. Black American and West African mothers and fathers sacrifice to make this educational

Figure E.3. Envisioning Black Muslim Freedom Dreams. Collage by the author.

experience accessible not just to their own children, but other people's as well. Finally, young people journey on this path alongside sisters and brothers from Africa and beyond, striving to build family ties and ways of caring for each other that refuse impulses to differentiate and hierarchize their struggles.

Unlike approaches to Sufism where spiritual seekers disassociate from worldly affairs and worship Allah in solitude, the fayda calls people to care for one another because doing so is an act of worship that is truly beloved to Allah. Unlike Islamic education programs that offer students knowledge that is primarily transformative on an individual level, or capitalist norms of schooling that prioritize individual, upward socioeconomic mobility, the educational experience in Medina Baye teaches students that their knowledge is made manifest through their work to benefit others. These young people learn that they must share what they learn, even if there are limited or no financial rewards for doing so. Unlike approaches to Islam where the believers' focus on success in the afterlife alone can breed political quietism and complacency with oppression in this world, the fayda calls upon murids to utilize Islamic scriptures as divine weapons of resistance against modern systems of racist, political, and economic exploitation. Overall, Shaykh Ibrahim's Sufi movement offers lessons to all of us—to holistically emulate the sunnah of Prophet Muhammad, who cared deeply for others, feared only Allah, and fought tirelessly for the revolutionary transformation of his society.

In September 2024, Shaykh Ibrahim's grandson, Shaykh Mahy Cisse, delivered the keynote lecture for the Second Annual English Gamou in Medina Baye, which was held on the rooftop of the AAII School. Officially hosted by the International Bureau of African Diaspora Affairs, the event was planned primarily by Black American Tijanis, at least three of whom were alumni of AAII. In the audience gathered that day were locals as well as Tijanis who had come to Medina Baye to celebrate Prophet Muhammad's birthday. The event was also livestreamed online, with viewers tuning in from different time zones throughout the world. In his lecture, Shaykh Mahy shared the hadith of a man who asked Prophet Muhammad what act was most pleasing to Allah. The Prophet replied, "Feeding the people." This hadith, found in collections of hadith including Sahih al-Bukhari and Sahih al-Muslim, is yet another prophetic proof of the sacred esteem given to those who engage in collective care and an affirmation of its continued emphasis within the fayda.

This idea of collective care is a reminder that being a good Muslim is determined not only by how much one prays, fasts, or makes dhikr. These are certainly essential actions that allow Muslims to show gratitude to Allah and garner His pleasure, and they are also tools Muslims can use in their efforts to achieve liberation. But they are part of a broader arsenal that Muslims have at their disposal. Doing what is pleasing to Allah also means engaging in mass struggle on the streets to oppose the greatest evils of our time. Doing what is pleasing to Allah also means using one's wealth to help relocate a family out of a war zone. Doing what is pleasing to Allah also means treating someone else's daughter as your own, so that she has the chance not just to survive but also to thrive. Doing what is pleasing to Allah also means gathering as a group to do a Qur'an khatm as part of a spiritual war of liberation on behalf of our sisters and brothers under attack. All of these are among the relational acts of piety that the Islamic educational experience in Medina Baye encourages young people to embrace. These are acts of collective care that the knowers of Allah undertake as they strive to emulate the prophetic example, become beloved to Allah, and freedom dream of better worlds, in this life and the next.

GLOSSARY

ADHAN the Islamic call for prayer
ALLAH the Arabic word for God
ASR late afternoon prayer
ASSALAMUALIKUM an Arabic greeting meaning "peace be unto you"
AYAT a verse of the Qur'an
BARAKA religious blessing
BAYE the Wolof word for father
BISMILLAH an Arabic phrase meaning "in the name of Allah"
DAARA the Wolof word for classical Qur'an schools
DHIKR phrases of remembrance of Allah; plural: dhikrs or adhkar
DEEN the religion of Islam
DUA supplication
DUNYA temporal world
FAJR early morning prayer
FAYDA the Arabic word for flood, also the name often used to refer to Shaykh Ibrahim Niasse's branch of the Tijani tariqa
GAMOU the Wolof word for the event commemorating Prophet Muhammad's birthday; mawlid in Arabic
HAFIZ, HAFIZA, HUFFAZ a person who has memorized the entire Qur'an in Arabic. Feminine: hafiza, masculine: hafiz, plural: huffaz
HADITH narration that describes Prophet Muhammad's sayings, actions, or teachings
HADIYA gift or gift-giving
HAJJAH, HAJJI a title for a Muslim who has completed the Islamic obligatory pilgrimage of hajj. Feminine: Hajjah, masculine: Hajji
HARAM forbidden according to Islamic legal rulings
HIJRA migration
HIZB a section of the Qur'an. The Qur'an is divided into 60 hizbs.
IMAM a title for one who leads a community. Most often, Muslims use it to describe a religious leader.

ISHA late evening prayer
JUMMAH Friday afternoon prayer
JUZ a part of the Quran. The Qur'an is divided into 30 juz (also rendered as ajza in the plural).
KHIDMA act of service, also translated as work or labor
KHUTBA sermon delivered during jummah
KUFI hat worn by Muslim men
LA ILLAHA ILLALLAH an Arabic statement and dhikr meaning "There is no God but God"
MAAGI DAARA a Wolof phrase describing a Qur'an teacher's assistant
MAGHRIB sunset prayer
MARIFA experiential knowledge of Allah. Tijanis seek to attain marifa by doing tarbiya.
MASJID mosque
MAQAM sacred burial grounds
MAWLID the Arabic word for the event commemorating Prophet Muhammad's birthday; gamou in Wolof
MURID, MURIDA, MURIDS Sufi disciple or spiritual seeker. Feminine: murida, masculine: murid, plural: murids
MELFA a women's garment stretching several yards of fabric and originating in Mauritania
SALLALLAHU ALAYHI WA SALLAM an Arabic phrase meaning "peace and blessings be upon him" that Muslims utter after mentioning Prophet Muhammad
SALAWAT Prayers of praise upon Prophet Muhammad; Tijanis consider salatul fatih to be the most blessed salawat.
SALAT Islamic prayer
SALATUL FATIH a salawat on Prophet Muhammad that is a core Tijani dhikr
SAYYIDA, SAYYIDI, SIDI a title of respect. Feminine: Sayyida, masculine: Sayyidi or Sidi
SHAHADA declaration of Islamic faith
SHAYKH, SHAYKHA, SHUYUKH a title given to a Muslim who is regarded as a Sufi spiritual guide or Islamic scholar. Masculine: Shaykh, feminine: Shaykha, plural: shuyukh
SHUKR gratitude
SUNNAH Prophet Muhammad's habits or practices

SURAH a chapter of the Qur'an
TALIBE the Wolof derivation of the Arabic word for student (talib)
TAFSIR exegesis, usually used to refer to an exegesis of the Qur'an
TARBIYA a specific, formalized approach to spiritual education in Shaykh Ibrahim's branch of the Tijani tariqa where shuyukh guide their disciplines towards marifa
TARAWEEH optional late night prayers during Ramadan
TARIQA Sufi path
UMMAH global community of Muslims
USTADHA, USTADH a religious teacher. Feminine: Ustadha, masculine: Ustadh
WAZIFA obligatory dhikr done once a day by Tijanis, preferably in congregation and aloud
ZAWIYA Sufi community center
ZIYARA visitation

NOTES

INTRODUCTION

1. Throughout the book, I use numerous Arabic and Wolof words repeatedly. In most cases, these words describe Islamic concepts. I choose to use these Arabic or Wolof words instead of their English translation if my interlocuters do the same when speaking in English with fellow Muslims, even if they switch to using the English term when speaking to non-Muslims. Recognizing that my interlocuters change their language based on who they are talking to, I opt for the Arabic or Wolof word in order to mirror the ethos of community members speaking to one another, rather than translating meaning for non-Muslims or other outside audiences. For example, I use the Arabic word "Allah" instead of its English translation "God." For the first usage of each non-English word in a chapter, I use italics and include the English translation. As the chapter continues, I use the word without italics or the translation. The glossary lists all Arabic and Wolof words that appear repeatedly in the book.
2. In keeping with the ways in which Tijanis tend to address one another, I often refer to people as "sisters" or "brothers." These naming practices reflect the familial and relational ethos among community members, who see and treat one another as kin. I elaborate on this ethos throughout the book.
3. Imam is an Arabic title for one who leads a community. Most often, Muslims use it to describe a religious leader.
4. This is his real name. Throughout the book, I use people's real names rather than pseudonyms when I am documenting their contributions for the historical record. I refer to people by their chosen Islamic names, even in cases where their birth name is different, out of respect for their desires to be known and remembered as Muslims.
5. By Black American, I mean African-descended people from throughout the Americas, including in the U.S. and Caribbean.
6. Nadirah is a pseudonym. I use pseudonyms for all young people and their family members, as well as adults whose contemporary experiences I describe. I do not use pseudonyms for adults whose perspectives and accomplishments bear testament to the historical record.
7. Hajjah is an Arabic title for women who have completed the Islamic obligatory pilgrimage of hajj. Men who have completed hajj are called Hajji.
8. Shaykh is an Arabic title for a Muslim man who is a spiritual guide or religious scholar. A woman held in this regard is called a Shaykha. Shuyukh is the non-gendered plural form.

9 Most people at the Tijani zawiya in Brooklyn and in Shaykh Ibrahim's branch of the Tijani tariqa are Black (i.e., Black American, Afro-Caribbean, African, or Black British). However, there is a small but growing number of disciples from other ethnic and racial groups.
10 While Shaykh Ibrahim's branch is the largest and most prominent branch of the Tijani tariqa globally, there are other branches of the tariqa. In Senegal, another notable Tijani branch is associated with al-Hajj Malick Sy (d. 1922).
11 Imam Cheikh is a two-part honorific title. Imam indicates his role as the top religious leader in Medina Baye. Cheikh is a French spelling of the title Shaykh.
12 Sayyida is an Arabic title of respect for Muslim women.
13 This notion of care builds upon Marcel Mauss's (1925) theory of gift exchanges. Mauss argues that gift exchanges foster enduring relationships of reciprocity between givers and recipients. These reciprocal gift-giving practices fuel social reproduction and indicate the existence of collective (rather than individual) values. For more anthropological works on gift exchange and reciprocity in West Africa, see Buggenhagen (2012) and Piot (1999).
14 For a critique of the term "African Traditional Religion" as a homogenizing category of analysis, see Shaw (1990).
15 For an important exception, see Prickett (2021).
16 Some anthropological studies on piety among Black Muslims have explored the relational aspects of their subject formation. See, for instance, Jouili (2021), Prickett (2021), and Rouse (2004). Notably, the majority of Jouili's interlocuters are publicly known as members of Shaykh Ibrahim's branch of the Tijani tariqa, though she does not elaborate upon their Sufi affiliation.

CHAPTER 1. THE PROPHETIC AND THE POLITICAL

1 All English translations from the Qur'an are from Mustafa Khattab's (2015) *The Clear Quran*, unless otherwise stated.
2 Jibril is the Arabic equivalent of the English name Gabriel.
3 Shaykh Ahmad al-Tijani recommended that his disciples be balanced as well. In *The Fifth Letter of Orientation: On Methods of Giving Charity*, a letter Shaykh Ahmad al-Tijani sent to Sidi Hashim ibn Ma'zuz, the Shaykh advised: "Take the middle road between them both—meaning take the middle road between miserliness and squandering." I thank Imam Talut Dawood for translating this letter from Arabic into English, sharing it with me, and offering this point of clarification.
4 This English translation is from M.A.S. Abdel Haleem's (2008) *The Qur'an*.
5 The concept of khidma is also emphasized among other tariqas from Senegal, such as the Muridiyya (see Babou 2007, 90–92) and the Mustafawiyya (see Carter 2020).
6 The Muridiyya tariqa similarly understands hadiya as a "solidarity system" (Mbacké 42, as cited in Kane 2011, 153) and way of sharing resources (Babou 2007, 93–94). Villalón (1995) also observed this ethical framing among Sufis in the

Senegalese town of Fatick, where shuyukh from the Muridiyya and Tijani tariqas oversaw networks of economic redistribution (191). As Babou (2007) asserts, these ethical framings of hadiya overlap with what Marcell Mauss (1925) terms the gift economy. My analysis of the hadiya economy as an ethical and political system of collective care is based on the model described by Shaykh Hassan and that I observed from Imam Cheikh and Shaykh Mahy—the two main shuyukh who host Black American Tijanis in Medina Baye. However, as some scholars have shown, not all shuyukh who receive hadiya redistribute it. For instance, hadiya has been used to exploit disciples and to create transactional, fee-for-service relationships between disciples and shuyukh (Soares 2005). It has also been perceived as a way to "entertain lazy shaykhs" (Kane 2011, 153). However, Babou (2007) points out that some of these critiques are misguided: "Unable to see the material returns of disciples' donations to their tariqa, many scholars concluded that hadiyya was a mere ploy through which clever sheikhs exploited their naive followers" (94).

7 I thank Imam Talut Dawood for finding and translating this dua from Arabic to English.

8 Imam Talut Dawood, who translated *Al-Kanz Al-Masun* into English, initially translated this to "Save for me my foundation." However, in a personal communication, Dawood clarified that he incorrectly translated an Arabic word into the English phrase "my foundation." Given the context of the passage, Dawood later realized that the Arabic word was actually a transliteration of the Akan name Kwame, which was a reference to Kwame Nkrumah.

9 Sanusi is a reference to Shaykh Ibrahim's Nigerian murid al-Hajji Muhammadu Sanusi I, who served as the Emir of Kano from 1954 to 1963. Sanusi became Shaykh Ibrahim's murid after the shaykh visited Kano in 1937 (Hutson 1999, 55).

CHAPTER 2. LAUNCHING THE DREAM

1 This is her real name. For more on when I use real names, please see Footnote 4 of the introduction. For more on when I use pseudonyms, please see Footnote 6 of the introduction.

2 *Huffaz* is the plural term for *hafiza* (female) and *hafiz* (male).

3 As esteemed community elders, these women were almost always addressed by religious or familial titles that preceded their first name. These titles included *Hajjah* (an Arabic word used to describe a woman who has completed the Islamic pilgrimage of *hajj*), *Umm* (an Arabic word for mother), Aunty, and Sister.

4 A comprehensive history of all the parents who helped bring these freedom dreams to life is beyond the scope of this chapter. Among the many parents who played an important role were Imam Sayed Abdus-Salaam, Hajjah Ashaki Taha-Cisse, Brother Sufi Muhammad, Shaykh Abdul-Azeem Shabazz, Uncle Abdul Azeem Mustafa, Imam Bilal Fareed, Hajjah Ayisha Jeffries-Cisse, Sister Hajar Robinson, Hajji Abdullah Robinson, and Imam Salim Joseph.

5   The two exceptions are Dr. Khadijah and Hajjah Kareemah. Dr. Khadijah was the focus of an article in a magazine for North American Muslim women (Muhammad 2001) and a short article in a newspaper published by Imam Warith Deen Mohammed's community (Muhammad 2012). Hajjah Kareemah was featured in an academic book chapter that draws upon an oral history she did with the author (Miller 2020).

6   While I interviewed Hajjah Kareemah, Dr. Karimah, and Dr. Khadijah for this book, they also shared their stories for "The Students of Shaykh Hassan" series, a community-led collaborative effort started in 2020 to document and preserve the history of Tijani tariqa (http://bit.ly/StudentsofShaykhHassan). The series is facilitated by a team of community members including myself. As of 2025, we had conducted semi-structured interviews with over two dozen Tijanis. The interviews covered disciples' journeys to and in Islam, journeys to and in the tariqa, and their time with Shaykh Hassan. We conducted the interviews virtually in front of a live audience and solicited questions posed by attendees (many of whom had been present during the events that interviewees recollected). I interviewed Hajjah Kareemah for the series, while other community members interviewed Dr. Karimah and Dr. Khadijah. This chapter draws upon information shared in interviews I conducted for my own research and for the series, interviews conducted by other community members for the series, and an oral history conducted by another scholar (Abdul Kareem 2016). I use citations when quoting interviews that I did not conduct. All uncited quotes are from interviews that I conducted.

7   Abdul-Kareem, Kareemah. Interview by Rasul Miller, July 10, 2016.
8   Ibid.
9   Ibid.
10 Ibid.
11 Ibid.
12 Ibid.
13 Ibid.
14 Joseph, Dr. Karimah. Students of Shaykh Hassan Cisse (RTA). Interview by Jamillah Karim, November 29, 2020. https://www.youtube.com/live/WrW6Hf2KqNo.
15 Ibid.
16 Ibid.
17 Ibid.
18 Ibid.
19 Askari, Dr. Khadijah. Students of Shaykh Hassan (RTA). Interview by Ihsan Muhammad, September 27, 2020. https://www.youtube.com/watch?v=zFmHeNlxusE.
20 Ibid.
21 Ibid.
22 Abdul-Kareem, Kareemah. Interview by Rasul Miller, July 10, 2016.
23 Joseph, Dr. Karimah. Students of Shaykh Hassan Cisse (RTA). Interview by Jamillah Karim, November 29, 2020. https://www.youtube.com/live/WrW6Hf2KqNo.
24 Ibid.

25 Askari, Dr. Khadijah. Students of Shaykh Hassan (RTA). Interview by Ihsan Muhammad, September 27, 2020. https://www.youtube.com/watch?v=zFmHeNlxusE.
26 Ibid.
27 Ibid.
28 Ibid.
29 Due to space constraints, I am unable to offer an in-depth treatment of the African Tijanis who served as adoptive fathers and mothers during the 1980s and 1990s. Some of these individuals included Mallam Barayah (the Togolese man who was the main male caretaker at the Yellow House dormitory), Cheikh Biteye (the Senegalese man who was one of the first teachers at AAII), and Ya Fatou (the Senegalese woman who was Shaykh Hassan's mother).

CHAPTER 3. PEDAGOGY OF PLACE

1 Medina Baye prescribes to a model of African Muslim self-determination that has historically been associated with West African Muslim (often Sufi) communities. It therefore shares but also lacks some of the features that characterize Sufi spaces in other parts of the world. For more on the dynamics of Sufi spaces in the Middle East, see Grewal (2014), Ho (2006), and Knysh (2001). For more on Sufi spaces in North America, see Carter (2019, 2026) and Xavier (2018).
2 Other such cities include Touba (headquarters for the Muriddiyya tariqa), Tivaouane (headquarters of al-Hajj Malick Sy's branch of the Tijani tariqa), and Medina Gounass (home to Fulani disciples in the Tijani tariqa). For a general history of these cities, see Ross (2020). For more on Touba, see Babou (2005) and Ross (2006). For more on Medina Gounass, see Glovsky (2021) and Smith (2008).
3 This approach was also common in the Muridiyya tariqa's headquarters in Touba, Senegal. In 1926, Shaykh Amadu Bamba urged his Muridiyya disciples to raise money to build the community's main mosque, which they finished in 1963; Muridiyya shuyukh also later called upon disciples to raise money to refurbish the mosque (Babou 2007, 94).
4 Recall that Chapter 2 discussed the Black American Tijani women who served as othermothers, or what Patricia Hill Collins (1990) defines as women who share mothering responsibilities for other people's children. In the Tijani community, othermothers and adoptive fathers sustained the collective care networks that made it possible for Black American youth to live and learn in Medina Baye.
5 Shaykh Hassan encouraged and prepared Sayyida Kubra to serve as an othermother. Even while she was a student at AAII, Shaykh Hassan assigned her to care for several West African children. In 2001, after Sayyida Kubra became a hafiza, got married, and moved into her own home, Shaykh Hassan encouraged her to host and care for international students in that home.

CHAPTER 4. TO BE YOUNG, GIFTED, AND BLACK

This chapter was revised from an article originally published as "Black Muslim brilliance: Confronting antiblackness and Islamophobia through transnational educational migration," *Curriculum Inquiry* 51, no. 1 (2021): 57–74. https://doi.org/10.1080/036 26784.2020.1831368. Reprinted by permission of the publisher, Taylor & Francis Ltd., http://www.tandfonline.com.

1. By Black, I am referring to all people of African descent. I recognize that some people of African descent may not self-identify with the term Black (i.e., a person may instead associate with the ethnic identity of being Fulani or the national identity of being Senegalese). However, I employ the term "Black" when discussing "Black Muslim brilliance" because this was the primary racial category ascribed to and adopted by my Black American interlocuters, who overwhelmingly made meaning of the scholarly accomplishments of Africans in Medina Baye as those by fellow Black people.
2. Many Muslim educators frame Islamic education as primarily an individual endeavor focused on personal piety. For instance, Aisha Lemu (1940–2019), the British Muslim educator who oversaw massive Islamic education campaigns in Nigeria during the late twentieth century, wrote: "*Tahdhib (Moral Education)* is very important for every Muslim. It guides him or her to happiness and peace of mind in this world and in the Hereafter" (Lemu 1986, 15, as cited in Renne 2021, 126).
3. The 99 names are collectively referred to as *al-Asma ul-Husna*, or the Most Beautiful Names. For more on the names and their meanings, see Al-Ghazali's *The Ninety-Nine Beautiful Names of God*.
4. Students who are considered to be able to read the Qur'an in Arabic are those who can fluently decipher and pronounce its letters and words. Such students may or may not be able to understand the meaning of the words. In this context, reading, literacy, and fluency are therefore associated with the ability to verbalize the sounds and words of the Qur'an, not with the ability to comprehend the substance of the words. For this reason, Qur'anic education has been critiqued by some as a meaningless form of rote memorization. For a refutation of such critiques in North and West Africa, see Moore (2006), Wagner and Lotfi (1983), and Ware (2004).
5. Several works have investigated the religious value and stigma around Qur'anic education, particularly amidst the U.S.-led global War on Terror. For works that address these debates in West Africa, see Launay (2016) and Hoechner (2018). For works that address these debates in South Asia, the Middle East, and North Africa, see Moosa (2015) and Hefner and Zaman (2007). For a discussion on how American Muslim adults reconcile these debates through their education in Syria, Jordan, and Egypt, see Grewal (2014).
6. In 1992, the Senegalese government partnered with UNICEF to launch a program to improve the plight of talibes (Loimeier 2002, 130). The program provided technical and financial support for daaras in rural areas. As a precondition for joining the program, administrators had to agree to abandon practices of begging and corporal discipline (ibid., 130–131). AAII was one of a few daaras awarded funds through the program (Wiegelmann and Naumann 1997, 288). This perhaps

contributed to AAII's exceptional reputation, leading to the conclusion that the "documentation of misery contrasts with a few positive cases such as the school of Hassan Cisse" (Loiemier 2002, 132).

7   Rudolph Ware (2014) similarly resists the impulse to prove the merits of Qur'anic education in Senegal and instead demonstrates the problematic qualities inherent in capitalist societies: "In the Qur'an school, people learn to make and live in a community. This sense of communal responsibility is under assault from individualistic materialism," "the consumer culture of late capitalism," and a modern society that "liberates and valorizes, stimulates and celebrates this endless pursuit of individualistic consumption" (239).

8   For an extensive treatment of Shaykh Ibrahim as well as other Black African Muslim intellectuals' embrace of their racial identity, see Wright (2022).

9   Ustadh is an Arabic word for a male teacher. At AAII, male teachers were usually called by this title followed by their last name.

10 This hadith is frequently cited in the works of Muslim scholars, including by shuyukh in Medina Baye. The Senegalese Tijani scholar, Ustadh Barham Mahmud Diop, cited this hadith in his introduction to Shaykh Ibrahim's *tafsir* (exegesis) of the Qur'an (Niasse 2014, 38).

11 Most African Muslims, like their Arab and South Asian counterparts, also immigrated to the U.S. from lands with sizable and long-standing Muslim populations. However, both community and scholarly discourses on Muslim in the U.S.—particularly those documenting the relationships between Black American Muslims and Muslims from immigrant backgrounds—often overlook the experiences of Africans. For some exceptions, see Abdullah (2010), Babou (2021), Kane (2011), and Stoller (2002).

12 Several students and teachers gave context for these numbers by explaining that memorization became cognitively more difficult as individuals got older. The average starting age for a Black American was 11—an age at which many of their Senegalese peers had neared completion, if not already become huffaz. This was not to say that Black Americans could not finish due to their later start; many who became huffaz tended to finish around 14 years old or later. However, the rarity of Black American huffaz underscored the cognitive difficulty of the task, especially for older students.

CHAPTER 6. FROM AMERICAN TO CISSE

1   Kincraft is what Todne Thomas (2021) defines as a relational ethos and community praxis among Afro-diasporic religious people who see and treat one another as spiritual kin. For a discussion of how Black American and Senegalese disciples forge pan-African Tijani modes of kincraft, see Chapters 2 and 3.

2   Shaykh Hassan selected the name Kossi Atlanta to pay tribute to two places that were significant to him. The first was Kossi, the village where Shaykh Ibrahim received the *fayda* (flood) and began his spiritual movement. Given this history, the village is now known as Kossi Baye. The second is Atlanta, which is one of the U.S.

cities with the most active Black American Tijani communities, as well as the city that Shaykh Hassan's then-wife, the Black American disciple Dr. Khadijah Askari, was connected to.

EPILOGUE

1 I thank Hafiz Ahmed Sufi Muhammad for sharing this interview with me.

BIBLIOGRAPHY

"237. Memorandum from the Director of the Office of West African Affairs (Trimble) to the Assistant Secretary of State for African Affairs (Williams)." 1964. Department of State, Central Files, POL 1 GHANA–US. https://history.state.gov.
Abdel Haleem, M. A. S. 2008. *The Qurʾan*. Oxford University Press.
Abdul Khabeer, Suʾad. 2016. *Muslim Cool: Race, Religion, and Hip Hop in the United States*. New York University Press.
———. 2017. "Africa as Tradition in U.S. African American Muslim Identity." *Journal of Africana Religions* 5 (1): 26. https://doi.org/10.5325/jafrireli.5.1.0026.
———. 2021a. "Umi's Archive: One Life, Many Stories." *NewBlackMan (in Exile)* (blog). April 2021. https://newblackmaninexile.net.
———. 2021b. "Planning Notes from M.E.A.R.C. Dawah Luncheon." Umi's Archive. https://umisarchive.com.
Abdul-Kareem, Kareemah. 2016. Interview by Rasul Miller, July 10.
Abdullah, Zain. 2010. *Black Mecca: The African Muslims of Harlem*. Oxford University Press.
Abdur-Rahman, Sufiya. 2021. *Heir to the Crescent Moon*. University of Iowa Press.
"About Nasrul Ilm America." 2021. *Nasrul Ilm America* (blog). 2021. www.nasrulilmamerica.org.
Aidi, Hisham. 2014. *Rebel Music: Race, Empire, and the New Muslim Youth Culture*. Vintage.
Al-Ghazali, Abū-Ḥāmid Muḥammad Ibn-Muḥammad al-. 2007. *The Ninety-Nine Beautiful Names of God: Al-Maqṣad al-Asnā Fī Sharḥ Asmāʾ Allāh al-Ḥusnā*. Translated by David B. Burrell and Nazih Daher. Reprint. Islamic Texts Society.
Ali, Kamal Hasan. 1981. "Muslim School Planning in the United States: An Analysis of Issues, Problems and Possible Approaches." Doctoral diss., University of Massachusetts Amherst.
Al-Islam, Amir. 2010. "Sunni Islam in the African American Experience: The Dialectic and Dialogic of Race, Ethnicity, and Islamicity Mapping and Decoding The Mosque of Islamic Brotherhood, 1964–2001." Ph.D. diss., New York University.
Al-Nawawi, Imam. 2013. *Etiquette with the Quran (Al Tibyan Fi Adab Hamalat al-Qurʾan)*. Translated by Musa Furber. Islamosaic.
Anderson, James D. 1988. *The Education of Blacks in the South, 1860–1935*. University of North Carolina Press.
Armstrong, Karen. 2006. *Muhammad: A Prophet for Our Time*. HarperCollins.
Asante, Molefi Kete. 1980. *Afrocentricity*. Africa World Press.

Askari, Dr. Khadijah. 2020. Students of Shaykh Hassan (RTA) Interview by Ihsan Muhammad. https://www.youtube.com/watch?v=zFmHeNlxusE.

Aslan, Reza. 2005. *No God but God: The Origins, Evolution, and Future of Islam*. Random House.

Atlanta Daily World. 1979. "EUF Awards $500 Scholarship," September 4.

———. 1991. "APA Annual African Village," June 23.

———. 1992. "Church News," February 13.

———. 1993. "Second Annual Malcolm X Commemorative Banquet," February 18.

Austin, Algernon. 2022. "High Joblessness for Black Youth: More Than 500,000 Jobs Are Needed." Center for Economic and Policy Research. https://cepr.net/.

Austin, Allan. 1984. *African Muslims in Antebellum America: Transatlantic Stories and Spiritual Struggles*. Routledge.

Ba, Cheick Oumar, Jérémy Bourgoin, and Djibril Diop. 2017. "Senegal: The Fluidity of Internal Migration as an Answer to Local Constraints," 32–33.

Babou, Cheikh Anta. 2007. *Fighting the Greater Jihad: Amadu Bamba and the Founding of the Muridiyya of Senegal, 1853–1913*. Ohio University Press.

———. 2008. "Migration and Cultural Change: Money, 'Caste,' Gender, and Social Status among Senegalese Female Hair Braiders in the United States." *Africa Today* 55 (2): 3–22.

———. 2021. *The Muridiyya on the Move: Islam, Migration, and Place Making*. Ohio University Press.

Bass, Lisa. 2012. "When Care Trumps Justice: The Operationalization of Black Feminist Caring in Educational Leadership." *International Journal of Qualitative Studies in Education* 25 (1): 73–87. https://doi.org/10.1080/09518398.2011.647721.

Bathily, Abdoulaye, Mamadou Diouf, and Mohamed Mbodj. 1995. "The Senegalese Student Movement from Its Inception to 1989." In *African Studies in Social Movements and Democracy*, edited by Mahmood Mamdani and Ernest Wamba-dia-Wamba, 369–408. CODESRIA.

Baum, Sandy, and Michael S. McPherson. 2022. *Can College Level the Playing Field? Higher Education in an Unequal Society*. Princeton University Press.

Bear, Laura. 2016. "Time as Technique." *Annual Review of Anthropology* 45 (1): 487–502. https://doi.org/10.1146/annurev-anthro-102313-030159.

Beauboeuf-Lafontant, Tamara. 2002. "A Womanist Experience of Caring: Understanding the Pedagogy of Exemplary Black Women Teachers." *Urban Review* 34 (1): 71–86.

Bedasso, Monique. 2017. *Jah Kingdom: Rastafarians, Tanzania, and Pan-Africanism in the Age of Decolonization*. University of North Carolina Press.

Beliso-De Jesús, Aisha M. 2015. *Electric Santería: Racial and Sexual Assemblages of Transnational Religion*. Columbia University Press.

Bell, Derrick. 1993. *Faces at the Bottom of the Well: The Permanence of Racism*. Basic Books.

Bin Omar, Azmi. 1993. "In Quest of an Islamic Ideal of Education: A Study of the Role of the Traditional Pondok Institution in Malaysia." Ph.D. diss., Temple University.

Black, Steven P. 2018. "The Ethics and Aesthetics of Care." *Annual Review of Anthropology* 47 (1): 79–95. https://doi.org/10.1146/annurev-anthro-102317-050059.
Bleck, Jaimie, and Alison Lodermeier. 2020. "Migration Aspirations from a Youth Perspective: Focus Groups with Returnees and Youth in Mali." *Journal of Modern African Studies* 58 (4): 551–77. https://doi.org/10.1017/S0022278X20000567.
Blum, Susan Debra, ed. 2020. *Ungrading: Why Rating Students Undermines Learning (and What to Do Instead)*. West Virginia University Press.
Bonilla, Yarimar. 2015. *Non-Sovereign Futures: French Caribbean Politics in the Wake of Disenchantment*. University of Chicago Press.
Bonilla-Silva, Eduardo. 2003. *Racism Without Racists: Color-Blind Racism and the Persistence of Racial Inequality in America*. Third edition. Rowman & Littlefield Publishers.
Bowen, Patrick D. 2017. *A History of Conversion to Islam in the United States: 1920–1975*. Brill.
Bowles, Samuel, and Herbert Gintis. 1977. *Schooling in Capitalist America: Educational Reform and the Contradictions of Economic Life*. Basic Books.
Boyce Davies, Carole. 2008. *Left of Karl Marx: The Political Life of Black Communist Claudia Jones*. Duke University Press.
Boyle, Helen N. 2004. *Quranic Schools: Agents of Preservation and Change*. Routledge Falmer.
———. 2006. "Memorization and Learning in Islamic Schools." *Comparative Education Review* 50 (3): 478–95. https://doi.org/10.1086/504819.
———. 2007. "Embodiment as a Conceptual Framework for Describing the Practice of Qur'anic Memorization." In *Recapturing the Personal: Essays on Education and Embodied Knowledge in Comparative Perspective*, edited by Irving Epstein. Information Age.
Brenner, Louis. 2001. *Controlling Knowledge: Religion, Power, and Schooling in a West African Muslim Society*. Indiana University Press.
Brown, Claude. 1965. *Manchild in the Promised Land*. Touchstone.
Buch, Elana D. 2015. "Anthropology of Aging and Care." *Annual Review of Anthropology* 44 (1): 277–93. https://doi.org/10.1146/annurev-anthro-102214-014254.
Buggenhagen, Beth A. 2012. *Muslim Families in Global Senegal: Money Takes Care of Shame*. Indiana University Press.
Burden-Stelly, Charisse, and Jodi Dean, eds. 2022. *Organize, Fight, Win: Black Communist Women's Political Writing*. Verso.
Butler, Judith. 2009. "Performativity, Precarity, and Sexual Politics." *AIBR* 4 (3): i–xxii.
Camara, Mouhamed. 2023. "150 Milliards de Budget Des Grands Chantiers de Médina Baye: Plus de Transparence Réclamée Au Promoteur." *Sene.News*, April 6, 2023. www.senenews.com.
Campt, Tina, and Deborah A. Thomas. 2008. "Gendering Diaspora: Transnational Feminism, Diaspora and Its Hegemonies." *Feminist Review* 90 (S1): 1–8.
Carey, Roderick L. 2014. "A Cultural Analysis of the Achievement Gap Discourse: Challenging the Language and Labels Used in the Work of School Reform." *Urban Education* 49 (4): 440–68. https://doi.org/10.1177/0042085913507459.

Carmichael, Stokely, and Michael Thelwell. 2005. *Ready for Revolution: The Life and Struggles of Stokely Carmichael (Kwame Ture)*. Scribner.
Carter, Youssef. 2019. "Black Muslimness Mobilized: A Study of West African Sufism in Diaspora." *American Journal of Islam and Society* 36 (1): 1–28. https://doi.org/10.35632/ajis.v36i1.2954.
———. 2020. "Fisibilillah: Labor as Learning on the Sufi Path." *Religions* 12 (1): 3. https://doi.org/10.3390/rel12010003.
———. 2021. "Alchemy of the Fuqara: Spiritual Care, Memory, and the Black Muslim Body." In *Embodying Black Religions in Africa and Its Diasporas*, edited by Yolanda Covington-Ward and Jeanette Selma Jouili. Duke University Press.
———. 2026. *The Vast Oceans: Remembering Allah and Self on the Mustafawiyya Sufi Path*. University of North Carolina Press.
Cash, Floris Loretta Barnett. 2001. *African American Women and Social Action: The Clubwomen and Volunteerism from Jim Crow to the New Deal, 1896–1936*. Greenwood Press.
Casselberry, Judith. 2017. *The Labor of Faith: Gender and Power in Black Apostolic Pentecostalism*. Duke University Press.
Castor, N. Fadeke. 2017. *Spiritual Citizenship: Transnational Pathways from Black Power to IFÁ in Trinidad*. Duke University Press.
Causey, J., S. Lee, M. Ryu, A. Scheetz, and D. Shapiro. 2022. "Completing College: National and State Report with Longitudinal Data Dashboard on Six- and Eight-Year Completion Rates. (Signature Report 21)." National Student Clearinghouse Research Center. https://nscresearchcenter.org.
Chan-Malik, Sylvia. 2018. *Being Muslim: A Cultural History of Women of Color in American Islam*. New York University Press.
Chittick, William C. 2007. *Sufism: A Beginner's Guide*. Oneworld.
Cisse, Shaykh Hassan. 1984. "Shaykh Ibrahim Niasse: Revivalist of the Sunnah." In *Pearls from the Flood: Select Insights of Shaykh Al-Islam Ibrahim Niasse*, 197–211. Northwestern University: Fayda Books.
———. 2005. "Shaykh Hassan Cisse in Zawiya Guguletu Cape Town." Cape Town, South Africa. https://www.youtube.com/watch?v=vATaEkk9F5Y.
———. n.d. Interview by Timange Ma Bondi TV (TMB TV). https://www.youtube.com/watch?v=4XezKcsY7CU.
Clarke, Kamari Maxine. 2004. *Mapping Yorùbá Networks: Power and Agency in the Making of Transnational Communities*. Duke University Press.
Clarke, Kamari Maxine, and Deborah A. Thomas, eds. 2006. *Globalization and Race: Transformations in the Cultural Production of Blackness*. Duke University Press.
Cohen, Stanley. 1972. *Folk Devils and Moral Panics: The Creation of the Mods and Rockers*. Routledge.
Collins, Patricia Hill. 1990. *Black Feminist Thought: Knowledge, Consciousness and the Politics of Empowerment*. Unwin Hyman.
———. 1994. "Shifting the Center: Race, Class, and Feminist Theorizing About Motherhood." In *Mothering: Ideology, Experience, and Agency*, edited by Evelyn Nakano Glenn, Grace Chang, and Linda Rennie Forcey, 45–65. Routledge.

Cooper, Camille Wilson. 2007. "School Choice as 'Motherwork': Valuing African-American Women's Educational Advocacy and Resistance." *International Journal of Qualitative Studies in Education* 20 (5): 491–512. https://doi.org/10.1080/09518390601176655.

Covington-Ward, Yolanda. 2016. *Gesture and Power: Religion, Nationalism, and Everyday Performance in Congo*. Duke University Press.

Covington-Ward, Yolanda, and Jeanette Selma Jouili. 2021. "Introduction: Embodiment and Relationality in Religions of Africa and Its Diasporas." In *Embodying Black Religions in Africa and Its Diasporas*, edited by Yolanda Covington-Ward and Jeanette Selma Jouili, 1–19. Duke University Press.

Cox, Aimee Meredith. 2015. *Shapeshifters: Black Girls and the Choreography of Citizenship*. Duke University Press.

Cruse, Lindsey, Eleanor Eckerson, and Barbara Gault. 2018. "Understanding the New College Majority: The Demographic and Financial Characteristics of Independent Students and Their Postsecondary Outcomes." Institute for Women's Policy Research. https://iwpr.org.

Curtis, Edward E. 2002. *Islam in Black America: Identity, Liberation, and Difference in African-American Islamic Thought*. State University of New York Press.

Daaru, Abdulsalam Mohammed. 2020. "Nkrumah Kept a Muslim Prayer Mat at the Flagstaff House Sheikh Salis Shaban Reveals!" *Modern Ghana*, September 21, 2020. www.modernghana.com.

Dannin, Robert. 2002. *Black Pilgrimage to Islam*. Oxford University Press.

Daulatzai, Sohail. 2012. *Black Star, Crescent Moon: The Muslim International and Black Freedom Beyond America*. University of Minnesota Press.

Davis, Elizabeth Lindsay. 1996. *Lifting as They Climb: African-American Women Writers, 1910–1940*. Prentice Hall International.

de Sá, Celina. 2024. "The Afro-Paradox: Diasporic Chauvinism and Cultural Expertise in Afro-Brazilian Capoeira." *Diaspora: A Journal of Transnational Studies* 24, no. 1: 1–28. https://doi.org/10.3138/diaspora.24.1.2024.01.02.

———. 2025. *Diaspora Without Displacement: The Coloniality and Promise of Capoeira in Senegal*. Duke University Press.

"Déclaration Générale / General Declaration." 1974. *Présence Africaine*, no. 91, 204–19.

De Royston, Maxine McKinney, Sepehr Vakil, Na'ilah Suad Nasir, Kihana Miraya Ross, Jarvis Givens, and Alea Holman. 2017. "'He's More Like a "Brother" than a Teacher': Politicized Caring in a Program for African American Males." *Teachers College Record* 119, no. 4: 1–40. https://doi.org/10.1177/016146811711900401.

Detroit Historical Society. n.d. "Paradise Valley." In *Encyclopedia of Detroit*. https://detroithistorical.org.

Dimson, Ibrahim. 2016. "Publisher's Foreword." In *The Spirit of Good Morals*, edited by Ibrahim Dimson, translated by Talut Dawood. Third edition. Fayda Books.

Diouf, Mamadou. 1996. "Urban Youth and Senegalese Politics: Dakar 1988–1994." *Public Culture* 8: 225–49.

———. 2003. "Engaging Postcolonial Cultures: African Youth and Public Space." *African Studies Review* 46 (2): 1. https://doi.org/10.2307/1514823.

Diouf, Sylviane A. 1998. *Servants of Allah: African Muslims Enslaved in the Americas*. New York University Press.

———. 1999. "'Sadaqa' Among African Muslims Enslaved in the Americas." *Journal of Islamic Studies* 10 (1): 22–32.

———. 2014. *Slavery's Exiles: The Story of the American Maroons*. New York University Press.

Dixon, Travis L. 2019. "Black Criminality 2.0: The Persistence of Stereotypes in the 21st Century." In *Race/Gender/Class/Media: Considering Diversity across Audiences, Content, and Producers*, edited by Rebecca Ann Lind. Routledge.

Dow, Dawn Marie. 2019. *Mothering While Black: Boundaries and Burdens of Middle-Class Parenthood*. University of California Press.

Drake, St. Clair. 1959. "Pan Africanism: What Is It?" *Africa Today* 6 (1): 6–10.

———. 1993. "Diaspora Studies and Pan-Africanism." In *Global Dimensions of the African Diaspora*, edited by Joseph E. Harris, second edition, 451–514. Howard University Press.

Dubay, Lisa, Joshua Aarons, K. Steven Brown, and Genevieve M. Kenney. 2020. "How Risk of Exposure to the Coronavirus at Work Varies by Race and Ethnicity and How to Protect the Health and Well-Being of Workers and Their Families." Urban Institute. www.urban.org.

Du Bois, W.E.B. 1921. "Manifesto of the Second PanAfrican Congress." *Crisis*, November 1921, 23 edition, sec. Opinion.

Dumas, Michael J. 2014. "'Losing an Arm': Schooling as a Site of Black Suffering." *Race Ethnicity and Education* 17 (1): 1–29. https://doi.org/10.1080/13613324.2013.850412.

Ebony Magazine. 1978. "Medical School's Mission Is to Serve Minorities and the Poor," December 1978.

Ebron, Paulla A. 2002. *Performing Africa*. Princeton University Press.

Eickelman, Dale F. 1978. "The Art of Memory: Islamic Education and Its Social Reproduction." *Comparative Studies in Society and History* 20 (4): 485–516. https://doi.org/10.1017/S0010417500012536.

El-Mekki, Sharif Dawud, Mikyeil Saifullah El-Mekki, Nzinga El-Mekki Abdullah-Aziz, Husayn Bilal El-Mekki Abdullah-Aziz, and Haajar Shakurah El-Mekki Abdullah-Aziz. 2020. "The Legacy of Aisha Kusaidia El-Mekki (Saundra Marie Dickerson): A Life Rooted in Faith and Justice." http://phillymuslimfreedomfund.org.

El-Sharif, Farah. 2021. "'If All the Legal Schools Were to Disappear': Umar Tal's Approach to Jurisprudence in Kitab al-Rimah." In *Islamic Scholarship in Africa: New Directions and Global Contexts*, edited by Ousmane Kane, 169–83. James Currey.

———. 2024. "The Palestine Letters of Shaykh Ibrahim Niasse: Missives of Love and Resistance from West Africa to Jerusalem." Sermons at the Court (blog). July 16. https://sermonsatcourt.substack.com.

Espinosa, Lorelle L., Jonathon M. Turk, Morgan Taylor, and Hollie M. Chessman. 2019. "Race and Ethnicity in Higher Education: A Status Report." American Council on Education. www.equityinhighered.org.

Essien-Udom, E. U. 1962. *Black Nationalism: The Search for an Identity in America*. University of Chicago Press.

Estruch, Elisenda, Lisa Van Dijck, David Schwebel, and Josee Randriamamonjy. 2019. "Youth Mobility and Its Role in Structural Transformation in Senegal." In *Youth and Jobs in Rural Africa*, by Elisenda Estruch, Lisa Van Dijck, David Schwebel, and Josee Randriamamonjy, 251–76. Oxford University Press. https://doi.org/10.1093/oso/9780198848059.003.0009.

Fadil, Nadia. 2011. "Not-/Unveiling as an Ethical Practice." *Feminist Review* 98 (1): 83–109. https://doi.org/10.1057/fr.2011.12.

Fong, Vanessa L. 2011. *Paradise Redefined: Transnational Chinese Students and the Quest for Flexible Citizenship in the Developed World*. Stanford University Press.

Gadsden, Vivian L., Ralph L. Smith, and Will J. Jordan. 1996. "The Promise of Desegregation: Tendering Expectation and Reality in Achieving Quality Schooling." *Urban Education* 31 (4): 381–402.

Gaines, Kevin Kelly. 2006. *American Africans in Ghana: Black Expatriates and the Civil Rights Era*. University of North Carolina Press.

Garcia, Marito H., and Fares Jean, eds. 2008. *Youth in Africa's Labor Market*. The World Bank. https://doi.org/10.1596/978-0-8213-6884-8.

Gholson, Maisie, Erika Bullock, and Nathan Alexander. 2012. "On the Brilliance of Black Children: A Response to a Clarion Call." *Journal of Urban Mathematics Education* 5 (1): 1–7.

Gilligan, Carol. 1982. *In a Different Voice: Psychological Theory and Women's Development*. Harvard University Press.

Gilmore, Ruth Wilson. 2007. *Golden Gulag: Prisons, Surplus, Crisis, and Opposition in Globalizing California*. University of California Press.

Gilroy, Paul. 1993. *The Black Atlantic: Modernity and Double-Consciousness*. Harvard University Press.

Ginwright, Shawn A. 2010. *Black Youth Rising: Activism and Radical Healing in Urban America*. Teachers College Press.

Givens, Jarvis R. 2021. *Fugitive Pedagogy: Carter G. Woodson and the Art of Black Teaching*. Harvard University Press.

Glovsky, David Newman. 2021. "Medina Gounass: Constructing Extra-National Space in a West African Borderland." *African Studies Review* 64 (3): 569–94. https://doi.org/10.1017/asr.2020.130.

Gomez, Michael. 1998. *Exchanging Our Country Marks: The Transformation of African Identities in the Colonial and Antebellum South*. University of North Carolina Press.

———. 2005. *Black Crescent: The Experience and Legacy of African Muslims in the Americas*. Cambridge University Press.

Grewal, Zareena. 2014. *Islam Is a Foreign Country: American Muslims and the Global Crisis of Authority*. New York University Press.

Guend, Hani. 2018. "Senegal Muslim Population: A Demographic Profile." *Revue Algérienne Des Etudes de Population* 2 (1): 130–57.

Gutman, Herbert George. 1977. *The Black Family in Slavery and Freedom, 1750–1925*. Vintage.

Hall, Amanda Joyce. 2022. "Black Students and the U.S. Anti-Apartheid Movements on Campus, 1976–1985." *Zanj: The Journal of Critical Global South Studies* 6 (1): 8–28.

Han, Clara. 2012. *Life in Debt: Times of Care and Violence in Neoliberal Chile*. University of California Press.

———. 2018. "Precarity, Precariousness, and Vulnerability." *Annual Review of Anthropology* 47 (1): 331–43. https://doi.org/10.1146/annurev-anthro-102116-041644.

Hannaford, Dinah. 2016. "Intimate Remittances: Marriage, Migration, and MoneyGram in Senegal." *Africa Today* 62 (3): 93. https://doi.org/10.2979/africatoday.62.3.93.

———. 2017. *Marriage Without Borders: Transnational Spouses in Neoliberal Senegal*. University of Pennsylvania Press.

Harris, Christopher Paul. 2023. *To Build a Black Future: The Radical Politics of Joy, Pain, and Care*. Princeton University Press.

Hartman, Saidiya V. 2007. *Lose Your Mother: A Journey Along the Atlantic Slave Route*. Farrar, Straus and Giroux.

Hefner, Robert W., and Muhammad Qasim Zaman, eds. 2007. *Schooling Islam: The Culture and Politics of Modern Muslim Education*. Princeton University Press.

Hernández-Carretero, María. 2015. "Renegotiating Obligations through Migration: Senegalese Transnationalism and the Quest for the *Right* Distance." *Journal of Ethnic and Migration Studies* 41 (12): 2021–40. https://doi.org/10.1080/1369183X.2015.1045462.

Herrera, Linda. 2010. "Young Egyptians' Quest for Jobs and Justice." In *Being Young and Muslim: New Cultural Politics in the Global South and North*, edited by Asef Bayat and Linda Herrera, 127–43. Oxford University Press.

Hersey, Tricia. 2022. *Rest Is Resistance: A Manifesto*. New York: Little, Brown Spark.

Hill, Joseph. 2013. "Sovereign Islam in a Secular State: Hidden Knowledge and Sufi Governance Among 'Taalibe Baay.'" In *Tolerance, Democracy, and Sufis in Senegal*, edited by Mamadou Diouf, 99–124. Columbia University Press.

———. 2018. *Wrapping Authority: Women Islamic Leaders in a Sufi Movement in Dakar, Senegal*. University of Toronto Press.

Hill, Sean. 2017. "Precarity in the Era of #BlackLivesMatter." *WSQ: Women's Studies Quarterly* 45 (3–4): 94–109. https://doi.org/10.1353/wsq.2017.0046.

Hinton, Elizabeth. 2016. *From the War on Poverty to the War on Crime: The Making of Mass Incarceration in America*. Harvard University Press.

———. 2021. *America on Fire: The Untold History of Police Violence and Black Rebellion since the 1960s*. Liveright.

Hirschkind, Charles. 2006. *The Ethical Soundscape: Cassette Sermons and Islamic Counterpublics*. Columbia University Press.

Ho, Engseng. 2006. *The Graves of Tarim: Genealogy and Mobility across the Indian Ocean*. University of California Press.

Hobson, Maurice J. 2017. *The Legend of the Black Mecca: Politics and Class in the Making of Modern Atlanta*. University of North Carolina Press.

Hoechner, Hannah. 2018. *Quranic Schools in Northern Nigeria: Everyday Experiences of Youth, Faith, and Poverty*. Cambridge University Press.

Holsey, Bayo. 2008. *Routes of Remembrance: Refashioning the Slave Trade in Ghana*. University of Chicago Press.

Honwana, Alcinda. 2012. *The Time of Youth: Work, Social Change, and Politics in Africa*. Kumarian Press.

Howell, Sally. 2014. *Old Islam in Detroit: Rediscovering the Muslim American Past*. Oxford University Press.

Hugon, Clothilde. 2015. "Sëriñ Daara and the Reform of Qur'anic Schools in Senegal." *Politique Africaine* 139 (3): 83–99.

Hutson, Alaine. 1999. "The Development of Women's Authority in the Kano Tijaniyya, 1894–1963." *Africa Today* 46 (3/4): 43–64.

Ibrahim, Jaffaru. 2021. "Concerning Praying for Kwame Nkrumah: Letter of Sheikh Ibrahim Niass." January 3. www.smilebakglobal.com.

Ikuenobe, Polycarp, ed. 2006. *Philosophical Perspectives on Communalism and Morality in African Traditions*. Lexington Books.

Jackson, Sherman A. 2005. *Islam and the Blackamerican: Looking Toward the Third Resurrection*. Oxford University Press.

Jaji, Tsitsi. 2014. *Africa in Stereo: Modernism, Music, and Pan-African Solidarity*. Oxford University Press.

James, C.L.R. 1938. *The Black Jacobins: Toussaint l'Ouverture and the San Domingo Revolution*. Secker & Warburg.

James, Stanlie M. 1993. "Mothering: A Possible Black Feminist Link to Social Transformation?" In *Theorizing Black Feminisms: The Visionary Pragmatism of Black Women*, edited by Stanlie M. James and Abena P. A. Busia, 45–55. Routledge.

Jeffrey, Craig. 2010. *Timepass: Youth, Class, and the Politics of Waiting in India*. Stanford University Press.

Joseph, Dr. Karimah. 2020. Students of Shaykh Hassan Cisse (RTA) Interview by Jamillah Karim. https://www.youtube.com/live/WrW6Hf2KqNo.

Jouili, Jeanette Selma. 2015. *Pious Practice and Secular Constraints: Women in the Islamic Revival in Europe*. Stanford University Press.

———. 2021. "Embodying Black Islam: The Ethics and Aesthetics of Afro-Diasporic Muslim Hip-Hop in Britain." In *Embodying Black Religions in Africa and Its Diasporas*, edited by Yolanda Covington-Ward and Jeanette Selma Jouili, 197–221. Duke University Press.

Kaba, Mariame, and Andrea J. Ritchie. 2022. *No More Police: A Case for Abolition*. The New Press.

Kane, Ousmane. 1997. "Shaikh Islam Al-Hajj Ibrahim Niasse." In *Le Temps Des Marabouts*, edited by David Robinson and Jean-Louis Triaud, 299–316. Karthala.

———. 2011. *The Homeland Is the Arena: Religion, Transnationalism, and the Integration of Senegalese Immigrants in America*. Oxford University Press.

———. 2016. *Beyond Timbuktu: An Intellectual History of Muslim West Africa*. Harvard University Press.

Karim, Jamillah Ashira, and Dawn Marie Gibson. 2014. *Women of the Nation: Between Black Protest and Sunni Islam*. New York University Press.

Kashani, Maryam. 2023. *Medina by the Bay: Scenes of Muslim Study and Survival*. Duke University Press.

Kelley, Robin D. G. 2002. *Freedom Dreams: The Black Radical Imagination*. Beacon Press.

———. 2012. *Africa Speaks, America Answers: Modern Jazz in Revolutionary Times*. Harvard University Press.

Khattab, Mustafa. 2015. *The Clear Quran*. Book of Signs Foundation.

Kleinman, Arthur. 2013. "From Illness as Culture to Caregiving as Moral Experience." *New England Journal of Medicine* 368 (15): 1376–77. https://doi.org/10.1056/NEJMp1300678.

Knysh, Alexander. 2001. "The 'Tariqa' on a Landcruiser: The Resurgence of Sufism in Yemen." *Middle East Journal* 55 (3): 399–414.

Kohli, Rita, R. N. Johnson, and Lindsay Perez Huber. 2006. "Naming Racism: A Conceptual Look at Internalized Racism in US Schools." *Chicano/Latino Law Review*, 183–206.

Kurashige, Scott. 2017. *The Fifty-Year Rebellion: How the U.S. Political Crisis Began in Detroit*. University of California Press.

Ladson-Billings, Gloria. 1994. *The Dreamkeepers: Successful Teachers of African American Children*. Jossey-Bass.

———. 2006. "From the Achievement Gap to the Education Debt: Understanding Achievement in US Schools." *Educational Researcher* 35 (7): 3–12.

———. 2007. "Pushing Past the Achievement Gap: An Essay on the Language of Deficit." *Journal of Negro Education* 76 (3): 316–23.

Ladson-Billings, Gloria, and William F. Tate. 1995. "Toward a Critical Race Theory of Education." *Teachers College Record: The Voice of Scholarship in Education* 97 (1): 47–68. https://doi.org/10.1177/016146819509700104.

Lahti, Sara. 2019. "A Tale of Two NGO Discourses: NGO Stories of Suffering Qur'anic School Children in Senegal." In *Disadvantaged Childhoods and Humanitarian Intervention: Processes of Affective Commodification and Objectification*, edited by Kristen Cheney and Aviva Sinervo. Palgrave Macmillan.

Lapidus, Ira M. 1984. "Knowledge, Virtue, and Action: The Classical Muslim Conception of Adab and the Nature of Religious Fulfillment in Islam." In *Moral Conduct and Authority: The Place of Adab in South Asian Islam*, edited by Barbara Daly Metcalf, 38–61. University of California Press.

Launay, Robert, ed. 2016. *Islamic Education in Africa: Writing Boards and Blackboards*. Indiana University Press.

———. 2021. "The Qur'an School and Trajectories of Islamic Education." In *Routledge Handbook of Islam in Africa*, edited by Terje Østebø. Routledge.
Leonard, Jacqueline, and Danny Bernard Martin, eds. 2013. *The Brilliance of Black Children in Mathematics: Beyond the Numbers and toward New Discourse*. Information Age Publishing.
Leonardo, Zeus, and Warner Norton Grubb. 2018. *Education and Racism: A Primer on Issues and Dilemmas*. Second edition. Routledge.
Levtzion, Nehemia. 1994. *Islam in West Africa: Religion, Society and Politics to 1800*. Variorum.
———. 2000. "Islam in the Bilad Al-Sudan to 1800." In *The History of Islam in Africa*, edited by Nehemia Levtzion and Randall Lee Pouwels, 63–92. Ohio University Press.
Lewis, I. M., ed. 1966. *Islam in Tropical Africa*. Oxford University Press.
Lincoln, C. Eric. 1961. *The Black Muslims in America*. Africa World Press.
Loimeier, Roman. 2002. "Je Veux Étudier sans Mendier: The Campaign Against the Qur'anic Schools in Senegal." In *Social Welfare in Muslim Societies in Africa*, edited by Holger Weiss, 116–35. Nordic Africa Institute.
Lomotey, Kofi. 1992. "Independent Black Institutions: African-Centered Education Models." *Journal of Negro Education* 61 (4): 455–62.
Lumbard, Joseph. 2020. "Love and Beauty in Sufism." In *Routledge Handbook on Sufism*, edited by Lloyd V. J. Ridgeon. Routledge.
Lydon, Ghislaine. 2011. "A Thirst for Knowledge: Arabic Literacy, Writing Paper and Saharan Bibliophiles in the Southwestern Sahara." In *The Trans-Saharan Book Trade: Manuscript Culture, Arabic Literacy, and Intellectual History in Muslim Africa*, edited by Graziano Krätli and Ghislaine Lydon, 35–72. Brill.
Mack, Beverly. 2018. "Fodiology: African American Heritage Connections to West African Islam." *Journal of West African History* 4 (2): 103–30. https://doi.org/10.14321/jwestafrihist.4.2.0103.
Mahon, Maureen. 2008. "Eslanda Goode Robeson's African Journey: The Politics of Identification and Representation in the African Diaspora." In *Transnational Blackness: Navigating the Global Color Line*, edited by Manning Marable and Vanessa Agard-Jones, 115–34. Palgrave Macmillan.
Mahmood, Saba. 2004. *Politics of Piety: The Islamic Revival and the Feminist Subject*. Princeton University Press.
Mains, Daniel. 2013. *Hope Is Cut: Youth, Unemployment, and the Future in Urban Ethiopia*. Temple University Press.
Marable, Manning. 1983. *How Capitalism Underdeveloped Black America: Problems in Race, Political Economy, and Society*. South End Press.
———. 2008. "Introduction: Blackness Beyond Boundaries: Navigating the Political Economies of Global Inequality." In *Transnational Blackness: Navigating the Global Color Line*, edited by Manning Marable and Vanessa Agard-Jones, 1–8. Palgrave Macmillan.

Marable, Manning, and Vanessa Agard-Jones, eds. 2008. *Transnational Blackness: Navigating the Global Color Line*. Palgrave Macmillan.

Marshall, Katherine. 2015. A Discussion with Seyda Rokhaya Ibrahima Niass, Islamic Scholar and Woman Religious Leader in the Tijaniyya Sufi Order, Senegal. https://berkleycenter.georgetown.edu.

Martin, Danny Bernard. 2019. "Equity, Inclusion, and Antiblackness in Mathematics Education." *Race Ethnicity and Education* 22 (4): 459–78. https://doi.org/10.1080/13613324.2019.1592833.

Martin, Elmer P., and Joanne Martin. 1978. *The Black Extended Family: A Theological Essay on Festivity and Fantasy*. University of Chicago Press.

Martin, Jane Roland. 1992. *The Schoolhome: Rethinking Schools for Changing Families*. Harvard University Press.

Marty, Paul. 1917. *Etudes Sur l'Islam Au Senegal*. Paris: Leroux.

Masquelier, Adeline Marie. 2019. *Fada: Boredom and Belonging in Niger*. University of Chicago Press.

Matory, J. Lorand. 2005. *Black Atlantic Religion: Tradition, Transnationalism, and Matriarchy in the Afro-Brazilian Candomblé*. Princeton University Press.

Mauss, Marcel. 2015. *The Gift: Forms and Functions of Exchange in Archaic Societies*. Andesite Press.

Mazama, Ama, and Garvey Lundy. 2015. "African American Homeschooling and the Quest for a Quality Education." *Education and Urban Society* 47 (2): 160–81.

Mazrui, Ali. 2005. "Pan-Africanism and the Intellectuals: Rise, Decline and Revival." In *African Intellectuals: Rethinking Politics, Language, Gender and Development*, edited by Thandika Mkandawire, 56–77. CODESRIA Books in association with Zed Books.

Mbembe, Achille, and Sarah Balakrishnan. 2016. "Pan-African Legacies, Afropolitan Futures." *Transition* 120: 28–37. https://doi.org/10.2979/transition.120.1.04.

McCloud, Aminah Beverly. 2004. "Conceptual Discourse Living as a Muslim in a Pluralistic Society." In *Muslims' Place in the American Public Square: Hope, Fears, and Aspirations*, edited by Zahid Hussain Bukhari, 73–83. AltaMira Press.

McGrath, Susan M. 1995. "From Tokenism to Community Control: Political Symbolism in the Desegregation of Atlanta's Public Schools, 1961–1973." *Georgia Historical Quarterly* 79 (4): 842–72.

McKay, Ramah. 2018. *Medicine in the Meantime: The Work of Care in Mozambique*. Duke University Press.

McKinney De Royston, Maxine, Tia C. Madkins, Jarvis R. Givens, and Na'ilah Suad Nasir. 2021. "'I'm a Teacher, I'm Gonna Always Protect You': Understanding Black Educators' Protection of Black Children." *American Educational Research Journal* 58 (1): 68–106. https://doi.org/10.3102/0002831220921119.

Mednick, Sam, and Monika Pronczuk. 2024. "Chad Ends a Defense Cooperation Agreement with France, Its Former Colonial Ruler," November 29. https://apnews.com.

Melly, Caroline. 2010. "Inside-out Houses: Urban Belonging and Imagined Futures in Dakar, Senegal." *Comparative Studies in Society and History* 52 (1): 37–65.

Miescher, Stephan F. 2014. "'Nkrumah's Baby': The Akosombo Dam and the Dream of Development in Ghana, 1952–1966." *Water History*, 341–66.

Miller, Rasul. 2019. "Black Muslim Cosmopolitanism: The Global Character of New York City's Black Muslim Movements, 1929–1990." Ph.D. diss., University of Pennsylvania. https://repository.upenn.edu.

———. 2020. "When the Flood Reached New York: The Tijani Sufi Order Among Black American Muslims in NYC." In *Varieties of American Sufism*. SUNY Press.

———. 2024. "Black Muslim Racial Reimagining: Traditions of Racial and Religious Self-Making Among Black Sunni Muslims in the US." *Journal of Africana Religions* 12 (2): 223–51. https://doi.org/10.5325/jafrireli.12.2.0223.

Mills, Charles. 1997. *The Racial Contract*. Cornell University Press.

Milner, H. Richard. 2013. "Rethinking Achievement Gap Talk in Urban Education." *Urban Education* 48 (1): 3–8. https://doi.org/10.1177/0042085912470417.

Mkwananzi, Faith. 2018. *Higher Education, Youth and Migration in Contexts of Disadvantage: Understanding Aspirations and Capabilities*. Palgrave Macmillan. https://doi.org/10.1007/978-3-030-04453-4.

Mohammed Schools of Atlanta. 2022. https://www.mohammedschools.org.

Mol, Annemarie. 2008. *The Logic of Care: Health and the Problem of Patient Choice*. Routledge.

Moore, Celeste Day. 2021. "Producing a 'Black World': William Greaves, '*Black Journal*,' and the Creation of a New Medium of Black Internationalism, 1968–1970." *Journal of African American History* 106 (4): 626–49. https://doi.org/10.1086/716495.

Moore, Leslie C. 2006. "Learning by Heart in Qur'anic and Public Schools in Northern Cameroon." *Social Analysis* 50 (3). https://doi.org/10.3167/015597706780459421.

Moosa, Ebrahim. 2015. *What Is a Madrasa?* University of North Carolina Press.

Morris, Jerome E. 1999. "A Pillar of Strength: An African American School's Communal Bonds with Families and Community since Brown." *Urban Education* 33 (5): 584–605. https://doi.org/10.1177/0042085999335003.

Morris, Monique. 2016. *Pushout: The Criminalization of Black Girls in Schools*. New Press.

Moses, Wilson Jeremiah, ed. 1998. *Liberian Dreams: Back-to-Africa Narratives from the 1850s*. Pennsylvania State University Press.

Muhammad, Ahmed Sufi. 2018. "Journey to Becoming Hafiz." *Ruhul Adab Newsletter*, February.

Muhammad, Gholdy. 2020. *Cultivating Genius: An Equity Framework for Culturally and Historically Responsive Literacy*. Scholastic Teaching Resources.

Muhammad, Opal. 2001. "Dr. Khadijah Askari-Cisse: Healing on 2 Continents." *Azizah Magazine* 1 (3): 44–47.

Muhammad, Sabir K. 2012. "Dr. Khadijah Askari Earns Trust of Those She Serves." *Muslim Journal* (Atlanta, GA), May 4.

Mullings, Leith. 1996. *On Our Own Terms: Race, Class, and Gender in the Lives of African American Women*. Routledge.

———. 2008. "Race and Globalization from Below." In *Transnational Blackness Navigating the Global Color Line*, edited by Manning Marable and Vanessa Agard-Jones, 11–18. Palgrave Macmillan.

Murch, Donna. 2010. *Living for the City: Migration, Education, and the Rise of the Black Panther Party in Oakland, California*. University of North Carolina Press.

———. 2015. "Crack in Los Angeles: Crisis, Militarization, and Black Response to the Late Twentieth-Century War on Drugs." *Journal of American History* 102 (1): 162–73. https://doi.org/10.1093/jahist/jav260.

Murphy, David. 2016. *The First World Festival of Negro Arts, Dakar 1966: Contexts and Legacies*. Liverpool University Press.

Nadasen, Premilla. 2023. *Care: The Highest Stage of Capitalism*. Haymarket Books.

Nash, Michael. 2008. *Islam Among Urban Blacks: Muslims in Newark, New Jersey: A Social History*. University Press of America.

Nasir, Na'ilah Suad. 2004. "'Halal-Ing' the Child: Reframing Identities of Resistance in an Urban Muslim School." *Harvard Educational Review* 74 (2): 153–74. https://doi.org/10.17763/haer.74.2.x203671222708725.

Neal, Larry. 1968. "The Black Arts Movement." *Drama Review*.

Neely, Cheryl L. 2015. *You're Dead—So What? Media, Police, and the Invisibility of Black Women as Victims of Homicide*. Michigan State University Press.

Nembhard, Jessica Gordon. 2014. *Collective Courage: A History of African American Cooperative Economic Thought and Practice*. Pennsylvania State University Press.

Neverdon-Morton, Cynthia. 1989. *Afro-American Women of the South and the Advancement of the Race, 1895–1935*. University of Tennessee Press.

Niasse, Aminah Abdul-Kareem. 2015. "Fifth Annual Shaykh Hassan Cisse Commemoration." Schomburg Center for Research in Black Culture, Harlem, New York City, December 5. https://www.youtube.com/watch?v=SP69qW8ie08&t=169s.

Niasse, Shaykh Ibrahim. 1941. *On Upholding Khidmah*. Translated by Adnan Wood-Smith. https://bayeniasse.blogspot.com.

———. 2001. *Spirit of Good Morals (Ruhul Adab)*. Compiled and Edited by Alhajj Abdul Hakim Halim. Translation and Commentary by Shaykh Hassan Cisse. Second edition. The African American Islamic Institute.

———. 2010. *The Removal of Confusion: Concerning the Flood of the Saintly Seal Aḥmad Al-Tijānī: A Translation of the Kāshif al-Ilbās ʿan Fayḍa Al-Khatm Abī al-ʿAbbās*. Translated by Zachary Wright, Muhtar Holland, and Abdullahi El-Okene. Fons Vitae.

———. 2014. *In the Meadows of Tafsir for the Noble Qur'an*. Translated by Moctar Boubakar M. Ba. Fayda Books.

———. 2016. *The Spirit of Good Morals*. Edited by Ibrahim Dimson. Translated by Talut Dawood. Third Edition. Fayda Books.

———. 2017. *The Guarded Treasure: Al-Kanz Al-Masun Wa'Lu'Lu Al-Maknun*. Translated by Talut Dawood. Fayda Books.

Niasse, Shaykha Ruqayya bint Ibrahim. 2015. *Volume I: Path to the Garden: Foundational Knowledge for Believing Women & Men*. Fayda Books.

Nkrumah, Kwame. 1963. *Africa Must Unite.* Praeger.
———. 1965. *Consciencism: Philosophy and Ideology for De-Colonization.*
———. 1972. "A Letter of Consolation to Dr. Kofi A. Busia: On the Coup in Ghana." *Black Scholar* 3 (9): 23–26.
Noddings, Nel. 1984. *Caring: A Feminine Approach to Ethics and Moral Education.* University of California Press.
Noguera, Pedro. 2008. *The Trouble with Black Boys: . . . And Other Reflections on Race, Equity, and the Future of Public Education.* Jossey-Bass.
Nyang, Sulayman S. 1993. "Islamic Revivalism in West Africa: Historical Perspectives and Recent Developments." In *Religious Plurality in Africa*, edited by Jacob K. Olupona and Sulayman S. Nyang. De Gruyter. https://doi.org/10.1515/9783110850079.231.
Nyerere, Julius K. 1968. "Education for Self-Reliance." *CrossCurrents* 18 (4): 415–34.
———. 1974. *UJAMAA: Essays on Socialism.* Oxford University Press.
O'Brien, John. 2017. *Keeping It Halal: The Everyday Lives of Muslim American Teenage Boys.* Princeton University Press.
Ogunnaike, Oludamini. 2020. *Deep Knowledge: Ways of Knowing in Sufism and Ifa, Two West African Intellectual Traditions.* Pennsylvania State University Press.
Ojogho, Dennis O. 2014. "Op Eds: Affirmative Reaction." *Harvard Crimson*, March 13. www.thecrimson.com.
Oliver, Melvin L., and Thomas M. Shapiro. 1997. *Black Wealth/White Wealth: A New Perspective on Racial Inequality.* Routledge.
Onaci, Edward. 2015. "Revolutionary Identities: New Afrikans and Name Choices in the Black Power Movement." *Souls* 17 (1–2): 67–89. https://doi.org/10.1080/10999949.2015.998584.
Orfield, Gary, and Carole Ashkinaze. 1991. *The Closing Door: Conservative Policy and Black Opportunity.* University of Chicago Press.
Oya, Carlos. 2006. "From State Dirigisme to Liberalisation in Senegal: Four Decades of Agricultural Policy Shifts and Continuities." *European Journal of Development Research* 18 (2): 203–34. https://doi.org/10.1080/09578810600708163.
Palmer, George. 1967. "Tavern Topics." *New York Amsterdam News*, August 5, 1967.
———. 1969. "Tavern Topics." *New York Amsterdam News*, July 26, 1969.
Parreñas, Rhacel Salazar. 2001. *Servants of Globalization: Migration and Domestic Work.* Stanford University Press.
Payne, Charles M., and Carol Sills Strickland, eds. 2008. *Teach Freedom: Education for Liberation in the African-American Tradition.* Teachers College Press.
Perkins, Alisa. 2015. "Muslim Sound, Public Space, and Citizenship Agendas in an American City." *Citizenship Studies* 19 (2): 169–83. https://doi.org/10.1080/13621025.2015.1005948.
Perry, Donna. 2004. "Muslim Child Disciples, Global Civil Society, and Children's Rights in Senegal: The Discourses of Strategic Structuralism." *Anthropological Quarterly* 77 (1): 47–86.

Pew Research Center's Forum on Religion & Public Life. 2012. "The World's Muslims: Unity and Diversity." Pew Research Center's Forum on Religion & Public Life. https://www.pewresearch.org.

Pierre, Jemima. 2012. *The Predicament of Blackness: Postcolonial Ghana and the Politics of Race*. University of Chicago Press.

———. 2020. "Slavery, Anthropological Knowledge, and the Racialization of Africans." *Current Anthropology* 61 (S22): S220–31. https://doi.org/10.1086/709844.

Piot, Charles. 1999. *Remotely Global: Village Modernity in West Africa*. University of Chicago Press.

Price, Paula Groves. 2009. "African-Centered Pedagogy and Womanist Caring: Reclaiming Black Children for Success." In *African American Perspectives on Leadership in Schools: Building a Culture of Empowerment*, edited by Lenoar Foster and Linda C. Tillman, 57–72. Rowman & Littlefield.

Prickett, Pamela J. 2021. *Believing in South Central: Everyday Islam in the City of Angels*. University of Chicago Press.

Prothmann, Sebastian. 2020. "Je Suis Sañse Rëkk, Mais Auma Xaalis (I'm Dressed Up, but I Don't Have Money): Pretense, Camouflage, and the Search for a Lifestyle by Young Men in Pikine, Senegal." *Mande Studies* 22 (57).

Ralph, Michael. 2008. "Killing Time." *Social Text* 26 (4): 1–29. https://doi.org/10.1215/01642472-2008-008.

Rahman, Samiha. 2025. "Living and Learning Islam in Black America: Education and Self-Determination in the Dar-ul-Islam Movement." *Journal of the American Academy of Religion*.

Ransby, Barbara. 2013. *Eslanda: The Large and Unconventional Life of Mrs. Paul Robeson*. Yale University Press.

Rashid, Hakim, and Zakiyyah Muhammad. 1992. "The Sister Clara Muhammad Schools: Pioneers in the Development of Islamic Education in America." *Journal of Negro Education* 61 (2): 178–85.

Ratcliff, Anthony J. 2014. "When Négritude Was in Vogue: Critical Reflections of the First World Festival of Negro Arts and Culture in 1966." *Journal of Pan African Studies* 6 (7): 167–86.

Redkey, Edwin S. 1969. *Black Exodus: Black Nationalist and Back-to-Africa Movements, 1890–1910*. Yale University Press.

Renne, Elisha P. 2021. "Covered Bodies, Moral Education, and the Embodiment of Islamic Reform in Northern Nigeria." In *Embodying Black Religions in Africa and Its Diasporas*, edited by Yolanda Covington-Ward and Jeanette Selma Jouili, 122–51. Duke University Press.

Riccio, Bruno. 2005. "Talkin' about Migration: Some Ethnographic Notes on the Ambivalent Representation of Migrants in Contemporary Senegal." *Stichproben: Wiener Zeitschrift Für Kritische Afrikastudien* 8 (5): 99–118.

Richardson, Joseph B., Mischelle Van Brakle, and Christopher St. Vil. 2014. "Taking Boys out of the Hood: Exile as a Parenting Strategy for African American Male

Youth." *New Directions for Child and Adolescent Development* 2014 (143): 11–31. https://doi.org/10.1002/cad.20052.

Rickford, Russell. 2016. *We Are an African People: Independent Education, Black Power, and the Radical Imagination*. Oxford University Press.

Robbins, Joel. 2013. "Beyond the Suffering Subject: Toward an Anthropology of the Good." *Journal of the Royal Anthropological Institute* 19 (3): 447–62.

Roberts, Dorothy E. 1997. *Killing the Black Body: Race, Reproduction, and the Meaning of Liberty*. Pantheon Books.

Roberts, Mari Ann. 2010. "Toward a Theory of Culturally Relevant Critical Teacher Care: African American Teachers' Definitions and Perceptions of Care for African American Students." *Journal of Moral Education* 39 (4): 449–67. https://doi.org/10.1080/03057241003754922.

Roberts, Neil. 2015. *Freedom as Marronage*. University of Chicago Press.

Robinson, Cedric J. 1983. *Black Marxism: The Making of the Black Radical Tradition*. Zed Press.

Robinson, David. 1985. *The Holy War of Umar Tal: The Western Sudan in the Mid-Nineteenth Century*. Oxford University Press.

Rodney, Walter. 1972. *How Europe Underdeveloped Africa*. Bogle-L'Ouverture Publications.

———. 1975. *Pan-Africanism: Struggle against Neo-colonialism and Imperialism – Documents of the Sixth Pan-African Congress*, edited by Horace Campbell. Toronto: Afro-CaribPublications, 1975, 18–41.

Rodriguez, Anne-Line. 2015. "Three Stories About Living Without Migration in Dakar: Coming to Terms with the Contradictions of the Moral Economy." *Africa* 85 (2): 333–55. https://doi.org/10.1017/S0001972015000042.

Rose, Khadijah (Um Husein). 2016. Interview by Sapelo Square. https://sapelosquare.com.

Ross, Eric. 2006. *Sufi City: Urban Design and Archetypes in Touba*. University of Rochester Press.

———. 2020. "Senegal's Sufi Cities: Places Beyond the State." In *Saintly Spheres and Islamic Landscapes*, edited by Daphna Ephrat, Ethel Sara Wolper, and Paulo G. Pinto, 366–93. Brill. https://doi.org/10.1163/9789004444270_014.

Rouse, Carolyn Moxley. 2004. *Engaged Surrender: African American Women and Islam*. University of California Press.

sadiki, dequi kioni-. 2023. Look for Me in the Whirlwind: Panther 21—hosted by MapSO Freedom Schools. https://www.youtube.com/watch?v=ZULV1ApXMDw.

Safi, Omid, ed. 2018. *Radical Love: Teachings from the Islamic Mystical Tradition*. Yale University Press.

Said, Omar ibn. 1925. "Autobiography of Omar Ibn Said, Slave in North Carolina, 1831." Edited by John Franklin Jameson. *American Historical Review* 30 (4): 787–95.

Sanneh, Lamin O. 1989. *The Jakhanke Muslim Clerics: A Religious and Historical Study of Islam in Senegambia*. University Press of America.

Scheld, Suzanne. 2007. "Youth Cosmopolitanism: Clothing, the City and Globalization in Dakar, Senegal." *City & Society* 19 (2): 232–53. https://doi.org/10.1525/city.2007.19.2.232.

Schleifer, S. Abdallah. 2016. "The World's 500 Most Influential Muslims, 2017." The Muslim 500. https://www.themuslim500.com/wp-content/uploads/2018/05/TheMuslim500-2017-low.pdf.

Schneider, Eric C. 2008. *Smack: Heroin and the American City*. University of Pennsylvania Press.

Seck, Aminata, and Fatiha Terki. 2020. "WFP Senegal Country Brief." World Food Programme.

Seesemann, Rüdiger. 2011. *The Divine Flood: Ibrahim Niasse and the Roots of a Twentieth-Century Sufi Revival*. Oxford University Press.

———. 2015. "Work Ethics among Sufis in Sub-Saharan Africa." *Religions*, 66–73.

Seesemann, Rudiger, and Benjamin Soares. 2009. "'Being as Good Muslims as Frenchmen': On Islam and Colonial Modernity in West Africa." *Journal of Religion in Africa* 39:91–120.

"Senegal: Nutrition Profile." 2018. USAID.

Shange, Savannah. 2019. *Progressive Dystopia: Abolition, Anthropology, and Race in the New San Francisco*. Duke University Press.

Shaw, Rosalind. 1990. "The Invention of 'African Traditional Religion.'" *Religion* 20 (4): 339–53. https://doi.org/10.1016/0048-721X(90)90116-N.

Shepperson, George. 1962. "Pan-Africanism and 'Pan-Africanism': Some Historical Notes." *Phylon* 23 (4): 346. https://doi.org/10.2307/274158.

Shepperson, George, and St. Clair Drake. 2008. "The Fifth Pan-African Conference, 1945 and the All African Peoples Congress, 1958." *Contributions in Black Studies* 8 (5): 35–66.

Shrider, Emily A. 2024. *Poverty in the United States: 2023*. P60-283. U.S. Census Bureau, Current Population Reports. www2.census.gov.

Smith, Christen A., Erica L. Williams, Imani A. Wadud, Whitney N. L. Pirtle, and The Cite Black Women Collective. 2021. "Cite Black Women: A Critical Praxis (A Statement)." *Feminist Anthropology* 2 (1): 10–17. https://doi.org/10.1002/fea2.12040.

Smith, Gina Gertrud. 2008. *Medina Gounass: Challenges to Village Sufism in Senegal*. København: Books on Demand.

Soares, Benjamin. 2005. *Islam and the Prayer Economy: History and Authority in a Malian Town*. University of Michigan Press.

Sommers, Marc. 2012. *Stuck: Rwandan Youth and the Struggle for Adulthood*. University of Georgia Press.

Souleymane, Barry. 2023. "Travaux de Médina Baye : Le Très Beau Geste Du Khalif Général Des Mourides, Serigne Mountakha." *Sene.News*, April 14, 2023. www.senenews.com.

Speciale, Teresa. 2021. "'We're Not Used to Racism at All': Race, Language, and Becoming 'Global' at the Bilingual Academy of Senegal." *Anthropology & Education Quarterly* 53 (1): 65–83. https://doi.org/10.1111/aeq.12397.

"Speeches & Statements Made at the First Organization of African Unity (O.A.U.) Summit." 1963. Addis Ababa, Ethiopia. https://au.int.

Stack, Carol B. 1974. *All Our Kin: Strategies for Survival in a Black Community*. Basic Books.

Stoller, Paul. 2002. *Money Has No Smell: The Africanization of New York City*. University of Chicago Press.

Stone, Joel. 2017. *Detroit 1967: Origins, Impacts, Legacies*. Wayne State University Press.

Stovall, David. 2020. "On Knowing: Willingness, Fugitivity and Abolition in Precarious Times." *Journal of Language and Literacy Education* 16 (1): 1–7.

Sugrue, Thomas J. 1996. *The Origins of the Urban Crisis: Race and Inequality in Postwar Detroit*. Princeton University Press.

Suleiman, Omar. 2021. "7 Ways to Increase Baraka in Your Time." Yaqeen Institute, November 19. https://www.youtube.com/watch?v=4YTfDUqGlZs&t=1335s.

Taylor, Keeanga-Yamahtta. 2016. *From #BlackLivesMatter to Black Liberation*. Haymarket Books.

——. 2019. *Race for Profit: How Banks and the Real Estate Industry Undermined Black Homeownership*. University of North Carolina Press.

Western Sunrise. 1979. "The Mosque of Islamic Brotherhood, Inc. Announces Registration 1980 of Its School of Islamic & Arabic Studies." *Western Sunrise* 8 (1), July 1979–October 1980.

Thomas, Todne. 2021. *Kincraft: The Making of Black Evangelical Sociality*. Duke University Press.

Thompson, Audrey. 1998. "Not the Color Purple: Black Feminist Lessons for Educational Caring." *Harvard Educational Review* 68 (4): 522–55. https://doi.org/10.17763/haer.68.4.nm436v83214n5016.

——. 2004. "Caring and Colortalk: Childhood Innocence in White and Black." In *Race-Ing Moral Formation: African American Perspectives on Care and Justice*, edited by Vanessa Siddle Walker and John R. Snarey, 23–37. Teachers College Press.

Thompson, Heather Ann. 2010. *Whose Detroit? Politics, Labor, and Race in a Modern American City*. Cornell University Press.

Tilton, Jennifer. 2010. *Dangerous or Endangered? Race and the Politics of Youth in Urban America*. New York University Press.

Todd-Breland, Elizabeth. 2018. *A Political Education: Black Politics and Education Reform in Chicago since the 1960s*. University of North Carolina Press.

Touré, Ahmed Sekou. 1977. *Islam for the People's Benefit*. African Democratic Revolution.

Tuck, Eve. 2009. "Suspending Damage: A Letter to Communities." *Harvard Educational Review* 79 (3): 409–28. https://doi.org/10.17763/haer.79.3.n0016675661t3n15.

Turner, Richard Brent. 1997. *Islam in the African-American Experience*. Indiana University Press.

——. 2000. "Pre-Twentieth Century Islam." In *Down by the Riverside: Readings in African American Religion*, edited by Larry G. Murphy, 69–80. New York University Press.

———. 2021. *Soundtrack to a Movement: African American Islam, Jazz, and Black Internationalism*. New York University Press.
Turner, Victor. 1987. "Betwixt and Between: The Liminal Period in Rites of Passage." In *Betwixt & Between: Patterns of Masculine and Feminine Initiation*, edited by Louise Carus Mahdi, Steven Foster, and Meredith Little, 3–19. Open Court Publishing.
Umoja, Akinyele Omowale. 2013. *We Will Shoot Back: Armed Resistance in the Mississippi Freedom Movement*. New York University Press.
Umoren, Imaobong Denis. 2018. *Race Women Internationalists: Activist-Intellectuals and Global Freedom Struggles*. University of California Press.
UNESCO, ed. 2015. *Education for All 2000–2015: Achievements and Challenges*. EFA Global Monitoring Report, 12.2015. Unesco Publications.
Uzoigwe, G. N. 1984. "Reflections on the Berlin West Africa Conference, 1884–1885." *Journal of the Historical Society of Nigeria* 12 (3/4): 9–22.
Valk, Anne M., and Leslie Brown. 2010. *Living with Jim Crow: African American Women and Memories of the Segregated South*. Palgrave Macmillan.
Vaught, Sabina Elena. 2011. *Racism, Public Schooling, and the Entrenchment of White Supremacy: A Critical Race Ethnography*. SUNY Press.
Villalón, Leonardo Alfonso. 1995. *Islamic Society and State Power in Senegal: Disciples and Citizens in Fatick*. Cambridge University Press.
Wagner, Daniel A. 1993. *Literacy, Culture, and Development: Becoming Literate in Morocco*. Cambridge University Press.
Wagner, Daniel A., and Abdelhamid Lotfi. 1983. "Learning to Read by 'Rote.'" *International Journal of the Sociology of Language* 1983 (42). https://doi.org/10.1515/ijsl.1983.42.111.
Walker, Vanessa Siddle. 1996. *Their Highest Potential: An African American School Community in the Segregated South*. University of North Carolina Press.
Walters, Tracey Lorraine. 2021. *Not Your Mother's Mammy: The Black Domestic Worker in Transatlantic Women's Media*. Rutgers University Press.
Ware, Rudolph. 2014. *The Walking Qur'an: Islamic Education, Embodied Knowledge, and History in West Africa*. University of North Carolina Press.
Ware, Rudolph, Zachary Wright, and Amir Syed. 2018. *Jihad of the Pen: The Sufi Literature of West Africa*. American University in Cairo Press.
Weisenfeld, Judith. 2017. *New World A-Coming: Black Religion and Racial Identity during the Great Migration*. New York University Press.
Weller, Christian. 2019. "African Americans Face Systematic Obstacles to Getting Good Jobs." Center for American Progress. www.americanprogress.org.
White, Deborah G. 2008. "Introduction: A Telling History." In *Telling Histories: Black Women Historians in the Ivory Tower*, edited by Deborah G. White, 1–27. University of North Carolina Press.
White, Monica M. 2018. *Freedom Farmers: Agricultural Resistance and the Black Freedom Movement*. University of North Carolina Press.
Wiegelmann, Ulrike, and Craig Naumann. 1997. "Zwischen Ausbildung Und Ausbeutung: Die Talibes Mendiants Im Senegal." In *Strassenkinder Und Kinderarbeit:*

Sozialisationstheoretische, Historische Und Kulturvergleichende Studien, edited by Christel Adick, 273–91. Frankfurt.

Wilder, Craig Steven. 2013. *Ebony and Ivy: Race, Slavery, and the Troubled History of America's Universities.* Bloomsbury.

Williams, Bianca C. 2018. *The Pursuit of Happiness: Black Women, Diasporic Dreams, and the Politics of Emotional Transnationalism.* Duke University Press.

Williams, Eric. 1944. *Capitalism & Slavery.* University of North Carolina Press.

Williams, Heather Andrea. 2005. *Self-Taught: African American Education in Slavery and Freedom.* University of North Carolina Press.

Winston, Celeste. 2021. "Maroon Geographies." *Annals of the American Association of Geographers*, May, 1–15. https://doi.org/10.1080/24694452.2021.1894087.

———. 2023. *How to Lose the Hounds: Maroon Geographies and a World Beyond Policing.* Duke University Press.

Wolcott, Victoria W. 2013. *Remaking Respectability: African American Women in Interwar Detroit.* University of North Carolina Press.

World Bank Microdata Library. 2009. "Migration and Remittances: Household Survey in Senegal." World Bank.

Wright, Willie Jamaal. 2020. "The Morphology of Marronage." *Annals of the American Association of Geographers* 110 (4): 1134–49. https://doi.org/10.1080/24694452.2019.1664890.

Wright, Zachary. 2005. *On the Path of the Prophet: Shaykh Ahmad Tijani (1737—1815) and the Tariqa Muhammadiyya.* The African-American Islamic Institute.

———. 2012. "Biographies: Shaykh Hassan Cisse (1945–2008), Imam of the Fayda Tijaniyya." *Annual Review of Islam in Africa*, no. 11: 60–63.

———. 2013. "Islam and Decolonization in Africa: The Political Engagement of a West African Muslim Community." *International Journal of African Historical Studies* 46 (2): 205–27.

———. 2015a. *Living Knowledge in West African Islam: The Sufi Community of Ibrahim Niasse.* Brill.

———. 2015b. *Pearls from the Flood: Select Insights of Shaykh Al-Islam Ibrahim Niasse.* Translated by Zachary Wright. Fayda Books.

———. 2018. "'The Spirit of Etiquette' (Ruh al-Adab)." In *Jihad of the Pen: The Sufi Literature of West Africa*, 169–81. American University in Cairo Press.

———. 2020. *Realizing Islam: The Tijāniyya in North Africa and the Eighteenth-Century Muslim World.* University of North Carolina Press.

———. 2022. "Islam, Blackness, and African Cultural Distinction: The Islamic Negritude of Shaykh Ibrahim Niasse." *Journal of Africana Religions* 10 (2): 237–65.

Xavier, Merin Shobhna. 2018. *Sacred Spaces and Transnational Networks in American Sufism: Bawa Muhaiyaddeen and Contemporary Shrine Cultures.* Bloomsbury Academic.

X, Malcolm. 1963. "Message to the Grass Roots." Presented at the Northern Negro Grass Roots Leadership Conference, King Solomon Baptist Church, Detroit, MI, November 10. https://ccnmtl.columbia.edu.

Yakub, Rukayat. 2024. "Black Belonging: Assessing Antiblackness in Full-Time US Islamic Schools." Master's Thesis, Chicago Theological Seminary.

Yeboah, Thomas. 2021. "Future Aspirations of Rural-Urban Young Migrants in Accra, Ghana." *Children's Geographies* 19 (1): 45–58. https://doi.org/10.1080/14733285.2020.1737643.

Young, Alden, and Keren Weitzberg. 2022. "Globalizing Racism and De-Provincializing Muslim Africa." *Modern Intellectual History* 19 (3): 912–33. https://doi.org/10.1017/S1479244321000196.

Yount-André, Chelsie. 2018. "Gifts, Trips and Facebook Families: Children and the Semiotics of Kinship in Transnational Senegal." *Africa* 88 (4): 683–701. https://doi.org/10.1017/S0001972018000426.

Yun, Lawrence, Jessica Lautz, Nadia Evangelou, Brandi Snowden, and Meredith Dunn. 2025. *2025 Snapshot of Race and Home Buying in America*. National Association of Realtors. www.nar.realtor.

Zuberi, Tukufu, and Eduardo Bonilla-Silva, eds. 2008. *White Logic, White Methods: Racism and Methodology*. Rowman & Littlefield.

ACKNOWLEDGMENTS

It has taken a long time to get to this point, but alhamdulilah, we're here! This book would not have been possible without the inspiration, support, encouragement, and duas of so many people. I wish I had the space to publicly acknowledge all the family, friends, community members, students, mentors, coworkers, and comrades who rooted for my success.

This book wouldn't exist without the patience and blessings of the parents who trusted me to speak with their children, the young people who let me hang out and ask a million questions, and the adults and elders who shared their stories with me. Thank you to Shaykh Mahy, Sayyida Kubra, and everyone who welcomed me to Medina Baye. I am also immensely grateful to Imam Sayed (may Allah be pleased with him) and Sister Najah. I would like to express my sincere appreciation for all my Tijani sisters and brothers who provided me with a community more beautiful than anything I could ever imagine. May Allah bless you with the best in this life and the hereafter. Please forgive my errors.

To my husband, Rasul, thank you for being the absolute best thought partner, sounding board, and champion. To my sons, thank you for always reminding me that there is more to life than doing conference calls and typing away on the computer. To my mother-in-law, thank you for taking care of your grandbabies while I worked and traveled. To Bhaijan (Shakeer), thank you for all your support and encouragement. Maa, thank you for feeding us, watching the boys, and so much more. Ami tumaderke onek bhalo bashi.

I have been blessed to be in community with scholars who understand that academia is not a competition, who never hesitated to put me on, and who believe that we all win when we support one another. My deepest appreciation and respect go to Wintre Foxworth-Johnson, Celina de Sá, Alden Young, Keon McGuire, Eziaku Nwokocha, Amber Henry, Zachary Mondesire, Oliver Rollins, Dana Cypress, Jasmine Blanks Jones, Ezgi Cakmak, Beeta Baghoolizadeh, Ali Karjoo-Ravary,

Wendell Marsh, Youssef Carter, Fatima Siwaju, Bryon Maxey, Lamin Manneh, Saquib Usman, Karishma Desai, Tahereh Aghdasifar, Bianca Murillo, Preeti Sharma, Rhea Rahman, and Ezgi Güner. I am immensely grateful to Sohail Daulatzai, Zachary Wright, Arshad Ali, Esa Syeed, Maryam Kashani, Junaid Rana, Su'ad Abdul Khabeer, Butch Ware, Ousmane Kane, and Zareena Grewal for modeling what it means to be a principled Muslim scholar.

I express my sincere thanks to my academic mentors. Dr. Vivian Gadsden, thank you for supporting me as a student, educator, scholar, and mother. From the first day I met you and every day since, you have shown such deep investment in my well-being and success. John Jackson, thank you for making me believe that I can accomplish anything I put my mind to. Thank you also to Krystal Strong and Cheikh Anta Babou for sharing your wisdom and insights with me. Robin D. G. Kelley, thank you for being so generous with your time and feedback. It has been a true gift to connect with you. You are the model of what it means to be in academia, but not of it.

I would like to thank the staff at New York University Press, especially Jennifer Hammer, Brianna Jean, and Ainee Jeong, who shepherded my manuscript through the review and production processes. Many thanks to Kali Handelman, an excellent developmental editor who provided thoughtful feedback on my full manuscript. Thank you also to the staff and my colleagues in the Department of Human Development at California State University, Long Beach, as well as my comrades in the College of Liberal Arts. Additional gratitude goes to Ms. Carol Davis, Ms. Teya Campbell, and Ms. Lorraine Hightower for their care and support during my days at the University of Pennsylvania.

I benefited from the material support of the Fulbright-Hays, the National Academy of Education, the Spencer Foundation, the CSULB College of Liberal Arts, the American Council of Learned Societies, the Institute for Citizens and Scholars, and the Mellon Foundation.

INDEX

Page numbers in italics indicate Figures and Photos

AAII. *See* African American Islamic Institute
AAII Legacy Academy, 140–41, 185
AAPRP. *See* All-African People's Revolutionary Party
Aaqil, 101, 102–3, 133–35, 137
Abdul-Fattaah, Sidi Kaba, 220–21
Abdul-Kareem, Brother Jamil, 61–63, 74–75, 94–95
Abdul-Kareem, Hajjah Kareemah, 57–58, 72, *84*, 284nn5–6; AAII and, 53–54; Cisse, Shaykh Hassan Aliou, and, 83, 84–86; Donia, Dr. Sulaiman and, 63; at Islamic Cultural Center, 61–62; in Medina Baye, 7, 59–60, 81, *96*, 97–98; motherwork of, 74–75; as *muqaddama*, 6, 7; as othermother, 83, 84, 89–90, 100
Abdul Khabeer, Su'ad, 58, 145–46, 173
Abdullah, Imam Luqman, 76–77
Abdus-Salaam, Hajjah Najah, 4, 237–38
Abdus-Salaam, Hajji Ajib, 252–53
Abdus-Salaam, Imam Sayed, 2, 4; AAII and, 7; in Medina Baye, 82; as *muqaddam*, 81
Abedeen, Hajjah Tauhidah, 53–55, *56*, 57–59, 63, *64*, *65*; Cisse, Shaykh Hassan Aliou, and, 86–88; in Medina Baye, *98*; motherwork of, 75–76
Abyssinia, 20, 112
achievement gap, 159
adhan (call to prayer), 2, 149
adl (justice), 38, 163, 273

adoptive father, 181, 285n4; Cisse, Shaykh Hassan Aliou, as, 100; Cisse, Shaykh Mouhamadou Mahy, as, 9, 133, 135, 174; collective care and, 241; kincraft and, 89, 260
African American Islamic Institute (AAII), 6, 7, 8, 101, *164*; alumni of, 203–5, 208, 210; Black Americans and, 91–92, 183, 188; classroom observations at, 27; collective care and, 26, 51, 56, 60; corporal discipline at, 184, 286n6; daily schedule at, 149–50; hadiya economy relation to, 157–58; huffaz at, 155, 161; jangi kamil relation to, 179; Journey to Africa and, 253, 254–55; kincraft at, 89–90; Mahmoud at, 199; NGO, 85; pan-Africanism of, 209, 235; peer-to-peer learning at, 165, 166–68, 170; public schools compared to, 168–69; Sadia at, 110; Salah, Aminah, at, 53–54; tuition for, 238–39; Yahya at, 223
African diaspora, 275; Blackness and, 235–36; Black Radical Tradition in, 271; collective care in, 16–17, 265; fashion of, 145–46; heritage tourism of, 237, 248; kincraft in, 89, 287n1; pan-Africanism relation to, 24–25, 51, 70–71, 233, 261–62, 264–65; transatlantic slave trade relation to, 263; wealth in, 264
African Diaspora Studies, 24
Ain Shams University, 80
akhira (afterlife), 36

313

Akosombo Dam, 47
Aksum, 20
Ali, Yusuf, 67
All-African People's Revolutionary Party (AAPRP), 71, 78; Askari, Dr. Khadijah relation to, 70
Alliance of Sahel States, 271
alumni: of AAII, 203–5, 208, 210; of Islamic education, 202, 203; moral compass of, 209–10, 228
Alvin Ailey American Dance Theater, 75
al-Amin, Imam Jamil, 71
Anan, Hajji Yusuf, 80, 81
anti-Black racism, 22, 87, 146, 159, 188; Arab Muslims and, 91; fashion relation to, 145–46; at Harvard, 69; motherwork relation to, 74; at Muslim schools in the U.S., 173, 204; in Philadelphia, 68; police brutality and, 117–18, 249; in public schools, 160, 188; resistance to, 22, 207; safe harbors from, 121; in the U.S. Muslim community, 29, 91, 146, 159
anti-colonial movements, 19; Medina Baye as, 113, 115; Muslim International and, 47; Niasse, Shaykh Ibrahim, relation to, 47, 50, 116; pan-Africanism relation to, 45
anti-Muslim violence, 118, 121, 147
Arabic language, 155, 161, 187, 201, 281n1; peer-to-peer learning of, 165, 166–67; Qur'anic education and, 286n5. *See also* huffaz
Arab League, 47
Arab Muslims, 90, 91, 173
Asian-African Conference in Bandung, 234
Askari, Abubakr, 95
Askari, Aminufu, 69–70, 94–95
Askari, Dr. Khadijah, 56, 57–59, 68–71, 284nn5–6; Cisse, Shaykh Hassan, and, 93, 95–97; in Medina Baye, 97, 97–98; membership in AAPRP, 70; motherwork of, 77–79; pan-African ideologies of, 69–71; at Shifa-al-Asqam Socio Medical Center, 98, 140
Askari-Cisse, Sayyida Kubra, 8–9, 29, 78–79, 100, 132; at AAII, 101; *Born in Gaza* and, 267–68; Cisse, Shaykh Hassan Aliou, and, 183–84; domestic khidma of, 123, 125, 142–43; fashion of, 145–46; as hafiza, 60, 140, 141, 187, 285n5; jangi kamil and, 180; Kamal and, 190–91; kincraft of, 133–34; as othermother, 133, 142, 285n5; Qur'anic education and, 152; as role model, 140–42; Yahya and, 223
asr (late afternoon prayer), 137, 180, 277
Association of Black Students, Wayne State University, 66–67
Atlanta, Georgia, 77–78, 135, 182–83, 208, 287n2
Atlanta Progress Academy, 78–79
The Autobiography of Malcolm X, 24
axiomatic stance: of Black Muslim brilliance, 158–59, 168, 171–72, 179, 188; collective care and, 185
ayats (verses), 34–35, 152–53, 277

Balaby, Malam, 49
Bamba, Shaykh Amadu, 161
baraka (blessings), 153–54, 194, 223, 226, 277
Barayah, Mallam, 285n29
bayat (oath of allegiance), 35
Baye (father), 260, 277
Berlin Conference, 44
Bey, Sadiq, 66–67
Bey community, 67–68, 90
Biafra war, 61
bint Khuwaylid, Sayyida Khadijah, 144
Biteye, Cheikh, 285n29
bizaan fabric, 3
Black Americans, 264, 281n5; AAII and, 91–92, 183, 188; African diaspora relation to, 24–25, 262–63, 275; Arab Mus-

lims relation to, 173; Black internationalism and, 90, 234–35; Black Muslim brilliance and, 286n1; caring traditions among, 14–15; Cisse, Shaykh Hassan Aliou, relation to, 95–96, 231, 239–41; communal networks, 88; disenfranchisement of, 252; education and literacy, 14, 160, 169; financial support for, 241–43; heritage tourism of, 237; HFH and, 256; hijra of, 287n11; home ownership for, 247; as huffaz, 185, 287n12; in Jamaica, 119, 120; khidma of, 244; kincraft and, 89; othermothers and, 83–84, 88, 89–90, 100; pan-Africanism and, 233–35; poverty rates among, 251; precarity of, 214–15; racial identity of, 191; renaming and, 259–60; safe harbors for, 121–23; Senegal relation to, 24–25, 157; social movements, 15, 22; structural inequities and, 232; student loan debt, 198; Tijani tariqa and, 51, 231, 273, 274, 282n9; toubab relation to, 248; workplace discrimination, 213

Black American Students' U.S. School Enrollment Prior to AAII, *160*

Black Arts Movement, 74–75

Black consciousness movements, 259–60

Black feminism, 14–15; praxis of, 158

Black Marxism (Robinson, Cedric), 18

Black Muslim brilliance, 26; axiomatic stance of, 158–59, 168, 171–72, 179, 188; Black Americans and, 286n1; Qur'anic education and, 151–52

Blackness, 24, 77; African diaspora and, 235–36; Islam relation to, 162, 191; Niasse, Shaykh Ibrahim, on, 161–63, 287n8

Black Radical Tradition: collective care in, 11, 43–44; definition of, 19; in Islam, 21–23; khidma in, 147–48; maroon geographies and, 125; Medina Baye and, 113; origins of, 18; pan-Africanism in, 46; racial capitalism relation to, 18–19; Tijani tariqa and, 19–20; in the twentieth century, 9; in the twenty-first century, 15, 271

Black religious female personhood, 141–42, 146

Black Star, Crescent Moon (Daulatzai, Sohail), 19

Black women: historical contributions of, 57; as living mirrors, 140–47; oral histories of, 57–58; pan-Africanism and, 59. *See also specific women*

Born in Gaza (documentary), 267–68

Boyle, Helen, 125, 127, 205

Brown v. Board of Education (1954), 72

Burkina Faso, 271

capitalist conceptions: of education, 192, 197–98; of grind culture, 213; of hoarding wealth, 41, 136, 139, 196; of human being's value, 227; of parenting, 88; of time, 195–96, 213, 215. *See also* racial capitalism

Casselberry, Judith, 141

Castor, N. Fadeke, 174–75

Chad, 271

Chan-Malik, Sylvia, 121

Cisse, Cheikh Diery, 239–40

Cisse, Hajji Isa Mama, 81–82, 238

Cisse, Imam Cheikh Tijani, 6, 132, 189, 282n11; as an adoptive father, 260; Bayyinah and, 258–59; Black Americans relation to, 133, 157, 187, 231; collective care of, 147, 217, 259, 282n6; financial support from, 242; Kareem and, 242; as a living mirror, 132; on Niasse, Shaykh Ibrahim, 162–63; partial family tree of, *7*

Cisse, Mallam Muhammad Barayah Niasse, 181–82

Cisse, Sayyida Ya Bilquis, 252–53

Cisse, Sayyidi Aliou, 82, 240–41; Cisse, Shaykh Ibrahim Niasse, and, 41, 175, 220; on farming, 40; in maqam, 107; partial family tree of, *7*

Cisse, Shaykh Hassan Aliou: AAII and, 6–7, 51, 53, 85; Abdul-Kareem, Hajjah Kareemah and, 81–86; Abedeen, Hajjah Tauhidah, and, 86–88; as adoptive father, 100; Askari, Dr. Khadijah, and, 93, 95–96, 97; Askari-Cisse, Sayyida Kubra and, 183–84; Black Americans relation to, 231, 239–41; collective care and, 33–34, 282n6; Dimson, Hajji Ahmed, and, 81–82; jangi kamil and, 180; Joseph, Dr. Karimah, and, 91; on khidma, 219; kincraft of, 89–90, 99–100, 241; Kossi Atlanta and, 247, 287n2; love and, 102–3; in maqam, 107; Niasse, Shaykh Ibrahim, and, 4, 48, 51, 80, 272; pan-Africanism and, 51, 80, 85, 96, 239; partial family tree of, 7; Salah, Aminah, and, 53, 86–88; The Students of, 284n6; at Tijani zawiya, 194, 195, 195; ziyara of, 30, 208–9, 212, 238

Cisse, Shaykh Mouhamadou Mahy, 6, 8–9, 116, 138; at AAII, 101; as adoptive father, 9, 133, 135, 174; Black Americans relation to, 133, 157, 187, 231; collective care of, 136, 147, 217, 221, 243–44, 259, 282n6; on corporal discipline, 184; educational hopes, 199–200; financial support from, 137–40, 241–43; hadiths shared by, 191, 275; jangi kamil and, 174, 179–80; Kamal and, 190–91; kincraft of, 133–35, 260; Mahmoud and, 199–200; Niasse, Shaykh Ibrahim, and, 116, 182–83; pan-African consciousness of, 191; partial family tree of, 7; at Second Annual English Gamou, 275; as "Voice of the Fayda," 116, 132, 174; wealth of, 135–37, 142; Yahya and, 223

Cisse, Sulaiman Amadi, 219
Cite Black Women Collective, 58
Civil Rights Movement, U.S., 19, 66, 234
Clarke, John Henrik, 70
classroom observations, at AAII, 27
Cobb, Charles, Jr., 69

Cohen, Stanley, 156
collaboration, 14, 169
collective care: AAII and, 26, 51, 56, 60; in African diaspora, 16–17, 265; baraka and, 194; Black Americans and, 231, 262–63, 264; Cisse, Shaykh Hassan Aliou, on, 33–34, 282n6; communal obligation for, 259; at daaras, 157; dhikr as, 268, 275; education and, 14, 159, 191, 202, 241, 276; financial support for, 244; hadith on, 175, 196, 275; hadiya as, 43–44, 200; hadiya economy as, 41–43, 282n6; of HFH, 256; humanitarianism and, 258; ihsan and, 38; in Islamic education, 11–12, 206–7; jangi kamil as, 180; Journey to Africa and, 254–55; as khidma, 11, 43–44, 192, 222, 227; kincraft relation to, 89–90; liberation and, 43, 49, 235, 275–76; material resources and, 135–36; of othermother, 285n4; pan-Africanism and, 10–12, 34, 236; peer-to-peer learning as, 171, 188; poverty and, 251, 264; precarity relation to, 216; prophetic lifestyle and, 132, 148; Qur'anic education and, 151–52, 154, 182, 188; relational piety and, 111, 153, 185, 195, 221; of shuyukh, 117, 136, 147, 217, 221, 243–44, 259, 282n6; as social welfare programs, 242; as societal norm, 127; sunnah and, 13, 125; for talibes, 243; Tijani tariqa and, 11–13, 18, 25–26, 102, 111; time relation to, 196, 219; wealth relation to, 139
collectivism, in African diaspora, 16–17
Collins, Patricia Hill, 74, 83, 285n4
communalism: in African diaspora, 16–17; Qur'anic education and, 287n7
communal meals, 123, 125
communal obligation: for collective care, 259; Islamic education and, 200–201
communal worship, 175; khatms as, 186–87; wazifa as, 3, 81, 91, 103–4
corporal discipline, 184, 286n6

corruption, 36, 44, 51
COVID-19 pandemic, 209, 211

daaras (classical Qur'an school), 155–57, 161, 168, 230, 277
Dakar, Senegal, 62, 119, 216, 246, 253
dan Fodio, Shaykh Usman, 21, 22
Darul Islam Movement, 73, 76–77
dashikis, 3
Daulatzai, Sohail, 19
Dawawin al-Sitt (Niasse, Shaykh Ibrahim), 44
Detroit, Michigan, 65–66, 67, 135, 172–73; Masjid al-Haqq, 76–77; wazifa in, 91
Detroit Public Schools, 76–77
dhikr (remembrance), 1–2, 54–55, 82; in the Bronx, 81, 86, 238; as collective care, 268, 275; in Detroit, 91; dua and, 50; at Grand Mosque, 101, 103; for spiritual war of liberation, 180. *See also dhikrul jummah*; wazifa
dhikr beads, *104*
dhikrul jummah (Friday dhikr), 2, 54–55
diasporic hegemonies, 235–36
Dimson, Hajji Ahmed, 81–82
Diop, Ustadh Barham Mahmud, 176, 287n10
Diouf, Sylviane, 18
domestic khidma, 123, 125, *126*, 142–43
Donia, Dr. Sulaiman, 63
Drake, St. Clare, 48–49
dua (supplication), 41–42, 50, 277
Du Bois, W. E. B., 233–34
dunya (temporal world), 36, 193, 277
Dyula community, 178

economic exploitation, 233–35
education: at AAII Legacy Academy, 140–41; African American traditions of, 14, 73, 169, 190–91; capitalist conceptions of, 197–98; collective care and, 14, 159, 191, 202, 241, 276; financial support for, 211, 212; higher education, 199, 203, 211–12, 250; for khidma, 192; moral, 132; Nasrul Ilm America and, 208; peer-to-peer learning in, 165, 166–69; precarity relation to, 244–45; state-sponsored, 198; in sunnah, 125, 127. *See also* African American Islamic Institute; Islamic education; Qur'anic education
emotional attachment, 13
Envisioning Black Muslim Freedom Dreams, 274
European colonization, 16, 44, 235; education and, 156, 160, 168, 196; liberation from, 44–45, 180–81; Niasse, Shaykh Ibrahim's resistance to, 44, 50, 113, 180, 272; resistance to, 206–7; wealth extracted from, 232–33
An Exposition on the Etiquette of the Bearers of the Qur'an (al-Nawawi), 152–54
extended community, collective care in, 202
extrinsic motivation, 184

FAFSA. *See* Free Application for Federal Student Aid
fajr (early morning prayer), 149, 277
Fanon, Frantz, 69
faqir, 36–37
farming, 41; autonomy and, 113; International Monetary Fund and, 216; as khidma, 39–40
fashion, 3, 145–46
fayda (flood), 6, 277; Medina Baye and, 112–13; of Niasse, Shaykh Ibrahim, 44; spiritual liberation and, 51. *See also* Tijani tariqa
Faye, Bassirou Diomaye, 271
female huffaz. *See* hafiza
The Fifth Letter of Orientation (al-Tijani), 282n3
financial support: for Black Americans, 241–43; for collective care, 244; for education, 211, 212; for spiritual transformation, 262

first-generation college students, 212
Flint water crisis, 209
flood. *See* fayda
Floyd, George, 180
food insecurity, 117, 251
France, 115, 233, 271. *See also* European colonization
Free Application for Federal Student Aid (FAFSA), 211
Freedom Dreams (Kelley, Robin D. G.), 9, 12, 15, 54, 272
Freedom Institute, 78
fugitive infrastructure, 113, 116, 137, 147, 157
fugitivity, 113, 120

gamou, 6, 42, 267, 275, 277
gendered piety, 130, 146
gender norms: love, 102–3; in Medina Baye, 130; in Senegal, 246
generational wealth, 225
Ghana, 50, 62, 75
Gibson, Dawn-Marie, 57–58
gift-giving. *See* hadiya
globalization, 214, 240, 262
Global War on Terror, 236, 286n5
Gorée Island, 237, 238
government assistance, Medina Baye relation to, 115–16
graduation rates, 211
Grand Mosque, of Medina Baye, *102, 104, 106, 176, 270*; *adhan* and, 149; dhikr at, 101, 103; jangi kamil at, 175, 176, *177*, 178, 179; maqam of, *107, 269*
gratitude (*shukr*), 36, 193–94, 278
Great Migration, 60, 65, 88
greed, 34
Grewal, Zareena, 285n1, 286n2
grind culture: capitalism relation to, 213; imagination relation to, 225; resistance to, 213, 226; time relation to, 215

hadith (narration), 33, 275, 277; on collective are, 175, 196, 275; on hadiya, 42–43; of Jibril, 35, 39, 152; on knowledge, 201; on Qur'anic education, 152–54, 170–71, 196; on relational piety, 123, 125, 153, 196
hadiya (gift-giving), 40–41, 110, 277, 282n6; of Bayyinah, 259; as collective care, 43–44, 200; hadith on, 42–43; marifa and, 116–17; misconceptions of, 283n6
hadiya economy, 35, 41, 110, 139, 147–48; AAII relation to, 157–58; as collective care, 41–43, 282n6; as fugitive infrastructure, 137, 147, 157; maroon geographies and, 116–17; relational piety and, 153; wealth relation to, 41, 137, 139
hafiz (male huffaz), 7, 8, 140, 152, 277; Cisse, Shaykh Mouhamadou Mahy, as, 174; Ismail as, 211; Kamal as, 190–91; Muhammad, Ahmed, as, 180
hafiza (female huffaz), 107, 169–70, 277; Askari-Cisse, Sayyida Kubra as, 60, 140, 141, 187, 285n5; Hafsa and, 150; Niasse, Aminah Abdul-Kareem as, 60
Hafsa, 125, 127, 160, 172, 208; hafiza and, 150; on sunnah, 123
Hajji, 281n7. *See also specific Hajji*
al-Hajj Malick Sy, 282n10, 285n2
Hanaan, 143–45, 146, 149, 161, 172–74, 185, 207
Haqq, Amina Amatul, 58
haram (forbidden), 36, 128–29, 277
Harlem, 60–61, 74–75
Harlem School of Arts, 74–75
hats (*kufis*), 3
Hausa ethnic group, 3, 21–22, 49, 222–23
hegemony: in African Diaspora Studies, 24; diasporic, 235–36; of U.S., 265
Help for Humanity (HFH), 209, 252–53, 255, 256, 257, 257–58
heritage tourism, 245, 248; to Medina Baye, 4–5; in Senegal, 237
Hersey, Tricia, 213, 225

HFH. *See* Help for Humanity
hijab (hair covering), 17, 145
hijra (migration), 277; to Abyssinia, 20, 112; of Black Americans, 287n11; to Medina al-Munawwara, 112; to Medina Baye, 216–17
Hill, Joseph, 115, 130
Hinton, Elizabeth, 72
Hispaniola, 21
home ownership, in Medina Baye, 247
House of Slaves, 237
Howard University, 69, 189, 198–99
huffaz, 53, 150, 152–53, 161, 277; Black Americans as, 185, 287n12; hadith on, 170–71; transatlantic slave trade and, 154–55
humanitarianism, 209; of HFH, 256, 257–58; pan-Africanism and, 236

idleness, 222, 227
Ifriqiya ila al-ifriqiyin (Niasse, Shaykh Ibrahim), 45, 47, 116, 271
ihsan (excellence), 35, 36; collective care and, 38–39; marifa and, 43; in Tijani tariqa, 39
imagination, 225–26
imperialism, 232, 271; militarism and, 272; pan-Africanism relation to, 49; resistance to, 207
import-export businesses, 204
International Bureau of African Diaspora Affairs, 275
International Monetary Fund, 216, 233
isha (late evening prayer), 105, 149, 278
Islam: Black Americans relation to, 10, 22–23; Blackness relation to, 162, 191; Black Radical Tradition in, 21–23; collective care and, 11, 16–17; Darul, 73, 76–77; justice and, 38, 273; liberation and, 10, 13, 18, 19, 59, 272–73; in Mecca, 34; pan-Africanism and, 51; resistance relation to, 275; safe harbors relation to, 121; Salafism and, 129; Shi'a, 65;

Sunni, 23, 59, 67, 71, 73, 189; in West Africa, 20–21, 160. *See also* Sufism
Islamic boarding school: AAII, 3, 85; AAII Legacy Academy, 140–41, 185
Islamic Cultural Center, 61–62, 63, 75
Islamic education: alumni of, 202, 203; collective care and, 11–12, 206–7; communal obligation and, 200–201; as individualistic, 201; khidma and, 198; material resources relation to, 197; moral compass in, 206–7; piety in, 286n2. *See also* Qur'anic education
Islamic legal rulings, 129
Ismail, 6, 7, 8, 207, 211–12, 214; hijra of, 216; khidma of, 217
Isra, 149–50, 160, 172, 185, 187, 207
Israel: genocide in Palestine, 267–68, 271; Zionism and, 46–47

Jackson, Sherman, 22, 173
Jakhanke, 20–21
jalabiyas (long hooded gowns), 3
Jamaica, 119, 120, 256
"Jamiat Nasrul Ilm," 84–85, 208
jangi kamil, 174–79, *177*; as collective care, 180; Qur'anic education and, 182
Jawahir al-Ma'ani (al-Tijani), 194
Jeffries-Cisse, Hajjah Ayisha, 97
Jersey City, New Jersey, 76
Jibril, hadith of, 35, 39, 152
Joseph, Hajjah Karimah, 56, 57–60, 65–68, 284n6; Arab Muslims and, 90; Cisse, Shaykh Hassan Aliou, and, 91; Joseph, Imam Salim, and, *94*; in Medina Baye, 92–93; motherwork of, 76; Shifa-al-Asqam Socio Medical Center, 98
Joseph, Imam Salim, 66, 67–68, 77; Joseph, Dr. Karimah, and, *94*; Tijani tariqa and, 90
Joseph, Yusuf, 91–93
Journey to Africa, 253, *254*, 254–55

jummah (Friday afternoon prayer), 176, 179, 189, 278
justice (*adl*), 38, 163, 273

Kamal, 190–91
Al-Kanz Al-Masun (Niasse, Shaykh Ibrahim), 50, 283n8
Kaolack, Senegal, 5, 112, 117, 216
Kareem, 236, 244, 259, 260; on precarity, 245–46; on toubab, 248; tuition of, 242; on U.S., 251; Usman and, 229, 230–31, 263
Karim, Jamillah, 57–58, 284n14
Kashif al-Ilbas (Niasse, Shaykh Ibrahim), 28, 39, 162, 175, 221
Kelley, Robin D. G., 9, 272
Kenya, 271
keur Pa, 107, 108
khalwa (solitary spiritual retreats), 37
khatm, 174; as collective care, 180–82, 186–87; merits of, 176
al-Khawas, Sidi Ali, 175
khidma (service), 3–4, 110, 217; baraka from, 223, 226; of Black Americans, 244; in Black Radical Tradition, 147–48; collective care as, 11, 43–44, 192, 222, 227; domestic, 123, 125, 126, 142–43; farming, 39–40; gender norms and, 130; hadiya and, 40–41, 50; Islamic education and, 198; marifa and, 116–17; Muridiyya tariqa and, 282n5; Niasse, Sayyida Fatima Zahra, and, 109; for Niasse, Shaykha Ruqayya, 105; opposed to capitalist labor, 220; ritual practice and, 220; safe harbors for, 122–23; at Shifa-al-Asqam Socio Medical Center, 219; Sufism relation to, 221; of Taha-Cisse, Hajjah Ashaki, 238; time and, 217–18, 225, 226
Khomeini, Ayatollah Ruhollah, 65
khuluq (character), 35–36
kincraft, 134–35, 287n1; at AAII, 89–90; adoptive father and, 89, 260; HFH as, 256; othermother and, 133; pan-Africanism and, 91–92, 239; of Tijani tariqa, 96, 99–100
kioni-sadiki, dequi, 30
knowledge, 197; communal obligation and, 201; experiential, 2, 35, 39, 43, 116–17, 278; Nasrul Ilm America and, 208
Korhogo, Côte d'Ivoire, 178
Kossi Atlanta, 247, 287n2
Kossi Baye, 112, 287n2
kufis (hats), 3, 278

Labor of Faith (Casselberry, Judith), 141, 220
LaRocque Bey School of Dance Theatre, 74
Launay, Robert, 168, 178–79
Layla, 167–68, 170, 207–8
leisure, 128
Lemu, Aisha, 286n2
liberation, 23; collective care and, 43, 49, 235, 275–76; education for, 169; from European colonization, 44–45, 180–81; grind culture relation to, 213; Islam and, 10, 13, 18, 19, 59, 272–73; pan-Africanism and, 46, 50, 272–73; spiritual, 5, 34, 51, 180–81
Louis, Joe, 60–61
love: at AAII, 102–3; Sufism relation to, 38
Lumumba, Chokwe, 30

maagi daara, 167, 278
maghrib (sunset prayer), 2, 101, 150, 278
Mahmood, Saba, 221
Mahmoud, 198–202, 227
Maimouna, 204–5, 206, 207, 209, 214, 227
Mains, Daniel, 215
Malcolm X Grassroots Movement, 30
Malcolm X Self-Determination Award, 78–79
male huffaz. *See* hafiz
Malê uprising, 21–22

Manasik Ahl-al Widad (Niasse, Shaykh Ibrahim), 44
mandatory minimum sentences, 72
maqam (sacred burial grounds), 107, *107*, 182, 269, 278
Mariama, 248–49, 250, 251–52
marifa (experiential knowledge), 2, 35, 39, 43, 116–17, 278
market liberalization, 233
maroon geographies, 113, 119–20; Black Radical Tradition and, 125; in Medina Baye, 115, 116, 117, 121, 147–48, 226, 251
Masjid al-Haqq, 76–77
Masjid Muhammad, 189–90
material resources: collective care and, 135–36; Islamic education relation to, 197; redistribution of, 137, 139
Mauss, Marcel, 282n6, 282n13
MEARC. *See* Muslim Educational Action and Resource Committee
Mecca, 34, 112
Medina al-Munawarra, 112, 128, 148
Medina Baye, 6, 8, 26–27, 117–19; Abdul-Kareem, Hajjah Kareemah, in, 7, 59–60, 81, *96*, 97–98; Abedeen, Hajjah Tauhidah, in, *98*; Asiya in, 213; Askari, Dr. Khadijah, in, *97*, 97–98; collective care in, 242, 252; farming in, 40; gender norms in, 130; government assistance relation to, 115–16; hadiya economy in, 116–17; heritage tourism to, 4–5; HFH in, 252; hijra to, 216–17; home ownership in, 247; huffaz in, 161; idleness in, 222; Islamic boarding school in, 85; Ismail in, 212; Joseph, Dr. Karimah, in, 92–93; Journey to Africa in, 253; liberation and, 10; as a maroon geography, 115, 116, 117, 121, 147–48, 226, 251; material resources in, 136; moral education in, 110–12; Nasira in, 210–11; Niasse, Shaykh Ibrahim, and, 112–13, *114*; pan-Africanism and, 235; police in, 120; prophetic lifestyle in, 127–28, 132, 140; al-Quds Day in, 267; Qur'anic education in, 151–52, 158, 173, 188; as safe harbor, 121–23, 147; Salah, Aminah, in, 53–54; self-determination and, 285n1; time in, 214; Yahya in, 223. *See also* Grand Mosque, of Medina Baye
Medina Baye Fund, 115–16
melfa, 3, 278
"Message to the Grass Roots" speech, 234
Miftah al-Arab fi ma li al-' Abd mina al-Talab (dua), 41–42
migration. *See* hijra
militarism, 272
Millinder, Lucky, 60–61
minimax principle, 184
mobility, 122
Mohammed, Imam Warith Deen, 59, 73, 189
Mol, Annemarie, 13–14
Moorish Science Temple of America, 22–23
moral compass, 227; of alumni, 209–10, 228; in Islamic education, 206–7; in Qur'anic education, 205–6, 208–9
moral education, 110–12, 132
moral panic, 156, 230
Morehouse School of Medicine, 70
Mosque of Islamic Brotherhood, 2
Mother Blues Café, 61
Mothers of the Believers (*Ummahat-ul-Mu'mineen*), 144
motherwork, 99; of Abdul-Kareem, Hajjah Kareemah, 74–75; of Abedeen, Hajjah Tauhidah, 75–76; of Askari, Dr. Khadijah, 77–79; of Joseph, Dr. Karimah, 76–77. *See also* othermother
Moynihan, Daniel Patrick, 69
Moynihan Report, 69
Muhammad (Prophet), 272; character of, 34–35; on collective care, 33, 275; habits of giving, 37; hijra of, 20; Medina al-Munawarra and, 112, 128, 148; sunnah and, 13, 125, 127, 278

Muhammad, Brother Bilal, 90
Muhammad, Hafiz Ahmed Sufi, 180, 187, 239–40
Muhammad, Sister Amina, 65, 86, 95
Muhammad, The Honorable Elijah, 189
Muhammad Speaks (newspaper), 69
muqaddam (man in spiritual leadership), 81
muqaddama (woman in spiritual leadership), 6, 7, 238
Muridiyya tariqa, 161, 282nn5–6, 285n3
murids (disciples). *See specific murids*
muruwah, 34
Musa, 183, 184–85, 187, 217
Muslim Cool (Abdul Khabeer, Su'ad), 145–46
Muslim Educational Action and Resource Committee (MEARC), 63
Muslim International, 23; collective care and, 18, 43–44; pan-Africanism and, 19–20, 47
Muslim Mosque Inc., 2
Muslim schools in the U.S.: anti-Black racism in, 173, 204; Dar-ul-Islam, 73; Masjid al-Haqq, 76–77; NOI, 73; Sister Clara Muhammad Schools, 73, 79
Mustafawiyya, 282n5

al-Najashi, 20
Nasira, 210–11, 214, 218–19, 225–26; hijra of, 216; khidma of, 217
Nasrul Ilm America, 208–9, 238, 252
Nasser, Gamal Abdel, 47–48
A Nation at Risk (report), 72–73
Nation of Islam (NOI), 2, 22, 23, 59; Abedeen, Hajjah Tauhidah, relation to, 63; Black women and, 57–58; Masjid Muhammad, 189–90; *Muhammad Speaks*, 69; Muslim school of, 73; Sunni Islam relation to, 67
al-Nawawi, Imam, 152–54
Négritude, 45–46
neocolonialism, 46, 232, 271

neoliberalism, precarity and, 214–15
New York City, 60–61, 74–75, 135
NGO. *See* nongovernmental organization
Niasse, al-Hajj Abdoulaye, 6
Niasse, Aminah Abdul-Kareem, 83, *84*; as first Black American hafiza, 60
Niasse, Cheikh Ahmed Tijani Cheikh Ibrahim, 115
Niasse, Sayyida Fatima Zahra "Ya Fatou," 107, *108*, 108–9, *186*, 285n29; collective khatm for, 186–87; partial family tree of, *7*
Niasse, Shaykha Ruqayya, 105, *106*, 109
Niasse, Shaykh Ibrahim, 4, 5–6, 80, 182–83, *274*; anti-colonial resistance and, 47, 50, 116; on Blackness, 161–63; branch of Tijani tariqa, 6, 10, 19, 83, 282n10; Cisse, Sayyidi Aliou, and, 41, 175, 220; Cisse, Shaykh Hassan Aliou, and, 4, 51, 80, 272; on communal worship, 175; farming and, 39–40; fayda of, 44, 162, 262, 272–73; on government assistance, 116; on hadiya, 117; ihsan and, 38; jangi kamil and, 176, 182; on khidma, 220, 221; liberation and, 44–45, 180–81; in maqam, 107; Medina Baye and, 112–13, *114*; *Miftah al-Arab fi ma li al-' Abd mina al-Talab*, 41–42; Nasser, Gamal Abdel, and, 47–48; Nkrumah, Kwame, and, 47–48, 50; Palestine and, 46, 268; partial family tree of, *7*; poetry of, 28; al-Quds Day and, 267; revolutionary pan-Africanism and, 26–27, 47–49, 51–52, 235, 272–73; Sanusi I and, 283n9; as a spiritual father, 260; Touré, Ahmed Sékou, and, 50; on wealth, 139
Niasse-Cisse family tree, Partial, *7*
Nigeria, 61, 222, 271
Nkrumah, Kwame, 47–48, 50, 69, 70–71
NOI. *See* Nation of Islam
nongovernmental organization (NGO): AAII as, 85; financial support from, 241

Northern Negro Grass Roots Leadership Conference, 234
Nyerere, Julius, 196, 232

oral histories, 57–58, 162, 284n6
Organization of African Unity, 47
othermother, 83, 84, 88, 89–90, 100; Askari-Cisse, Sayyida Kubra as, 133, 142, 285n5; collective care of, 285n4; Jeffries-Cisse, Hajjah Ayisha as, 97; kincraft and, 133; Niasse, Sayyida Fatima Zahra, as, 109, 186–87

Palestine, 47, 267–68, 271; Niasse, Shaykh Ibrahim, support of, 46, 268
Pan-African Congress: Second, 233–34; Sixth, 46
pan-Africanism, 45, 271; of AAII, 209, 235; African diaspora relation to, 24–25, 51, 70–71, 233, 261–62, 264–65; Alliance of Sahel States and, 271; Askari, Dr. Khadijah, and, 69–71; Atlanta Progress Academy and, 78–79; among Black Americans, 69–70, 234–35; Black women and, 59; collective care and, 10–12, 34, 236; as cultural, 45; fashion of, 145; hijra and, 217; kincraft and, 91–92, 239; liberation and, 46, 50, 272–73; Muslim International and, 19–20, 47; Niasse, Shaykh Ibrahim, and, 26–27, 47–49, 51–52, 235, 272–73; as revolutionary, 46; in Senegal, 271; as small-p and capital P, 48–49; solidarity and, 237, 261, 265; Sufism and, 4, 13, 51, 273; Tijani tariqa and, 19–20, 99, 191, 264; Tuskegee Institute relation to, 69; in the twenty-first century, 236
Pays de la Teranga, 251
peer-to-peer learning, 165, 166–69, 170, 172; as collective care, 171, 188; in Sufism, 173–74
Philadelphia, Pennsylvania, 68–69

Philadelphia Public Schools, 77
Pierre, Jemima, 252
piety, 18; collective care as, 10–12, 17; education relation to, 192; gendered, 130, 146; in Islamic education, 286n2; khidma and, 221, 225; personal, 17, 221, 286n2; poverty relation to, 42; structural inequities relation to, 193; in Sufism, 135; time relation to, 219; wealth relation to, 139. *See also* relational piety
poetry, of Niasse, Shaykh Ibrahim, 28
police, in Medina Baye, 120
police brutality, 72, 117–18, 249
political quietism, 275
positionality, 29–30
poverty, 72; collective care and, 251, 264; piety relation to, 42; racial capitalism and, 136; safe harbors from, 121
power dynamics, of humanitarianism, 258
precarity, 214–16, 223, 227–28; education relation to, 244–45; idleness and, 222, 227; khidma relation to, 219; time and, 215; in Washington D.C., 245–46
Prickett, Pamela, 193, 282n15
prophetic lifestyle, 127–28, 132; collective care and, 132, 148; wealth and, 139–40
pseudonyms, 281n6
public schools, 75–76, 79, 167; anti-Black racism in, 160; in Atlanta, 77–78; in Detroit, 76; in Philadelphia, 68; Qur'anic education compared to, 168–69
The Pursuit of Happiness (Williams, Bianca), 24–25, 119–20

al-Quds Day, 267
queens, 144–45
Qur'an, 9, 67, *165*, *181*; jangi kamil and, 174–75; khatm of, 174, 176; as-Siddiq, Sayyida Abu Bakr and, 154; Surah al-Fatiha, 155; Surah an-Naba, 165, 166. *See also* hafiz; hafiza; huffaz

Qur'anic education, 153; Arabic language and, 286n5; Blackness relation to, 163; collective care and, 151–52, 154, 182, 188; communalism and, 287n7; Global War on Terror relation to, 286n5; jangi kamil and, 182; in Medina Baye, 151–52, 158, 173, 188; moral compass in, 205–6, 208–9; of Musa, 184; peer-to-peer learning in, 171, 172; public schools compared to, 168–69; in Senegal, 156–57; time for, 196; transatlantic slave trade and, 155. *See also* African American Islamic Institute

Quraysh, 34, 112

racial capitalism, 55, 227, 271; Black Radical Tradition relation to, 18–19; collective care relation to, 12–13, 14; Islam relation to, 158; piety relation to, 193; poverty and, 136; precarity relation to, 216; relational piety relation to, 27, 231; resistance to, 17, 207, 226; spiritual liberation from, 5; time relation to, 196; transatlantic slave trade as, 232; white supremacy relation to, 11

racial formation, collective care and, 12

racial identity, 29, 204–5, 256; of Black Americans, 191; education and, 159; motherwork relation to, 74

racism. *See* anti-Black racism

radical Black praxis of community, 113, 116–17, 125

Rahman, Safa Abdur, 93, 94–95

Rashida, 255, 256, 258

Reagan, Ronald, 72–73

reciprocity, 14, 169, 282n13

redistribution: of hadiya, 41; of material resources, 137, 139; of wealth, 142, 144, 282n6

relational piety, 26, 38, 148; collective care and, 111, 153, 185, 195, 221; education in, 151; hadith on, 33, 123, 125, 153, 196; in Islamic education, 206–7; Qur'anic education and, 154, 188; racial capitalism relation to, 27, 231; role models of, 147; in Tijani tariqa, 43

religious identity, 16, 29

religious multi-tasking, 141–42

renaming, 62, 70, 144, 259–60, 271

reparations, 239

Republic of New Arika, 30

resistance: to grind culture, 213, 226; Islam relation to, 275; to transatlantic slave trade, 206; to white supremacy, 17, 59, 207, 226

revolutionary pan-Africanism, 46; Malcolm X and, 234–35; Niasse, Shaykh Ibrahim, relation to, 47–50; in the twenty-first century, 271

Robinson, Bill "Bojangles," 60–61

Robinson, Cedric, 18

Rodney, Walter, 232

Rogers, J. A., 69

role models, 132–34, 140–42, 145–47, 148

Ruhul Adab (Niasse, Shaykh Ibrahim), 28, 41, 161

Ruqiyyah, 199–200, 204

sadaqa (charity), 22

Sadia, 101, 102–3, 105, 107, 127–28; at AAII, 110; Niasse, Sayyida Fatima Zahra, and, 109

safe harbors, 121–23, 147

Safi, Omid, 38

Salaam, Brother Mahmoud, 90–91

Salafism, 129

Salah, Abdullah, 63

Salah, Aminah, 53–54, 65, 86–88

salat (prayer), 2, 149–50, 278

salawat (prayers of praise), 3, 278; salatul fatih and, 107, 278

Sall, Macky, 115

Samira, 163, 164–65, 166, 171, 185

Sankara, Thomas, 271

Sanusi I, al-Hajji Muhammadu, 283n9

Sayyida, 282n12. *See also specific Sayyida*
scholarly authority, 202
School and Employment Status of Black American Alumni, *203*
School of Oriental and African Studies, University of London, 80
Sea Islands, 22
Second Annual English Gamou, 275
Second Pan-African Congress, 233–34
Seerah, 129, 130, 132, 157, 159, 160
segregation, 65–66, 72, 99
self-criticism, 30
self-determination, 116, 285n1
Senegal, 115; Black Americans relation to, 24–25, 157; daaras in, 168; Dakar, 62, 119, 216, 246, 253; economic development in, 233; farming in, 40; gender norms in, 246; heritage tourism in, 237; Kaolack, 117; Ministry of National Education, 241; precarity in, 215–16; Qur'anic education in, 156–57; Touba, 285n3; U.S. compared to, 250–52. *See also* Medina Baye
Senghor, Léopold Sédar, 45
service. *See khidma*
Shabaab al-Fayda (Youth of the Flood), 120
shahada (declaration of faith), 62, 278
Sharubutu, Shaykh Osman Nuhu, 75
Shaykh, 281n8. *See also specific Shaykh*
Shaykha, 281n8. *See also specific Shaykha*
Shepperson, George, 48
Shi'a Islam, 65
Shifa-al-Asqam Socio Medical Center, 98, 140, 219, 239
shukr (gratitude), 36, 193–94, 278
shuyukh (spiritual guides), 281n8; collective care of, 117; hadiya economy and, 35, 110; safe harbors for, 121–22. *See also specific shuyukh*
as-Siddiq, Sayyidina Abu Bakr, 154
Siddiqa, 218, 223
Simone, Nina, 187

Sister Clara Muhammed Schools, 73, 79, 95
Sixth Pan-African Congress, 46
SNCC. *See* Student Nonviolent Coordinating Committee
social adulthood, 201–2, 211, 215
socialism, 46, 232
social welfare programs, collective care as, 242
societal norms, collective care as, 127
socioeconomic mobility, 197–98; through capitalist education, 196
sociopolitical action, spiritual liberation and, 34
solidarity: with oppressed peoples, 234–35; with Palestine, 268; pan-Africanism and, 237, 261, 265
Sonko, Ousmane, 271
spiritual labor, 141–42
spiritual liberation, 5, 34, 50–51, 180–81
spiritual transformation, 241, 262
state-sponsored education, 198
strategic entanglement, 113, 120
structural inequities, 193, 232
student debt, 198–99, 200
Student Nonviolent Coordinating Committee (SNCC), 69
"The Students of Shaykh Hassan," 284n6
Sufism: asceticism and, 36; *faqir* and, 36; hadiya relation to, 40–41; justice relation to, 38; khidma relation to, 39, 221; liberation and, 272–73; love relation to, 38; marifa and, 35; pan-Africanism and, 4, 13, 51, 273; peer-to-peer learning in, 173–74; piety in, 135; tarbiya and, 39–40; Tijani tariqa relation to, 37–38, 111, 132. *See also* Tijani *tariqa*
sugar, 36
sunnah (habits), 13, 125, 127, 278
Sunni Islam, 23, 59; Community Masjid, 71; Darul Islam Movement relation to, 73; Mohammed, Imam Warith Deen, and, 189; NOI relation to, 67

Surah al-Fatiha, 155
Surah al-Kahf, 125
Surah an-Naba, 165, 166
surahs, 107, 279

Taal, Shaykh Umar Futi, 21, 38–39, 175
Taal, Ustadh, 163, 165
Tabaski, 117
Taha, Papa Khari, 238
Taha-Cisse, Hajjah Ashaki, 238
Tahanee, 256, 257
talibes (students), 156–57, 229, 230–31, 243, 279, 286n6
tarbiya, 39–40, 279
tariqa (path), 1–2. *See also* Tijani *tariqa*
tawakkul, 116
teranga (hospitality), 251
Thiam, Shaykh Ahmed, 80
Thomas, Todne, 89, 287n1
Thompson, Audrey, 14, 83, 84
al-Tijani, Shaykh Ahmad, 36–37, 112, 194, 282n3; on corruption, 44, 51; ihsan and, 38; on knowledge, 197; on wealth and habits of giving, 139, 282n3
Tijani tariqa, 6, 8, 26–27, 39, 282n10; Black Americans and, 51, 231, 273, 274, 282n9; collective care and, 11–13, 18, 25–26, 102, 111; ihsan and, 36; kincraft of, 96, 99–100; liberation and, 10; marifa in, 39; Palestine relation to, 268; pan-Africanism and, 19–20, 99, 191, 264; piety and, 17; relational piety in, 43; in Senegal, 115; Shaykh Ibrahim Niasse's branch of, 6, 10, 19, 83, 282n10; shukr and, 193–94; wealth relation to, 139
Tijani zawiya, 194, 195, *195*, 197, 208, 212
time, 201; capitalist conceptions of, 195–96, 213, 215; Islamic ethical conceptions of, 193–95, 213; khidma and, 217–18, 225, 226; in Medina Baye, 214; piety relation to, 219; shukr for, 194; as at a standstill, 215, 244
Touba, Senegal, 285n3

toubab, 248
Touré, Ahmed Sékou, 46, 47; Niasse, Shaykh Ibrahim, and, 50; Nkrumah, Kwame, and, 48
transatlantic slave trade, 11, 89, 235; African diaspora relation to, 263; African Muslims' resistance to, 18, 21–22, 206; Black Radical Tradition relation to, 18; huffaz and, 154–55; as racial capitalism, 232
Traore, Ibrahim, 271
Tuck, Eve, 15
tuition: for AAII, 238–39; financial support for, 241–42
Ture, Kwame, 70
Tuskegee Institute, 69–70
Tuubanaan movement, 21

Umarian Caliphate, 21, 175
ummah (global community), 10, 47, 279
Ummahat-ul-Mu'mineen (Mothers of the Believers), 144
underdevelopment, 232–33, 247, 252, 263
unemployment rate, 211, 250, 252
UNICEF, 286n6
United States (U.S.), 25; Civil Rights Movement, 19, 66, 234; hegemony of, 265; home ownership in, 247; precarity in, 215, 216, 245–46; Senegal compared to, 250–52; wealth in, 246, 249–50; white supremacy in, 226
University of London, School of Oriental and African Studies, 80
Usman, 229, 230–31, 235, 236, 260, 263
Ustadh, 287n9. *See also specific Ustadh*

vice, wealth as, 37, 41, 139
Vietnam War, 66
"Voice of the Fayda," 116, 132, 174. *See also* Cisse, Shaykh Mouhamadou Mahy

Wade, Abdoulaye, 253
waged labor, 200

Ware, Rudolph, 125, 206, 287n7
Washington D.C., 118, 160; Masjid Muhammad, 189–90; precarity in, 245–46
Wayne State University, 66–67, 77
wazifa, 3, 54–55, 81–82, 279; Cisse, Shaykh Hassan Aliou, and, 86; in Detroit, 91; at Grand Mosque, 101, 103–4; grind culture relation to, 213; Niasse, Shaykha Ruqayya, and, 105; safe harbors for, 121
wealth, 136, 140; in African diaspora, 264; capitalist conceptions of, 196; extracted through European colonization, 232–33; hadiya economy relation to, 41, 137, 139; hijra for, 246–47; piety relation to, 42; redistribution of, 142, 144, 282n6; Sufism relation to, 37; talibes relation to, 229, 230–31; Tijani tariqa relation to, 139; in U.S., 246, 249–50; as vice, 37, 41, 139
West Africa: Islam in, 20–21; Sufi societies in, 113, 115, 285nn1–2
White, Deborah Gray, 57
white supremacy, 29, 55, 144, 227, 271; collective care relation to, 12–13, 14; grind culture relation to, 213; Islam's resistance to, 158; piety relation to, 193; precarity relation to, 216; racial capitalism relation to, 11; relational piety relation to, 27, 231; resistance to, 17, 59, 158, 207, 226; safe harbors from, 121;

spiritual liberation from, 5; time relation to, 196. *See also* racial capitalism
Williams, Bianca, 24, 25, 119, 120, 256
Winston, Celeste, 113, 115
Wolof ethnic group, 21–22
Women of the Nation (Karim, Jamillah and Gibson, Dawn-Marie), 57–58
World Bank, 233
worldly asceticism (*zuhd*), 37
Wright, Zachary, 37, 50, 130, 132, 180–81, 206

X, Malcolm, 24, 30, 78–79; "Message to the Grass Roots" speech, 234; Muslim Mosque Inc., 2; revolutionary pan-Africanism and, 234–35

Yahya, 222–23, 225–26
Yathrib, 112
Yellow House, 239, 285n29
Yoruba ethnic group, 21–22
Yusuf, Ibrahim, 62

Zakariya, 217
Zionism, 46–47; Niasse, Shaykh Ibrahim's opposition to, 47, 268; revolutionary pan-Africanism's opposition to, 46
ziyara (visitation), 109, 279; of Cisse, Shaykh Hassan Aliou, 30, 208–9, 212, 238; to maqam, 107, 182
Zuberi, Tukufu, 29
zuhd (worldly asceticism), 37

ABOUT THE AUTHOR

SAMIHA RAHMAN is a scholar-activist who examines how youth and their families engage race, religion, and education to achieve justice and liberation. She holds a Ph.D. in Africana Studies and Education from the University of Pennsylvania and a bachelor's degree in History and Ethnicity & Race Studies from Columbia University. She is currently Assistant Professor of Human Development at California State University, Long Beach.

www.ingramcontent.com/pod-product-compliance
Ingram Content Group UK Ltd.
Pitfield, Milton Keynes, MK11 3LW, UK
UKHW040226050326
468667UK00005B/263